PERSECUTION, PRIVILEGE & POWER

Reconsidering The Zionist Narrative in American Life

Thirty Essential Articles on the Most Pressing Issue of our Time

Edited by Mark Green

PREFACE

Not long ago, the US-Israeli alliance was commonly called "the special relationship". Today, this entanglement is marketed more indirectly, as either a joint struggle against 'terror' or as a way to secure a democratic beachhead in the Middle East. In both cases however, there remains a mystery: why exactly is the United States so *committed* to Israel, and why is our posture elsewhere in the region so *confrontational?* What is the driving force(s) behind America's disparate policies in the Middle East? Is it oil, 'strategic interests', Empire, or Zionism?

As for Israel, the case can be made that the source of the Jewish State's affection for the U.S. can be reasonably traced to ordinary matters involving economic security, military supremacy and long-term objectives concerning 'disputed' territories and demographic purity. But it must noted that Israel's long-term aspirations can be achieved *only* through targeted intervention by the mother of all political patrons, namely Washington D.C.

As for rank and file Americans, they must be content to invest precious tax dollars and blood in the Middle East for less-tangible objectives. These include 'democracy spreading', nation-building, energy security, global military preparedness, and the ongoing pursuit of cave-dwelling terror suspects. And the costs? Washington's foreign policies are making American civilization less admired, less prosperous and less secure. Yet few understand how these plans came to be or why they should endure. This volume intends to supply some of the missing explanations to this veiled mystery.

The essays selected for this purpose explore political terrain that is often excluded from mainstream discourse. As such, "PERSECUTION, PRIVILEGE & POWER" does not pretend, nor seek, to supply favorable or "even-handed" chatter about the Zionist project in Israel-Palestine. For that brand of news, simply turn on your TV, pick up a newspaper, or peruse a bookstore in your local mall.

Lastly, for those who inevitably plan to smear this book as "anti-Semitic", let me say plainly that this volume is a critical examination of organized political conduct that has been widely identified and thoroughly catalogued. It is certainly not an attack upon Jews "just for being Jewish" whatever that is supposed to imply.

With hundreds of thousands dead or in exile, from Afghanistan to Iraq and beyond, and Washington's ruling establishment threatening to embark upon yet another military mission in the Middle East, the time for this collection has surely arrived.

Mark Green, *editor*, November 2007

ACKNOWLEDGEMENTS

I want to thank all the bold and informed contributors to this book, most of whom have generously donated their articles.

In particular, I am greatly indebted to the extraordinary research, effort and labor done by groups and individuals associated with Antiwar.com, Counterpunch.org, dissidentvoice.org, GlobalResearch.org, IHR.org, IfAmericansKnew.org, JewishTribalReview.org, Rense.com, VDARE.com, The Barnes Review, The Occidental Quarterly, The Washington Report on Middle East Affairs, among others.

I am especially grateful that the Internet remains (mostly) free of political censorship, though it must be said that a considerable array of inter-connected advocacy groups representing the narrow interests of global Zionism are toiling to undermine free expression even there. It is in fact no exaggeration to say that their appetite to control political discourse is without equal, and that their desire to censor their critics and adversaries is similarly unparalleled. These anti-democratic pressures constitute a genuine threat to free speech and intellectual liberty worldwide.

Finally, I wish to thank my wife, Wendy Campbell, for her invaluable encouragement and advice on this project.

CONTENTS

Articles Of Faith

*When two eminent US scholars wrote about the
'Israel lobby' they were vilified.*

by Ed Pilkington

The London Guardian, Saturday September 15, 2007

Given the reception John Mearsheimer and Stephen Walt received for their London Review of Books essay last year on what they called the Israel Lobby, it would have been understandable had they crawled away to a dark corner of their respective academic institutions to lick their wounds. Their argument that US foreign policy has been distorted by the stultifying power of pro-Israeli groups and individuals was met with a firestorm of protest that has smoldered ever since.

The authors were assailed with headlines such as the Washington Post's: "Yes, it's anti-Semitic." The neocon pundit William Kristol accused them in the Wall Street Journal of "anti-Judaism" while the New York Sun linked them with the white supremacist David Duke.

The row became a focal point of a much wider debate about the limits of permitted criticism of the state of Israel and its American-based supporters that has ensnared several academics and writers, including a former president. Jimmy Carter was castigated earlier this year when he published a plea for a renewed engagement in the Middle-East peace process under the admittedly provocative title, Palestine: Peace Not Apartheid. He was labeled an anti-Semitic "Jew hater" and even a Nazi sympathiser. Meanwhile, a British-born historian at New York University, Tony Judt, has been warned off or disinvited from four academic events in the past year. On one occasion, he was asked to promise not to mention Israel in a speech on the Holocaust. He refused.

For Walt, the explosion of criticism after the LRB publication in March 2006 struck particularly close to home as two members of his own Harvard faculty turned on him. Ruth Wisse, professor of Yiddish literature, compared Walt and his University of Chicago co-author's work to that of a notorious 19th-century German anti-Semite. Alan Dershowitz, the Harvard criminal law professor who represented OJ Simpson, charged them with culling some of their references from neo-Nazi websites.

Given the battering he has taken, Walt is remarkably upbeat. "We were surprised by how nasty it got," says the Harvard professor. "The David Duke reference, the neo-Nazi websites - these were intended to smear us and swing attention on to us rather than to what we were saying. It wasn't pleasant, but it never made me doubt what we had written or doubt myself." Standing tall in the face of attack is one thing; to raise your head above the parapet for a second round is quite another. But that is what the Mearsheimer/Walt double act are doing: they have gone on the offensive with the publication of a book-length version of their original treatise.

As night follows day, the dispute has started anew. The New York Sun has dedicated a section of its website to the controversy; Dershowitz has revved up again, calling the book "a bigoted attack on the American Jewish community"; and Abraham Foxman, director of the Anti-Defamation League, has gone to the trouble of writing his own book in riposte - and it's in the bookshops a week before The Israel Lobby appears.

There is one obvious question to put to Walt: why do it to yourself? Wasn't one stoning enough? "We did ask ourselves, did we want to go through this again?" he admits, but only to add: "It didn't take us all that long to figure out we had more to say and it was our job to say it."

By writing a 496-page book, as opposed to the original article's mere 13,000 words, the authors hope to present a more nuanced version of their case. They have taken in new examples to support their thesis, notably the second Lebanon war, which broke out in the interim, and have sought to address some of the points raised by critics.

The book follows the structure of the original article fairly faithfully, and its argument can be summarised thus: in recent years the US government has given Israel unconditional support, showering it with three billion dollars a year a year irrespective of the human rights violations it inflicts on the Palestinians. It was not always this way - think of the Suez crisis of 1956 when America stepped in to frustrate Israel's (and Britain's) ambitions. But from the 1960s onwards the relationship deepened to the extent that today American and Israeli interests are deemed by many Americans to be essentially identical.

The authors ask why this is the case, and argue that strategically there is no reason for it. The end of the cold war removed a central justification for the special relationship, as Israel no longer provided the US with a barrier to communism in the region. Post 9/11, the US and Israel are presented as partners against terrorism, but America's vulnerability to attack partly stems from its support for Israel, which has provoked hostility in the Muslim world. Nor is there a moral argument for indiscriminately backing Israel - as a towering military presence in the Middle East, Israel is no longer under existential threat.

So what explains this ongoing largesse? The authors conclude that the answer lies with the Israel lobby, a loose coalition of individuals and organisations that wants US leaders to treat Israel as though it were the 51st state. The lobby stifles debate, inhibits criticism of the Israeli occupation of Palestinian lands and maintains the special relationship despite the fact that it has become a liability both for the US and for Israel itself.

3

In its transition from literary journal essay to stand-alone book, the authors have made a few telling alterations of presentation and emphasis. The most vivid is that in the body of the text they have demoted lobby to lower case: the Israel Lobby has become the Israel lobby. Walt sees that as the most minor of changes, remarking that: "John and I don't even remember how the capital L got used in the first place."

More substantially, perhaps, they have used the extra space to make several robust disclaimers, insisting that they have never questioned the right of Israel to exist or the legitimacy of the Israel lobby itself. They have also filed down some of the more jagged edges of their argument, such as their position on the role the lobby played in the build-up to the Iraq war. They still maintain that the war would "almost certainly not have occurred" were it not for the Israel lobby, but they soften the claim by adding that America's belligerent mood in the aftermath of the attacks on New York and Washington also had much to do with it.

Such nuances make for a more sophisticated read, but they fall far short of the revisions - the authors would say capitulations - that would be needed to satisfy their detractors.

Foxman is one of the most vocal critics. His new book, timed specifically to counteract the arrival on bookshelves of The Israel Lobby, pulls no punches. Its title is representative of the tone of the book: The Deadliest Lies. "This is a big lie that the Jewish people have lived with throughout history," he tells me from his New York office. "Up to now these anti-Semitic canards have been heard on the fringes, but to have two respected academics repeat them legitimises the debate and penetrates the mainstream."

More measured - though still forceful - criticism of the Mearsheimer and Walt book has come from those titans of US journalism, the New York Times and the New Yorker. The Times' book critic William Grimes takes a swipe at the authors' claim that it is time for the US to treat Israel as a normal country: "But it's not. And America won't. That's realism." David Remnick, editor of the New Yorker, suggests none too flatteringly that the book is symptomatic of a polarised era in which Americans are searching for an explanation to the evils of the times.

In the swirl of debate, the squabbling parties keep coming back to the core concept of an Israel lobby, case notwithstanding. The authors have been meticulously careful in the book to stress that they see the lobby as a loose coalition. It is not a single, unified movement and it is certainly not a cabal or conspiracy. Yet no matter how profuse their disclaimers, they have not assuaged those antagonists for whom any lumping together of Jews or Jewish interest groups sets alarm bells ringing. "Visit any anti-Semitic website and you'll hear the same old themes: the Jews have too much power; they exercise political influence not as individual citizens but as a cabal," writes Foxman. "Walt and Mearsheimer sound all the same notes, with a subtlety and pseudo-scholarly style that makes their poison all the more dangerous."

In our conversation, Walt accepts the phrase "the lobby" is "an awkward term as many of the groups and people in it don't operate on Capitol Hill. It's shorthand - you could call it the pro-Israel movement". One wonders why he and his co-author have stuck with it, then, when it has allowed their detractors to smear other more credible parts of their argument.

Take the slanging match over the causes of the Iraq war. Walt and Mearsheimer rightly lay a large part of the blame for this disastrous escapade on the neoconservatives within the Bush administration, but they then go on to define those neocons as an integral part of the Israel lobby. Books have been written about the various motivations of the neocons. Sympathy for Israel is one, but there are many others - the desire to spread democracy, a belief in the positive uses of military intervention, denigration of international institutions. To suggest that the neocons and the Israel lobby are one and the same is a conflation too far.

But the authors have brought into the open aspects of American intellectual life that needed airing. They cast light on the overweening activities of specific pro-Israeli groups, most importantly the American Israel Public Affairs Committee. AIPAC is a self-avowed lobby (it calls itself America's pro-Israel lobby) and has been ranked the second most powerful such body in the US. With a staff of more than 150 and a budget of $60m, it wields extensive influence among Congressmen, working to ensure criticism of Israel is rarely aired on Capitol Hill. The Guardian invited it to comment, but it declined.

Though Foxman insists the furor is proof that debate is alive and kicking, Walt and Mearsheimer have also put their finger on the limits of acceptable discourse in the US. It is notable that none of the candidates standing for president in 2008 have a word of criticism for Israeli state behaviour; this week Barack Obama pulled an advertisement for his campaign from the Amazon page selling The Israel Lobby, denouncing the book as "just wrong".

So what happened to America's commitment to free speech, the First Amendment? "We knew from De Tocqueville this country is driven by conformity," Judt says. "The law can't make people speak out - it can only prevent people from stopping free speech. What's happened is not censorship, but self-censorship." Judt believes that a few well-organised groups including AIPAC have succeeded in proscribing debate. He recalls a prominent Democratic senator confiding to him that he would never criticise Israel in public. "He told me that if he did so, for the rest of his career he would never be able to get a majority for what he cared about. He would be cut off at the knees."

In the final chapter of the book, Walt and Mearsheimer make a shopping list of reforms. They call for: a two-state solution to the Middle East crisis; greater separation of US foreign policy from Israel for both nations' sake; and campaign finance reform to reduce the power of pro-Israeli groups.

Nothing outlandish, or even controversial, there. Coming at the end of such a bumpy ride of claim and counter-claim, the conclusion feels almost disappointingly gentle. That in itself bears eloquent witness to the state of affairs in America today, where thoughts considered unremarkable elsewhere are deemed beyond the pale.

ARTICLES OF FAITH

Ed Pilkington is the Guardian's New York correspondent. He is a former national and foreign editor of the paper, and author of "Beyond the Mother Country".

Copyright Guardian News & Media Ltd 2007

The Cost of Israel to the American People

by Richard Curtiss

January 1999

By now many Americans are aware that Israel, with a population of only 5.8 million people, is the largest recipient of U.S. foreign aid, and that Israel's aid plus U.S. aid to Egypt's 65 million people for keeping the peace with Israel has, for many years, consumed more than half of the U.S. bi-lateral foreign aid budget world-wide.

What few Americans understand however, is the steep price they pay in many other fields for the U.S.-Israeli relationship, which in turn is a product of the influence of Israel's powerful U.S. lobby on American domestic politics and has nothing to do with U.S. strategic interests, U.S. national interests, or even with traditional American support for self-determination, human rights, and fair play overseas.

Besides its financial cost, unwavering U.S. support for Israel, whether it's right or wrong, exacts a huge price in American prestige and credibility overseas. Further, Israel's powerful U.S. lobby has been a major factor in delaying campaign finance reform, and also in the removal from American political life of some of our most distinguished public servants, members of Congress and even presidents.

Finally, the Israel-U.S. relationship has cost a significant number of American lives. The incidents in which hundreds of U.S. service personnel, diplomats, and civilians have been killed in the Middle East have been reported in the media. But the media seldom revisits these events, and scrupulously avoids analyzing why they occurred or compiling the cumulative toll of American deaths resulting from our Israel-centered Middle East policies.

Each of these four categories of the costs of Israel to the American people merits a talk of its own. What follows, therefore, is just an overview of such losses.

First is the financial cost of Israel to U.S. taxpayers. Between 1949 and 1998, the U.S. gave to Israel, with a self-declared population of 5.8 million people, more foreign aid than it gave to all of the countries of sub-Saharan Africa, all of the countries of Latin America, and all of the countries of the Caribbean combined – with a total population of 1,054,000,000 people.

In the 1997 fiscal year, for example, Israel received $3 billion from the foreign aid budget, at least $525 million from other U.S. budgets, and $2 billion in federal loan guarantees. So the 1997 total of U.S. grants and loan guarantees to Israel was $5.5 billion. That's $15,068,493 per day, 365 days a year.

If you add its foreign aid grants and loans, plus the approximate totals of grants to Israel from other parts of the U.S. federal budget, Israel has received since 1949 a grand total of $84.8 billion, excluding the $10 billion in U.S. government loan guarantees it has drawn to date.

And if you calculate what the U.S. has had to pay in interest to borrow this money to give to Israel, the cost of Israel to U.S. taxpayers rises to $134.8 billion, not adjusted for inflation.

Put another way, the nearly $14,630 every one of 5.8 million Israelis had received from the U.S. government by October 31, 1997, cost American taxpayers $23,241 per Israeli. That's $116,205 for every Israeli family of five.

THE COST OF ISRAEL TO THE AMERICAN PEOPLE

None of these figures include the private donations by Americans to Israeli charities, which initially constituted about one quarter of Israel's budget, and today approach $1 billion annually. In addition to the negative effect of these donations on the U.S. balance of payments, the donors also deduct them from their U.S. income taxes, creating another large drain on the U.S. treasury.

Nor do the figures above include any of the indirect financial costs of Israel to the United States, which cannot be tallied. One example is the cost to U.S. manufacturers of the Arab boycott, surely in the billions of dollars by now. Another example is the cost to U.S. consumers of the price of petroleum, which surged to such heights that it set off a world-wide recession during the Arab oil boycott imposed in reaction to U.S. support of Israel in the 1973 war.

Other examples are a portion of the costs of maintaining large U.S. Sixth Fleet naval forces in the Mediterranean, primarily to protect Israel, and military air units at the Aviano base in Italy, not to mention the staggering costs of frequent deployments to the Arabian Peninsula and Gulf area of land and air forces from the United States and naval units from the Seventh Fleet, which normally operates in the Pacific Ocean.

Many years ago the late Undersecretary of State George Ball estimated the true financial cost of Israel to the United States at $11 billion a year. Since then direct U.S. foreign aid to Israel has nearly doubled, and simply adjusting that original figure into 1998 dollars would send it considerably higher today.

Next comes the cost of Israel to the international prestige and credibility of the United States. Americans seem constantly astounded at our foreign policy failures in the Middle East. This stems from a profound ignorance of the background of the Israeli-Palestinian dispute, which in turn results from reluctance by the mainstream U.S. media to present these facts objectively.

Toward the end of the 19th century when political Zionism was created in Europe, Jews were a tiny fraction of the population of the Holy Land, much of which was heavily cultivated and thickly populated, and certainly not a desert waiting to be reclaimed by outsiders.

Even in 1947, after half a century of Zionist immigration and an influx of Jewish refugees from Hitler, Jews still constituted only one third of the population of the British Mandate of Palestine. Only seven percent of the land was Jewish-owned. Yet when the United Nations partitioned Palestine in that year, the Jewish state-to-be received 53 percent and the Arab state-to-be received only 47 percent of the land. Jerusalem was to remain separate under international supervision, a "corpus seperatum" in the words of the United Nations.

One of the myths that many Americans still believe is that the initial war between the Arabs and Israelis broke out on May 15, 1948 when the British withdrew and military units from Egypt, Jordan, Iraq and Syria entered Palestine, allegedly because the Arabs had rejected a partition plan that the Israelis accepted.

In fact, the fighting began almost six months earlier, immediately after the partition plan was announced. By the time the Arab armies intervened in May, some 400,000 Palestinians already had fled or been driven from their homes. To the Arab nations the military forces they sent to Palestine were on a rescue mission to halt the dispossession of Palestinians from the areas the U.N. had awarded to both the Jewish and the Palestinian Arab state. In fact history has revealed that the Jordanian forces had orders not to venture into areas the U.N. had awarded to Israel.

Although the newly created Israeli government didn't formally reject the partition plan, in practice it never accepted the plan. To this day, half a century later, Israel still refuses to define its borders.

In fact, when the fighting of 1947 and 1948 ended, the State of Israel occupied half of Jerusalem and 78 percent of the former mandate of Palestine. About 750,000 Muslim and Christian Palestinians had been driven from towns, villages and homes to which the Israeli forces never allowed them to return.

The four wars that followed, three of them started by Israel in 1956, 1967, and 1982, and one of them started by Egypt and Syria to recover their occupied lands in 1973, have been over the portions of Lebanon, Syria, Jordan and Egypt which the Israelis occupied militarily in those wars, the other half of Jerusalem, and the 22 percent of Palestine – comprising the West Bank and Gaza – which is all that remains for the Palestinians.

It is the unwillingness of successive U.S. governments to acknowledge these historical facts, and adjust U.S. Middle East policies to right these wrongs, that has resulted in such a devastating loss of international credibility. Americans, who once were identified with the modern schools, universities and hospitals they had established throughout the Middle East starting more than 150 years ago, now are identified with U.S. misuse of its veto in the United Nations to condone Israeli violations of the human rights of the Palestinians living in the lands Israel has seized by force. The Israeli occupation violates the preface to the United Nations Charter banning the acquisition of territory by war. What the Israeli government has been doing in the occupied territories also violates the Fourth Geneva convention, which forbids the transfer of populations to or from such areas.

Governments of Middle Eastern countries which once looked to the United States as their protectors from European colonialism, now find it very difficult to justify maintaining cordial relations with the United States at all. Friendly Arab governments are jeopardized by their U.S. alliances, and the fall of one, the Hashemite Kingdom of Iraq, was directly attributable to its premature withdrawal of its armed forces from Palestine during the 1948 fighting, and its subsequent membership in a military alliance with the U.S. and Britain.

Even our European and Asian allies have joined in deploring the perpetual American tilt toward Israel. In a recent vote on a U.N. General Assembly resolution calling upon Israel to curb further encroachments on Palestinian lands by Jewish settlers, only the United States and Micronesia voted with Israel. Of the 185 U.N. member nations, all of the others, without exception, voted against Israel or abstained.

Yet Americans seem oblivious to such examples of how their Israel-centered Middle East policies are isolating the United States in the world.

Next is the cost of Israel to the American domestic political system. In December 1997, Fortune magazine asked professional lobbyists to select the most powerful special interest group in the United States. They chose the American Association of Retired Persons (AARP), which lobbies on behalf of all Americans over 60.

In second place, however, was the American Israel Public Affairs Committee (AIPAC), Israel's official Washington, D.C. lobby, with a multi-million dollar budget—the sources of which AIPAC refuses to disclose—and 150 employees. AIPAC, in turn, can draw upon the resources of the Conference of Presidents of Major American Jewish Organizations, a roof group set up to coordinate the efforts on behalf of Israel of some 52 national Jewish organizations.

Among those organizations are groups such as B'nai B'rith's Anti-Defamation League (ADL), with a $45 million budget, and Hadassah, the Zionist women's group, which spends more than AIPAC and sends thousands of Americans every year to Israel on Israeli government-supervised visits.

Both AIPAC and the ADL maintain secret "opposition research" departments which compile files on politicians, journalists, academics and organizations, and circulate this information through local Jewish community councils to pro-Israel groups and activists in order to damage the reputations of those who dare to speak out and thus have been blackballed as "enemies of Israel." In the case of ADL, police raids on the organization's Los Angeles and San Francisco offices established that much of the information they had compiled was erroneous, and thus slanderous, and some also was illegally obtained.

THE COST OF ISRAEL TO THE AMERICAN PEOPLE

In the case of AIPAC, this is not the organization's most controversial activity. In the 1970s members of AIPAC's national board of directors set out to form deceptively named local political action committees (PACs) which could coordinate their efforts in supporting candidates in federal elections. To date, at least 126 pro-Israel PACs have been registered, and no fewer than 50 PACs, like AIPAC, can give a candidate who is facing a tough opponent and who has voted according to AIPAC recommendations up to half a million dollars. That's enough money to buy all the television time needed to get elected in most parts of the country.

What is totally unique about AIPAC's network of political action committees is that they all have deceptive names. Who could possibly know that the Delaware Valley PAC in Philadelphia, San Franciscans for Good Government in California, Cactus PAC in Arizona, Chili PAC in New Mexico, Beaver PAC in Wisconsin and even Ice PAC in New York are really pro-Israel PACs. So just as no other special interest can put so much hard money into any candidate's election campaign as can the Israel lobby, no other special interest has gone to such elaborate lengths to hide its tracks.

Some of America's wisest and most distinguished public servants have been kept from higher office by the blackballing of the Israel lobby. One such leader was George Ball, who served the Kennedy administration as Under Secretary of State and the Johnson administration as U.S. Ambassador to the United Nations. Given his unmatched brilliance in forecasting international developments, there is no doubt that he would have become secretary of state had he not publicly expressed the skepticism about the U.S. relationship with Israel which most Americans involved in foreign affairs privately feel.

In membership meetings which journalists are not allowed to attend, AIPAC presidents have boasted that the organization was responsible for the defeats of two of history's most distinguished chairmen of the Senate Foreign Relations Committee – Democrat J. William Fulbright of Arkansas and Republican Charles Percy of Illinois. The list of other senators and House members for whose election defeats AIPAC takes credit is too long to recount.

There is good evidence also that had it not been for complex maneuvers by the Israel lobby, including encouragement of third party candidates and unrelenting partisanship by pro-Israeli syndicated columnists and other media figures, Democratic President Jimmy Carter probably would have been reelected in 1980, and Republican President George Bush almost certainly would have been reelected in 1992.

The cost to our political system of losing national figures who refused to allow U.S. domestic political interests to dictate U.S. foreign policy has been enormous. So long as AIPAC and other powerful lobbies continue to thwart meaningful efforts on behalf of campaign finance reform, Americans will continue unknowingly paying such costs.

Finally, there is the cost of Israel in American lives. References to the attack by Israeli aircraft and torpedo boats on the USS Liberty in which 34 Americans were killed and 171 wounded on the fourth day of the Six-Day War of June 1967 often are met by disbelief. Very few Americans seem to have heard of the attack on the ship operated by the U.S. Navy for the National Security Agency to monitor Israel and Arab military communications during the fighting.

The Israeli government claimed it was a case of mistaken identity. The members of the crew and other naval officers who were stationed in the Mediterranean and in Washington at the time state that it was a deliberate attempt to sink the ship and blame Egyptian forces for the disaster. It is the only such event in U.S. Naval history the cause of which has never been formally investigated either by Congress or by the Navy itself.

Major losses of American lives at the hands of Arab forces opposing Israel are better known. These include the loss of 141 U.S. service personnel in the bombing of the U.S. Marine barracks in Beirut in 1984. They also include the loss of diplomats and local employees of the U.S. government in two bombings of the American Embassy in Beirut. Other such events include the bombing of the U.S. Embassy in Kuwait, the taking of U.S. hostages in Beirut of whom three were killed, the deaths of Americans in a series of Middle East related skyjackings, the deaths of 19 U.S. service personnel in the bombing of the Al Khobar Towers in Saudi Arabia, and the 1997 assassination of four U.S. accountants working for an American company in Karachi.

All of these incidents, and many more in which Americans have died, resulted directly from one-sided U.S. support for Israel in its refusal to participate in the land-for-peace settlement with the Palestinians and its other Arab neighbors envisioned in U.N. Security Council Resolution 242. The U.S. has given lip service to that resolution since November, 1967. But in practice the U.S. has done nothing to force Israel to comply, even though the resolution has been accepted by the members of the League of Arab States. That U.S. hypocrisy fuels rage and frustration throughout the Middle East and South Asia which will continue to take a toll of American lives until Israel finally gives back the lands it occupied in 1967, or the U.S. stops subsidizing Israeli intransigence.

Claims that there are positive aspects of the U.S.-Israeli relationship seldom stand up to scrutiny. During the Reagan administration it was labeled for the first time a "strategic relationship" conferring benefits on the U.S. as well as on Israel. The idea that Israel – smaller in both area and population than Hong Kong – can offer the United States benefits sufficient to offset the hostility that relationship arouses among 250 million Arabs living in a 4,000-mile strategic swath of territory stretching from Morocco to Oman is ludicrous. It becomes even more ludicrous when one realizes that the relationship also has alienated another 750 million Muslims who, together with the Arabs, control more than 60 percent of the world's proven oil and gas reserves.

Apologists for Israel also describe the U.S.-Israeli cooperation in weapons development. The fact is that the one or two successful joint weapons programs have been largely U.S. financed, while for their part the Israelis have repeatedly sold to rogue nations U.S. weapons turned over at no cost to Israel.

It is a sad but proven fact that the Israeli government also has obtained secret U.S. military technology which Israel has sold to other countries. For example, after the U.S. sent Patriot missile defense batteries on an emergency basis to help defend Israel during the Gulf War, the Israelis seem to have sold the Patriot missile technology to China, according to the U.S. State Department's inspector general. As a result, the U.S. has been forced to develop a whole new generation of missile technology able to penetrate the defenses China has developed as a result of the Israeli treachery.

Perhaps the most hypocritical rationalization offered by friends of Israel is that U.S. special treatment is justified because Israel is "the Middle East's only working democracy" and that Israel and the U.S. have many basic institutions in common. In fact, Israeli democracy does not work for non-Jews. In contrast to the United States, where by law all citizens have equal rights regardless of religion or ethnic origin, Muslim and Christian citizens of Israel do not have equal rights with regards to military service, the extensive social benefits available to veterans of Israeli military service, or even in terms of Israeli tax rates imposed on Arab citizens and Israeli government expenditures in Arab communities within Israel.

Further, Israeli citizenship is not available to the Muslim and Christian Palestinians driven from their homes in Israel in 1948, nor to their descendants. But a Jew, born anywhere in the world, can have Israeli citizenship for the asking.

Perhaps most shocking is the little-known fact that by now 90 percent of the land in Israel proper is held under restrictive covenants barring non-Jews, even those with Israeli citizenship, from owning the land or from earning a living on it. Unfortunately, the land held under such covenants is increasing, not decreasing. It would be difficult, therefore, to find two countries more profoundly different in their approaches to basic questions of citizenship and civil and human rights as are the United States and Israel.

Richard H Curtiss is the executive editor of the Washington Report on Middle East Affairs, *and is the author of two books on US policies in the Middle East. During WWII, Curtiss served in the US Army and later as a career foreign service officer with the Department of State and the U.S. Information Agency in Djakarta, Bonn, Stuttgart, Ankara, Beirut (three times), Baghdad, Damascus and Rhodes. Curtiss earned his degree in Journalism from the University of Southern California and is a recipient of the Edward R. Murrow Award for Excellence in Public Diplomacy, the U.S.I.A.'s highest professional recognition.*

This article is reprinted with permission from the *Washington Report on Middle East Affairs.*

Afterword by Mark Green

When Richard Curtiss' trenchant analysis of America's Israeli-centered policies first appeared, the attacks of 911 were still years away. Curtiss' ominous political assessment, and others like it, was widely ignored. And its deeper meaning, that Israel may indeed be a political liability, rather than a US asset, remains nearly as taboo now as then. If Curtiss is to be faulted, it may only be for the narrow formula he uses in assessing the decades-long economic "costs" connected with our nation's uninterrupted funding of the Zionist enterprise.

Indeed, according an analysis published in the Christian Science Monitor (12-9-02), indirect US costs associated with sustaining Israel since 1948 go far beyond Curtiss' straightforward aid figures. Thomas Stauffer, an independent Washington DC economist, estimates that the total US outlays (through 2002) for the Zion-American alliance lies in the area of some two trillion dollars, which is roughly twice the amount of money that the US squandered on the entire Viet Nam War.

It must be noted that Stauffer is famously at odds with the Israel Lobby, but his observations about the economic repercussions associated with the Washington's "special relationship" with Tel Aviv cannot be ignored, even though 'official' Washington and Big Media try.

Please also bear in mind that Stauffer's astounding estimates do *not* include Bush-Cheney's recent and ongoing *trillion-dollar makeover* of Iraq that began in 2003, only months after Stauffer's eye-popping report was first issued.

19

Among the real but unacknowledged US expenses that Stauffer identifies as being Israel-related are:

1973 Oil Embargo and subsequent tripling of oil prices.

In the midst of the Arab-Israeli 'October War' of 1973, the US secretly funneled tons of advanced and high-priced weaponry to the Jewish State. When the Arabs realized that the United States, their biggest trading partner, had orchestrated their humiliating defeat, the infamous Arab oil embargo ensued. This tripled the price of oil, sending the US economy into prolonged recession. Stauffer puts the economic toll at (in 2001 dollars) at 420 billion dollars, with the rise in oil prices costing an additional 450 billion dollars.

Strategic Petroleum Reserve:

Established to deter the impact of another oil embargo. This federally subsidized 'reserve' of oil has cost at least the taxpayer (in 2001 dollars) some 134 billion dollars.

Continued aid to Egypt and Jordan:

Since signing their peace agreements with Israel, these two autocratic governments have received well over 140 billion dollars in US aid. As long as they continue to play ball with the Israelis, US money will flow their way.

Special Loan and Tax Privileges:

Israel enjoys special trade status, commercial loan privileges, and unique benefits (including US-imposed sanctions against anti-Zionist regimes like Iran) that often fly under the radar but still cost US taxpayers billions. These special deals run the gamut from tax deductions that allow American Jews to deduct contributions to Israel (which drains our treasury) to Israeli housing loans, outright grants, and costly joint-development military programs with the Jewish State. The loss of trade (and degradation of our currency) that's attributable to America's political posture in the Middle East is surely massive but in the end, incalculable. -mg

Carter and the Swarm

by Israel Shamir

Publication of Jimmy Carter's *Palestine: Peace Not Apartheid* is a great event for America and for all of us. It's not that Carter said anything we did not already know about Palestine. Before Carter, we already knew that the Zionists had established a racist apartheid regime in the Holy Land where Jews have rights, and goyim have duties. Before Carter we knew a native Palestinian has no right to vote, move or work freely in his land — that he is locked up behind the twenty-foot wall. Before Carter we knew that the US support allowed the atrocities to occur and the apartheid regime to entrench. But what we did not know was that there are prominent Americans who would dare the wrath of organised Jewry and spell it out loud.

Why did President Carter do it? Why did he risk his peaceful old age and gently fading glory to endure an attack by Israel's Fifth Column as merciless as the Four Columns' onslaught on Gaza? He was moved by compassion, that supreme Christian virtue of feeling together with the suffering and the oppressed. He saw the suffering of Palestine and he could not keep quiet. He upheld an honourable American tradition: that of Mark Twain who condemned the US atrocities in Philippines, that of Henry Thoreau speaking against the Mexican War. This is a universal tradition, too: Multatuli unmasked the Dutch atrocities in Indonesia, Roger Casement did it to the

Belgians in Congo, Radishchev bewept the fate of the Russian peasant. And their voices changed our world, though not immediately. Carter is not a radical — a man of hotter temper would call to eliminate the infamy called 'The Jewish State' altogether. Carter's message is soft and gentle; so soft and compassionate that only the arrogant and power-intoxicated won't be able to live with it. Others (including me) have been harder and more explicit, but then, we others weren't former US presidents.

Why now? The apartheid system in Palestine was bad enough ten years ago to warrant his intervention, but this despondent helplessness we now witness is a new phenomenon. The hope kept alive by Camp David, by peace with Egypt, by the Madrid and Oslo conferences, is dead. A year of severe blockade has engendered a confrontation between the Palestinian parties and the Jewish wet dream of an inter-Palestinian civil war is about to come true. The Holy Land is on the verge of collapse. President Carter is 82, and he is not afraid of anything. At this age, in this stage of life, statesmen are likely to speak their mind, like the Malaysian PM Mohammad Mahathir did after his retirement. This is the time for unpalatable truth: the ideological and spiritual guidance of the West, dislodged from the hands of the Church, passed over to the usurpers of Zion. While they rule, Palestine has no chance.

Though most ordinary US Jews are sane and sensible, these decisions are made by super-rich, super-powerful, super-chauvinist Jews who are anything but. They are the power pushing for war. Carter wants to stop the disaster in the Middle East, by convincing the sane and rebutting the arrogant. Thus the President joined the fracas, as traditional WASP America tries to regain lost ground and save the country they love from destruction. The WASPs, with their immense property holdings, traditions and roots found themselves marginalised by the Jews, with their death grip on the media and universities: indeed, Spirit rules over Matter. The reports by the Baker-Hamilton Iraq Study Group and Walt – Mearsheimer are the first salvos fired by this WASP Intifada. A Jewish American columnist (a resident in Israel writing for Israel's Haaretz) named Burston correctly stated that "Carter's true intended target was the organized

American Jewish community." Carter pointed out the main reasons for apartheid in the Holy Land, says Burston:

- Jewish control of [the US] government: "It would be almost politically suicidal for members of Congress to espouse a balanced position between Israel and Palestine, to suggest that Israel comply with international law or to speak in defense of justice or human rights for Palestinians."

- Jewish control of the [US] media: "What is even more difficult to comprehend is why the editorial pages of the major newspapers and magazines in the United States exercise similar self-restraint, quite contrary to private assessments expressed quite forcefully by their correspondents in the Holy Land."

After Carter spoke, he was immediately counter-attacked by organised Jewry – you couldn't miss it! In my native Siberia, in its short and furious summer, you can watch a swarm of gnats attack a horse, each small bloodsucker eager for his piece of the action. After a while, the blinded and infuriated animal rushes headlong in a mad sprint and soon finds its death in the bottomless moors. The Jews developed the same style of attack. It is never a single voice arguing the case, but always a mass attack from the left and the right, from below and above, until the attacked one is beaten and broken and crawls away in disgrace.

Each attacker is as tiny and irrelevant as a single gnat, but as a swarm they are formidable. Observe them separately: Dershowitz, an advocate of torture and of hostage killing, an apprehended plagiarist who never was elected to any position of authority and commands no respect, demands to debate the president. It is indeed beyond chutzpah; but Dershowitz is supported by other Jews in prime positions and his ridiculous demand is seconded by both university and media until this thieving nonentity gets equal time on a TV channel to present "his case". Another gnat is a Deborah Lipstadt, a nonentity brought forth by the *Washington Post*. Plenty of others are even smaller than these two, for instance 14 Jews who gave up their positions at Carter Center. If they were not able to keep the media in their hands, they wouldn't be heard by anyone but their spouses.

Their technique is quite simple: They switch the focus of argument onto the personality of their adversary. Thus, instead of discussing apartheid in Israel, we discuss Jimmy Carter, whether he is a bigot and anti-Semite (thus Foxman, the "bad Jew") or he is not (Avnery, the "good Jew"). The correct answer is "irrelevant": Carter's love for Jews or lack of it has no bearing on the question of apartheid in Palestine. Likewise, if we discuss the situation in Bosnia or Kosovo, we do not go into our sentiments towards Serbs, Albanians or Croats. But Jews are different!

For instance, General Wesley Clark said that rich Jews, the great donors of Washington politicians, push for war with Iran. Well, this can be discussed, maybe even denied, but instead they derail the discussion into another topic, whether Clark is an anti-Semite. Matthew Yglesias provides the sources for the whole kosher hog, from comparison with *The Protocols,* to the inevitable quote from Foxman who says Clark had "bought into conspiratorial bigotry". From this moment, Clark will stick to defending himself, and the guys will take care that his hands will be full. Here again, the correct answer is a polite shrug: who cares whether Clark is a bigot? Maybe he is also a paedophile and usurer, but this *ad hominem* has no bearing on what he said. And an accusation "you do not love Jews" is not much different from "You do not love your aunt", and you probably have learned to live with it at the age of six.

A good book to accustom oneself to this sort of attack is Michael Bulgakov's The Master and the Margarita. This marvelous book shows the Jewish critics' swarm attack on a writer who dared to write about Christ. Indeed, whoever mentions Christ will experience it sooner or later.

I also had a personal taste of this swarm attack. During the Tsunami disaster in Thailand I discovered that the Jewish undertakers, Zaka, forced the Thais to delay mass burial of victims for a day or two, despite the real and immediate danger of epidemic diseases, in order to avoid a real calamity: that holy Jewish bodies might be inadvertently buried together with the goyim. I was told so by the members of Zaka team who were quite proud of their feat. I wrote about it (Tsunami in Gaza). It was republished by a few sites. Then, a British Jew named Manfred Ropschitz began an *ad hominem* campaign against me. Other Jews joined the fray, discussing whether I am a Jew, or a "Swedish-Russian Nazi anti-Semite", as if this had any bearing on the tsunami story. Instead of shrugging it off, other supporters of Palestine switched to this piquant subject. They carried their discussion from The Times to their email lists, until eventually, another Jewish "antizionist" commented with deep satisfaction: "Shamir is marginalised and brought into disrepute".

Ropschitz did not try to disprove the story, for the story was true. He wrote: "With an army of journalists crawling over the Tsunami story I'd expect to have heard such shocking news by now − if it's true. I am a journalist and I don't believe it." No, gentlemen, you won't hear a true story if it is not acceptable to Ropschitzes of this world. They will hunt you to the far-away corner of the world, and there are not many people who care to risk their well-planned attacks. Indeed, one ought to be a real kamikaze to enter this fight. The Ropschitzes, these quite ordinary Jews who fully identify with their community, are the key to the swarm attack. There are many Jewish media-lords, even more Jewish editors, but it is the Ropschitzes that clinch the party line. These willing executioners of our freedom, these footsoldiers of the media lords, automatically defend "the Jews" (i.e., the organised Jewish community) at any price. Ordinary human beings of Jewish origin can be of any opinion. Likewise, ordinary Americans do not decide whether their country will attack Iran or not. But Bush and Cheney alone can't fight the Iraqi war, and the Jewish media lords would be powerless without their willing executioners of freedom.

The Gentile philo-Semites are even worse, observed Eustace Mullins, the legendary American writer whose best-selling books (running into the millions) were never published or distributed by the mainstream press. He wrote:

> "It has long been common knowledge since the incorporation of the three [US] major national television networks that each of them was owned, operated and controlled by

Jews. Now at last, or so it seemed, the Christians of America would have their own Christian television network on which they could observe the tenets of the Christian religion. Or so it seemed. And when the CBN began its daily broadcasting, what was its daily message? We must love the Jews. We must support the State of Israel in all its depredations and its immoral devastation of the Holy Christian Shrines in the Birthplace of Our Saviour. We must help the Jews, and we must, above all, avoid the greatest sin, the sin of 'anti-Semitism', whatever that is. Even the Jewish networks do not broadcast as blatantly pro-Jewish propaganda as the Christian Broadcasting Network."

A man died this week in France, a real saint, who was known by the affectionate appellation of "Abbè Pierre", a priest who fought with the Resistance, helped the homeless, provided for the poor and was a great friend of the Palestinians. In 1996 he was hounded almost to death after he expressed his support for another friend of Palestine, Roger Garaudy, who wrote a book called "The Founding Myths of Israeli Politics". A victim of Jewish swarm attack, he went into seclusion in Italy and Switzerland, deserted by the very people he fought for. His sorry fate should be remembered by the French, and bother their conscience. If the Maid of Orleans was executed by the British Occupation regime (though using French collaborationists), no such excuse is available for those who ostracised the Abbè Pierre: they just got frightened by the swarm attack.

This fear of Jewish swarm attacks has already brought much sorrow to mankind. In 1930s, the famous American aviator Charles Lindbergh called for the US to stay out of the approaching war in Europe. He was attacked by the Jewish media as a Nazi and a Hitler sympathiser, was besmirched and "overnight Lindbergh went from cultural hero to moral pariah". Now again, the US is being pushed by the same forces into a new war, this time in the Middle East. Let us try and stop it by being fearless, for as a Jewish Hassid spiritual song hath it, "haikar lo lefahed bihlal" — the most important thing is not to be afraid at all. Carter brought us hope that there is an America the world can live with: a non-aggressive, democratic

America, whose policies aren't decided by the rich donors, but by the ordinary Americans who voted against the war, and who today gather in Washington calling to stop its escalation.

Israel Shamir is a prominent Russian-Israeli writer, translator and journalist. He is especially well known to Russian readers, thanks to his books "The Pine and the Olive" and "Travels in Japan", and for his translations of Joyce, Homer and Agnon.

Born in Siberia, Shamir is the grandson of a professor of mathematics and a descendant of a Rabbi from Tiberias, Palestine. He studied at the prestigious School of the Academy of Sciences, and read Math and Law at Novosibirsk University. He has written for Haaretz, worked at the BBC, and is a scholar in Judaic studies. A book of his collected essays "Flowers of Galilee" has earned considerable praise. Shamir is also a combat veteran of the Israeli Army and stands among the leading advocates of a 'One Man, One Vote, One State' solution to the Israel-Palestine dilemma. He is the father of three sons, and lives in Jaffa, Israel.

As The Arabs
See The Jews

by His Majesty King Abdullah

November, 1947

Summary

This fascinating essay, written by [the late] King Hussein's grandfather King Abdullah, appeared in the United States six months before the 1948 Arab-Israeli War.

In the article, King Abdullah disputes the mistaken view that Arab opposition to Zionism (and later the state of Israel) is because of longstanding religious or ethnic hatred. He notes that Jews and Muslims enjoyed a long history of peaceful coexistence in the Middle East, and that Jews have historically suffered far more at the hands of Christian Europe. Pointing to the tragedy of the holocaust that Jews suffered during World War II, the monarch asks why America and Europe are refusing to accept more than a token handful of Jewish immigrants and refugees. It is unfair, he argues, to make Palestine, which is innocent of anti-Semitism, pay for the crimes of Europe. King Abdullah also asks how Jews can claim a historic right to Palestine, when Arabs have been the overwhelming majority there for nearly 1300 uninterrupted years? The essay ends on an ominous note, warning of dire consequences if a peaceful solution cannot be found to protect the rights of the indigenous Arabs of Palestine. –The American Magazine, 1947

"As the Arabs see the Jews"

by His Majesty King Abdullah,

The American Magazine, November, 1947

I am especially delighted to address an American audience, for the tragic problem of Palestine will never be solved without American understanding, American sympathy, American support.

So many billions of words have been written about Palestine—perhaps more than on any other subject in history—that I hesitate to add to them. Yet I am compelled to do so, for I am reluctantly convinced that the world in general, and America in particular, knows almost nothing of the true case for the Arabs.

We Arabs follow, perhaps far more than you think, the press of America. We are frankly disturbed to find that for every word printed on the Arab side, a thousand are printed on the Zionist side.

There are many reasons for this. You have many millions of Jewish citizens interested in this question. They are highly vocal and wise in the ways of publicity. There are few Arab citizens in America, and we are as yet unskilled in the technique of modern propaganda.

The results have been alarming for us. In your press we see a horrible caricature and are told it is our true portrait. In all justice, we cannot let this pass by default.

Our case is quite simple: For nearly 2,000 years Palestine has been almost 100 per cent Arab. It is still preponderantly Arab today, in spite of enormous Jewish immigration. But if this immigration continues we shall soon be outnumbered—a minority in our home.

Palestine is a small and very poor country, about the size of your state of Vermont. Its Arab population is only about 1,200,000. Already we have had forced on us, against our will, some 600,000 Zionist Jews. We are threatened with many hundreds of thousands more.

Our position is so simple and natural that we are amazed it should even be questioned. It is exactly the same position you in America take in regard to the unhappy European Jews. You are sorry for them, but you do not want them in your country.

We do not want them in ours, either. Not because they are Jews, but because they are foreigners. We would not want hundreds of thousands of foreigners in our country, be they Englishmen or Norwegians or Brazilians or whatever.

Think for a moment: In the last 25 years we have had one third of our entire population forced upon us. In America that would be the equivalent of 45,000,000 complete strangers admitted to your country, over your violent protest, since 1921. How would you have reacted to that?

Because of our perfectly natural dislike of being overwhelmed in our own homeland, we are called blind nationalists and heartless anti-Semites. This charge would be ludicrous were it not so dangerous.

No people on earth have been less "anti-Semitic" than the Arabs. The persecution of the Jews has been confined almost entirely to the Christian nations of the West. Jews, themselves, will admit that never since the Great Dispersion did Jews develop so freely and reach such importance as in Spain when it was an Arab possession. With very minor exceptions, Jews have lived for many centuries in the Middle East, in complete peace and friendliness with their Arab neighbors.

Damascus, Baghdad, Beirut and other Arab centers have always contained large and prosperous Jewish colonies. Until the Zionist invasion of Palestine began, these Jews received the most generous treatment—far, far better than in Christian Europe. Now, unhappily, for the first time in history, these Jews are beginning to feel the effects of Arab resistance to the Zionist assault. Most of them are as anxious as Arabs to stop it. Most of these Jews who have found happy homes among us resent, as we do, the coming of these strangers.

I was puzzled for a long time about the odd belief which apparently persists in America that Palestine has somehow "always been a Jewish land." Recently an American I talked to cleared up this mystery. He pointed out that the only things most Americans know about Palestine are what they read in the Bible. It was a Jewish land in those days, they reason, and they assume it has always remained so.

Nothing could be farther from the truth. It is absurd to reach so far back into the mists of history to argue about who should have Palestine today, and I apologize for it. Yet the Jews do this, and I must reply to their "historic claim." I wonder if the world has ever seen a stranger sight than a group of people seriously pretending to claim a land because their ancestors lived there some 2,000 years ago!

If you suggest that I am biased, I invite you to read any sound history of the period and verify the facts.

Such fragmentary records as we have indicate that the Jews were wandering nomads from Iraq who moved to southern Turkey, came south to Palestine, stayed there a short time, and then passed to Egypt, where they remained about 400 years. About 1300 BC (according to your calendar) they left Egypt and gradually conquered most—but not all—of the inhabitants of Palestine.

It is significant that the Philistines—not the Jews—gave their name to the country: "Palestine" is merely the Greek form of "Philistia."

Only once, during the empire of David and Solomon, did the Jews ever control nearly—but not all—the land which is today Palestine. This empire lasted only 70 years, ending in 926 BC. Only 250 years later the Kingdom of Judah had shrunk to a small province around Jerusalem, barely a quarter of modern Palestine.

In 63 BC the Jews were conquered by Roman Pompey, and never again had even the vestige of independence. The Roman Emperor Hadrian finally wiped them out about 135 AD. He utterly destroyed Jerusalem, rebuilt under another name, and for hundreds of years no Jew was permitted to enter it. A handful of Jews remained in Palestine but the vast majority were killed or scattered to other countries, in the Diaspora, or the Great Dispersion. From that time Palestine ceased to be a Jewish country, in any conceivable sense.

This was 1,815 years ago, and yet the Jews solemnly pretend they still own Palestine! If such fantasy were allowed, how the map of the world would dance about!

Italians might claim England, which the Romans held so long. England might claim France, "homeland" of the conquering Normans. And the French Normans might claim Norway, where their ancestors originated. And incidentally, we Arabs might claim Spain, which we held for 700 years.

Many Mexicans might claim Spain, "homeland" of their forefathers. They might even claim Texas, which was Mexican until 100 years ago. And suppose the American Indians claimed the "homeland" of which they were the sole, native, and ancient occupants until only some 450 years ago!

I am not being facetious. All these claims are just as valid—or just as fantastic—as the Jewish "historic connection" with Palestine. Most are more valid.

In any event, the great Moslem expansion about 650 AD finally settled things. It dominated Palestine completely. From that day on, Palestine was solidly Arabic in population, language, and religion. When British armies entered the country during the last war, they found 500,000 Arabs and only 65,000 Jews.

If solid, uninterrupted Arab occupation for nearly 1,300 years does not make a country "Arab", what does?

The Jews say, and rightly, that Palestine is the home of their religion. It is likewise the birthplace of Christianity, but would any

Christian nation claim it on that account? In passing, let me say that the Christian Arabs—and there are many hundreds of thousands of them in the Arab World—are in absolute agreement with all other Arabs in opposing the Zionist invasion of Palestine.

May I also point out that Jerusalem is, after Mecca and Medina, the holiest place in Islam. In fact, in the early days of our religion, Moslems prayed toward Jerusalem instead of Mecca.

The Jewish "religious claim" to Palestine is as absurd as the "historic claim." The Holy Places, sacred to three great religions, must be open to all, the monopoly of none. Let us not confuse religion and politics.

We are told that we are inhumane and heartless because do not accept with open arms the perhaps 200,000 Jews in Europe who suffered so frightfully under Nazi cruelty, and who even now— almost three years after war's end—still languish in cold, depressing camps.

Let me underline several facts. The unimaginable persecution of the Jews was not done by the Arabs: it was done by a Christian nation in the West. The war which ruined Europe and made it almost impossible for these Jews to rehabilitate themselves was fought by the Christian nations of the West. The rich and empty portions of the earth belong, not to the Arabs, but to the Christian nations of the West.

And yet, to ease their consciences, these Christian nations of the West are asking Palestine—a poor and tiny Moslem country of the East—to accept the entire burden. "We have hurt these people terribly," cries the West to the East. "Won't you please take care of them for us?"

We find neither logic nor justice in this. Are we therefore "cruel and heartless nationalists"?

We are a generous people: we are proud that "Arab hospitality" is a phrase famous throughout the world. We are a humane people: no one was shocked more than we by the Hitlerite terror. No one pities the present plight of the desperate European Jews more than we.

But we say that Palestine has already sheltered 600,000 refugees. We believe that is enough to expect of us—even too much. We believe it is now the turn of the rest of the world to accept some of them.

I will be entirely frank with you. There is one thing the Arab world simply cannot understand. Of all the nations of the earth, America is most insistent that something be done for these suffering Jews of Europe. This feeling does credit to the humanity for which America is famous, and to that glorious inscription on your Statue of Liberty.

And yet this same America—the richest, greatest, most powerful nation the world has ever known—refuses to accept more than a token handful of these same Jews herself!

I hope you will not think I am being bitter about this. I have tried hard to understand that mysterious paradox, and I confess I cannot. Nor can any other Arab.

Perhaps you have been informed that "the Jews in Europe want to go to no other place except Palestine."

This myth is one of the greatest propaganda triumphs of the Jewish Agency for Palestine, the organization which promotes with fanatic zeal the emigration to Palestine. It is a subtle half-truth, thus doubly dangerous.

The astounding truth is that nobody on earth *really* knows where these unfortunate Jews *really* want to go!

You would think that in so grave a problem, the American, British, and other authorities responsible for the European Jews would have made a very careful survey, probably by vote, to find out where each Jew actually wants to go. Amazingly enough this has never been done! The Jewish Agency has prevented it.

Some time ago the American Military Governor in Germany was asked at a press conference how he was so certain that all Jews there wanted to go to Palestine. His answer was simple: "My Jewish advisors tell me so." He admitted no poll had ever been made. Preparations were indeed begun for one, but the Jewish Agency stepped in to stop it.

The truth is that the Jews in German camps are now subjected to a Zionist pressure campaign which learned much from the Nazi terror. It is dangerous for a Jew to say that he would rather go to some other country, not Palestine. Such dissenters have been severely beaten, and worse.

Not long ago, in Palestine, nearly 1,000 Austrian Jews informed the international refugee organization that they would like to go back to Austria, and plans were made to repatriate them.

The Jewish Agency heard of this, and exerted enough political pressure to stop it. It would be bad propaganda for Zionism if Jews began leaving Palestine. The nearly 1,000 Austrian are still there, against their will.

The fact is that most of the European Jews are Western in culture and outlook, entirely urban in experience and habits. They cannot really have their hearts set on becoming pioneers in the barren, arid, cramped land which is Palestine.

One thing, however, is undoubtedly true. As matters stand now, most refugee Jews in Europe would, indeed, vote for Palestine, simply because they know no other country will have them.

If you or I were given a choice between a near-prison camp for the rest of our lives—or Palestine—we would both choose Palestine, too.

But open up any other alternative to them—give them any other choice, and see what happens!

No poll, however, will be worth anything unless the nations of the earth are willing to open their doors—just a little—to the Jews.

In other words, if in such a poll a Jew says he wants to go to Sweden, Sweden must be willing to accept him. If he votes for America, you must let him come in.

Any other kind of poll would be a farce. For the desperate Jew, this is no idle testing of opinion: this is a grave matter of life or death. Unless he is absolutely sure that his vote means something, he will always vote for Palestine, so as not to risk his bird in the hand for one in the bush.

In any event, Palestine can accept no more. The 65,000 Jews in Palestine in 1918 have jumped to 600,000 today. We Arabs have increased, too, but not by immigration. The Jews were then a mere 11 per cent of our population. Today they are one third of it.

The rate of increase has been terrifying. In a few more years—unless stopped now—it will overwhelm us, and we shall be an important minority in our own home.

Surely the rest of the wide world is rich enough and generous enough to find a place for 200,000 Jews—about one third the number that tiny, poor Palestine has already sheltered. For the rest of the world, it is hardly a drop in the bucket. For us it means national suicide.

We are sometimes told that since the Jews came to Palestine, the Arab standard of living has improved. This is a most complicated question. But let us even assume, for the argument, that it is true. We would rather be a bit poorer, and masters of our own home. Is this unnatural?

The sorry story of the so-called "Balfour Declaration," which started Zionist immigration into Palestine, is too complicated to repeat here in detail. It is grounded in broken promises to the Arabs—promises made in cold print which admit no denying.

We utterly deny its validity. We utterly deny the right of Great Britain to give away Arab land for a "national home" for an entirely foreign people.

Even the League of Nations sanction does not alter this. At the time, not a single Arab state was a member of the League. We were not allowed to say a word in our own defense.

I must point out, again in friendly frankness, that America was nearly as responsible as Britain for this Balfour Declaration. President Wilson approved it before it was issued, and the American Congress adopted it word for word in a joint resolution on 30th June, 1922.

In the 1920s, Arabs were annoyed and insulted by Zionist immigration, but not alarmed by it. It was steady, but fairly small, as even the Zionist founders thought it would remain. Indeed for some years, more Jews left Palestine than entered it—in 1927 almost twice as many.

But two new factors, entirely unforeseen by Britain or the League or America or the most fervent Zionist, arose in the early thirties to raise the immigration to undreamed heights. One was the World Depression; the second the rise of Hitler.

In 1932, the year before Hitler came to power, only 9,500 Jews came to Palestine. We did not welcome them, but we were not afraid that, at that rate, our solid Arab majority would ever be in danger.

But the next year—the year of Hitler—it jumped to 30,000! In 1934 it was 42,000! In 1935 it reached 61,000!

It was no longer the orderly arrival of idealist Zionists. Rather, all Europe was pouring its frightened Jews upon us. Then, at last, we, too, became frightened. We knew that unless this enormous influx stopped, we were, as Arabs, doomed in our Palestine homeland. And we have not changed our minds.

I have the impression that many Americans believe the trouble in Palestine is very remote from them, that America had little to do with it, and that your only interest now is that of a humane bystander.

I believe that you do not realize how directly you are, as a nation, responsible in general for the whole Zionist move and specifically for the present terrorism. I call this to your attention because I am certain that if you realize your responsibility you will act fairly to admit it and assume it.

Quite aside from official American support for the "National Home" of the Balfour Declaration, the Zionist settlements in Palestine would have been almost impossible, on anything like the current scale, without American money. This was contributed by American Jewry in an idealistic effort to help their fellows.

The motive was worthy: the results were disastrous. The contributions were by private individuals, but they were almost entirely Americans, and, as a nation, only America can answer for it.

The present catastrophe may be laid almost entirely at your door. Your government, almost alone in the world, is insisting on the immediate admission of 100,000 more Jews into Palestine—to be followed by countless additional ones. This will have the most frightful consequences in bloody chaos beyond anything ever hinted at in Palestine before.

It is your press and political leadership, almost alone in the world, who press this demand. It is almost entirely American money which hires or buys the "refugee ships" that steam illegally toward Palestine: American money which pays their crews. The illegal immigration from Europe is arranged by the Jewish Agency, supported almost entirely by American funds. It is American dollars which support the terrorists, which buy the bullets and pistols that kill British soldiers—your allies—and Arab citizens—your friends.

We in the Arab world were stunned to hear that you permit open advertisements in newspapers asking for money to finance these terrorists, to arm them openly and deliberately for murder. We could not believe this could really happen in the modern world. Now we must believe it: we have seen the advertisements with our own eyes.

I point out these things because nothing less than complete frankness will be of use. The crisis is too stark for mere polite vagueness which means nothing.

I have the most complete confidence in the fair-mindedness and generosity of the American public. We Arabs ask no favors. We ask only that you know the full truth, not half of it. We ask only that when you judge the Palestine question, you put yourselves in our place.

What would your answer be if some outside agency told you that you must accept in America many millions of utter strangers in your midst—enough to dominate your country—merely because they insisted on going to America, and because their forefathers had once lived there some 2,000 years ago?

Our answer is the same.

And what would be your action if, in spite of your refusal, this outside agency began forcing them on you?

Ours will be the same.

King Abdullah bin Al-Hussein (1882–1951) gradually established, in the wake of WWI, the first centralized governmental system in the Hashemite Kingdom of Jordan. Over three decades, he transformed a mostly tribal and nomadic society into a constitutional monarchy and acted as a mentor to his grandson and eventual heir, the late King Hussein I of Jordan.

Christian Zionism as a Representation of American Manifest Destiny

by Lawrence Davidson

Department of History, West Chester University, Pennsylvania, USA

The Bipolar Worldview

We swim in a sea of culture. Our culture and its traditions set parameters for perception that still, despite the 'globalizing' nature of our
world, create in-groups and out-groups, and tell us what is comfortable and uncomfortable, right and wrong. Matthew Arnold once put
it this way: culture creates a picture of societal 'perfection' and then
sends us out to 'make it prevail.'[1] That is what the West has been
doing for at least the past 200 years (led for the last 60 years by the
United States). Mesmerized by the power drawn from its industrial
and scientific revolutions, the West has glorified its own culture as one
of modernity and progress. To this claim it has added the champion-
ship of Judeo-Christian values and, more recently, the democratic
political system. And then, with a sense of divinely granted manifest
destiny, the West has gone out into the rest of the world and sought
to universalize that culture. In truth this expansion, this process
of self-glorification, has been pursued mainly through imperialist

conquest and economic penetration. However, the parameters set by their cultural paradigm do not allow most Westerners to see it that way. Instead, they have traditionally seen their own actions through the rationalizing lens of a bipolar worldview.

The bipolar world view marries the positive and romantic self-conception of the West as a modern, progressive, moral, and democratic place, with a corresponding negative perception of the East as a backward, fanatical, immoral, and tyrannical zone in need of guidance and control. As the work of Edward Said work has shown, this perception of the non-West is essential to the West's own idea of itself: 'The Orient has helped to define Europe (or the West) as its contrasting image, idea, personality, experience.'[2] Thus, one really cannot separate the two. It also allows the West to perceive the universalization of its culture—its manifest destiny—as a pursuit, in Arthur Balfour's words, of 'the general welfare of mankind.' [3] *Ipso facto*, imperialism becomes altruistic.

One particularly important aspect of the bipolar worldview—important because of its continuing impact on perception and policy in the United States—is its religious content. This speaks specifically to the Western claim to possess in Protestant Christianity a superior, or 'true,' religion. Here the West's altruistic mission to bring the East the virtues of good government and the hardware of progress is melded to the proselytizing zeal of Protestant evangelical fundamentalism.

This religious aspect of the bipolar world view has taken on a special meaning when applied by Americans to the Holy Land, or what is now Israel and Palestine. Most Americans have understood the Holy Land principally in terms of its biblical representation.[4] Having learned a romantic version of Western and American history in public school, they have also learned romanticized variants on the biblical history of the Holy Land in Sunday and Hebrew schools. One consequence of this is that the mythical Palestine of the Bible is much more meaningful to many than the Palestine actually inhabited by millions of contemporary Palestinian Arabs. Another consequence is that for as many as 40 million Americans who characterize themselves as Christian fundamentalists,[5] Palestine has primary meaning in terms of its place in prophetic interpretation.

There is a parallel, pseudo-historical storyline to all this that fits neatly with the bipolar world view: That in the dim past the 'real' (biblical) Palestine that is the Holy Land was stolen from Christendom (the West) by heathen Muslims (the East) who, over the centuries, have transformed the 'land of milk and honey' into a 'land of dust.'[6] Rectification of this situation has been a longstanding objective of conservative Protestants. Beginning in the nineteenth century, rectification started to appear possible. The Ottoman Empire, in whose territory the Holy Land rested, was on the wane, and the imperialist, expanding West was correspondingly waxing. This growing Western strength would express itself, in part, through the dispersal of Western evangelical missionaries throughout the world, including the Middle East.

America as the Spearhead of Western Manifest Destiny

Among the most avid of these missionaries were American Protestants trained specifically for such overseas efforts at colleges and seminaries in New England beginning in the 1830s. Their efforts were coordinated and financed by a long-lived organization named the American Board of Commissioners for Foreign Missions (ABCFM). What is particularly interesting about their efforts is that they merged their mission to redeem the Holy Land (and the rest of the world as well) with the firm belief that the American political, economic, and social culture was the God-ordained ideal version of the already glorified Western culture. This means that Western manifest destiny should be spearheaded by the advancement of American culture, which was as important to spread about as Protestant Christianity. In fact, in the minds of American missionaries, the two were almost synonymous. For example, the Reverend John Codman addressed supporters of American missionaries in 1836 in the following way:

How can we better testify our appreciation of [America's] free institutions, than by laboring to plant them in other lands? For where the Gospel goes in its purity and power, there will follow in its train the blessings of civilization, and good government. ... Coming himself from a land of freedom, he [the missionary] will naturally spread around him an atmosphere of liberty.[7]

Codman was expressing a connection between God, Western civilization and the United States that was more or less taken for granted, not only by American clergymen but also by American politicians and other spokesmen. That is how America has seen its own manifest destiny. It comes from God. The sincere belief in this proposition can be seen as early as 1630 when John Winthrop proclaimed New England as the home of his divinely blessed 'City upon a Hill' in which God would 'delight to dwell among us as his own people.'[8] The settlements of the Pilgrims and Puritans were generally thought of as a 'new Israel' linking the sacred history of biblical 'covenant lands' to the destiny of America. This outlook still prevailed in the mid-nineteenth century when the editor and essayist John L. O'Sullivan declared that America's divinely sanctioned project was to overrun the continent and then to establish 'on earth the moral dignity and salvation of man.'[9] He coined the term 'manifest destiny.' This idea, that America has a God-given destiny, has been reaffirmed in the inaugural speeches of US presidents. One finds that God is identified with a 'divinely blessed' America and its mission in the world in every single one of them except the one for Thomas Jefferson's second inauguration (which was only several paragraphs long).[10] As Albert Weinberg has demonstrated in his comprehensive study of the phenomenon of American manifest destiny, westward expansion across the continent (and the near genocidal displacement of 'heathen' native Americans) was rationalized repeatedly by references to providence, 'natural right,' the 'creator,' and 'God's will.'[11] When William McKinley decided to retain the Philippines as an American colony following the Spanish-American War, he did so only after staying up praying all night. In the morning God had given him the needed justification: America would keep the Philippines to 'uplift, and civilize and Christianize' the (Catholic and Muslim) natives. One result was a colonial war that (officially) lasted from 1899 to 1902 and took the lives of 4,234 Americans and at least 220,000 Filipinos.[12]

With time this integration of God into what Benedict Anderson might call America's 'imagined community'[13] has taken on even greater proportions. What was originally only an alliance between God and America's continental destiny, has now become God's alleged assertion that American manifest destiny is synonymous with the world's destiny. The fact that President George W. Bush's crusade for democratic freedom—'our democratic faith is more than the creed of our country, it is the inborn hope of humanity ... a trust we bear and pass along'[14] will be 'passed along,' with the help of American troops, is the modern metamorphosis of the bipolar worldview.

American Manifest Destiny and the Zionist Connection

This identification of the United States and its manifest destiny with a God that has plans for mankind constitutes an implicit identification of America with the biblical Israelites and their own God-given manifest destiny in the Holy Land. This orientation creates a seemingly natural American sympathy for the Zionist movement. In the nineteenth century, those who recognized and acted on this identification were American Protestant evangelicals who sought not only to promote the return of the Jews to Palestine so as to rescue the Holy Land from heathen Muslim rule but also to promote what they believed to be prophetic steps leading to the second coming of Christ. The most energetic of these believers in 'pre-millennial dispensationalism' [15] was William Eugene Blackstone, for whom the Bible was oracular. He was a prolific writer and tireless campaigner for a modern reincarnation of ancient Israel. In 1891 Blackstone drew up a petition addressed to President Benjamin Harrison and Secretary of State James G. Blaine asking for the 'use of their good offices and influence with the governments of the European world to secure the holding, at an early date, of an international conference to consider the condition of the Israelites and their claims to

Palestine as their ancient home.'[16] Significantly, it was signed by 413 well-known Americans, including the Speaker of the House of Representatives, the Chief Justice of the Supreme Court, J. P. Morgan, and John D. Rockefeller.

This petition is early evidence of the power of this subject to attract a wide range of influential Americans. Against this backdrop of prophetic expectation, those with pre-millenarian inclinations would automatically connect Zionism with a Palestine qua Holy Land in need of redemption. Thus, during World War I and the subsequent British capture of Jerusalem, American Protestants in general assumed that the Jews, led by an active Zionist movement, had the right—the manifest destiny—to 'return home.'

In terms of the bipolar worldview and altruistic imperialism, the Zionists (who were Westerners, and 'modern, progressive people'), allied to the British, soon became perceived as the major vehicle for the physical and spiritual revitalization of Palestine, as well as the realization of prophecy. Simultaneously the natives, the indigenous Arabs (both the Muslim majority and what American Protestants considered the 'pseudo' Christian Arabs of the Greek Orthodox and Catholic 'degenerate churches') became less noticed except in as much as they stood in 'barbaric' opposition to prophecy and modernity alike. This took the form of a process of 'perceptual depopulation' that erased the demographic and cultural/religious realities of contemporary Palestine. Thus Palestine became a 'land without a people for a people without a land.'[17] It was a form of ethnic cleansing at the conceptual level.

America's discovery of Zionism was the apparent discovery of biblical Israelites who had come alive once more. Building on deep national memories going back to the Puritans, Americans were soon identifying with the Zionists through more recent parallels that made it seem as if they shared two versions of the same divine destiny. For example, the Reverend John Hubers, the Reformed Church in America's Mission Coordinator for the Middle East and South Asia, critically described the basis for this shared 'manifest destiny' as:

[T]he belief that the settlement and taming of …largely uninhabited land …was a divinely destined event. Here's how the story goes: a brave pioneering people, escaping from religious and political oppression in [Europe or Egypt] meet great obstacles in realizing their dreams of a free land for free people in an untamed wilderness. Among these obstacles are 'savage' natives [native Americans or Canaanites or contemporary Palestinians] who use terrorist tactics to attempt to thwart their designs. With God's help the brave settlers defeat the 'savages' and force them off the land, at least the best land, thus making way for those who are better able to exploit the God given resources that it yields.[18]

American Zionists, starting soon after the issuance of the Balfour Declaration (1917), began to promote this identification extensively. Throughout the 1920s and into the 1930s, representatives of the Zionist Organization of America strategically placed articles in American newspapers describing the Zionist 'pioneers' as modern-day versions of American settlers. For example, study the following quotes from a typical article that appeared in the New York Times on 11 June 1922: 'These immigrants to Palestine are indeed the Jewish Puritans'; their settlements are 'the Jamestown and Plymouth of the new House of Israel'; they are 'building the new Judea even as the Puritans built New England'; the settlers are like the 'followers of Daniel Boone who opened the West for American settlers' while 'facing the dangers of Indian warfare'; and in the process 'the Jews are bringing prosperity and happiness in Palestine.'[19]

Correspondingly, many of the rationalizations for settlement, expansion and appropriation that Americans used in their continental conquest were those later used by Zionists to explain and justify to the American people and government their colonization of Palestine. One can compare the categories of argument researched by Albert Weinberg in his book Manifest Destiny with positions taken by David Ben-Gurion between 1918 and 1948 and reiterated by many American Zionists. The similarity of arguments for American manifest destiny and Zionism included propinquity or the notion of natural boundaries. Americans used this argument to justify expansion from the Appalachian Mountains to the Mississippi River, then to the Rocky Mountains, and then to the Pacific coast. Ben-Gurion used the same argument for a northern Israeli boundary at the

Litani River in Lebanon and the 'furthest edge of the Transjordan.'[20] Another similar argument was based on a 'destined use of the soil' or the notion that God wanted the land to go to those who could develop it. As Weinberg pointed out, Americans often used this rationale,[21] and Ben-Gurion used the same tack when he claimed that the Arabs had left Palestine 'undeveloped' and therefore they had no 'right ...to rule the country.' The Jews, however, were the 'builders' Palestine 'awaits.'[22] Other parallel arguments were 'extension of freedom,' 'paramount interest,' and 'true title.'[23]

By using the same arguments to the same purpose of expansion and colonization, Zionists both in the United States and Palestine helped Americans to feel that the whole Zionist effort was somehow running parallel to American history. Thus, as early as January 1923, while attending an American Zionist celebration in his honor, Representative Hamilton Fish could make the following statement:

I see a vision that if such a [Jewish] state is created [in Palestine] ...there will be a great republic, built on democratic principles ...They will fashion their government after the ideals of ours and believe in our flag ... because it represents freedom, liberty and justice and that is what we want to see eventually in Palestine.' [24]

Christian Zionism's Impact on Twentieth-century Presidents

Representative Fish's 'vision' had no relation to real Zionist policies in Palestine, all of which at that time reflected a socialist model that was utter anathema in an America beset by Red Scares. But reality mattered little, because Americans had become convinced that Zionism reflected an American style, destiny and way of life. The Americans who most enthusiastically bought into this fanciful story of parallel manifest destinies turned out to be the spiritual heirs of William Blackstone. And, as the signers of Blackstone's original petition presaged, they were men of influence. For instance, there was Woodrow Wilson, US president from 1913 to 1921. He believed that America had a God-ordained political destiny to reform the world.

'It is surely the manifest destiny of the United States,' he proclaimed, to demonstrate democracy's 'power to prevail.'[25] Wilson had grown up in a strong Presbyterian environment (his father was a clergyman and his mother was the daughter of one), read the Bible daily, and was fascinated with the Zionist movement. His friend and ally Louis Brandeis had described Zionism to him as a variant on American Progressivism, and so he saw it as a sort of Americanized biblical endeavor. Thus, after lending his support to the Balfour Declaration, he marveled that 'I, a son of the manse, should be able to help restore the Holy Land to its people.' In March of 1919 he informed the Zionist leader Rabbi Stephen Wise: 'don't worry Dr. Wise, Palestine is yours.'[26]

Every president since Wilson has drawn connections between the United States and God. Most have referenced the Bible as a source of inspiration and alleged a similarity between the destiny of America and the experiences of the ancient Hebrews. This attitude constitutes a powerful illusion that continued strongly. For example, Harry Truman (president, 1945–53) believed that 'the fundamental basis of this nation's law was given by Moses on the Mount. The fundamental basis of our Bill of Rights comes from the teaching of Exodus and St. Matthew, from Isaiah and St. Paul.'[27] The divinely ordained destiny of the United States was to create a 'free world' and to protect it against 'godless communism.' Truman believed part of that mission entailed the establishment of the State of Israel. He thought that his knowledge of the Old Testament made him an expert on contemporary Palestine, and it was his 'expert' opinion that the Holy Land was the proper patrimony of the Jews. He took personal offense at those (particularly in the State Department) who disagreed with this judgment.[28] Having helped in the establishment of the State of Israel, he said of himself: 'I am Cyrus. I am Cyrus.'[29]

Lyndon B. Johnson (president, 1963–69) said that every time he thought of the Israelis, he either equated them with the biblical heroes of his youth or with his native Texan ancestors who, as another 'frontier people,' fought off the Mexicans.[30] In a speech to the B'nai B'rith, he explained that his 'very deep ties with the land and people of Israel' were a function of 'my Christian faith' and 'the Bible stories woven into my childhood memories.'[31] Consequently, as president,

Johnson acted as if the United States had a spiritual connection to both the ancient and modern Israelites. 'Our society is illuminated by the spiritual insights of the Hebrew prophets.' Therefore, he asserted, 'America and Israel have a common love of human freedom, and they have a common faith in a democratic way of life.'[32]

Ronald Reagan (president, 1981–89) had similar views. He thought that the United States was the product of a 'divine plan,' just as was Israel. He identified the United States with Israel as two 'stable and democratic' countries sharing the same Judeo-Christian heritage. A believer in the literal truth of the Bible, Reagan also believed in its prophetic predictions. On at least seven public occasions he alluded to Bible prophecies about the coming of Armageddon (and thus the destruction of most of the Jewish people as a prelude to the second coming of Christ), and in 1983 he explicitly told Thomas Dine of the America-Israel Public Affairs Committee that these prophecies were true.[33]

Contemporary American Christian Zionists

Christian Zionists continue to express these same religious passions and obsessions. Furthermore, they are well positioned and equipped to spread their ideas. Utilizing televangelist techniques, religious radio, evangelical newspapers and even novels, once more they have taken up pre-millennial prophecy as a key motivator for American support of Israel. Simultaneously, according to Robert Pyne, a theologian who works at the Dallas Theological Seminary, these same evangelicals 'identify the American cause…as the cause of Christ.'[34] Thus, for these evangelicals the fate of American and Israel are tied together by divine prophecy.

One should not think of today's Christian Zionists as a fringe group. Those who think of themselves as Christian conservatives accept the Bible as the literal or inspired word of God, believe in prophecy, and expect the end of the world in the relatively near future, make up close to 20 percent of the American electorate. [35] This constituency has become the voting core of the Republican Party, or as Karl Rove,

Bush's political adviser, describes it, the Republican Party's 'base.'[36] And it is an effective and highly motivated base acting against the backdrop of a general population known for its political apathy and record of non-voting.

The Christian Zionists are represented by several groups: The Christian Coalition of America, for example, was founded by Pat Robertson who, on a November 2002 program of the Christian Broadcasting Network that reaches 180 countries, called Muslims 'worse than Nazis.' He also characterized the efforts to bring peace to the Middle East as an illusion: 'The idea that you're going to make peace with the Muslim world by giving them territory is an absolute illusion.'[37] The Moral Majority founded by Jerry Falwell is another Christian Zionist group. In October 2002, Falwell called the Muslim prophet Muhammad 'a terrorist,' and in June of 2003 he remarked that 'it is my belief that the Bible belt in America is Israel's only safety belt right now.'[38] The National Unity Coalition for Israel (NUCI), an important lobbying arm of the American Christian Zionist movement that maintains close contacts with neo-conservative Washington think tanks and Bush administration personnel, is presently claiming to represent 40 million Americans and is the originator of a 'Save Israel [from any compromises to the Palestinians] Campaign.'[39] The Religious Roundtable is run by Ed McAteer, the self-styled 'godfather' of the modern Religious Right. In his opinion, 'the best friends that Israel has are not those people who believe the Bible contains the word of God, but that the Bible is the word of God.'[40] In addition to the above there are other well-known tele-evangelist personalities such as Billy Graham and his son Franklin Graham (who gave the benediction at George W. Bush's first presidential inaugural).[41]

All of these individuals and groups had been galvanized by the 1967 'Six Day War' and Israeli expansion into the Occupied Territories. Just as in the case of General Allenby's capture of Jerusalem in December of 1917, they saw the hand of God in Israeli expansion into the West Bank and Gaza Strip, and interpreted these events as a big step toward the fulfillment of biblical prophecy. Their faith seemingly re-confirmed by events, Christian Zionists since 1967 have been energized to move prophecy forward. Thus, they take hardline positions on the Israeli-Palestinian conflict, attempting to block any American government support for a Palestinian state or the trading of land for peace.[42] In essence they support the ethnic cleansing of Palestine.[43]

Thus a revitalized and politically potent Christian Zionism has built on the legacy of identification with biblical and contemporary Israel and allied itself to the American Zionist movement and neo-conservative political philosophy. In doing so, it has been able, especially since the advent of the George W. Bush administration in 2001, to exercise a major influence on the formulation of US policy as it relates to Israel. In this effort they once more have close allies in the government. For instance, the 2002 convention of the Christian Coalition, held in Washington, DC, opened with a videotaped benediction that came straight from the Oval Office. The most powerful Republicans in Congress addressed the Convention (as did the Zionist mayor of Jerusalem). Tom Delay, who was then the majority whip of the House of Representatives, told the crowd: We are 'standing up for Jews and Jesus.' [44] Later, as the majority leader in the House of Representatives, Delay went to Israel with the same message and addressed the Knesset directly. Under these circumstances, according to Doug Bandow, a senior fellow at the conservative Cato Institute and himself an evangelical, the Christian Zionist message 'colors the environment in which [government foreign policy] decisions are made.' [45] Even the weakest and essentially meaningless demand on Israel by the White House results in tens of thousands of angry protest letters from the Christian Zionist camp. It is no surprise, then, that this administration often turns a blind eye to Israeli behavior no matter how brutal. The oppression of the Palestinians and the confiscation of their land is simply 'God's way' of keeping his promise to 'bless' the Israelites along with those who aid them (most of all America), and 'curse' those who oppose Israel. In other words, since the Jews are God's chosen people and Israel plays a central role in prophecy, the Israelis can do no wrong.

This unquestioning support for Israel fits neatly into the neo-consevative, pro-Zionism of Bush's secular advisers such as Vice President Richard Cheney, Defense Secretary Donald Rumsfeld, former National Security Adviser and current Secretary of State Condoleezza Rice, and influential actors such as Douglas Feith, Richard Pearle, and Paul Wolfowitz. Thus, there is an intertwining alliance of neo-conservative government leaders and the Christian Zionist movement. It should be noted that all these people and groups also believe that the United States has a duty, and a divine manifest destiny, to reshape the world in terms of its own interests (which, of course, allegedly represent the interests of the whole Judeo-Christian world). The same neo-conservative advisers who support Israel with the assistance and blessing of the Christian Coalition, planned the invasion of Iraq, and assert America's right to remake the Middle East in the name of, as the Reverend John Codman put it some 167 years ago, 'spreading the atmosphere of liberty.' As American troops bombed Baghdad, Franklin Graham prepared his army of missionaries as a second wave of invaders.[46]

In the pursuit of their goals, be they in terms of American or Israeli manifest destiny, Christian Zionists do not recognize the applicability of UN resolutions, international treaties, or for that matter, US law and policy. When, in 1997, John Hagee, a prominent American Christian Fundamentalist who had raised a million dollars to help settle Soviet Jews on the West Bank, was asked whether he had any concern that such efforts went against US policy (at that time) on expansion of the settlements, he adamantly said no. 'I am a Bible scholar and a theologian,' he said, 'and from my perspective the law of God transcends the laws of the United States government and the US State Department.' To the extent that the Executive Branch and Congress are populated by men and women with a Christian Zionist ideology, adherence to US law becomes either secondary or an obstacle to be worked around. It is perhaps within this context that the Patriot Act, the establishment of the 'detention camp' at Guantanamo Bay, and the Bush administration's policy of exaggeration, evasion, and lying, in part, can be understood.

Enter President George W. Bush

George W. Bush is an evangelical Christian conservative who embraces a belief in the parallel, divinely sanctioned, manifest destinies of the United States and Israel. Christian Zionism and neo-conservatism are the two guiding philosophies of his administration's Middle East foreign policy. He and his policies can be judged to represent the logical outcome of the triumph of nationalist mythology and religious fantasy over fact-based national interest and analysis. For example, Bush has said that he makes decisions by 'gut instinct.' [48] There seems little doubt that his instinct is basically that of an evangelical Christian with an unquestioning commitment to a divinely inspired American manifest destiny. In effect, the president believes that God is using the United States as an instrument toward some preordained end, as can be seen in his 2002 and 2003 State of the Union addresses: 'the loving God behind all of life and all of history' once more has called on the United States to spread 'the liberty we prize' which, according to the president, is 'the right of every person and the future of every nation.' [49]

American-style democracy also turns out to be identical with 'God's gift to humanity.' A Newsweek article that examined Bush and religion concluded that the Bush administration is 'the most resolutely "faith-based" in modern times, an enterprise founded, supported and guided by trust in the temporal and spiritual power of God.' [50] The same article provided a series of quotes from the President that meld Christian fundamentalist thought and American manifest destiny: 'Our Nation is chosen by God and commissioned by history to be a model to the world of justice'; [51] the United States has been called upon to bring God's gift of liberty to 'every human being in the world'; [52] 'freedom and fear, justice and cruelty have always been at war, and we know that God is not neutral between them...we are in a conflict between good and evil, and we will call evil by its name'; [53] in Saddam Hussein 'we are encountering evil' that must be destroyed, even if it means war—an action about which Mr. Bush says: 'if anyone can be at peace, I am at peace about this.' [54] Other national print media have also published stories on this subject, and all have concluded that, as one reporter put it, 'The sense of divine calling is hard to miss in the White House.' [55]

The above quotes strongly suggest that Bush has interpreted his evangelical faith in the reductive fashion of Presidents McKinley and Wilson. However, perhaps even more than his fundamentalist predecessors, Christian evangelicalism melded to American nationalism marks the boundaries of Bush's world view, and he seems incapable of the self-examination and reflection required to see beyond it. The implications can be frightening for those who happen not to share the president's world view. For instance, decisions made from 'the gut' and guided by 'providence' do not have to be thought through. This approach helps to explain Bush's well-known lack of intellectual curiosity. In the Bush White House there is no one to play the cynic, the devil's advocate, the 'what if' critic. Indeed, this attitude means, according to a member of Bush's staff, that 'no one is allowed to second guess, even when you should.' [56] David Frum, a former speech writer for Bush, has said that the president's attitude is 'You do your best and accept that everything is in God's hands … things will work out.' [57] There is a powerful feeling of certainty that comes with knowing, absolutely, that one is on God's side. According to former Commerce Secretary Don Evans, the president's faith gives him 'a very clear sense of what is good and what is evil.' [58] Consequently, he knows who are the 'terrorists' and the 'evildoers.' Iran and North Korea are 'evil.' Saddam Hussein is 'evil.' Correspondingly, the president's gut and faith tell him who is 'good.' In the Middle East, the good guys are the Israelis.

Even before he was president, Bush had told the American Jewish Committee: 'I am a Christian. But I believe with the Psalmist that the Lord God of Israel neither slumbers nor sleeps. We will stand up for our friends in the world. And one of the most important friends is the state of Israel.' [59] Thus, the way George W. Bush interprets his Christian fundamentalist faith and, for instance, how he interprets scripture follow in the line of Wilson, Truman, Johnson, and Reagan and lead to the same result—an a priori sympathy for, and identification with, Israel. There is every evidence that this religiously inspired identification, along with the influence of neo-conservative advisors who see Israeli behavior as a model for American action in the Middle East, is now the basis for American policy formulation in that region.

Conclusion

An historical conflation of the United States and the biblical Hebrews is as old as the country itself. Many Americans feel a sense of purpose that they say comes from God and constitutes a parallel manifest destiny with both the ancient and modern Israelites. As the above has demonstrated, this belief can be found in the speeches of American political leaders at all levels. It is a deeply held belief that manifests itself in the rationalizations and policies of Congress and American presidents. Today, this orientation is backed up by organized religious groups that have effectively taken over the Republican Party.

An intricate and ideologically driven alliance now exists between the political elites of the United States (and their mythology of manifest destiny), Israel (and its mythology of Greater Israel necessitating the expansion into 'covenant lands'), and millions of Christian Zionists (with their mythology to a sacred prophetic plan for the world).

It is this last group, the Christian Zionists, who subsume the first two mythologies under the third, creating a vision of divine destiny in which the two sacred nations of the United States and Israel play a shared central role. This has produced an ultimately non-rational basis for policy formulation in that it forgoes real-world analysis and in its place puts ideological and religious fantasy. The consequences have been radical and violent. Manifest destiny has always been a bloody and disastrous notion. In its American manifestation it has led to the killing of millions of native Americans, Mexicans, and Filipinos. Now, American political leaders resort to this ideology once more. Now, as in the past, they invoke God and religion to justify policies they proclaim as good but which in practice bring death and destruction to millions who remain invisible victims to those who are convinced of the righteousness of their cause. In effect, Bush along with his neo-conservative allies and Christian Zionist boosters have resurrected imperialism and colonialism as legitimate pursuits in the name of religion and security.

In this new international order the United States and Israel go forward hand in hand, each actualizing these at once very old and newly devastating policies: Israel in the territories of occupied Palestine, and the United States in Afghanistan and Iraq. Both try to hide the horror that results—the deaths of tens of thousands and the destruction of whole cultures—through the propaganda and 'spin' of a mutual admiration society that touts the notions of progress, democracy, and God's will. Such is the allied legacy of manifest destiny: American, Zionist, and Christian Zionist.

Notes

1. 'The great aim of culture [is] the aim of setting ourselves to ascertain what perfection is and to make it prevail.' The Oxford Dictionary of Quotations, 2nd ed. (Oxford: Oxford University Press, 1955), p. 19.

2. Edward Said (1978) Orientalism (New York: Vintage Books), pp. 1–2.

3. Lawrence Davidson (2001) America's Palestine: Popular and Official Perceptions from Balfour to Israeli Statehood (Gainesville, FL: University Press of Florida), p. 22. These are the words Balfour used to characterize the post-World War I mandate regime. Rudyard Kipling would call it the taking up of the 'white man's burden.'

4. 'See Davidson, America's Palestine, chap. 1.

5. 'See Newsweek, 1 November 2000.

6. 'See Fuad Sha'ban (1991) Islam and Arabs in Early American Thought (Durham, NC: Acorn Press), p. 91.

7. Clifton Phillips (1969) Protestant America and the Pagan World (Cambridge, MA: Harvard University Press), p. 243.

8. 'khttp://www.mtholyoke.edu/acad/intrel/winthrop.html.

9. John L. O'Sullivan (1839) 'The great nation of futurity,' The United States Democratic Review, 6(23), pp. 426–430.

10. See the addresses posted by the Avalon Project of Yale University Law School at khttp://www.yale.edu/lawweb/avalon/presiden/inaug/inaug.html.

11. Albert Weinberg (1963) Manifest Destiny (Chicago: Quadrangle Books).

12. Cited in Howard Zinn (1980) A People's History of the United States (New York: Harper &Row), pp. 305–306.

13. See Benedict Anderson (1991) Imagined Communities: Reflections on the Origin and Spread of Nationalism (London: Verso).

14. George W. Bush, Inaugural Address, 20 January 2001.

15. 'Dispensationalism' is the regulation or ordering of events by God. History is divided into periods that witness certain divinely set events. A 'pre-millennial' reading of biblical prophecy dictates that certain events must occur prior to the Second Coming of Christ. Paul S. Boyer defines it as 'a series of last-day signs' signaling the end of the world. One of these signs is the return of the Jews to the 'promised land' and the recreation of an exclusively Jewish state of Israel (see Boyer's piece in the Chronicle of Higher Education, 14 February 2003, p. B10). The pre-millennial period ends with the battle of Armageddon and the defeat of the Anti-Christ. This signifies the 'end of times' and the end of history. We then get the return of Christ, and the Rapture in which the faithful are transported to heaven; those few surviving Jews not slaughtered at the battle of Armageddon are then converted to Christianity. See also 'Christian Zionism summarized' posted on the Globalist.org. Website at khttp://globalist.

org/world_regions/asia/palestine-israel/020423_christian_zi-onism.htmll.

16. Paul C. Merkley (1998) The Politics of Christian Zionism, 1898–1948 (London: Frank Cass), p. 68.

17. The phrase was coined originally by the British Christian Zionist Lord Shaftesbury in 1853. It was used consistently by Zionist propagandists in the United States and elsewhere to argue that Palestine was essentially unpopulated. Today, the Zionist Organization of America (ZOA) disingenuously claims that 'the phrase...was used occasionally by early Zionists to refer to the fact that the Arab residents of Turkish-ruled Palestine did not consider themselves a "people" separate from the Arabs of surrounding countries...' See khttp://www. zoa.org/pressrel2001/20011220a.html.

18. See 'Christian Zionism and the myth of America' at khttp://www.mecchurches.org/newsreport/wol14_2/ christianzionism.aspl.

19. See Davidson, America's Palestine, pp. 46–47.

20. See Nur Masalha (1992) Expulsion of the Palestinians: The Concept of Transfer in Zionist Thought, 1882– 1948 (Washington, DC: Institute for Palestine Studies), p. 87.

21. Weinberg, Manifest Destiny, pp. 73, 79.

22. Shabtai Teveth (1985) Ben Gurion and the Palestinian Arabs: From Peace to War (Oxford: Oxford University Press), p. 38.

23. See Weinberg, Manifest Destiny, pp. 143–154. See also David Ben-Gurion quotes based on declassified documents and personal diaries at khttp://www.palestineremembered.com/Acre/Famous-Zionist-Quotes/ Story638.htmll.

24. Cited in Davidson, America's Palestine, pp. 51–52.

25. Woodrow Wilson, 8th State of the Union Message, 7 December 1920.

26. Davidson, America's Palestine, pp. 16, 21.

27 See khttp://www.errantskeptics.org/quotes_by_presidents.html.

28 Davidson, America's Palestine, p. 174.

29. Merkley, Politics of Christian Zionism, p. 191.

30 Davidson, America's Palestine, p. 220.

31 khttp://www.us-israel.org/jsource/US-Israel/presquote.htmll.

32 khttp://www.eyeranian.net/2003/11/19,518.shtmll.

33. Andrew Lang, 'Convergence: the politics of Armageddon,' at khttp://www.prop1.org/inaugur/85reagan/ 85rrarm.html.

34. Cited in Lee Mcauliffe Rambo, 'Bush believes he is leading a Holy War,' Atlanta Journal-Constitution, 13 April 2003.

35. This comes to approximately 40 million Americans; see the following polls: New York Times poll published on 7 December 1997; Newsweek polls (conducted by Princeton Research Associates) on 24 October 1999 and 1 May 2000; and the CNN/USA Today poll of 22 November 2002. See also the BBC report, 'President Bush and religion,' 7 May 2002; Jane Lampman's article in the Christian Science Monitor, 17 March 2003; and Newsweek, 'Year 2000 and the history of prophecy,' 1 November 2000.

36. Cited in Guardian Weekly, 21–27 November 2002, p. 23. Rove has argued that in the 2000 presidential election some four million American evangelicals, 'all natural Bush supporters,' did not vote. His goal for the 2004 election was to get a significant portion of these potential voters to the polls; see Rupert Cornwell, 'In God he trusts—how George Bush infused the White House with a religious spirit,' The Independent, 21 February 2003.

37 Cited in the Jordan Times, 14 November 2002.

38. khttp://www.cbsnews.com/stories/2002/10/03/60minutes/main524268.shtmll.

39. khttp://www.israelunitycoalition.com/l.

40. Cited in Ken Silverstein & Michael Scherer, 'Born again Zionists,' Mother Jones, September/October 2002. McAteer also hopes to be the 'first evangelical ambassador to Israel.'

41. A minority of conservative Christians disapprove of the one-sidedness of the Bush administration's foreign policy. About 'forty evangelical leaders' wrote to the president in the summer of 2002 asking for an 'evenhanded US policy toward Israel and the Palestinians.' They also pointedly rejected 'the way some have distorted biblical passages for their rationale for uncritical support for Israel'; see further Lampman, Christian Science Monitor, 17 March 2003. Some of these disapproving evangelicals assert that Bush has distorted Christian theology into an 'American civil religion'; see further Jim Wallis, 'Dangerous religion,' Sojourners Magazine, September/October 2003. See also Corinne Whitlatch, 'Christian commitment to peacemaking is distorted by Christian Zionists,' at khttp://www.pcusa.org/washington/issuesnet/me-030610.html.

42. For instance, they adamantly oppose something as mild as Bush's 'Roadmap to Peace'; see Giles Fraser, 'Evangelicals in the US believe there is a biblical basis for opposing the Middle East Road Map,' Guardian, 9 June 2003. Attacking the road map, Ed McAteer said: 'It's not a road map. It's a roadblock. Every grain of sand in that piece of real estate backed up by the Jordan River, the Dead Sea and the Mediterranean belongs to the Jewish people because God gave it to them'; cited in Carol Eisenberg, 'Road Map testing their faith,' Newsday, 10 June 2003. McAteer's position mimics closely those of fanatical Jewish settlers who in a June 2003 rally in Jerusalem held up signs that read 'To Divide Our Land is to Defy God'; see Haaretz, 4 June 2003. The Fourth Geneva Convention, which makes the Israeli settlement movement illegal under international law is disregarded or held in disdain by both McAteer and the Israeli colonists.

43. For instance, on 1 May 2002 Congressmen Richard Armey, a Christian Zionist and then leader of the Republican Party in the

House of Representatives, told MSNBC talk show host Chris Mathews that he supported the expulsion of Palestinians from the Occupied Territories (West Bank and Gaza).

44. See the American Jewish newspaper Forward, 18 October 2002. Appearing at the 2002 Christian Coalition convention in Washington, along with House Majority leader Tom Delay, was Benny Elon, the leader of Israel's Moledet Party. Elon drew cheers from thousands of attendees waving Israeli flags when he called for the 'relocation' of West Bank Palestinians to Jordan.

45. khttp://www.motherjones.com/news/feature/2002/37/ma_109_01.htmll.

46. See the Guardian, 4 April 2003, (http://www.guardian.co.uk/Iraq/Story/0,2763,929399,00.html).

47. Donald Wagner, 'The interregnum: Christian Zionism in the Clinton years,' The Daily Star, 13 October 2003.

48. In an interview with Bob Woodward in 2002 Bush said: 'I am not a textbook player. I'm a gut player'; cited in Richard Brookhiser, 'The mind of George Bush,' The Atlantic Monthly, April 2003, p. 62. See also Jane Lampman, Christian Science Monitor, 17 March 2003.

49. khttp://www.jimpix.co.uk/words/bush_speech.aspl.

50. Howard Fineman, 'Bush and God,' Newsweek, 10 March 2003, p. 25.

51. Ibid. p. 33.

52. Ibid. p. 24.

53. Ibid. p. 28.

54. Ibid. p. 21.

55. Philadelphia Inquirer, 9 February 2003, p. A11.

56. White House Staff quote.

57. Frum quote.

58. Evans quote.

59. See Bush speech in Atlanta, Georgia, 8 November 2001.

References

Anderson, B. (1991) Imagined Communities: Reflections on the Origin and Spread of Nationalism (London: Verso). Davidson, L. (2001) America's Palestine: Popular and Official Perceptions from Balfour to Israeli Statehood (Gainesville, FL: University Press of Florida). Masalha, N. (1992) Expulsion of the Palestinians: The Concept of Transfer in Zionist Thought, 1882–1948 (Washington, DC: Institute for Palestine Studies). Merkley, P. C. (1998) The Politics of Christian Zionism, 1898–1948 (London: Frank Cass). O'Sullivan, J. L. (1839) The great nation of futurity, The United States Democratic Review, 6(23), pp. 426–430. Phillips, C. (1969) Protestant America and the Pagan World (Cambridge, MA: Harvard University Press). Said, E. (1978) Orientalism (New York: Vintage Books). Sha'ban, F. (1991) Islam and Arabs in Early American Thought (Durham, NC: Acorn Press). Teveth, S. (1985) Ben Gurion and the Palestinian Arabs: From Peace to War (London: Oxford University Press). Weinberg, A. (1963) Manifest Destiny (Chicago: Quadrangle Books). Zinn, H. (1980) A People's History of the United States (New York: Harper & Row).

Correspondence address: Lawrence Davidson, Department of History, West Chester University, 500 Main Hall, West Chester, Pennsylvania 19383, USA. Email: ldavidson@wcupa.edu

A War Culture

by Charley Reese

Our country, if you look at its history, has fought an awful lot of wars, and it's no wonder that militarism is always just beneath the surface of our culture, even in times of peace.

Americans fought in the French and Indian War, the American Revolution, the War of 1812, the Mexican War, the War Between the States, the Spanish-American War, the Philippines Insurrection, World War I, World War II, the Korean War, the Vietnam War, the war against the Serbs, the war in Afghanistan and the Iraqi wars.

Interspersed among all of those are about 300 years of Indian wars and minor military incursions into such places as China, Lebanon, Panama, Nicaragua, Haiti, Grenada, Libya, Somalia and perhaps others that I have missed. Our national anthem is a war song based on a poem written during the War of 1812. Many television stations, when they sign off, run a film of military jets flying above the flag.

Even our language is full of references to war. Politicians, pink-fingered and manicured, nevertheless always "fight" for this or that program or policy. The expression "lock, stock and barrel" does not refer to whiskey barrels but to the parts of a rifle. To say that someone has "shot his wad" is a reference to soldiers who forgot to put the bullets into their black-powder rifles. We say winning an election is a "victory." We sometimes talk about a "double-barreled" threat or say that something is "on target." Election efforts are called "campaigns." We often speak of sports teams "battling back." We conduct "wars" on social problems such as poverty and drug abuse. As an aside, I should point out that the Arabic word "jihad" is like our English word "war." It can mean either physical combat or a personal, social or political struggle.

I'm sure you can think of more expressions or words. We often use a World War II acronym, "snafu," which stands for "situation normal, all f— up." We sometimes say "ground zero," which is a reference to the impact point of a nuclear weapon.

Of course, in addition to our real and historical involvement in wars, our entertainment culture is saturated with violence. Our civilian police departments are being militarized. It's an odd country indeed for anyone to suggest gun control, and, of course, the peace movement in the United States has always been a minority faction. Pacifism has often been equated with treason, and to many Americans patriotism means simply a willingness to go to war (or, more often, a willingness for some of our younger citizens to go to war).

My own life has been molded by the war culture. I was 2 years old when World War II started in Europe and 8 when it ended in the Pacific. Thus, most of my childhood was filled with war. I saw so much newsreel footage of American bombs falling on German cities that I used to carry a hard-rubber ball in my pocket to "bomb" columns of ants on the sidewalk. I assumed as a given that I would take my turn in uniform. I have always assumed that violence itself is a given. Except for a few trips, I've never slept in a house without a loaded gun. I've always been psychologically prepared to kill if the need arises.

I confess that I was less upset by the Sept. 11 attack than many people. Having become calloused with the massive casualties of World War II, with so many images of destroyed cities and dead bodies stored in my brain, my first reaction was: "Only 3,000 dead? That's not too bad."

A WAR CULTURE

Thank God I realized how warped by the war culture I was and tried hard to rear my own children differently. In the world as it is, we probably cannot avoid war, but we should certainly stop glorifying it and should crack down on the gratuitous violence on television, in movies and in video games. Exposure to violence, even make-believe violence, does produce emotional calluses.

We need for our children and grandchildren a culture of life, not a culture of death.

January 26, 2004

Time To Choose

by Charley Reese

Most politicians, when they talk about reducing spending, chatter on about cutting waste and fraud. That's OK, but it's a mere nick on the federal budget. If you really want to reduce spending, you must dismantle the overseas empire.

Excluding Iraq, Afghanistan and the other facilities in the Gulf States that have been built since the Republican war, the Pentagon lists 702 overseas bases in 130 foreign countries on which are stationed more than 250,000 uniformed troops. There are also dependents and civilian employees on many of those bases.

One of the oldest military clichés is that the generals always want to fight the last war over again. Well, there's some truth to that. In fact, though, we will never again fight World War II, so why in the heck do we have bases still in Germany, Italy, Japan, Guam and South Korea?

Just whom do we expect to fight from these bases? How do they contribute to the defense of the U.S.? They don't. They are, frankly, a residue of World War II and a reminder that the military is, after all, a bureaucracy and hates the very idea of "losing" any facilities and billets. We don't need to have troops permanently stationed in any of these countries. Nor do we need to maintain our membership in the North Atlantic Treaty Organization, which is a residue from the Cold War.

I don't wish to disillusion anyone, but Asia and Europe are not our responsibilities. If there is any need for defense, it is the responsibility of the countries on those continents. We know from personal experience that Japan and Germany can field large and competent armies if they should decide they need them. They do not need our protection.

At the present, there are only two countries in the world that have the capability of waging war against us. Those are China and Russia. In both cases, the war would be fought with intercontinental ballistic missiles. We are never going to see a land war with either of those countries. It should be the No. 1 priority of our foreign-policy establishment to see that we never have a war at all with either of these countries.

Wars start when empires wish to expand. That was the cause of the Spanish-American War, World War I and World War II. The Korean and Vietnam wars were civil wars in which our politicians involved us. The wars against Afghanistan and Iraq are again wars of an empire trying to expand. In these cases, we are the empire, and you might as well face the ugly truth that our invasions of both countries were no different from the Nazi invasions that led to World War II. Neither Afghanistan nor Iraq had attacked us or were even capable of attacking us.

In Afghanistan, we could have gone after al-Qaeda without overthrowing the Taliban government. In the case of Iraq, like Adolf Hitler did with Poland, we simply published a pack of lies to justify our invasion.

Americans need to realize that we are not the police force of the world. It is not our responsibility to overthrow dictators or effect regime change in other people's countries. It is not our responsibility to stop slaughters such as seem to be a permanent feature of Africa.

TIME TO CHOOSE

If we could only learn to mind our own business and see to the needs of our own people, we could lead a peaceful, prosperous and happy existence. As for the terrorists, they are mainly a problem for intelligence and police. If any military force is necessary, one company of Rangers or Marines would be enough.

You can't have a free republic and an empire. It is time to choose.

October 23, 2007

Charley Reese has been a journalist for 49 years, reporting on everything from sports to politics. From 1969–71, he worked as a campaign staffer for gubernatorial, senatorial and congressional races in several states. He was an editor, assistant to the publisher, and columnist for the Orlando Sentinel from 1971 to 2001. Reese served two years active duty in the U.S. Army as a tank gunner.

Vanishing the Palestinians

by Ghada Karmi

When the Zionists decided in 1897 to establish a Jewish state in Palestine, the Jews of Vienna dispatched a delegation to examine the country for its suitability. The delegation reported back as follows: "the bride is beautiful but she is married to another man". They had found that Palestine to their dismay was already inhabited by another people. And this has been Zionism's central problem ever since. How to "vanish the Palestinians" and get an empty land? The latest manifestation of this imperative is the barrier wall, which Israel is currently building to separate and enclose Palestinian towns and villages in the lands it occupied after 1967. There are those who rightly point to the wall's illegality and infringement of human rights. And the International Court of Justice has just affirmed this view resoundingly in its ruling, passed on 9.7.04 by 14 of the 15 judges, that the wall was an illegal structure when in the occupied Palestinian territories and that Israel would have to tear it down and make restitution for the damage it has caused to thousands of Palestinians. This position is entirely valid, but critics, in my view, have missed one crucial aspect of the wall's purpose, which is, to "vanish" the Palestinians, to make them so invisible that Israelis can go on pretending that there is no "other man".

Observers of Palestinian history have long been familiar with Israel's position on this issue. But few realize how successful, subtle and far reaching this Israeli policy has been. Arriving in Haifa recently I could see how hard Israel had tried to make that wish to send the Palestinians into oblivion come true. Haifa prides itself on being the best example of a 'mixed' Arab-Jewish city in Israel, practicing a much-vaunted mutual tolerance and cooperation. In fact, it is over-whelmingly Jewish, the Arabs forming less than ten per cent of the population. Haifa is a picturesque city; its famous Carmel Mountain, where the city's Arab notables used to live before 1948, overlooks a beautiful harbor.

Today, Jews inhabit those houses and the Arab minority that re-mained after the 1948 expulsions lives in a rundown district by the port below, segregated in all but name. The old Haifa street names have been replaced by Jewish ones. To me, an "original" Palestinian exiled in England since 1948, the place was ineffably depressing. Beneath the phony friendliness in public there was no disguising the unequal relationship between the two sides: the menial jobs in which Arabs are concentrated, the discrimination in housing, jobs and edu-cation, implicit rather then legislative, and the aversion to meaning-ful social contact. One woman described her struggle to buy into the exclusive website Carmel district. People had said Arabs in the neighborhood would depress property prices, rather as blacks are said to do in some Western countries.

Israeli Jews look down on Arabs. Even recently arrived Ethiopian "Jews", themselves fighting discrimination, affect to despise Arabs. Walking along Haifa's streets, a disturbing hybrid of modern Eu-ropean and old Arab, I had a sense of a city gutted and soulless, its true past barely discernible beneath the new constructions. People showed me where my uncle's house had once stood; it is now a mu-nicipal car park, demolished by the authorities in 1983. The van-ishing process I could see was well advanced here. It had started with the Zionist slogan of Palestine as 'a land without a people', to which end the Israelis expended much effort. In 1948, a majority of Palestine's population was expelled (my family amongst them) and was never allowed to return. A campaign to eradicate the Palestinian presence swiftly followed. Over 500 Palestinian villages were demolished and replaced with Israeli settlements; Hebrew place names were substituted for the previous Arabs ones; the country's history was re-written to claim that Palestine had been a wasteland, home to a few wandering Bedouin tribes. Israeli schoolchildren were reared for decades on this mythology. Palestinian customs were appropriated as "Israeli", and the minority of Palestinians that remained became invisible.

This was the narrative I grew up with in Britain. It was so effective that no one here doubted its truth for decades and Israelis themselves were astonished to "discover" the Palestinians of the West Bank and Gaza after 1967. However, in occupying them, Israel was back to the old problem of how to keep the new land without the people. Since physical expulsion was no longer an option, the alternative has been to make the Palestinians disappear as a nation by destroying their society. The history of the last 37 years of Israeli occupation can perhaps be best understood in this context. The Israeli colonization of land and resources has strangled the Palestinian economy and made statehood unviable. At the same time, the destruction of Palestinian history proceeds unabated. One of the least noted aspects of Israel's 1982 invasion of Lebanon was the removal to Israel of truckloads of crucial Palestinian archives and documents from the PLO Research Centre in Beirut. The Israelis did the same in 2002 when they invaded Ramallah. Vital statistics, computer hard drives, population statistics and land registers were taken out with the aim of destroying the Palestinian collective memory, history and national existence.

Israel had meanwhile denigrated the PLO, which threatened to give the Palestinian cause international stratus, as terrorists. In 1969, Golda Meir, Israel's prime minister, made the now notorious statement that "there was no such thing as a Palestinian people". The world was supposed to understand that, even if there were Palestinians, they did not amount to a separate people with national rights. Our route from Haifa to Jerusalem took us past the barrier wall, which is the subject of the ICJ's preoccupation and snakes its way down to Jerusalem; it is obscenely high in some places up to eight meters clearly on the principle that what you don't see does not exist. When we reached East Jerusalem and saw the shriveled Palestinian community there that tries to survive in this truncated part of the original homeland, I saw another kind of vanishment. So-called Arab Jerusalem now consists effectively of three main streets and is surrounded by Jewish settlements. Israel considers the city "Jewish forever" and the previous Arab population preponderance has been deliberately overturned from 72 to 28 per cent by vigorous Israeli colonization.

I was born in Jerusalem and yet I hate to see it now, The Old City, with its magnificent Islamic architecture, once the glory of Jerusalem and beyond into the Arab and Islamic worlds, is now a place of aggressive competition for ownership. Extremist religious settlers harass the Arabs, aiming to evict them, and threaten openly to build the Jewish Temple in place of the Aqsa mosque. Sad shopkeepers tell a story of poor business, encroaching Jewish settlement, unfair competition from Israeli traders and tourist guides who warn visitors against buying from "cheating Arabs", and high taxes imposed by a state of which they are not citizens. It is an unnatural place, but not yet a ghost town like Haifa, though with Israeli strictures against Jerusalemites, I wondered for how long? Friends who worked in Jerusalem were now barred from entry there (or anywhere else). Visiting them in Ramallah one night, I left later than I should, forgetting that the checkpoints close at arbitrary times in the evening. I just made it to the no-man's land beyond the second checkpoint and stood waiting for a taxi to take me on. None came, and in the eerie stillness with the shapes of heavily armed Israeli soldiers just discernible in the night gloom, I felt I was in a war-zone. But what war and with whom? With a poor people whose only crime is that they are not Jewish?

The wall, the stifling restrictions on movement, the impoverishment, and the daily killings are all designed to encourage flight. Unconfirmed reports say that 200,000 West Bank people have already left. The deliberate targeting of Palestinian leaders, (Sheikh Yassin, the head of Hamas and his replacement were both killed within weeks of each other earlier this year and Arafat is threatened with a similar fate), aims to create a chaotic people incapable of articulating their case. The constant reiteration that "there is no one to talk to" on the Palestinian side, when such interlocutors have been effectively eliminated, is another tactic towards the same end. These extreme antics bespeak an Israeli desperation to preserve the Jewish state "pure", perhaps understandable in those who perceive, however wrongly, that without it their very survival is at stake. But what continues to baffle and frustrate is America's unwavering support for Israel and thereby its collusion with this campaign to render the Palestinians invisible. President Bush backed Ariel Sharon's unilateral 'plan' for the Palestinians in April and his Administration vetoed the Security Council Resolution condemning Israel's wall. The US of course is only following on British precedent when, in 1917, the Balfour Declaration decided the Palestinians' fate over their heads and cancelled their identity by re-defining them as "non-Jewish communities".

The world, meanwhile, looks on ineffectually, as if there were a tacit consensus to see the Palestinians vanish. Of course the rhetoric is beguiling; it speaks of a Palestinian state that even Bush supports. The ICJ's condemnation of Israel's barrier wall has encouraged Palestinians to feel hopeful. But the facts speak otherwise. Compare the treatment of the Kosovans in 1999. Then every effort was made to safeguard their integrity as a people; NATO, the EU and the US strove to return them to their homes. Compare also the case of the Iraqi Kurds, protected since 1991 by US and British no-fly zones, and now given special status by the Coalition in Iraq. So why are the Palestinians denied the same treatment? Why are their national identity, aspirations and right of return to their homeland under such vicious, concerted attack? They have retaliated by largely standing their ground, refusing to repeat the tragic exodus of 1948 and 1967, though for how long they can withstand this multi-pronged attack on their society is anyone's guess. As for Israel, racing against time to hold back the Arab "demographic" tide, it is also anyone's guess how long it can put off its inevitable absorption into the Arab world by such antics.

Ghada Karmi

Ghada Karmi is a Palestinian writer and academic living in London. She is Research Fellow at the Institute of Arab and Islamic Studies, and the author of a memoir called, "In Search of Fatima" (Verso). Her latest book is "Married to a man: Israel's dilemma and the one-state solution" (Pluto Press).

New York Times Distortion: Up Close and Personal

by Alison Weir

Founder of **If Americans Knew**

April 24, 2005

A little over a week ago, some members of our organization, If Americans Knew, met with *New York Times* Public Editor Daniel Okrent to discuss the findings of a detailed study we had completed of two years worth of *Times* news stories on the Israeli-Palestinian conflict. Okrent was going to be writing a column discussing the paper's coverage of Israel/Palestine, and we felt our study would be an important resource.

Using a PowerPoint presentation, we explained our findings and gave him copies of the 23-page report, along with approximately 40 pages of supporting documentation.

In order to find as clear and objective a measure as possible, our studies examine how news organizations report deaths among both populations, Israelis and Palestinian. Basically, we simply count the deaths reported on both sides of the conflict, and then compare these to the actual number of deaths that had occurred. It is our view that all deaths are equally tragic regardless of race, religion, or ethnicity; we hoped that the *Times* shared that perspective.

Findings:

We found that in every single category, The *Times* coverage reported Israeli deaths at rates three or more times greater than Palestinian deaths.

Our statistical analysis of their coverage, however, showed that there was startling disparity in how deaths were reported, depending on the ethnicity of the victim.

For example, we found that in 2004, at a time when 8 Israeli children and 176 Palestinian children were killed – a ratio of 1 to 22 – *Times* headlines and lead paragraphs reported on Israeli children's deaths at a rate almost seven times greater than Palestinian children's deaths.

A one-month sub-study indicated that this disparity grew even larger when the entire article was analyzed, with Israeli children's deaths mentioned (through repetitions of deaths reported on previous days) at a rate ten times greater than Palestinian children's deaths.

Times coverage of deaths of all ages, while less dramatically skewed, showed similar distortion. In the first year of the current Palestinian uprising, which began in fall of 2000, we discovered that the *Times* reported prominently on 42 percent of Palestinian deaths, and on 119 percent of Israeli deaths (follow-up headline articles, we find, frequently push coverage of Israeli deaths over 100 percent). In other words, the *Times* reported Israeli deaths at a rate approximately three times greater than Palestinian deaths.

During this period over three times more Palestinians were being killed than Israelis.

Overall, we found that in every single category *Times* coverage reported Israeli deaths at rates three or more times greater than Palestinian deaths.

Such patterns of distortion gave readers the impression that equal numbers of people on both sides were being killed – or that more Israelis were being killed – when the reality is that Palestinians have always been killed in far greater numbers. In particular, we found that *Times* stories so often repeated reports of Israeli children's deaths that in some periods they were reporting on Israeli deaths at a rate of 400 percent.

In contrast, the majority of Palestinian deaths – particularly children's deaths – were never reported by the *Times* at all.

According to Israeli human rights groups and others who assiduously gather data on all children killed in the conflict, at least 82 Palestinian children were killed before any Israeli children were killed – and the largest single cause of these Palestinian children's deaths was "gunfire to the head." Yet, almost no one is aware of this, since *Times* coverage consistently omitted or minimized coverage of these Palestinian deaths.

In other words, we found that *New York Times* coverage of Israel-Palestine exhibited highly disturbing patterns of bias.

To make matters worse, since the *Times* is often considered "the newspaper of record," with hundreds of newspapers subscribing to the *New York Times* News Service, the paper's distortions become replicated throughout the country.

Unintentionally, editors around the country are reporting this issue with a distortion based on ethnicity that most would oppose, if they were aware that they were doing it.

The Full Report can be found online at:
http://www.ifamericansknew.org/media/nyt-report.html

New York Times Reaction

We came away with the very strong impression that Okrent, who is himself, Jewish, felt basically that only Jewish reporters could cover this issue.

We presented these findings, complete with charts, spread-sheets, clear sourcing, and extensive additional documentation, to Okrent and his assistant. We gave him the names and details of 32 Palestinian children who had been killed during the first month of the uprising – none of whom had been the subject of *Times'* articles. (28 of these children, it was found, had been killed by gunfire to the head or chest.)

Okrent appeared to accept our findings readily – even commenting at one of our findings that he "wasn't surprised."

His subsequent column, purporting to examine *Times* coverage of Israel-Palestine, given all of the above, is perplexing. There is no mention whatsoever of our report, no mention of our two-year study, no mention of the 40-some pages of supporting evidence, no mention, even, of our lengthy face-to-face meeting (despite the fact that it appears we were one of the few groups to present our information in person).

In his 1,762-word column, there are a total of three mentions of *If Americans Knew*.

One is an off-hand sentence claiming that we "say" that the *Times* "ignores" the deaths of Palestinian children, whom, we "say" are often shot in the head or chest by Israeli soldiers. Instead of this loose, somewhat flawed paraphrase, Okrent could simply have quoted our report directly, perhaps even mentioning our substantial evidence. One wonders why he didn't.

A second reference, potentially damaging, significantly misrepresents what we said. (We have phoned the *Times* asking for a correction and space for rebuttal to Okrent's allegations.)

In his column, Okrent writes: "During my research, representatives of If Americans Knew expressed the belief that unless the paper assigned equal numbers of Muslim and Jewish reporters to cover the conflict, Jewish reporters should be kept off the beat. I find this profoundly offensive."

Actually, Okrent is referring to his own words at the meeting, not ours. Let us tell you the complete version. It is quite illuminating.

Even before we had finished presenting our findings, Okrent interrupted to ask us why there was such distortion in *Times* coverage, what was causing the bias. He asked what we would suggest doing about it.

I replied that I wondered if there was a lack of diversity in the reporters and editors working on the issue. I pointed out that since this was a conflict between a state whose identity and purpose of existence was to be a Jewish state, it seemed to me that the number of Jewish-American reporters covering it should be balanced by approximately an equal number of Arab/Muslim-American reporters, or that there be reporters and editors working on it – for example, Asian-American or African-American journalists – without predisposition to partisanship toward either side.

Okrent said that it was impossible to find equal numbers of Arab/ Muslim journalists of sufficiently high quality to balance out the number of Jewish reporters available to cover it, and ignored the suggestion that other groups be included in the reportorial/editorial pool. He said that there shouldn't be an "ethnic litmus test" and that Jewish reporters shouldn't be excluded just because there weren't enough Muslims for the *Times* to employ. I agreed with him that there should not be a litmus test, and then asked him if he thought only Jewish reporters could cover it.

No, he said, the problem, he felt, was that *Times* reporters only lived in Israel and didn't live in the Palestinian territories. He then said that when he had suggested to reporters that they also live in the West Bank or Gaza, a person he "trusted" told him that this was too dangerous; they would be kidnapped. I then said that he needed to reconsider the reliability of this anonymous person, since I myself had traveled throughout Gaza and the West Bank as a freelance reporter without any danger from the Palestinian population.

We were astounded at his assumption that it would be impossible for the *Times* to find sufficient numbers of high quality journalists of Muslim or Arab heritage to work on this issue.

Finally, I said that fundamentally it was up to the *Times* to figure out how to improve their system of reporting – that I only saw the results. I said that we had provided free outside consultation, had found patterns I was sure they would find as disturbing as we did, and that it was now up to the *Times* to determine and remedy the cause.

Overall, I found this exchange bizarre. We had expected some questions about our study, its methodology, what additional patterns we had noticed, etc. Almost none of this took place. On the other hand, we came away with the very strong impression that Okrent, who is himself Jewish, felt basically that only Jewish reporters could cover this issue and that, while their reporting would be more accurate if some of them lived in the West Bank or Gaza, they probably wouldn't do this because it would be too dangerous for them (despite the fact that such Jewish Israeli journalists as Amira Haas have lived there for years).

The fact that it could be both possible and valuable to have additional ethnic groups involved in covering this issue, including some without ethnic connection to this ethnic dispute, seemed incomprehensible to him. Finally, we were astounded at his assumption that it would be impossible for the *Times* to find sufficient numbers of high quality journalists of Muslim or Arab heritage to work on this issue.

Still disturbed at the oddness of this meeting, afterwards I sent a follow-up email again explaining my view. I will print it below:

Email to Dan Okrent

Dear Dan,

Thank you for meeting with us, and for your willingness to take on what is certainly one of the most volatile issues in the news today – and one of the most urgent. I hope our study will help alert the New York Times to patterns of omission that I'm sure you find as disturbing as we do.

Regarding your important question about what changes I would suggest: Truthfully, it is difficult for me to offer solutions, since I only see the results, and have no idea what the internal dynamics are of the *Times'* reporting and editing that have created these patterns. It seems to me that news organizations themselves, once alerted to flaws in their coverage, are in the best position to undertake thorough analyses of the causation, and then to implement whatever changes are required.

I suspect that your idea that coverage would improve greatly if reporters lived in the West Bank and Gaza as well as Israel is quite correct. One possibility, of course, is that the *Times* could hire some of the excellent Palestinian journalists living in these areas. When I visited Birzeit University a few months ago, I met a professor and a number of students in the journalism department that I found quite impressive. I haven't visited any journalism departments in Gaza, but I did visit some classes in American literature at Islamic University in Gaza City in 2001, and found a level of teaching equivalent to the finest in US universities.

At the same time, of course, it is important that those editing these reports be as unpartisan as possible – which, I suspect, requires that those in this position have diverse backgrounds. While I'm not Jewish, I can imagine similar situations in which I might believe that I had arrived at a neutral position, not realizing that I was still influenced by what my mother had believed, or what my aunt would say, or the narrative I had absorbed as a child – in other words, I might write and edit within parameters that would interfere with the accuracy of my work. Finally, below is some more recent information about the disturbing – and unreported, in the *Times* – pattern of Israeli forces shooting and abusing children and other civilians.

1. Here is the link to the Remember These Children information: http://www.rememberthesechildren.org/remember 2000.html. Again, please note the high number of young people shot in the head, neck, and chest in 2004 and 2005. Please ask Mr. Erlanger why *Times'* readers have not learned of these patterns. At least 29 Palestinian children have already been killed through March of this year, and one Israeli child. As you know, several more Palestinian young people have been killed this month.

2. The fact that Israeli forces have been targeting children and civilians has been noted in diverse reports. For example, Physicians for Human Rights reported: "Physicians for Human Rights analysis of fatal gunshot wounds in Gaza reveals that approximately 50% were to the head. This high proportion of fatal head wounds suggests that given broad rules of engagement, soldiers are specifically aiming at peoples' heads." Following are a few of the excellent and thorough articles on this topic that have appeared in the Israeli press, and some of the Human Rights reports on this topic. Gideon Levy article from Ha'aretz, "Suffer the Little Children"
Another Gideon Levy article (I highly recommend his column 'twilight zone'): http://www.jerusalemites.org/articles/english/ oct2004/19.htm
Defence for Children International report: "Status of Palestinian Children's Rights" ... http://www.dci-pal.org/english/display.cfm?DocId=287&CategoryId=2

Report on child prisoners: http://www.dci-pal.org/english/doc/ reports/2005/apr03.pdf

3. I understand that *Times* reporters are reluctant to spend much time in the West Bank and Gaza. Nevertheless, I would like to offer to personally take *Times* reporters to visit Palestinian

hospitals to verify the high number of young people being shot by Israeli forces. In return, it would be excellent if *Times'* reporters would then take me to visit Israeli prisons, so that we might investigate the conditions in which Palestinian prisoners – particularly children – are being kept.

Again, thanks for your time. It was nice seeing you again – it has certainly resurrected many memories of Ann Arbor and *The Michigan Daily.*

Best Wishes,

Alison

(As the last sentence of this email indicates, Dan Okrent and I were friends and fellow student journalists many years ago.)

Editor's Admission (by Alison Weir)

In his column, Okrent makes one other statement purportedly about us, but that actually seems to be a personal confession: "I don't think any of us can be objective about our own claimed objectivity." Given that admission, it seems that it would have been appropriate for Okrent to at least note the existence of our statistical study, so that his readers could examine our findings for themselves.

Truthfully, however, it is not rare for newspapers to cover up negative information about their organization, and for their ombudsmen to participate in the attempt to suppress such information.

Alison Weir is an independent journalist and executive director of the non-profit organization, If Americans Knew. Some of her most recent work can be found in Censored 2005: The Top 25 Censored Stories (Seven Stories Press). She lives in Washington, D.C.

What about Mel?
Hollywood's Passionate Attachment

by Mark Green and Wendy Campbell

The Greeks gave us theater, and Edison, the 'motion picture'; but it was Jewish immigrants who "invented" Hollywood. Remarkably, in the near century since Louis B. Mayer, the Warner brothers and an assemblage of other Ashkenazi Jewish immigrants created Hollywood's studio system, business there still retains a Yiddish accent.

Some critics however claim that Hollywood doesn't play fair or live up to its responsibilities, since it employs the mesmerizing power of cinema to manipulate the mindset of complacent viewers. How? By relentlessly injecting sordid images and denigrating scenarios of once-respected American archetypes and institutions. Today's targets: Christianity in general, the Catholic Church in particular, and Arabs and Muslims most pointedly.

One memorable example of this kind of cinematic propaganda is the comic-book-styled action film "Sin City" (2005), where oddball villains, many adorned with gaudy layers of crucifixion crosses, go about their merry, murderous ways. The film's arch-villain, in fact, turns out to be nothing less than a cannibalistic and Satan-worshiping Catholic cardinal.

True to form, the movie's two leading characters, portrayed by Mickey Rourke and Bruce Willis, were bereft of any unseemly Christian symbols. I don't want to spoil the ending, but it's Willis who finally manages to exterminate the evil Catholic priest. It's a stirring moment the whole family can enjoy.

Yes, artistic freedom is an essential element to a free society, and "Sin City" wasn't an altogether bad action film; but these insulting depictions are not only common, but they may become in the long term, harmful, since they *selectively* demean faith and arouse ill will. This describes our own culture's dilemma since there are unique double standards at play in American film involving ethnic and religious portrayal. Jewish archetypes, Jewish history and Jewish religious beliefs are generally handled delicately and respectfully. Hollywood's take on the 'Christian community however is far less admiring, running the gamut of characters from spiritually deluded to oafishly hypocritical. And Muslim depictions certainly fare no better.

Consider, for instance, the number of incidents in film or television where a highly religious character is portrayed as having a deep connection to Jesus or "Allah" during the commission of an unspeakable crime. These hell-bent, religious nut cases are so commonplace that they've become cliché. But when the shoe is on the other foot, and well-documented patterns of lethal intolerance are observed, let's say, among Israeli 'settlers' in the Occupied Territories, these stories go unseen by Hollywood. Why? Entertainment is 'news'. And news shapes the political world.

Therefore, don't hold your breath waiting for the release of a major Hollywood film that critically explores the espionage activities of Jewish-American super-spy Jonathan Pollard, or Julius and Ethel Rosenberg, or jailed political power broker, Jack Abramoff. What you may find instead are news stories, recurring TV documentaries and even two full-length films about convicted (Catholic) spy Robert Hanssen, whose cunning deceptions are detailed in "Breach" (2007) and "Master Spy" (2002).

The highly-publicized death of an American Jew, Leon Klinghoffer, at the hands of Palestinian hijackers in 1985 has yielded "Voyage of Death" (1990) starring Burt Lancaster and the opera "The Death of Klinghoffer" (1991). Similarly, Jewish journalist, Daniel Pearl—executed by radical Jihadists in Pakistan in 2002—instantly became a media sensation used to exemplify innocent Jewish suffering at the hands of Islamic terror. Pearl's tragedy is the moral centerpiece of "A Mighty Heart" (2007) starring Angelina Jolie.

Conversely, non-Jewish peace activists Rachael Corrie and Tom Hurndall, (killed by Israeli security forces in 2003 and 2004) have been dutifully ignored by Hollywood. In a similar vein, nuclear whistleblower Mordechai Vanunu--who spent 18 years in an Israeli prison (eleven years in solitary confinement) for revealing that the Jewish State had secretly developed an arsenal of nuclear bombs—is ignored. Similarly, the entire scandal involving Israel's treacherous and murderous assault upon the USS Liberty on June 8, 1967 has been shunned by Hollywood and most mainstream news media. Indeed, historic facts are often highlighted or airbrushed away in Hollywood for political purposes. This surely explains why the amount of movies and documentaries devoted to the Holocaust have uniquely *increased* in number in each successive decade since WWII.

Venus Envy

As a side note, among the slew of heavies in "Sin City", the presence of blue eyes correlated strongly with moral failure. This has been observed in other films as well, including the mixed pattern of casting blonde-haired men in unlikable roles. Is Hollywood sending out another subliminal message? If this seems improbable, please note that it was Hollywood that invented (and maintains) the ever-present 'dumb blonde' stereotype.

Indeed, whereas gratuitously denigrating imagery of most ethnic minorities is now taboo in American film, in its place is a new array of politically-correct bogeymen. Today's baddies (besides being Islamo-fascists) are greedy white guys in suits, Italian mobsters,

Southern racists, wretched suburban housewives, duplicitous Christians, or hillbilly rednecks. Jewish characters on the other hand are generally virtuous. If a Jewish character does turn out to be a jerk, he's invariably complex and probably lovable. Indeed, under Hollywood's gaze there are many Jewish heroes, *many*, many Jewish victims, but no Jewish villains. When a (historically Jewish) criminal does emerge in an American movie, as in "Bugsy" (1991), he's nevertheless depicted as a pretty swell guy (even a business visionary in this case) and the issues of race and ethnicity within Judaism go unexplored. Having WASPy and debonair Warren Beatty play Busy Siegel keeps this matter off-screen and under wraps. Jewish?

Hollywood producers clearly understand that these fictional scenarios, when acted out repeatedly, have a subliminal and genuine impact. This is surely why we don't see any Hollywood-fabricated psychopaths sporting a *Star of David* adornment on their chest, or any rabid, murderous rabbis dished up for popular amusement.

In fact, Jewishness is both exalted and disguised in Hollywood. When a heroic cop-lawyer saves the day in "American Gangster" (2007) it is ultra-goy movie star Russell Crowe (adorned with a *Star of David*) who is cast to play this incorruptible Jewish lion. Yet Crowe finds himself engulfed in a sea of cultural dishonesty throughout "American Gangster". Is it his Jewishness that allows him to reach and sustain this elevated moral stature? After all, even his fellow (non-Jewish) cops are depicted as mostly *low-lifes*. The viewer is left to guess. But virtue and Jewishness are bound together tightly in Hollywood lore, just as they are in the nightly news where heroic Israeli commandos 'retaliate' against murdering 'terrorists'.

Indeed, Judaism is customarily presented to the American public as either the source of an ethnic identity that's senselessly under siege, or as a morally centered (and universal) worldview that's fully compatible with Christianity and American law. Rarely is Judaism depicted as a potentially adversarial or exclusivist creed with its own agenda and array of victims. In American media, the underlying problems associated with Jewishness invariably boils down to this: Muslim fanaticism or white supremacism.

The unwary consumer of American news and entertainment is therefore trained to think pleasant (or guilty) thoughts about this unique victim/success group and favor them over all their cardboard adversaries. This culminates in taboo. And its power is sustained through repeated Holocaust imagery that subconsciously connects the *expression of criticism* about Jewish behavior with the *act of committing genocide* against Jewish people. The result: stigma and self-censorship.

When Movie Stars Go Bad

Indeed, it took an actor/director/producer with the stature of Mel Gibson to re-test this inviolable rule when, in the midst of a DUI arrest back in 2006, he ran into a brick wall otherwise known as the Hollywood establishment.

In Malibu one night, Gibson was pulled over for speeding. Though he tested slightly intoxicated, he proclaimed his innocence and pleaded not to be arrested. Finally Gibson angrily accused the arresting cop: "Are you a Jew"?—(it turned out that he was). That was the beginning of the end for Mel. Thirty months into the US war on Iraq, Gibson drunkenly proclaimed to an arresting policeman "Jews start all the world's wars". Tinsel Town went wild, or at least its media did.

As a result, Mel's not only forever *off* the Hollywood A-list, but he's forever *on* the 'watch list' of virulent "Jew-haters", "neo-Nazis", "white supremacists" and maybe even "terrorist enablers". Don't expect Oscar-winner Gibson to eventually emerge from this as if his comments were just a forgettable and embarrassing *faux pas*. This isn't a mere drug bust, assault charge, sex crime, or even a formal statement disparaging motherhood. Mel Gibson has gone way, way over the top: he's made "anti-Semitic comments".

Yet there are countless successful and ruthless people (gentile and Jew alike) who do unethical things each and every day. If it turns out that they're absolutely hog-wild *in love* with Zionist Israel, does this make them virtuous? Conversely, why should an upstanding and accomplished artist like Mel Gibson be judged to be 'beyond the pale' if he concludes that the warmongering politics of the neocons and international Jewry are deplorable?

It's worth remembering that well before Gibson's international media incident played itself out, powerful forces within organized Jewry were trying to sabotage his Biblically faithful but allegedly anti-Semitic film "The Passion". Abe Foxman of the Anti-Defamation League (ADL) even went so far as to demand that Gibson edit out "incendiary" portions of his film. Later, Foxman not only called for a boycott of the "The Passion" but supported efforts to undermine its distribution. So Gibson's alleged paranoia over organized Jewish subterfuge was not without warrant.

The brouhaha over the Gibson affair, and others like it, becomes especially ironic when you factor in Tinsel Town's ignominious levels of infidelity, billion-dollar porn casting, glorification of violence, routine defamation of Islam and Christianity, and open-faced warmongering. Just who exactly is it among that highfalutin crowd that's entitled to cast stones at Mel?

Let's also recall that Hollywood distribution moguls Bob and Harvey Weinstein declined to circulate Gibson's "The Passion" because its storyline upset a wide spectrum of Jewish activists whose job it is to scan for anti-Semitic blips on the cultural radar screen. So Gibson was already being watched, and watched closely. At the same time, the Weinstein brothers did elect to distribute "Sin City" as well as Michael Moore's much ballyhooed "Fahrenheit 9/11". Why? Both of these films respected the unwritten Hollywood code: vilification of Arab and/or Christians is acceptable, but one must never—even in the context of analyzing terrorism or the forces which shape U.S. war policies in the Middle East—undermine the legitimacy of Israel and Zionism before an American audience.

Could Big Media and Big Government really be in cahoots to advance an ethno-political agenda? Stranger things have happened. Writing in the Los Angeles Times (12/19/08) columnist Joel Stein adds humor and realism to the stunning reality of ethnic monopoly in Big Media/Entertainment. He writes:

> "How deeply Jewish is Hollywood? When the studio chiefs took out a full-page ad in the Los Angeles Times a few weeks ago to demand that the Screen Actors Guild settle its contract, the open letter was signed by: News Corp. President Peter Chernin (Jewish), Paramount Pictures Chairman Brad Grey (Jewish), Walt Disney Co. Chief Executive Robert Iger (Jewish), Sony Pictures Chairman Michael Lynton (surprise, Dutch Jew), Warner Bros. Chairman Barry Meyer (Jewish), CBS Corp. Chief Executive Leslie Moonves (so Jewish his great uncle was the first prime minister of Israel), MGM Chairman Harry Sloan (Jewish) and NBC Universal Chief Executive Jeff Zucker (mega-Jewish). If either of the Weinstein brothers had signed, this group would have not only the power to shut down all film production but to form a *minyan* with enough Fiji water on hand to fill a *mikvah*."

Stein clears the air. And he's pretty funny about it, adding:

> "The Jews are so dominant, I had to scour the trades to come up with six Gentiles in high positions at entertainment companies. When I called them to talk about their incredible advancement, five of them refused to talk to me, apparently out of fear of insulting Jews. The sixth, AMC President Charlie Collier, turned out to be Jewish."

These stunning facts surely help explain why "Fahrenheit 911", Michael Moore's 'controversial' documentary about 911 and the Bush Administration, actually managed to sidestep mentioning "Israel", "Palestine", "Zionism" or "neo-conservatism" throughout the entire film! 'Controversial'?

With that in mind, it's important that the aspiring filmmaker remember these three things:

1) Jewish Americans tend to occupy the top of the Hollywood food chain.

2) They plan to remain there.

3) Don't forget the first two things.

OK, Moore did provide requisite doses of Saudi-bashing, as well as enough oily innuendo to bolster the politically correct but dubious view that U.S. policies in the Middle East are all about 'corporate greed and oil'. He's been the darling of liberal Hollywood ever since. Unfortunately, Moore's war-for-oil thesis is mostly bunk since US energy and foreign policies have historically yielded to Israel's hegemonic ambitions.

Indeed, with Israel locked in a semi-continuous state of war, Zionist media-mavens have the means and motive to make political mischief as needed, and with far-reaching consequences. This includes the option of manufacturing the kind of headlines that makes preemptive war against any of Israel's numerous foes appear prudent and just. As one considers the unrivaled Jewish presence in Hollywood and American journalism, is it not possible, even *inevitable*, that many of our country's most influential writers, commentators, producers, pundits and editors suffer from a deep and profound *conflict of interest* on political matters involving the Jewish state?

Put another way: how can they not?

Zionists may spin this criticism as anti-Semitism, but don't be fooled, since the term itself is an undefined and over-reaching smear. In fact, the allegation of "anti-Semitism" is designed to communicate one simple idea: "You are evil. Now shut up".

As the *pogrom* against non-Jews in Palestine grinds on, Zionism's terrible excesses cry out for scrutiny and reform.

Mark Green is a businessman, writer, editor of this book, and the former host of the TV talk show "Flashpoint". He can be reached at markgreen@flashpoint-tv.net. Wendy Campbell is a documentary filmmaker. Her web sites are MarWenMedia.com and ExposingIsraseliApartheid.com

The Jews of Prime Time

by Edmund Connelly

Introduction

Given that Jews numerically prevail in some of our cultural institutions, and that in others they are represented in numbers and positions that automatically give them major influence, and given further that Jews have a Jewish sensibility, it follows that Jewish sensibility is likely to dominate some of our cultural institutions. It does.

Ernest van den Haag[i]

It makes no sense at all to try to deny the reality of Jewish power and prominence in popular culture. . . . Any Martian monitoring American television . . . would view Seinfeld, Friends, The Nanny, Northern Exposure, Mad About You, *and other shows and be surprised to learn that fewer than 1 in 40 Americans is Jewish . . .*

Michael Medved[ii]

The way Steven Spielberg sees the world has become the way the world is communicated back to us every day.

Stephen Schiff[iii]

Amid the Turbulence of the Sixties

In the wake of the turbulent Sixties, one could do worse than identify a change in the prime-time television line-up to mark the beginning of the end of the dominance of Euro-derived people in
the United States. For in the early 1970's, the "hayseed" shows about
the heartland and American Majority vanished from the three major
networks' evening offerings and were replaced by decidedly more
ethnic fare. In a few short years, essentially all-white shows like *The
Beverly Hillbillies, The Andy Griffith Show/Mayberry R.F.D., Green Acres,*
and *Petticoat Junction* gave way to "hip, urban" shows that "pushed
the socially engaged agenda into the ethno-racial arena." In place of
Andy Griffith and Don Knotts, viewers were now watching characters from "ethnicoms" in shows like *Sanford and Son,* The Jeffersons,
and *Chico and the Man.* Alongside these shows came socially conscious
sitcoms often critical of mainstream values, led by Norman Lear's *All
in the Family.* What did all this mean for representation of life in modern America, and where has it led in the ensuing thirty-five years?

Perhaps Wilmot Robertson was right when he wrote about the dispossession of Majority white Christians in modern America. The
present essay focuses on one aspect of that dispossession: the role of
prime-time television, which in the years 1960–2000 was possibly
the most powerful medium in existence for delivering scripted cultural messages to the American masses.

To understand the changes that have been made on the small screen,
it is necessary to focus on who the people are that have been in a position to make those changes and who have, in fact, been making them.
We find that the primary producers of this form of anti-majority
cultural representation are essentially the same group as that pro-
ducing media images more generally. That the members of this
group are not themselves drawn from the Majority has had a critical
impact on the final products Americans see on TV.

Readers may suspect that the group in question is composed largely of immigrant Eastern European Jews and their descendants, an
argument that has been made by *Occidental Quarterly* contributor

Kevin MacDonald. In the paperback preface of *The Culture of Critique*, MacDonald describes the Hollywood aspects of a wider culture struggle between Jews and Gentiles. The kings of Hollywood branched out easily from their first visual mass medium into the electronic media of radio, and then, as technology advanced, into television. The same themes and conflicts evident in a hundred years of Hollywood film can therefore be found in TV offerings as well. For a few crucial reasons, though, television was late in explicitly addressing them.

[4]We are fortunate to have not only extensive studies of "the Jewish invention of Hollywood" but insightful scholarship into the role of Jews in the creation of television fare as well. For instance, we have Jonathan and Judith Pearl's *The Chosen Image: Television's Portrayal of Jewish Themes and Characters* (1999); Vincent Brook's *Something Ain't Kosher Here: The Rise of the "Jewish" Sitcom* (2003); David Zurawik's *The Jews of Prime Time (2003)*; and Paul Buhle's *From the Lower East Side to Hollywood: Jews in American Popular Culture* (2004). These books delineate and discuss the scores of Jewish programs and characters featured on American TV in the last three decades, with names familiar to even the most casual TV viewer: *Mad About You, Northern Exposure, The Nanny, Friends, Brooklyn Bridge, Dharma and Greg, The Larry Sanders Show*, and most of all, *Seinfeld.*

I. Jews on TV

In their book titled *The Chosen Image*, the Pearls offer a fascinating look at the Jewish themes Americans have been exposed to by prime-time TV. There have been portraits of *bar* and *bat mitzvahs*, Jewish weddings, anti-Semitism, Chanukah, and, of course, the Holocaust. "Jewish matters," the Pearls write, "have driven story lines, shaped characters, defined issues, and made appearances on countless TV shows throughout the decades. Indeed, the presence of Jewish themes on television has been a constant throughout the history of television. From its earliest days until today, the great reflector of American life has simply recognized the active place of Jews within that life."

In the same year that *The Beverly Hillbillies* and *Green Acres* disappeared from television screens, *All in the Family* made its debut, placing before the American people a completely different representation of American character and culture. Jewish liberal Norman Lear had created Archie Bunker, an icon that became familiar to and loved by millions of television viewers. In an important sense, Archie's primary role was to usher out the older era of a white, male-dominated America, represented by people like himself, and to instruct this soon-to-be disestablished class in the manners and attitudes befitting a new, multicultural America, one in which blacks could own their own businesses and homosexuals could come out of the closet.

Most of all, this new, multicultural America was one in which Jews and all things Jewish had a new-found prominence. "By the end of his twelve years on prime-time television," the Pearls inform us, "Archie Bunker, America's best-known bigot, had come to raise a Jewish child in his home, befriend a black Jew, go into business with a Jewish partner, enroll as a member of Temple Beth Shalom, eulogize his close friend at a Jewish funeral, host a Sabbath dinner, participate in a *bat mitzvah* ceremony, and join a group to fight synagogue vandalism."[7]

Cultural historians and other astute observers have seen clearly that this shift in focus from America's Majority Christian whites to a broad cast of minorities was far from inevitable, for humans themselves construct all cultural products. Although the vast majority of the important players in determining TV programming were Jews, they were at first reluctant to project themselves and their concerns too directly into what appeared on broadcast TV, at least for the first few decades of American television. This was the "too Jewish" conundrum that American Jews had earlier encountered—and conquered—with respect to literature and film.

David Zurawik takes this as his starting point in *The Jews of Prime Time*, asking, "What is 'too Jewish' yet not Jewish enough?" Answer: "the strange history of Jewish characters on prime-time network television." The incongruence to which he refers comes from the fact that nearly all the top TV executives and producers were Jewish, yet they were ambivalent about portraying their own high status or that of Jews in other important areas of American life. To illustrate, he begins with an interview with Jewish comedian Al Franken. Zurawik's direct access to Franken and TV mogul Brandon Tartikoff provides an inside view of Jewish thinking on the "too Jewish" issue.

Tartikoff was concerned about a sketch on NBC Entertainment's highly popular *Saturday Night Live* show, in which actor Tom Hanks plays a fictional emcee of a game show called "Jew/Not-a-Jew." Alluding to *Laverne & Shirley* co-star Penny Marshall, Hanks asks, "Okay, panelists, Jew or not a Jew?" Tartikoff allowed that it was funny "but was it anti-Semitic?" After agonizing over it for a week, he gave the skit a green light, whereupon his phone rang off the hook on Sunday morning "with calls from colleagues, many of whom were Jewish." The most troubling call, said Tartikoff, came from his mother. "I cannot believe it. I'm embarrassed to call you my son. This Jew/Not-a-Jew sketch was the most anti-Semitic thing I've ever seen."

While Tartikoff may have erred in this instance, there were other times he pulled the plug because a sketch or show was "too Jewish." Why did Tartikoff and other Jewish executives so often react this way? To Franken, it was because "there's a feeling among some Jews that 'Hey, let's not get too out front in our Jewishness, because people might not like it.' . . . 'Hey, let's not . . . draw fire. There's a lot of us in this business, let's not call attention to it, you know.'" This may well explain why so many Jewish network executives and TV programmers shaded or avoided any connection between Jewish identity and what characters said or did on so many shows. In fact, Tartikoff in 1991 nearly canceled *Seinfeld* after just one episode for being—surprise—"too Jewish."

Zurawik finds David Sarnoff and William Paley, respective founders of NBC and CBS, responsible for leading the way in Jewish self-censorship. While many other powerful Jewish executives respected this censorship, Zurawik believes that Paley set the bar when it came to avoiding "surplus Jewish visibility." He wrote, "There is no doubt that Paley is one of the primary reasons there were no Jewish characters on network television from 1955 to 1972." Given the "incredible power Paley wielded in television during those years," it is understandable that his strong desire not to see Jewish characters on television would be honored.[8]

Of course, Zurawik's observations go only so far, for, in addition to mid-70's shows like *Archie Bunker*, one could also find heavily Jewish-inflected shows like *Bridget Loves Bernie, Rhoda, Welcome Back Kotter, Barney Miller* and *Taxi*. In any case, the taboo vanished in many respects around the same year that Tartikoff gave the okay to *Seinfeld*, after which overtly Jewish shows became the norm across the spectrum, from sitcoms to late-night shows on cable (think of Comedy Central's *The Daily Show with Jon Stewart* [born Jonathan Stuart Leibowitz in 1962] or *Larry King Live* with Larry King [born Lawrence Harvey Ziegler]). Mostly, however, the Jewish shows that blossomed in the 1990s were of the *Mad About You* variety, which brings us to the issues that became the ones most featured: assimilation and intermarriage.

Both Zurawik and the Pearls devote extensive space to these issues, which in most ways mirror earlier analyses from film, when critics and scholars could mine the likes of *Marjorie Morningstar* (1958), *Funny Girl* (1968), *Goodbye Columbus* (1969), *Portnoy's Complaint* (1972) or *Annie Hall* (1977) for cultural ore. As in film, when television approached these themes, the drama centered almost exclusively around the Jewish male courting the Gentile female, or, as critics so lovingly referred to her, the *shiksa*. Of the *shiksa*, one critic wrote:

> In the 1990s, it seems that the mother of every fictional female on television is advising her daughter to find a nice Jewish boy. And the daughters are listening. From hour-long dramas, "Sisters," "Chicago Hope," and "Murder One," to 30-minute comedies, "Mad About You," "Cybill," "Partners," "Bless This House," "The Single Guy," "The Larry Sanders Show," "Friends," "Love and War," "Seinfeld," and "Murphy Brown," Jewish men are dating—and marrying—Gentile women in numbers far exceeding any other interethnic relationships currently on television.

The most likely reason for such images, the critic argues, is that Jewish men run Hollywood. But do Jews really have that much power in television?

II. Jewish Power in TV

From its origins, Hollywood has been stamped with a Jewish identity, but nobody else was supposed to know about it. But somehow, no matter how thorough the attempt to suppress or disguise it, Jewishness is going to bob to the surface anyway.

Stephen J. Whitfield[x]

Mogul Hollywood

Hollywood has always been a Jewish milieu. This fact has been well documented by Neal Gabler, Michael Medved, Ben Stein, and others who have chronicled Hollywood's initial and continuing Jewish makeup and sensibility, however masked it may at times be. In his 1988 book *An Empire of Their Own: How the Jews Invented Hollywood,* author Neal Gabler celebrates the period of Hollywood's founding through the end of the studio and mogul era, thus buttressing the belief that "The American Dream—is a Jewish invention." Indeed, as Medved documents:

> The storefront theaters of the late teens were transformed into the movie palaces of the twenties by Jewish exhibitors. And when sound movies commandeered the industry, Hollywood was invaded by a battalion of Jewish writers, mostly from the East. The most powerful talent agencies were run by Jews. Jewish lawyers transacted most of the industry's business and Jewish doctors ministered to the industry's sick. Above all, Jews produced the movies."[12]

Social scientist and media gadfly Ernest van den Haag adds further comments to how power is employed and how Jews in particular use it, in this case with respect to cinema's younger sibling, television:

"The Jewish cultural establishment goes far beyond the strictly intellectual and academic milieu. It is spread throughout the communications industry and thereby enters almost every home in America. Hollywood has always been a largely Jewish institution . . . On the other hand, the television industry was founded and staffed by a much later generation of Jews."[13] What are the consequences that flow from this state of affairs?

MacDonald notes that "Jewish contributions to entertainment and the media have often had the function of promoting positive images of Judaism and multi-culturalism and negative images of Christianity and European ethnic interests and identification."[14] Both a cursory and an in-depth analysis of this claim appear to be true. Take, for instance, the Pearls' conclusion about their exhaustive investigation of Jewish images on television, *The Chosen Image: Television's Portrayal of Jewish Themes and Characters*:

> Since the inception of network television half a century ago, hundreds of popular TV shows have portrayed Jewish themes. Such topics as anti-Semitism, intermarriage, Jewish lore and traditions, Israel, the Holocaust, and questions of Jewish identity have been featured in a wide range of television genres. . . . What is the television image of Jews and Judaism that emerges from this fascinating wealth of programming? In nearly every instance, the Jewish issues have been portrayed with respect, relative depth, affection, and good intentions, and the Jewish characters who appear in these shows have, without any doubt, been Jewish—often depicted as deeply involved in their Judaism.[15]

One interesting outcome of the Jewish-controlled portrayal of religion has been "the unraveling of the TV-melded Christmas-Chanukah holiday" into one where Chanukah can stand on its own merits. In an episode of *Frank's Place*, for example, when a non-Jew is invited to a Chanukah dinner at the home of lawyer Bubba Weisberger, the audience is treated to a lengthy and positive account of the holiday, one "without any thought of Christmas." On an episode of the 1992 *WIOU*, "Chanukah held center stage. The defacing of a Chanukah menorah in a public park by anti-Semitic thugs became the occasion for series regular Willis Teitlebaum" to explore his feelings and Jewish identity. This linkage of Chanukah with anti-Semitism was also the theme of an episode of *Sisters*, when vandals attacked a Jewish restaurant. [16] Here, then, is the privileging of a small but powerful minority, while at the same time the Jew-as-victim message is reinforced.

The themes of anti-Semitism and Jewish victimhood have been and continue to be openly or subtly woven into story lines across the board, but the most urgent reminders of Jewish victimhood have come in the form of scores of highly graphic televised Holocaust specials, beginning with NBC's 1978 airing of the four-part miniseries *Holocaust*, which was seen by up to one hundred million Americans. In addition, notes historian Peter Novick,

> the Anti-Defamation League distributed ten million copies of its sixteen-page tabloid, *The Record*, to promote the drama. Jewish organizations successfully lobbied major newspapers to serialize Gerald Green's novelization of his television play, or to publish special inserts on the Holocaust. (*The Chicago Sun-Times* distributed hundreds of thousands of copies of its insert to local schools.) The American Jewish Committee, in cooperation with NBC, distributed millions of copies of a study guide for viewers; teachers' magazines carried other curricular material tied to the program. Jewish organizations worked with the National Council of Churches to prepare other promotional and educational materials, and organized advance viewings for religious leaders. The day the series began was designated "Holocaust Sunday"; various activities were scheduled in cities across the country; the National Conference of Christians and Jews distributed yellow stars to be worn on that day.[17]

Television viewers have likely also noticed the commercial-free Ford Motor Company-sponsored airing on NBC of Spielberg's *Schindler's List*. It seems unlikely that a major American corporation will soon sponsor a commercial-free viewing of Mel Gibson's *The Passion of the Christ*, especially now that Gibson has been involved in what some are calling an anti-Semitic affair. [18]

III. Hostility toward Gentiles

If the average American were asked if a culture war was currently being waged in America, the significant number likely to answer in the affirmative would point to the ongoing liberal-conservative split, or as it is now more commonly known, the battle between the blue states and red states. Were one to posit that Jews were waging an equally vitriolic (and not totally unrelated) war on Majority Americans, there would likely be strenuous denials. In fact, however, leading intellectuals have described such a war—or *kulturkampf*—in minute detail.

John Murray Cuddihy argued in his 1974 book, *The Ordeal of Civility: Freud, Marx, Levi-Strauss, and the Jewish Struggle with Modernity*, that at least since the Enlightenment, a significant segment of Jewry has considered itself to be at war with the Gentile world and has acted accordingly. He wrote, "the ordeal in question involves the pain felt by newly emancipated Eastern Jews who began to realize that the Christian societies of Western Europe had overtaken them culturally, financially, artistically, and intellectually." According to Cuddihy, the Jewish response to this trauma has been anger and "vindictive objectivity"; worse, "they continue unabated into our own time because Jewish Emancipation continues into our own time." [19]

Just as Cuddihy shows how the Jews of the title have prosecuted their war on Gentiles in terms of psychoanalysis, class struggle and structuralism, he also shows how it is being waged more recently, for example in American fiction of late 1950's and 1960's. He could probably have found endless examples in the decades of televised cultural messages as well.

Historian Albert Lindemann prefers an allegorical approach to this *kulturkampf*, beginning with one of the founding myths of the Jewish people, the story of feuding brothers Esau and Jacob (Gen. 25,

23–26). Lindemann argues that this Jewish-derived division between Jew and Gentile has relevance from ancient times to our own day, including a Jewish tendency (even "instinct," in Lindemann's words) "to view surrounding Gentile society as pervasively flawed, polluted, or sick." In modern times this tendency is to be found in ideologies such as "socialism (both Marxist and anarchist), Zionism, and various forms of the psychiatric worldview (Freudian psychoanalysis and related schools)." Remarkably, Lindemann makes these arguments with no indication that Cuddihy's work has informed him, suggesting a fortuitous simultaneous discovery on the order of the simultaneous but independent invention of calculus by Newton and Leibniz in the late 1600s.

Writing twenty-four years after Cuddihy and only a year after Lindemann, MacDonald makes a more straightforward case for a Jewish war on Gentiles. Applying a social identity approach, MacDonald illuminates Jews' "very deep antipathy to the entire gentile-dominated social order, which is viewed as anti-Semitic." MacDonald goes further than David Hollinger's claim that the increased Jewish presence in academia (and elsewhere) has resulted merely in a generic "cosmopolitanism," noting, "This antipathy toward gentile-dominated society was often accompanied by a powerful desire to avenge the evils of the old social order." Referring to the many Jewish families "which around the breakfast table, day after day, in Scarsdale, Newton, Great Neck, and Beverly Hills have discussed what an awful, corrupt, immoral, undemocratic, racist society the United States is," MacDonald argues that there were clearly elements of active hostility toward Middle American culture in general. [20] If so, it should be easy to find such hostility in modern TV fare.

Hostility Toward Religion

It is only natural that a group should find the symbols cherished by its perceived opponents threatening or irritating, which is a likely reason for the perennial Jewish attacks on Christian symbols in the United States. Norman Podhoretz admits that such heavily Jewish groups as the American Jewish Congress and the American Civil

Liberties Union often oppose Christian beliefs in America, ridiculing these beliefs and attempting to undermine their public position.[22]

This observation is consistent with the findings of Hollywood film critic Michael Medved, who has written and spoken about the fact that so much of what emanates from Hollywood has become shockingly anti-religious, particularly with respect to Christianity. While Medved does not state it explicitly, we are witnessing the effects of a kind of cultural hegemony being exercised by a distinct group of Hollywood writers, producers, etc. who, as we have seen, are predominately Jewish. Medved writes:

> In the ongoing war on traditional values, the assault on organized faith represents the front to which the entertainment industry has most clearly committed itself. On no other issue do the perspectives of the show business elites and those of the public at large differ more dramatically. Time and again, the producers have gone out of their way to affront the religious sensibilities of ordinary Americans.[23]

Citing a 1992 study that found that "89 percent of Americans claim affiliations with an organized faith," Medved describes in detail how Hollywood has produced fare that is hostile to its audience's beliefs. He notes that many made-for-television movies are consistently grim regarding Christian identification. For instance, in the miniseries *The Thorn Birds*, handsome Richard Chamberlain plays a tormented priest who has broken his vows of celibacy. William Shatner, in his role as *T.J. Hooker*, tracks down a "ruthless, Scripture-spouting crook who leaves Bibles as calling cards at the scene of his crimes." ABC's *The Women of Brewster Place* shows a preacher luring a woman to his bed, while in one episode of *Unsub* "Bishop Grace" murders two teenage girls in his congregation. NBC's *In the Heat of the Night* aired an episode in which "Reverend Haskell" expires just after enjoying an affair with one of his parishioners. Two "Bible thumpin' hayseeds" appear as kidnappers on *Shannon's Deal*, paired up with "a devout Christian who murders his wife and then justifies the killing as 'an act of God . . . unstoppable as a flood.' "

Christianity has fared just as poorly on animated TV shows. Fox Television Network's *The Simpsons* featured a scene in which the family gathered around the table to say grace, and Bart solemnly intones, "Dear God, we paid for all this stuff ourselves, so thanks for nothing." A more aggressive expression of disrespect was written into the Christmas episode from *South Park* entitled "Mr. Hankey, the Christmas Poo." A parody of the 1965 television special *A Charlie Brown Christmas*, this episode featured a human feces as the spirit of Christmas, the obvious message being that "Christmas is shit." What we can see being played out in the visual media, then, is one aspect of the Jewish-Gentile *kulturkampf* in modern America.

Hollywood insider Benjamin Stein confirms this impression. In the 1976 essay "Whatever happened to small-town America?" he explores television's consistent hostility toward rural (read Majority Christian) Americans. Stein begins by noting that "a truly great number of the people who write movies and television shows are Jewish," and given their largely urban upbringing, when they create TV fare they are not telling it "like it is."

> Instead they are giving us the point of view of a small and extremely powerful section of the American intellectual community—those who write for the mass visual media. . . . What is happening, as a consequence, is something unusual and remarkable. A national culture is making war upon a way of life that is still powerfully attractive and widely practiced in the same country. . . . Feelings of affection for small towns run deep in America, and small-town life is treasured by millions of people. But in the mass culture of the country, a hatred for the small town is spewed out on television screens and movie screens every day. . . . Television and the movies are America's folk culture, and they have nothing but contempt for the way of life of a very large part of the folk. . . . People are told that their culture is, at its root, sick, violent, and depraved, and this message gives them little confidence in the future of that culture. It also leads them to feel ashamed of their country

and to believe that if their society is in decline, it deserves to be.

IV. Denial and Deception Regarding Jewish Power

As we saw earlier, any number of Jewish observers are willing to acknowledge the immense power of Jews in American media, particularly in Hollywood film and television, although this view cannot yet be described as conventional wisdom as far as the general public is concerned. But for informed observers, identity always matters. In *Jews and the Left*, Arthur Liebman observes that "one of the most important pieces of information a researcher can gather on a social movement is the socioeconomic composition of its membership."[25] The same can be said about the ethnic composition of those openly commenting on Jewish power in the media: they are overwhelmingly Jews themselves. In contrast, Gentiles are routinely discouraged from noticing, yet alone analyzing, this phenomenon, which is crucial in a democracy. As MacDonald notes, "Jewish groups have made any critical discussion of Jewish issues off limits, and that's vitally important because, yes, Jews are a very powerful group.[26]

It appears that a regime of silence has been imposed, with ample rewards going to those Gentiles willing to toe the party line and a graduated range of punishments being administered to those unwilling to abide by the established rules of discourse. Prominent examples have been cited by MacDonald et al., including the case of young British journalist, William Cash. He is the one who, with innocent candor, noted the Hollywood presence of Michael Ovitz, Steven Spielberg, David Geffen, Jeffrey Katzenberg, Lew Wasserman, Sidney Sheinberg, Barry Diller, Gerald Levin, Herbert Allen and others and wrote of the Spielberg-Geffen-Katzenberg "Dream Team": "But in one respect at least this particular combination of talents, or 'talent combo' in the local argot, will start out on the right foot. Like the old mogul founders of the early studios—and unlike most other failed build-your-own studio merchants—they are Jewish."

This gaffe broke a cardinal rule, as articulated by columnist Joe Sobran: "Jewish control of the major media in the media age makes the enforced silence both paradoxical and paralyzing. Survival in public life requires that you know all about it, but never refer to it." Vincent Brook, author of *Something Ain't Kosher Here*, belongs to the camp that would enforce this silence among Gentiles, applauding the fact that a group critical of some TV portrayals "refrained from reviving the old canard of Jewish media control." Brook then elides attribution to a quote on the Cash affair, putting these words in Cash's mouth: "a self-perpetuating Jewish cabal had created an exclusive Power Elite in Hollywood."[30] Never mind that Brook's book is all about Jewish prominence in Hollywood.

Brook follows this censure of Cash with a condemnation of Marlon Brando for his unsettling statements on *Larry King Live*, claiming that Jews run Hollywood and exploit stereotypes of minorities. "Hollywood is run by Jews, it is owned by Jews," he began, "but we never saw the kike because they know perfectly well that's where you draw the wagons around." Two comments about Brando's observation are in order. First, Brando could easily have added Majority Christians to the list of exploited Hollywood stereotypes, as we saw above, but perhaps his greatest insight was about the "kike."[31] Though an unfortunate choice of words, it does point to the fact that we do not begin to see in Hollywood fare even a fraction of the real doings of real Jews.

Leaving aside the touchy issue of modern Israel, we can still focus on two crucial aspects of Jewish American behavior that are essentially absent from TV discourse: the numerous wrongdoings of individual Jews and Jewish groups,[32] and the pervasive power of Jews in media, finance, politics, education and a host of other important areas. Try to find a show that features the illegal activities of an Ivan Boesky or Michael Milken or dozens of other American Jews discussed in books like Connie Bruck's 1988 *Predators' Ball* or James B. Stewart's 1991 *Den of Thieves*.[33]

For detailed accounts of massive Jewish power in modern America, see what J. J. Goldberg, current editor of *The Jewish Forward*, wrote

in his 1996 book *Jewish Power*, or political scientist Benjamin Gins-
berg in his 1993 *The Fatal Embrace: Jews and the State*. Alone, these two
instances of Jewish privilege in acknowledging and describing Jewish power amply demonstrate the rule about selective silence on the
topic, but the greater point is that the American TV viewer does not
see any representations on television of this vast power, unless one
is willing to acknowledge the pervasive presence of Jewish reporters (Wolfe Blitzer, Barbara Walters, Mike Wallace, Ted Koppel et
al.), talk show hosts (Larry King, Jon Stewart et al.), actors, come-
dians, various spokespersons, etc. as an indirect display of Jewish
prominence and power. Where, however, is the *direct* portrayal of this
power? Miles Silverberg on *Murphy Brown?* If so, this kind of mock-
ing of the belief in Jewish power in the newsroom serves to trivialize
the debate, if not eliminate it completely. The absence of any narrative of Jewish power—political, financial, academic—forces us to
reconsider the concept of "surplus visibility" and its application to
American television.

V. How Hiding Their Power Helps the Jews

In *The Jews of Prime-Time*, Zurawik describes the sociological concept of "surplus visibility": "the feeling among minority members
and others that whatever members of that group say or do, it is too
much and, moreover, they are being too conspicuous about it." He
accepts the conventional wisdom that membership in a "particular
community of production" will result in less stereotypical images of
that community and images "more representative of social reality."
The paradox he finds is that this "is not what happened with Jews
and television."[34] The Jewish "self-censorship" exhibited by important gatekeepers of TV programming such as William Paley, David
Sarnoff and Brandon Tartikoff can best be described as a form of
deception in which Jewish producers of culture are highly conscious
of the perceived self-interests of the Jewish community and where
the question "Is it good for the Jews?" is often uppermost in their
thoughts.

Almost without exception, a refusal to note the sheer unreality of Jewish images in popular culture is found. For example, film critic Lester Friedman makes the same error: "Unlike films about other American minorities, movies with Jews were often scrutinized by one segment of that minority group with the power to decide how the entire group would be presented to society as a whole. The resulting images of Jews in films constitute a rich and varied tapestry woven by several generations of moviemakers responding to the world around them." This is fair enough as far as it goes, but he loses sight of reality when he continues, "Their works dynamically depict both the Jews' profound impact on American society and that society's perception of the Jews within its midst. . . . But whether they explain or exploit their Jewish characters, *all these films either implicitly or explicitly show how Jews affect American life* . . . [emphasis added]"[35]

This is precisely where he gets it wrong, for these films, and the voluminous *oeuvre* of TV shows, *hide* the reality of how Jews affect American life. Where have we seen explicit representations of how Jewish activists have marched through the institutions of psychoanalysis, anthropology or the Old and New Left? Where the Jewish role in Communism and its attendant infamies? Where the dramas featuring Jews agitating for open borders and other "immigration reform"? Most pointedly, where are the new shows starring Jewish neoconservatives in their quest for perpetual war in the Middle East?

As a reality counterbalance along the lines of the popular *24* series, in which indefatigable federal agent Jack Bauer (Keifer Sutherland) fights around the clock to protect the nation from terrorists, where is the series starring Ron Silver as Homeland Security Secretary Michael Chertoff, and Jewish actors as his Israeli-born mother and rabbi father? Richard Dreyfus could play veteran Jewish activist Gregg Rickman, who was recently sworn in as the State Department's Special Envoy for Monitoring and Combating Anti-Semitism. If pugnacious Ed Asner was unavailable to play the recurring role of Abraham Foxman of the Anti-Defamation League, perhaps Harvey Keitel could do the honors. What is the likelihood of seeing anything remotely similar in the new TV season?

VI. James Jaeger on *Crash*

This deception is no doubt what so aggravated film critic James Jaeger, prompting him to excoriate Paul Haggis for his racial and ethnic depictions in *Crash*, the 2005 Oscar winner for Best Picture. Echoing Brando, Jaeger notes the film's ensemble of a diverse array of characters "crashing" into each other in a racially tense Los Angeles but charges that "Nowhere is it shown that Jews also CRASH into Blacks, Whites, Latinos, Iranians, Asians and Persians and profoundly affect THEIR lives—especially in Hollywood where CRASH is set and Jews comprise a dominating minority in the Los Angeles area." Rather, Jaeger sees the same old display of select diversity on-screen but no mention of the lack of diversity behind-the-scenes. "Why doesn't Paul write a feature that is set in the executive suites of say Warner Bros. or Paramount where the dominating minority is properly and accurately acknowledged as Jewish?"

One of the consequences of this unbalanced ethnic representation in the executive suite is a plethora of images attacking the values of the American Majority. The films that are financed and/or distributed by the dominating minority comprised of liberal Jewish males "continue to emphasize the homosexual-lesbian agenda, Zionism, uncritical support for Israel and endless Holocaust movies to perpetuate the myth of Jewish victimology." Further, "stories that bash and invalidate the nuclear family unit or stay-at-home mothers thrive. Stories that divide or poke fun at the Christian community, invalidate its history or attempt to dilute and eradicate its holidays, beliefs and/or values are financed and released by Hollywood insiders with abandon."[36]

I would argue that Jaeger's description of Hollywood's film agenda differs not a whit from its TV agenda, which is to "make movies that tell the stories that an elite group of insiders agree with and want told to the exclusion of almost all other stories and themes."
[37]Clearly, this agenda produces winners and losers.

VII. The Propaganda Power of TV

Political scientist Michael Parenti has investigated how media power is wielded. *In Inventing Reality: The Politics of the Mass Media,* he writes:

> The existence of a common pool of culturally determined (systemic, nonconspiratorial) political values cannot be denied, but where did this common pool come from? Who or what determines the determining element in the culture itself? And can we reduce an entire culture . . . to a set of accumulated habituations and practices that simply build up over time? . . . A closer look reveals that the unconsciously shared "established" view . . . is not shared by everyone and is not in fact all that established. . . . In other words, it may be true that most media elites . . . share common views on these subjects, but much—and sometimes most—of the public does not. What we have then is an *"established establishment* view" which is given the highest media visibility, usually to the exclusion of views held by large dissident sectors of the populace. The "dominant shared values and beliefs" that are supposedly the natural accretions and expressions of our common political culture, are not shared by all or most . . . although they surely are dominant in that they tend to preempt the field of opinion visibility. . . .   In sum, media owners—like other social groups—consciously pursue their self-interest and try to influence others in ways that are advantageous to themselves.[38]

It is given "the highest media visibility" by being shown repeatedly on television. Such repetition is necessary for conditioning an uncritical audience to the message at hand. Media experts note, "There is little reason to believe that a single film or even group of films significantly influences audiences' views over the long haul." If, however, a constant and unwavering message is broadcast repeatedly, "it is reasonable to believe that such presentations will affect audiences to a significant extent." [39] Or, as Margaret Miles puts it, "No one film has iconic power, but the recurrence of similar images across films weaves those images into the fabric of the common life of American society . . . We get, at a subliminal and hence utterly effective level, not the narrative but the conventions of Hollywood film." [40] If movies can achieve this, imagine the power of television, which most people, including children, spend incomparably more time watching than film.

By way of an elegy for the American Majority, I note the conclusion MacDonald drew in 1998 about the Gentile response to the sustained ideological attacks on its culture and value. He believes that avoiding open ethnic strife in America means that "at least some ethnic groups be unconcerned that they are losing in the competition. I regard this last possibility as unlikely in the long run." [41] At least for the present, it appears that Majority Americans are indeed all too unconcerned about losing the competition, perhaps because they are so busy watching television and, to play on a title from Neil Postman, "amusing themselves to death." [42]

Edmund Connelly is a freelance writer, academic, and expert on the cinema arts.

Notes

1. Ernest van den Haag, *The Jewish Mystique* (New York: Stein and Day, 1969), 129.

2. "Is Hollywood Too Jewish?" *Moment*, Aug. 1996, 37.

3. "Seriously Spielberg," in *Steven Spielberg*, ed. Lester D. Friedman and Brent Notbohm (Jackson, Mississippi: University Press of Mississippi, 2000), 171.

4. Vincent Brook, *Something Ain't Kosher Here: The Rise of the "Jewish" Sitcom* (New Brunswick, New Jersey: Rutgers University Press, 2003), 49. Incidentally, *The Beverly Hillbillies*, *Green Acres* and *Petticoat Junction* were all creations of Jewish Paul Henning. See Paul Buhle, *From the Lower East Side to Hollywood: Jews in American Popular Culture* (New York, Verso 2004), 263 n39.

5. Neal Gabler coined this phrase for *An Empire of Their Own: How the Jews Invented Hollywood* (New York: Crown Publishers, 1988).

6. Jonathan Pearl and Judith Pearl, *The Chosen Image: Television's Portrayal of Jewish Themes and Characters* (Jefferson, North Caroline: McFarland & Company, Inc., 1999), 229.

7. Pearl and Pearl, *The Chosen Image*, 5.

8. David Zurawik, *The Jews of Prime* Time (Hanover and London: University Press of New England, 2003), 2–6, 62–63. Paley's dominance in the industry was such that for many years Paley's CBS took in 85 percent of the total profits for all three major networks.

9. Alina Sivorinovsky, "Images of Modern Jews on Television," *Midstream*, December 1, 1995 v.41n9, 39–40. It is interesting to note that the shiksa theme, as an internal, gendered Jewish narrative about the Jewish male's sexual conquest or attainment of the Gentile woman, appears as unproblematic, which is odd considering how sensitive interracial and inter-ethnic sexual encounters have been in American history. Modern scholars tend to strongly

condemn views of women as sexual objects. For example, one finds abundant accounts (and condemnations) of instances where white males portray and possess Asian women as sex objects. This theme is apparent from *Madame Butterfly* to scores of Hollywood films, and has been unpacked in works such as Mari Yoshihara's *Embracing the East: White Women and American Orientalism* (Oxford, 2002) and "re-education" documentaries like *Picturing Oriental Girls* and *Slaying the Dragon,* where the trope of a masculine, dominant West and feminine, submissive East is interrogated.

10. Stephen J. Whitfield, *American Space, Jewish Time: Essays in Modern Culture and Politics* (Armonk, NY: M.E. Sharpe, Inc., 1996), 151.

11. Quoted in Gabler, *An Empire of Their Own,* 1.

12. Gabler, *An Empire of Their Own,* 1–2.

13. van den Haag, *The Jewish Mystique,* 141–142.

14. See http://www.csulb.edu/~kmacd/books-derbyshire.html#2nl

15. Pearl and Pearl, *The Chosen Image,* 5.

16. Pearl and Pearl, The Chosen Image, 32-39.

17. Peter Novick, *The Holocaust in American Life* (Boston & New York: Houghton Mifflin Company, 1999), 210. Novick notes that Jewish agencies separately targeted Gentile and Jewish audiences, and in the case of the ADL, they appear to have engaged in deliberate deception, where the study guides for Jewish children emphasized Christian anti-Semitism and denigrated assimilated Jews.

18. In the early hours of July 28, 2006, Gibson was pulled over for possible drunken driving. Los Angeles County Sheriff's Deputy James Mee, who is Jewish, made the arrest, after which Gibson was quoted as blurting out "a barrage of anti-Semitic remarks about 'f—ing Jews,' including the claim that 'the Jews are responsible for all the wars in the world.' " Finally, Gibson asked the officer, "Are you a Jew?" (Gabriel Sanders, "Gibson's New

Line: Forgive Me, Foxman, For I Have Sinned ...", The Jewish Daily Forward, August 4, 2006).

19. John Murray Cuddihy, *The Ordeal of Civility: Freud, Marx, Levi-Strauss and the Jewish Struggle with Modernity* (Boston: Beacon Press, 1987, 1974), 68.

20. Albert S. Lindemann, *Esau's Tears: Modern Anti-Semitism and the Rise of the Jews* (New York: Cambridge University Press, 1997), 13-15.

21. Kevin MacDonald, *The Culture of Critique: An Evolutionary Analysis of Jewish Involvement in Twentieth-Century Intellectual and Political Movements* (Westport, CT: Praeger, 1998), 85-86.

22. Podhoretz in *Commentary*, 1995,30, cited in MacDonald, *The Culture of Critique*, 148.

23. Michael Medved, *Hollywood vs. America: Popular Culture and the War on Traditional Values* (New York: HarperCollins, 1992), 50.

24. Medved, Hollywood vs. America, 80-81.

25. Benjamin Stein, "Whatever happened to small-town America?" *The Public Interest*, Summer 1976, 22–23. In a later book, *The View from Sunset Boulevard: America As Brought To You By The People Who Make Television* (New York: Basic Books, 1979), Stein shows how Norman Lear had an extremely negative view of (Gentile) rural America: "In TAT, Norman Lear's production company, two shows set in small towns have appeared within the last two years—'Mary Hartman, Mary Hartman' and 'Fernwood 2Night.' In both shows, what Marx called 'the idiocy of rural life' comes across powerfully. The small Ohio town of Fernwood, not quite rural and not quite industrial, is full of bigots, Klansmen, quacks, hillbillies, and religious frauds" (72).

26. Arthur Liebman, Jews and the Left (New York: John Wiley & Sons, Inc., 1979), ix-xi. See http://www.csulb.edu/~kmacd/books-derbyshire.html#2nl.

28. William Cash, "Kings of the Deal," *The Spectator,* October, 29, 1994, 14.

29. Joe Sobran, "The Buchanan Frenzy," *Sobran's,* March 1996, 3. Though Cash found defense in the form of his Jewish editor, Dominic Lawson, he nonetheless was the target of strident rebuke from the American side of the Atlantic.

30. Brook, *Something Ain't Kosher Here,* 171.

31. Marlon Brando, *Larry King Live,* Friday, April 5, 1996.

32. For example, in 2002, the Anti-Defamation League settled a lawsuit in which they were accused of spying on San Francisco-area activists. The ADL's chief intelligence-gatherer in the Bay Area, Roy Bullock, was linked to San Francisco police inspector, Tom Gerard, who later pled no contest to a charge of illegally accessing government information. (Bob Egelko, "Jewish defense group settles S.F. spying suit," *San Francisco Chronicle,* February 23, 2002). In another case, in 2001, a federal judge upheld most of a $10 million defamation suit against the ADL for labeling a Denver-area couple as anti-Semites. (Marc Perelman, "Judge Slams ADL for Hurting Couple Tarred As 'Anti-Semites'," *The Forward,* April 13, 2001.) With respect to another important Jewish group, the American Israel Public Affairs Committee (AIPAC), two senior employees were fired after being accused of passing classified U.S. information to the government of Israel. According to documents, the two employees are policy director Steve Rosen and senior analyst Keith Weissman. (Dan Eggen and Jerry Markon, "2 Senior AIPAC Employees Ousted," *The Washington Post,* April 21, 2005, A8). In addition to AIPAC's problems with this scandal, a robust controversy has broken out over the level of clout held by the institution. John Mearsheimer, a West Point graduate and now distinguished professor of political science at the University of Chicago, and Stephen Walt, academic dean of Harvard's Kennedy School of Government, are credited with arguing that "a small group of Israel's supporters inside and outside of government have a disproportionate influence over American foreign policy toward

the Middle East, and this works to the detriment of U.S. security." Their essay, "The Israel Lobby," was published in the *London Review of Books* and continues to generate intense discussion and controversy. (See Michael C. Desch, "Prophets in Their Own Land: How to go from respected academic to anti-Semite—in one simple step," *The American Conservative,* June 19, 2006).

33. Connie Bruck, *The Predators' Ball: The Inside Story of Drexel Burnham and the Rise of the Junk Bond Traders* (New York: Penguin Books, 1988) and James B. Stewart, *Den of Thieves* (New York: Simon and Schuster, 1991). When director Oliver Stone put this issue on the big screen in *Wall Street* (1987), he only tangentially touched on the Jewish indentity of the corrupt trader, Gordon Gekko (Michael Douglas). In the sauna scene, Gekko contrasts his own origins with those of the wealthy WASPs in New York who are more interested in animals in the zoo than in real people.

34. Zurawik, *The Jews of Prime Time*, 6.

35. Lester D. Friedman, *The Jewish Image in American Film* (Secaucus, NJ: Citadel Press, 1987), 9.

36. Parallels with MacDonald's arguments in The Culture of Critique are manifest: "Institutions that promote group ties among gentiles (such as nationalism and traditional gentile religious associations) are actively opposed and subverted, while the structural integrity of Jewish separatism is maintained" (89).

37. James Jaeger, "Paul Haggis, Bigotry & CRASH,

38. http://www.mecfilms.com/universe/articles/crash.htm, 4 March 2006

39. Michael Parenti, *Inventing Reality: The Politics of the Mass Media* (New York: St. Martin's Press, 1986), 241-242.

40. Stephen Powers, David J. Rothman, and Stanley Rothman, *Hollywood's America: Social and Political Themes in Motion Pictures* (Boulder, CO: Westview Press, 1996), 10, 287.

41. Margaret R. Miles, *Seeing and Believing: Religion and Values in the Movies* (Boston: Beacon Press, 1996), 190-191.

42. MacDonald, *The Culture of Critique*, 309.

43. Neil Postman, Amusing Ourselves to Death: Public Discourse in the Age of Show Business (New York: Viking Adult, 1985).

"The Sopranos" and The Shapiros

by Giuseppe Furioso

11/05/02

To: Jonathan Alter, *Newsweek Magazine* From: Giuseppe Furioso

Dear Mr. Alter,

Please forgive me for taking so long to respond to your reply to my letter of Oct. 10, in which I was critical of your essay in which you compared New Jersey Senator, Robert Torracelli, with the fictitious crime boss, Tony Soprano. Regarding the comparison, you said you were merely, "trying to be funny".

As for the question of whether the show demeans Italians, you took the position that this is "much debated" and then gratuitously stated that, "the Italians who created the program and act in it obviously don't think so".

Ethnic disparagement that masquerades as humor is easiest when it is at someone else's expense. The fact that Italians act in the program and are among its creators does not get you or the program off the hook any more than the fact that the actors in the old "Amos and Andy" series were black. And why did you not mention the ethnic background of the producers of the series or of the ownership of HBO? They are certainly not Italians.

At any rate, since you obviously do not find the "Sopranos" offensive, perhaps you could use your tribal connections to the media to promote my idea for another series about an ethnically-defined "Crime Family". It could be called, "The Shapiros" and the following could be its leading characters:

* The patriarch of the family Morris Shapiro, a slumlord whose tenants are mostly minority and who is also suspected of being the nation's largest launderer of Colombian drug money.

* Uncle Yitsak who runs a chain of sub standard nursing homes and is currently out on bail for dealing in child pornography.

* Eldest son Dr. Mortimer Shapiro who runs a Medicare mill and several dozen "bingo" parlors in poor neighborhoods, the profits of which are used to finance illegal settlements on the West Bank.

* Cousin Irving Shapiro, a convicted insider trader who recently purchased a pardon from outgoing president Bill Clinton.

* Zviv Shapiro who languishes in a federal prison because he spied for Israel and his brother Lev, an Israeli General, who in addition to siphoning off millions from the six billion in aid the US gives Israel each year, was recently indicted for war crimes by a Belgian court for his role in the murder of 1600 Egyptian POW's during the Six Day War.

* Nephew Aaron who runs a 'Tolerance' institute that has destroyed the careers and ruined financially numerous public figures who were critical of Israel and her American supporters.

* Family attorney, Seth Ginzburg, who, when he is not providing the family with legal loopholes for their nefarious activities, is bringing class action lawsuits on behalf of Holocaust survivors with contingency fees that have netted him tens of millions, whereas the actual individual plaintiff awards have usually amounted to a few thousand dollars at most.

* Rabbi Joshua Goldstein spiritual councilor to the family who is currently under indictment for having hired a hit-man to kill his wife.

Then of course there are the Shapiro women:

* Bertha, the sister of Morris who wrote the new course of study for multiculturalism and diversity mandated for use in New York City public schools and who has also been linked to the world's largest white slavery network that traffics primarily in poor young women from the former Soviet Union;

* Tiffany her younger sister, who with her lesbian lover were the first same sex couple to adopt a child in New York;

* Daughter Beth and her Israeli husband, Yossi, who are the leading importers and distributors of the drug ecstasy into the United States;

* The voluptuous Cohen twins, Becky and Rachel, who allowed themselves to be taped by the Mossad during sexual trysts with the president and various congressional leaders for the purposes of political blackmail;

* Niece Sharon and her husband Herb Hymawitz, who as officers of the ACLU are actively lobbying for the passage of a federal hate crimes which would make, among other things, a series like "Shapiros" illegal. And no episode would be complete without a visit by one of the principle characters to family therapist and frequent "Oprah" guest, Dr. Sarah Sokoloff whose standard pattern of treatment calls for her to have sex with her patients.

Warmly, Giuseppe

A New Religion?

by Giuseppe Furioso

Is it just me, or does the story of the Holocaust exhibit a grotesque mimicry of Christianity?

1) Christianity centers on the crucifixion of God's only begotten son whereas the Holocaust centers on the annihilation of six million of God's chosen people.

2) For both Christianity and the Holocaust, the victims are entirely blameless.

3) For Christians, Jesus is the light of the world. Jews are the self-described "light of nations".

4) Both victims experience resurrection. Jesus rises on the third day after his crucifixion. Israel rises, Phoenix-like, out of the ashes of the Holocaust.

5) Christianity has its spotless virgin.
The Holocaust has Anne Frank.

6) On his way to Calvary, Jesus is helped by Simon the Cyrene.
The Holocaust, too, has its "righteous gentiles".

7) For Christians, Jesus' death makes human salvation possible. The Holocaust forever discredits racist nationalism (among gentiles) thereby insuring the triumph liberal democracy with its commitment to multiculturalism and diversity.

8) For both events the historical evidence is relatively thin, and both rely almost entirely on eyewitness testimony.

9) The Church regards deniers as heretics, tools of Satan, and will not debate them. Jews regard historical Revisionists as "Holocaust deniers" with a satanic political agenda, i.e. anti-Semitism. Laws now stipulate that these evil ones are to be ostracized and/or criminally prosecuted, as they now are in eleven European 'democracies' as well as Israel.

10) Pilate is the consummate bureaucrat, a mere cog in the machinery of imperial Rome. He does his job efficiently and without passion. His Holocaust counterpart is Adolf Eichmann who claimed to be "just following orders".
Eichmann was described by Hannah Arendt as exhibiting the "banality of evil".

11) Both Christianity and the Holocaust have their official houses of worship: churches for Christianity, museums and memorials for the Holocaust. In both 'traditions', their greatest institutions hold and preserve actual relics.

12) Both faiths have their official chroniclers. Christianity has the four Gospels.
The Holocaust has the accounts of Hillburg, Daswidowitz, Lipstadt and Levin.

13) Christianity had Paul, "Preacher to the Gentiles".
Elie Wiesel performs that same role for the Holocaust.

14) Both tales underwent extensive in-house revision. Some of the earlier accounts of Jesus—many of them quite popular—were eventually jettisoned by the early Church Fathers in favor of a more streamlined version. Holocaust lore was similarly edited. Some of the pre- and post-wartime claims

about how Jews were slaughtered (or used in lampshade or in soap production) have been quietly retired from the official narrative.

15) For both Christianity and the Holocaust, the actual instruments of death—the cross and the gas chambers—have become part of the official iconography.

16) Jesus was killed alongside two others but only his death is regarded as having cosmic importance. Similarly, it is only the Judeocide of six million among the 40-60 million total deaths during World War II that has achieved the status of supreme tragedy.

17) The spiritual elite of Christianity are the clergy. They claim legitimacy through apostolic succession which spiritually connects them to the Twelve Apostles.
Judaism has its elite "Holocaust Survivors" as well as "Children of Holocaust survivors", and so on. These survivors (as well as Holocaust scholars who study them) comprise a kind of "Holocaustic succession"

18) Christianity blamed the Jews for the crucifixion.
Jewry blames Christianity for the Holocaust.

19) Christians sometimes speak of a "Second Coming".
Jews never stop warning of a Second Holocaust.

20) A new religion has arrived: 'Holocaustianity'.

So Who's Afraid of the Israel Lobby?

by Ray McGovern

Who's afraid of the Israel Lobby? Virtually everyone: Republican, Democrat – Conservative, Liberal. The fear factor is non-partisan, you might say, and palpable. The American Israel Public Affairs Committee (AIPAC) brags that it is the most influential foreign policy lobbying organization on Capitol Hill, and has demonstrated that time and again – and not only on Capitol Hill.

Seldom has the Lobby's power been as clearly demonstrated as in its ability to suppress the awful truth that on June 8, 1967, during the [Arab-Israeli] Six Day War:

* Israel deliberately attacked the intelligence collection ship USS Liberty, in full awareness it was a U.S. Navy ship, and did its best to sink it and leave no survivors;

* The Israelis would have succeeded had they not broken off the attack upon learning, from an intercepted message, that the commander of the U.S. 6th Fleet had launched carrier fighters to the scene; and

* By that time 34 of the Liberty's crew had been killed and over 170 wounded.

Scores of intelligence analysts and senior officials have known this for years. That virtually all of them have kept a forty-year frightened silence is testament to the widespread fear of touching this live wire. Even more telling is the fact that the National Security Agency apparently has destroyed voice tapes and transcripts heard and seen by many intelligence analysts, material that shows beyond doubt that the Israelis knew exactly what they were doing.

The Ugly Truth

But the truth will come out – eventually. All it took in this case was for a courageous journalist (an endangered species) to listen to the surviving crew and do a little basic research, not shrinking from naming war crimes and not letting senior U.S. officials, from the president on down, off the hook for suppressing – even destroying – damning evidence from intercepted Israeli communications.

The mainstream media have now published an exposé based largely on interviews with those most intimately involved. A lengthy article by Pulitzer Prize winning investigative reporter John Crewdson appeared in the Chicago Tribune and Baltimore Sun on Oct. 2, 2007, titled "New revelations in attack on American spy ship." To the subtitle goes the prize for understatement of the year: "Veterans, documents suggest U.S., Israel didn't tell full story of deadly 1967 incident."

Better 40 years late than never, I suppose. Many of us have known of the incident and cover-up for a very long time and have tried to expose and discuss it for the lessons it holds for today. It has proved far easier, though, to get a very pedestrian Dog-Bites-Man article published than an article with the importance and explosiveness of this sensitive story.

A Marine Stands Up

On the evening of Sept. 26, 2006, I gave a talk on Iraq to an overflow crowd of 400 at National Avenue Church in Springfield, Missouri. A questioner asked what I thought of the study by John Mearsheimer of the University of Chicago and Stephen Walt of Harvard titled The Israel Lobby and U.S. Foreign Policy. The study had originally been commissioned by The Atlantic Monthly. When the draft arrived, however, shouts of "Leper!" were heard at the Atlantic. The monthly wasted no time in saying thanks-but-no-thanks, and the leper-study then wandered in search of a home, finding none among American publishers. Eventually the London Review of Books published it in March 2006.

I had read that piece carefully and found it an unusual act of courage as well as scholarship. That's what I told the questioner, adding that I did have two problems with the study:

First, it seemed to me the authors erred in attributing virtually all the motivation for the U.S. attack on Iraq to the Israel Lobby and the so-called "neoconservatives" running our policy and armed forces. Was Israel an important factor? Indeed. But of equal importance, in my view, was the oil factor and what the Pentagon now calls the "enduring" military bases in Iraq, which the White House and Pentagon decided were needed for the U.S. to dominate that part of the Middle East.

Second, I was intrigued by the fact that Mearsheimer and Walt made no mention of what I believe to be, if not the most telling, then perhaps the most sensational proof of the power the Lobby knows it can exert over our government and Congress. In sum, in June 1967, after deliberately using fighter-bombers and torpedo boats to attack the USS Liberty for over two hours in an attempt to sink it and kill its entire crew, and then getting the U.S. government, the Navy, and the Congress to cover up what happened, the Israeli government learned that it could – literally – get away with murder.

I found myself looking out at 400 blank stares. The USS Liberty? And so I asked how many in the audience had heard of the attack on the Liberty on June 8, 1967. Three hands went up; I called on the gentleman nearest me.

Ramrod straight he stood:

"Sir, Sergeant Bryce Lockwood, United States Marine Corps, retired. I am a member of the USS Liberty crew, Sir."

Catching my breath, I asked him if he would be willing to tell us what happened.

"Sir, I have not been able to do that. It is hard. But it has been almost 40 years, and I would like to try this evening, Sir."

You could hear a pin drop for the next 15 minutes, as Lockwood gave us his personal account of what happened to him, his colleagues, and his ship on the afternoon of June 8, 1967. He was a linguist assigned to collect communications intelligence from the USS Liberty, which was among the ugliest – and most easily identifiable – ships in the fleet with antennae springing out in all directions.

Lockwood told of the events of that fateful day, beginning with the six-hour naval and air surveillance of the Liberty by the Israeli navy and air force on the morning of June 8. After the air attacks including thousand-pound bombs and napalm, three sixty-ton torpedo boats lined up like a firing squad, pointing their torpedo tubes at the Liberty's starboard hull. Lockwood had been ordered to throw the extremely sensitive cryptological equipment overboard and had just walked beyond the bulwark separating the NSA intelligence unit from the rest of the ship when, he recalled, he sensed a large black object, a tremendous explosion, and sheet of flame. The torpedo had struck dead center in the NSA space.

The cold, oily water brought Lockwood back to consciousness. Around him were 25 dead colleagues; but he heard moaning. Three were still alive; one of Lockwood's shipmates dragged one survivor up the hatch. Lockwood was able to lift the two others, one-by-one, onto his shoulder and carry them up through the hatch. This meant alternatively banging on the hatch for someone to open it and swimming back to fish his shipmate out of the water lest he float out to sea through the 39-foot hole made by the torpedo.

At that Lockwood stopped speaking. It was enough. Hard, very hard – even after almost 40 years.

What Else We Know

John Crewdson's meticulously documented article, together with the 57 pages that James Bamford devotes to the incident in his book Body of Secrets and recent confessions by those who played a role in the cover-up, paint a picture that the surviving crew of the USS Liberty can only find infuriating. The evidence, from intercepted communications as well as testimony, of Israeli deliberate intent is unimpeachable, even though the Israelis continue to portray the incident as merely a terrible mistake.

Crewdson refers to U.S. Navy Captain Ward Boston, who was the Navy lawyer appointed as senior counsel to Admiral Isaac C. Kidd, named by Admiral John S. McCain (Sen. John McCain's father) to "inquire into all the facts and circumstances." The fact that they were given only one week to gather evidence and were forbidden to contact the Israelis screams out "cover-up."

Captain Boston, now 84, signed a formal declaration on Jan. 8, 2004 in which he described himself as "outraged at the efforts of the apologists for Israel in this country to claim that this attack was a case of 'mistaken identity.'" Boston continued:

"The evidence was clear. Both Admiral Kidd and I believed with certainty that this attack...was a deliberate effort to sink an American ship and murder its entire crew... Not only did the Israelis attack the ship with napalm, gunfire, and missiles, Israeli torpedo boats machine-gunned three lifeboats that had been launched in an attempt by the crew to save the most seriously wounded – a war crime...I know from personal conversations I had with Admiral Kidd that President Lyndon Johnson and Secretary of Defense Robert McNamara ordered him to conclude that the attack was a case of 'mistaken identity' despite overwhelming evidence to the contrary."

Why the Israelis decided to take the draconian measure of sinking a ship of the U.S. Navy is open to speculation. One view is that the Israelis did not want the U.S. to find out they were massing troops to seize the Golan Heights from Syria, and wanted to deprive the U.S. of the opportunity to argue against such a move. Another theory: James Bamford, in "Body of Secrets," adduces evidence, including reporting from an Israeli journalist eyewitness and an Israeli military historian, of wholesale killing of Egyptian prisoners of war at the coastal town of El Arish in the Sinai. The Liberty was patrolling directly opposite El Arish in international waters but within easy range to pick up intelligence on what was going on there. And the Israelis were well aware.

As for the why, well, someone could at least approach the Israelis involved and ask, no? The important thing here is not to confuse what is known (the deliberate nature of the Israeli attack) with the purpose behind it, which remains a matter of speculation.

Other Indignities

Bowing to intense pressure from the Navy, the White House agreed to award the Liberty's skipper, Captain William McGonagle, the Medal of Honor...but not at the White House, and not by the president (as is the custom). Rather, the Secretary of the Navy gave the award at the Washington Navy Yard on the banks of the acrid Anacostia River. A naval officer involved in the awards ceremony told one of the Liberty crew, "The government is pretty jumpy about Israel...the State Department even asked the Israeli ambassador if his government had any objections to McGonagle getting the medal."

Adding insult to injury, those of the Liberty crew who survived well enough to call for an independent investigation have been hit with charges of, you guessed it, anti-Semitism.

Now that some of the truth is emerging more and more, others are showing more courage in speaking out. In a recent email, an associate of mine who has followed Middle East affairs for almost 60 years, shared the following:

"The chief of the intelligence analysts studying the Arab/Israeli region at the time told me about the intercepted messages and said very flatly and firmly that the pilots reported seeing the American flag and repeated their requests for confirmation of the attack order. Whole platoons of Americans saw those intercepts. If NSA now says they do not exist, then someone ordered them destroyed."

Leaving the destruction of evidence without investigation is an open invitation to repetition in the future.

As for the larger picture, visiting Israel this past summer I was constantly told that Egypt forced Israel into war in June 1967. This does not square with the unguarded words of Menachem Begin in 1982, when he was Israel's prime minister. Rather he admitted publicly:

"In June 1967, we had a choice. The Egyptian army concentrations in the Sinai approaches do not prove that [Egyptian President] Nasser was really about to attack us. We must be honest with ourselves. We decided to attack him."

Israel had, in fact, prepared well militarily and mounted provocations against its neighbors, in order to provoke a response that could be used to justify an expansion of its borders. Israel's illegal 40-year control over and confiscation of land in the occupied territories and U.S. enabling support (particularly the one-sided support by the current U.S. administration) go a long way toward explaining why it is that 1.3 billion Muslims "hate us."

Ray McGovern is a U.S. Army veteran and was a CIA analyst for 27 years. He received an M.A. in Russian Studies from Fordham University, a certificate in Theological Studies from Georgetown University and is a graduate of Harvard Business School's Advanced Management Program. He has written extensively on US policies in the Middle East.

'Terrorism': The Word Itself is Dangerous

by John V. Whitbeck

The greatest threat to world peace today is clearly terrorism - not the behavior to which the word is applied but the word itself. For years, people have recited the truisms that one man's terrorist is another man's freedom fighter and that terrorism, like beauty, is in the eye of the beholder. However, with the world's sole superpower declaring an open-ended, worldwide war on terrorism, the notorious subjectivity of this word is no longer a joke. It is no accident there is no agreed definition of terrorism, since the word is so subjective as to be devoid of meaning. At the same time, the word is extremely dangerous, because people tend to believe that it does have meaning and to use and abuse the word by applying it to whatever they hate as a way of avoiding rational thought and discussion and, frequently, excusing their own illegal and immoral behavior.

There is no shortage of precise verbal formulations for the diverse acts to which the word terrorism is often applied. Mass murder, assassination, and sabotage are available (to which the phrase politically motivated can be added if appropriate), and such crimes are already on the statute books, rendering specific criminal legislation for terrorism unnecessary. However, such precise formulations do not carry the overwhelming, demonizing and thought-deadening impact of the word terrorism, which is precisely the charm of the word for its more cynical and unprincipled users and abusers. If someone commits politically motivated mass murder, people might be curious as to the cause or grievances which inspired such a crime, but no cause or grievance can justify (or even explain) terrorism, which, all right-thinking people agree, is the ultimate evil.

Most acts to which terrorism is applied (at least in the West) are tactics of the weak, usually (although not always) against the strong. Such acts are not a tactic of choice but of last resort. To cite one example, the Palestinians would prefer to fight for their freedom by respectable means, using F-16s, Apache attack helicopters and laser-guided missiles such as those the United States provides to Israel. If the United States provided such weapons to Palestine as well, the problem of suicide bombers would be solved. Until it does, and for so long as the Palestinians can see no hope for a decent future, no one should be surprised or shocked that Palestinians use the delivery systems available to them - their own bodies. Genuine hope for something better than a life worse than death is the only cure for the despairwhich inspires such gruesome violence.

In this regard, it is worth noting that the poor, the weak and the oppressed rarely complain about terrorism. The rich, the strong and the oppressors constantly do. While most of mankind has more reason to fear the high-technology violence of the strong than the low-technology violence of the weak, the fundamental mind-trick employed by the abusers of the epithet terrorism (no doubt, in some cases, unconsciously) is essentially this: The low-technology violence of the weak is such an abomination that there are no limits on the high-technology violence of the strong which can be deployed against it. Not surprisingly, since Sept. 11, virtually every recognized state confronting an insurgency or separatist movement has eagerly jumped on the war on terrorism bandwagon, branding its domestic opponents (if it had not already done so) terrorists and, at least implicitly, taking the position that, since no one dares to criticize the

United States for doing whatever it deems necessary in its war on terrorism, no one should criticize whatever they now do to suppress their own terrorists.

Even while accepting that many people labeled terrorists are genuinely reprehensible, it should be recognized that neither respect for human rights nor the human condition are likely to be enhanced by this apparent carte blanche seized by the strong to crush the weak as they see fit. Writing in the Washington Post on Oct. 15, Post Deputy Editor Jackson Diehl cited two prominent examples of the abuse of the epithet terrorism: With their handshake in the Kremlin, Sharon and Putin exchanged a common falsehood about the wars their armies are fighting against rebels in Chechnya and the West Bank and Gaza. In both cases, the underlying conflict is about national self-determination: statehood for the Palestinians, self-rule for Chechnya. The world is inclined to believe that both causes are just — Sharon and Putin both have tried to convince the world that all their opponents are terrorists, which implies that the solution need not involve political concessions but merely a vigorous counterterrorism campaign. Perhaps the only honest and globally workable definition of terrorism is an explicitly subjective one - violence which I don't support.

The Western press routinely characterizes as terrorism virtually all Palestinian violence against Israelis (even against Israeli occupation forces within Palestine), while the Arab press routinely characterizes as terrorism virtually all Israeli violence against Palestinians. Only this formulation would accommodate both characterizations, as well as most others. However, the word has been so devalued that even violence is no longer an essential prerequisite for its use. In recently announcing a multi-billion dollar lawsuit against 10 international tobacco companies, a Saudi Arabian lawyer told the press: We will demand tobacco firms be included on the lists of terrorists and those financing and sponsoring terrorism because of the large number of victims smoking has claimed the world over. If everyone recognized the word terrorism is fundamentally an epithet and a term of abuse, with no intrinsic meaning, there would be no more reason to worry about the word now than prior to Sept. 11. However, with the

United States relying on the word to assert, apparently, an absolute right to attack any country it dislikes (for the most part, countries Israel dislikes) and with President Bush repeatedly menacing that either you're with us or you're with the terrorists (which effectively means, either you make our enemies your enemies or you'll be our enemy - and you know what we do to our enemies), many people around the world must feel a genuine sense of terror (dictionary definition: a state of intense fear) as to where the United States is taking the rest of the world.

Meanwhile, in America itself, the Bush Administration appears to be feeding the US Constitution and America's traditions of civil liberties, due process and the rule of law into a shredder - mostly to domestic applause or acquiescence. Who would have imagined that 19 angry men armed only with knives could accomplish so much, provoking a response, beyond their wildest dreams, which threatens to be vastly more damaging to their enemies even than their own appalling acts? If the world is to avoid a descent into anarchy, in which the only rule is might makes right, every retaliation provokes a counter-retaliation and a genuine war of civilizations is ignited, the world - and particularly the United States - must recognize that terrorism is simply a word, a subjective epithet, not an objective reality and certainly not an excuse to suspend all the rules of international law and domestic civil liberties which have, until now, made at least some parts of our planet decent places to live.

John V. Whitbeck is an international lawyer who writes frequently on the Israeli-Palestinian conflict. Since 1988 his articles on behalf of Middle East peace have been published more than 450 times in over 70 Arab, Israeli, and international newspapers, magazines, journals and books. He is also the author of "The World According to Whitbeck.

James Petras' New Book: "The Power of Israel in the United States"

A Review by Stephen Lendman

James Petras is Professor Emeritus of Sociology at Binghamton University, New York. He's a noted academic figure on the US Left and a well-respected Latin American expert and longtime chronicler of the region's popular struggles. He's also an advisor to the landless workers in Brazil and the unemployed workers movement in Argentina. Along the way, he managed to find time to write many hundreds of articles and 62 books published in 29 languages including his latest one in which he discusses another vital world region he has extensive knowledge of and has written frequently about - the Middle East and specifically the state of Israel and its relations with its neighbors, the Palestinians and, most importantly and the subject of this book, the US.

Petras' powerful new book is titled "The Power of Israel in the United States". It's a work of epic writing and essential reading documenting the enormous influence of the pro-Israeli Lobby on US policy in the Middle East. It focuses like a laser to assure that policy conforms with Israel's long-term goal for regional hegemony. The Lobby's influence is broad and deep enough to include officials at the highest levels of government, the business community, academia, the clergy (especially the dominant Christian fundamentalists/Christian Zionists) and the mass media. Petras shows how together they're able to assure the full and unconditional US support for all elements of Israel's agenda going back decades even when that agenda harms our interests such as the unwinnable war in Iraq, any future one against Iran if it's undertaken, and the appalling and brutal subjugation and colonization of the Palestinian people that serves no US interest whatever. In spite of it, the Lobby is able to get the US to go along with Israel unconditionally with no serious opposition to it tolerated.

The book is divided into four parts. This review will cover each one in detail, and what's discussed will likely surprise any reader unfamiliar with the thoroughly documented account presented in it so compellingly. Petras sets the table in his introduction for what's to come in the later chapters. He notes what author JJ Goldberg reported in his book "Jewish Power: Inside the Jewish Establishment". Goldberg wrote in the early 1990s that 45% of the Democrat Party's fundraising and 25% of that for the Republicans came from Jewish-funded Political Action Committees (PACS). Petras then updates the numbers using the ones Richard Cohen published in the Washington Post showing them now at 60% and 35% respectively, and that this funding relates to a single core issue: unconditional US support for Israel's agenda including those parts of it human rights activists and observers of conscience judge most egregious and illegal. Petras stresses that no other single US lobby including Big Pharma, Big Oil, agribusiness, or any other one has this kind of dominant influence over the political process here. He refers to "Zioncon" ideologues and policymakers whose main goal is to make the Middle East into a "US-Israeli Co-Prosperity Sphere" under the fraudulent cover of promoting democracy in the region - but doing it through the barrel of a gun.

Petras explains the root of the Lobby's power lies in the high proportion of Jewish families who are among the wealthiest and most influential ones in the country. He cites Forbes magazine that reported 25 – 30% of the wealthiest families here are Jewish despite the small percentage of Jews in the population overall. They include billionaires with enormous influence, and along with all others comprising the pro-Israeli Lobby, have created a "tyranny of Israel over the US" with consequences grave enough to threaten world peace and stability, the global economy, and the very future of democracy in this country.

That democracy and our constitutionally protected rights now hang by a thread after the recent passage of the Military Commissions Act (aka the "torture authorization act" or more accurately the "US Constitutional annulment act") that makes everyone everywhere an "enemy combatant" subject to arrest and detention out of sight anywhere in the world without regard for our (no longer) constitutionally guaranteed rights. The new law also applies to US citizens as the Jose Padilla case showed. We've effectively lost our habeas and due process rights even though technically we still have them.

Because of the Lobby's power, Petras reports, the US has unconditionally supported Israel's wars of aggression since 1967. It's influence also led to the US Gulf war in 1991 and the second Iraq war begun in 2003, now raging out of control and seen by some noted analysts as unwinnable and causing potential irreparable economic and political harm to the nation. Nonetheless, it persists with no plan agreed on to end it. The Lobby also guaranteed this country's unconditional support for Israel's illegal wars of aggression against Lebanon and Palestine with all the devastation they caused and the horrendous consequences from them unresolved. The Palestinian conflict still rages under the radar, and the status in Lebanon hangs by a hair trigger ready to erupt again any time Israel decides to resume hostilities. But inflaming the Middle East powder keg to a near boiling point is the strong possibility the US and/or Israel will attack Iran because Israel wants it and the Jewish Lobby put its powerful support behind it. More on this, Palestine and Lebanon below.

Today the situation in the Middle East is so dire, Petras reports a large majority of Europeans and a growing number of Americans believe Israel is the greatest of all threats to world peace and stability. Nonetheless, the Bush administration, in acquiescence to the Lobby, has "bludgeoned" its European partners to go along with its uncompromising support for the Jewish state despite all the obvious perils from it. In this country, open debate is stifled, public figures and academics daring to air one truthfully are pilloried, ridiculed, called anti-Semitic and even threatened, and no serious dissent is ever tolerated in the corporate-run media or their funded and controlled so-called public radio or **PBS** parts of it.

No publication is more servile to, supportive of, or more influential than the nation's so-called "paper of record" publishing "All the News That's Fit to Print" - the New York Times. It's important because the stories it features prominently resonate around the country and the world. This dominant newspaper pledges unconditional support and fealty to the state of Israel whatever it does. The rest of the major media go along unquestioningly putting out regular one-sided, pro-Israel uber alles propaganda with no opposition voices allowed to represent other points of view. We call that a free press - but only for those who own one. The state of the corporate-controlled media in this country is now so pathetic that Reporters Sans Frontieres (Reporters without Borders - for press freedom) recently ranked the US 53rd in the world in press freedom behind countries like Benin, Namibia, Jamaica, France and Bolivia.

James Petras is a courageous independent voice who bucks this disturbing trend and refuses to go along. He proves it in his powerful and carefully documented new book that gives no quarter countering the mendacity, deceit and danger of the Lobby, its acolytes and hangers-on, and the corrupted major media. In his introduction, he calls for a "counter-hegemonic movement" to free us from our destructive "Israeli entanglements." It's needed to begin rebuilding our democracy and freedoms that are somewhere between life support and the crematorium. This book, he says, is his modest effort toward that goal. Because of the important information in it, it's considerably more than that. It needs widespread exposure so people will know about it. Hopefully this review will help arouse some of them to want to find out in more detail.

Part I - Zionist Power in America

Petras begins with a discussion of who fabricated the lies about Iraq's threat to our security and why. He mentions two competing channels of policy makers and advisors - the long-in-place formal structure of career military and civilian professionals in the Pentagon and State Department and a parallel one Bush administration neocons set up for this one purpose in the Pentagon, staffed by political appointees, and called the Office of Special Plans (OSP). It was the OSP's job to cook the books, come up with the idea of weapons of mass destruction while ignoring the clear evidence to the contrary and contrive a fraudulent case for war against Iraq. The people in it were those in Donald Rumsfeld's and Paul Wolfowitz's chain of command and were closely connected to a number of influential neoconservative and pro-Israel organizations. They planned a war agenda based on lies because Israel wanted it for its security and hegemony in the region - beginning with the overthrow of Saddam Hussein followed by regime change in Syria, Lebanon, Iran and even Saudi Arabia.

Petras points out, contrary to popular belief, this war happened largely due to the efforts of the Jewish Lobby representing the interests of Israel. Big Oil opposed the idea because it feared attacking Iraq would jeopardize its business prospects with other oil-producing states in the region. Still, Israel and the Jewish Lobby got their war, and aside from the gain from high oil prices, Big Oil may end up a longer-term loser from it. US oil interests always prefer stability and normal relationships with countries where they operate or wish to and were quite comfortable dealing with Saddam Hussein without wanting to risk a war that might upset an otherwise profitable arrangement. Their fears proved justified as the war they feared created such unresolved turbulence in Iraq, it's become too dangerous and unprofitable to undertake new ventures there except perhaps in parts of the Kurdish-controlled north.

Big Oil also chafes at not being allowed to deal with the Iranians for contracts now let to its European and other competitors because US sanctions prevent them from doing business there. It's hard to

imagine those interests would ever go along with US - Israeli bellig-
erence in the Middle East, but they dare not oppose it publicly.

Petras observes there's never a public discussion allowed about that
relationship in the mainstream nor will there ever be any, especially
any hint the US attacked Iraq in service to Israel. There should be
plenty of it though because the Iraq and Afghanistan wars have enraged hundreds of millions of Muslims and all people of conscience
worldwide. They've caused the US to be seen as a pariah state and
George Bush as a dangerous and morally depraved president of
a failed administration. He and those closest to him like Richard
Cheney and Donald Rumsfeld are reviled around the world and increasingly here at home as witnessed by the many thousands who
took to the streets on October 5, 2006, in over 200 US cities on The
World Can't Wait Day - Drive Out the Bush Regime. The cost of
Bush's wars far exceed any possible future benefits from them, our
security has been jeopardized, the nation's status has been compro-
mised, and some analysts believe the total dollar cost of the Iraq adventure may eventually top $2 trillion - an amount extremely harm-
ful to the nation's economy that's now worrying key business leaders
and responsible people in government.

The only clear beneficiary of the Bush war agenda is Israel. It removed its main adversary in the region and cut off the political and
economic support it gave the Palestinians. Petras points out that Iraq
along with Iran and Syria comprised the core resistance to Israel's
expansionist plans to crush the Palestinians (one down, two to go),
ethnically cleanse them from their homeland and seize their land as
one part of a long-term goal for a greater Israel and unchallengeable dominance in the region. Israel is the only country in the world
with undeclared borders. It's kept that status to give itself maximum
latitude to annex all the territory it can toward the goal of a greater
"Eretz Israel" Zionists want that includes the ancient lands of "Judea"
and "Summaria," the West Bank biblical parts of Israel Palestinians
claim as their homeland.

With US help, Israel removed one threat to its plan for regional supremacy, but it still faces determined resistance from the Palestinians

in spite of having crushed its democratically elected Hamas government. It also faces a resilient Hezbollah in Lebanon that humiliated the Israeli Defense Forces (IDF) in the summer war there as well as opposition from Iran and Syria. In addition, there's internal opposition within Israel over its war and colonization agenda because of its enormous cost plus the added insecurity it causes. It's resulted in a level of out-migration now exceeding new arrivals as well as an erosion of the nation's social programs because the state needs the resources for its aggression and annexation agenda. It's much like what's happening under the Bush administration where the people pay the price for imperial wars abroad and the moral decay and authoritarianism at home.

Obstacles and setbacks aside, Israel has pursued its goal to "democratize" the region through a belligerent policy of neutralizing its enemies in it by force. The plan they crafted is for a series of wars with its US ally taking the lead and the eventual goal of joint US - Israeli control over the entire region. Making it work depends on getting US administrations to go along, which so far hasn't been a problem and has never been easier with the Bush administration in power and the high-level pro-Zionist officials in it with long-standing ties to Israel. They have the most important policy-making positions in government or are closely associated with the ones who do. These officials have a history of dedication to Israel's interests even when they conflict with those here at home. They're in the administration, the Congress as well as in the most influential Jewish organizations and lobbying groups like the Conference of Presidents of Major Jewish Organizations, the Anti-Defamation League and what some observers believe is the single most powerful lobby in Washington - AIPAC.

Committed support for Israel also comes from the "Jewish Diaspora" that comprises thousands of dedicated activists here - doctors, dentists, philanthropists, key individuals on Wall Street, the major banks and the Federal Reserve and other key segments of business, the major media, the clergy and academics and journalists given special prominence because of their willingness to corrupt their integrity in return for the handsome benefits they get for their unconditional public support and contrived rationalizations for the US -Israeli agenda. This kind of influence and support has made Israel by far the largest recipient in the world of US financial aid that amounts upfront to about $3 billion a year with more forthcoming any time as needed in added funding, weapons transfers and large low or no-interest loans that may never have to be repaid.

Israel also gets the unheard of advantage of receiving the latest and most advanced US arms and technology, unrestricted US market access for its products and services, free entry of its immigrants, unconditional support for its aggressive wars and colonization of the Palestinians and South Lebanese, and guaranteed US vetoes in the Security Council against all UN resolutions unfavorable to its interests. It's also able to get prominent Washington officials and the dominant corporate-run and funded media to label all criticism of Israel anti-Semitic and freely uses this ruse whenever it serves its purpose.

Israel is allowed to get away with its intelligence operations here as well including its covert penetration of military bases, the FBI, IRS, INS, EPA and many other government agencies. In addition, it's believed its agents knew in advance about the 9/11 attacks but withheld the information knowing it would serve its interests to let it happen. There's also considerable evidence high US officials either knew about it themselves or were complicit in carrying it out because they also knew it would allow them the kind of reckless free reign at home and abroad they never could have gotten any other way. This is a story that won't go away nor should it, and one day we may finally learn all the parts of it we can only speculate about now.

Because of Israel's unparalleled ties to the centers of power and dominant media, Petras notes it's able get back $50 in return for every dollar it spends. That's how it's able to finance its military and colonial settlements in the Occupied Palestinian Territories (OPT) on annexed land. The Jewish networks here support these practices as justifiable compensation allowed victims of the "Holocaust" (the ones noted author John Pilger calls "worthy victims") and circulate that ideology in the corporate media. They also reinforce anti-Muslim hysteria labeling all Arabs untrustworthy, radical Islamic fundamentalists or Islamo-fascists ("unworthy" victims for John Pilger), claiming the right to arrest, torture and mete out summary justice to them in military tribunals or just attack and kill them in imperial wars of "liberation."

The result for Israel and its people has been disastrous because the Palestinians have refused for almost six decades to accede to this abuse and have waged two Intifadas to end it. With little more than a fierce determination, their bodies and crude weapons, they've fought back with suicide bombings and attacks on public facilities in Israel knowing what harsh retaliation they'll face afterward. People in the US have also paid a heavy price in the erosion of democracy and freedom. It's evidenced by the Bush administration's harsh legislation beginning with the infamous USA Patriot Act passed in short order right after the 9/11 attack, followed by other repressive laws and practices allowed like illegal surveillance and secret renditions of anyone targeted to torture-prisons with court acquiescence or silence about most of them.

Petras points out that none of this deters powerful supporters of Israel who raise billions of dollars to support the country's war machine and finance its colonization of annexed Palestinian land plus the Golan Heights (with its invaluable water resources) seized and never returned to Syria after the 1967 war. Israel's economy is not self-sufficient, and without this aid, it would have to make unacceptable cuts in social services, reduce its military budget and curtail its expansionary plans. With it, plus the $3 billion a year direct US contribution and lots more help, US taxpayers (like it or not) have the burden of funding Israel's belligerence and colonization agenda.

Petras itemizes what it all costs:

- $3 billion annually in direct aid.

- Billions more in loans as needed.

- Millions annually for resettlement help for Soviet (now Russian) and Ethiopian immigrants.

- a $10 billion loan guarantee in 1990 and a further $9 billion one in 2004 plus billions more for the asking and to be forthcoming to pay the costs of the 2006 Lebanon and Palestine wars.

- Since 1981, economic aid made in cash transfers, and since 1985 military aid done the same way.

- $45 billion in repayment waved loans since 1974 and billions more for the asking - free money at US taxpayer expense.

- Since 1982, ESF cash transfers in one early in the fiscal year lump sum with no strings attached while other countries receiving them are paid quarterly with their use monitored. Israel invests the money in US treasuries costing US taxpayers millions more annually and also gets special FMS funding arrangements costing US taxpayers well over $1 billion since 1991.

- Other privileged benefits include financial aid to develop Israel's defense industry, transfer of state-of-the-art technology and the latest US weapons, US guarantee for Israel's access to oil, and the likely massive aid still to come to defray the country's "special costs" for its Gaza "disengagement plan" morphing into the colonization of whatever parts of the OPT Israel wishes to annex for new settlements US taxpayers pay for.

- Add to this some $22 billion Israel got over the past 50 years through the sale of its below-market interest paying bonds that have financed half of its development - meaning the colonization of annexed Palestinian lands and military funding for its predatory imperial wars.

Petras explains the Zionist power structure in the US makes it all possible, but its reach extends well beyond the so-called "Jewish Lobby." He identifies a "Zionist power configuration (ZPC) that includes AIPAC as one part of a "complex network of interrelated formal and informal groupings, operating at the international, national, regional, and local levels" unconditionally supporting the state of Israel and all its policies including its wars, colonization and oppression. Its power is like a cancer infecting the highest levels of government and all the other centers of power and influence as already explained. It controls the selection of political candidates and can defeat incumbents or aspirants daring to criticize Israel. It also shapes the reporting on Israel in the mass media suppressing any of it that's unsupportive or critical. And it's powerful enough to get "uncooperative" journalists, and even some academics, fired and banished from the mainstream for daring to step out of line.

Petras reports the power of the ZPC was evident in the run-up to the Iraq war and the Gulf war before it in 1991. Going back to the GHW Bush administration, the US wanted regime change in Iraq, but that decision was heavily influenced by the ZPC that considered Saddam a mortal enemy of Israel who had to be removed. He managed to survive through the 1990s despite our efforts to destabilize the country and bring it to its knees. But once the GW Bush administration neocons took over in 2001, the ugly business of war planning and occupation took hold to complete what the Gulf war left unfinished, and powerful Zionists (like Paul Wolfowitz and Connecticut Senator Joe Lieberman - the senator from AIPAC) in key policy-making positions invented the threat to bring it about in March, 2003 - all based on lies, deceit and subservience to Israel's imperial agenda.

The US military finally removed Saddam and conducted a scorched-earth campaign to destroy Iraqi society, its infrastructure and historical treasures to "dismantle the secular state (and) turn the country in a desert kingdom - a loose collection of at least three 'tribal' client mini-states based on ethnicities, religious-tribal loyalties (and no viable threat against) Israeli expansionism, particularly in Northern Iraq." The effort to do this is now underway after the Iraq puppet parliament's passage of its federalism bill to take effect in 18 months that will effectively divide the country into the three US-ordered, designed and supposedly more easily governed parts it wants.

It's unlikely this can work, but it's clearer than ever now what the human cost of the war has been for Iraqis. It caused the violent deaths of about 655,000 of them attributable to the war according to a shocking new study published by the noted Lancet British medical journal which updated their two earlier ones done after March, 2003. The study used the statistically reliable technique known as random households "cluster sampling" with personal interviews conducted across the country that used death certificate verification in the great majority of cases to come up with the total. It's likely the true number of deaths is even much higher than this appalling number as the interviewers were unable to include in their count the most dangerous and violent parts of the country like Fallujah, Ramadi and other areas of al Anbar province where mass killing still goes on daily as well as families (likely in the thousands) in which all the members were killed.

This new information, just out and covering a period since March, 2003, compares to Human Rights Watch's estimate of 250,000 – 290,000 people killed by Saddam Hussein's Baathist regime over its 20 year existence. It amplifies the outrageous crime of this barbarous adventure to achieve a "Greater Middle East US-Israel Co-Prosperity Sphere" and to give Israel access to the extra water, oil, capital and markets it lacks. It was also part of Israel's greater agenda under the Sharon Likud, and now Olmert Kadima, governments to have free reign to pursue their stated policy of "annexation and separation" in the OPT. The Zionist influence in the Bush administration is so entrenched, it assured there'd be no opposition to it then or now.

It's all gone on in spite of mass anti-imperial resistance to what's seen as an arrogant disregard for the standards and norms of international behavior and laws in the pursuit of an expansionist agenda. Israel and the US today willfully violate the UN Charter, the Hague Regulations and Geneva Conventions relative to the conduct of war and when it may be legally waged, the treatment of prisoners, the use of torture, destruction of infrastructure and historical sites, and plunder of natural resources to establish client puppet-run regimes exploiting their people in service to the dominant capital and political interests of their imperial conquerors.

Then to quell resistance and tighten security, the US and Israel resort to the most extreme methods including mass arrests and detentions and the free use of torture and targeted assassinations as state policy. Amnesty International reports since the passage of the Military Commissions Act of 2006, the US and Israel are the only two countries in the world to have legalized the use of torture. Petras and others report the top leaders in the Pentagon up to Donald Rumsfeld specifically ordered its use "while the Justice and Defense Departments insisted that the President could override any laws - international or national as well as the US Constitution - in defending the empire." These top officials in key areas of government have audaciously given the President "de facto and de jure dictatorial powers" to do whatever he chooses to establish "Imperial Security." It makes our citizens at home no safer than the victims of US and Israeli imperial aggression in Iraq, Lebanon, Palestine or anywhere else in the world.

But Petras reports it's even worse than that, as the exposure of torture in Iraq revealed a highly organized network of US and Israeli assassins worldwide. They operate as international death squads engaged in "killing, kidnapping and torturing 'suspects' and sympathizers of resistance movements." Petras calls this a US-sponsored "Murder Incorporated" that's composed of Army Special Forces, Navy Seals and a DELTA force operating in a Special Agency Program (SAP). It follows the same practices long engaged in by Israel's Institute for Intelligence and Special Operations known as the Mossad, and its aim is to remove all opposition by whatever extralegal methods it chooses while ignoring international law. It then justifies this activity at the highest levels of government as a matter of policy.

Petras further points to the UN's International Leadership report on the destruction of civilian and military infrastructure in Iraq (much like what Israel did in the OPT discussed below). It showed "84% of Iraq's higher learning institutions have been burnt, looted or destroyed." Archeological museums and historic sites, libraries and archives have also been plundered, and targeted assassinations have been carried out against academics, other teachers, senior military personnel, journalists and other professionals including doctors.

In addition, there are random or targeted daily terror killings by US-directed "Salvador option" death squads as well as thousands of kidnappings and other systematic horrors making life intolerable for most everyone in the country outside the four square kilometer fortress-like Green Zone HQ in central Baghdad for "coalition" officials and the puppet "Iraq interim government."

It's all part of Washington's design to destroy the country's cultural identity as an Arab state, separate its oil resources from any large population base, and divide the nation into more easily governed parts just the way it was done in the breakup of Yugoslavia in the 1990s.

What's happening today in Iraq and Palestine is so outrageous and chaotic, Petras refers to a "House of Horrors" in both countries with the Zionist militarists at the Pentagon and their Israeli counterparts in charge of their respective "Horror Shows....under the big tent of a 'Mid-East Democratic Reform Initiative.' "This is the modus operandi of empire building and colonization - blast and tear a nation to shreds so it can never again exist as it once did. Then terrorize the people into submission and kill off all the ones who resist. It's a barbaric thumb in the eye to humanity, but this is the way rogue empires do things, especially when they're too powerful to challenge.

The US-led killing machine is in full operation in Iraq, and so is the Israeli one in the OPT. Petras calls the one there "Israel's Final Solution" or the "Palestinian Holocaust," and it's focal point is in Gaza which even unoccupied is the world's largest open-air prison for its 1.45 million people in the most densely populated space of its size in the world. Today the Strip and the West Bank are Israeli-directed killing fields targeting Palestinian civilians helpless to stop it beyond their courageous acts of desperation with crude weapons and their bodies against tanks, F-16s, helicopter gunships, and illegal and immoral terror weapons like white phosphorus bombs and shells, cluster bombs that never stop killing and maiming, and experimental new weapons that don't have publicly-known names yet.

Israel's war on Palestine has gone on for nearly six decades, and September 28 marked the sixth anniversary of the al-Aqsa Mosque

Intifada resistance against it that began with Ariel Sharon's provocative visit to the holy site in 2000. Israel dramatically escalated the conflict after the minor June 25, 2006 incident at an Israeli military post near Kerem Shalom crossing killing two IDF soldiers, injuring several others and capturing a third still held whose name the corporate media made sure everyone knows but won't ever reveal any of over-10,000 names of Palestinian prisoners held (the fate of "unworthy victims"). The June clash followed a series of bloody earlier in the month Israeli attacks on Gaza including the widely reported beach shelling that killed eight Palestinians and injured 32 others including 13 children. Much as it did in Lebanon (discussed below), Israel's response was swift, deadly, disproportionate to what happened and planned months in advance as revealed by General Yoav Galant, in charge of Gaza, in a candid interview he gave in Israel's Maariv daily.

The Palestinian Centre for Human Rights (PCHR) documented it all including the devastation of the past six years. Overall it created a state of mass-immiseration for the Palestinian people in Gaza and the West Bank:

- essential infrastructure affecting power, clean water and sanitation destroyed

- mobility restricted or denied

- imposition of an embargo threatening the collapse of an already weak economy creating unemployment up to 80% of the population

- hostile incursions into the OPT, daily killings, and frequent extra-judicial assassinations

- home and property demolitions

- mass arbitrary arrests, administrative detentions of thousands of Palestinians without charge, and the systematic use of torture on those held including against women and children

- the destruction of a viable Hamas-led Palestinian Authority (PA) through imprisonments of its democratically elected members held without charge or on contrived ones against them as well as the destruction of its civil and security facilities

All this and much more has been done (as in Iraq) to destroy the cultural identity and very existence of the Palestinian people to prevent them from ever having a viable independent state of their own as well as force a mass-Palestinian exodus to other Arab states willing to help them escape their intolerable situation in the OPT.

The plan to crush these defenseless people now includes credible evidence that the Bush and Olmert administrations have been arming, training and plotting with Palestinian President Mahmoud Abbas and his Fatah followers to lead a civil uprising against the Hamas-led Palestinian Authority (PA) and destroy it by force. It follows the Palestinians failed efforts to form a national unity government because Hamas refused Fatah's demand to govern as Israel's enforcer and abandon its own pledge to serve the welfare of its people. Now in an interview on October 8 in the London Sunday Times, Fatah militia leader Tawfig Tirawi, inflamed matters by accusing Hamas of "accumulating weapons" and that "a full-scale civil war can break out at any moment." He earlier said "civil war is inevitable." The paper also reported President Abbas "notified the US, Jordan and Egypt that he is preparing to take action against Hamas." These statements defy Hamas Prime Minister Ismail Haniyeh who firmly said he'll never allow a civil war to happen, and it's unimaginable the Palestinian people want one. But Haniyeh and his people may have no choice as this seems to be the current joint US-Israeli strategy to destroy Palestinian resistance and do it with help from Fatah President Abbas. This is the same man who pledged his fealty to Israel as a participant in crafting the Oslo Accords sellout of his people and being a principle in the Arafat-led corrupted and mismanaged Palestinian Authority until Hamas won a majority of the seats in the January, 2006 Palestinian Legislative Council (PLC) elections. The Bush and Olmert governments wouldn't tolerate that outcome, and the New York Times reported right after the election US and Israeli officials met at the "highest level" to plan the destruction of Hamas by "starving" the PA and making the people in the OPT pay the greatest price.

For Israel, this is part of its state policy of ethnic cleansing by slow-motion genocide and out-migration all leading to the destruction of the Palestinian identity. It wants to co-opt a corrupted PA leadership of its choice to act as Israel's enforcer and partner in the destruction of its own people. It's to fulfill the intent of what former Israeli Prime Minister Golda Meier meant by her racist comment that "There are no Palestinians" and what Prime Minister David Ben Gurion earlier said after Israel brutally expelled the Palestinians from their homes and land in the 1948 war establishing the state of Israel: "We have come and we have stolen their country....We must do everything to insure they (the Palestinians) never do return....(and 10 years earlier had written his son) We will expel the Arabs and take their places.... with the force at our disposal." He and his successors planned to include all the land of biblical Eretz Israel (the land of Israel) within the final fixed borders of a greater Israeli state whenever they're finally declared. The US unconditionally supports Israel's plan to do this as well as its policies of plunder and exploitation, but as Petras explains: "No one in their right mind can claim that the Israeli assault on Gaza advances US policies, interests or US imperial power." It doesn't matter because the power of the Jewish Lobby got the full support of the Bush administration for it anyway as well as the near unanimity for it in the Congress.

The Rape of Lebanon

What Israel did to the Palestinians in the OPT over decades, it did to Lebanon in 1978, 1982 and in about a five week blitzkrieg beginning July 12, ending formally but fragilely with a UN-brokered ceasefire on August 14. Petras compares the assault to the Nazi's November 9 and 10, 1938 infamous Kristallnacht pogrom in the German Reich against the Jews calling that event a "garden party" compared to the rape of Lebanon and vast devastation from it. It began with Hezbollah's cross-border incursion on July 12, killing eight IDF soldiers in the exchange that followed and capturing two others. There's still a dispute over which side of the Lebanese border the incident took place as for years Israel routinely makes hostile incursions into Lebanon by land and air, and still illegally occupies the 25 square kilometer Shebaa Farms area of South Lebanon it never relinquished after seizing it in the 1967 war.

As against Gaza, Israel again responded swiftly and disproportionately in a reign of terror against the Lebanese people by land, air and sea. It killed and wounded thousands and displaced a million or more Lebanese civilians. It also systematically destroyed the country's essential to life and other vital infrastructure and created an amount of physical devastation that could take a generation to recover from if Israel even allows it to happen. It was done in part to destroy Hezbollah as a political entity and as an effective resistance force against Israel's imperial designs on the country. But Israel's plans are much more far-reaching than that as explained below.

Petras reported Middle East expert Juan Cole claims Israel wanted the war and planned it at least a year in advance. Matthew Kallman of the San Francisco Chronicle Foreign Service also found and reported evidence that preparations for it began in May, 2000, immediately after Israel ended its occupation of the country that began with its invasion and brutal assault in 1982 that killed about 18,000 Lebanese. Kallman also reported that over a year before the conflict began a senior IDF official gave "PowerPoint presentations" off the record to US and other officials and unnamed journalists and think tanks explaining how the attack would unfold "in revealing detail."

Again, Israel got the full backing, funding and arming as needed from the Bush administration to carry it out, effectively making this gruesome adventure a joint US-Israeli operation. Besides wanting to neutralize Hezbollah's resistance, the goal was to destroy Lebanon as a functioning country and ethnically cleanse the southern part of it up to the Litani River Israel wants to control and eventually annex and keep as it did the Golan after the 1967 war. Israel claims this area (like the Golan) is important for security reasons, but its greatest value (again like the Golan) is as a source of fresh water from the Litani and from the Wazzani springs that feed into the Hasbani River that's a tributary of the Jordan River. The Hisbani flows into Israel two miles downstream from the Wazzani and runs into the Sea of Galilee that's Israel's largest source of fresh water.

Israel has had designs on Lebanon for 40 years or more and has kept the country in a state of instability, partial occupation and conflict over most of that time. Now the state of the country is a devastated near-wasteland monitored by so-called (Israel-approved and friendly) UN Blue Helmets and Lebanese Armed Forces replacing the IDF on the ground under a fragile UN brokered ceasefire arrangement that could end any time Israel wishes again to unleash its war machine and on any pretext. There's nothing to deter Israel from doing it as it has the unconditional support of the Jewish Lobby and whatever US administration is in power. Unless this changes, the people of Lebanon, like those in Iraq and Palestine, can only look ahead to more conflict and the pain and suffering from it.

That's because there's still unfinished business for both empires, and it's not likely either one will soon give up on what they're determined to achieve. So even though Iraq is a hopeless quagmire, the Bush administration says it will "stay the course." And as long as Israel has full US backing, it will continue pursuing its imperial agenda even though Hezbollah humiliated the IDF in Lebanon and the Palestinians show no signs of ending their determined resistance short of mass-annihilation or forced expulsion. But it's not all smooth sailing as the unholy US-Israeli alliance faces a threat it can't ignore that could derail it. It's a growing broad-based worldwide anti-imperialist movement against these two partnered pariah states. It remains to be seen how far it will go, whether it can achieve critical mass in the US and in Israel, and if it can succeed in changing the direction of these two belligerents so far unstoppable and determined to go on unchecked by what passes for the civilized western world.

Part II - Israel and Middle East Warfare

It now looks like the only lesson the US and Israel learned from past failure is to press on with a new adventure. It appears the likely prime target is the Islamic Republic of Iran, as ill-advised as it will be to attack it. Petras explains that "Israel's political and military leadership have repeatedly and openly declared (their intention) to attack Iran in the immediate future." And once again it looks like the power of the Jewish Lobby in the US has the Bush administration thinking the same way to help its Israeli partner free itself from another "irritant" in the region that stands in the way of both countries' imperial aims. Petras calls Israel's Iran-directed war preparations "the greatest immediate threat to world peace and political stability (today)." It's hard to disagree.

That threat was heightened following North Korea's nuclear test which Israeli officials were quick to jump on suggesting it will benefit Iran. It came from an inflammatory statement by Miri Eisin, Prime Minister Olmert's spokeswoman, who told the AP: "We should remind ourselves that the North Koreans have already been suppliers of launching platforms which could reach Europe and certainly Israel. As such, they have already shown their willingness to be suppliers to Iran." Then Israel's UN Ambassador Dan Gillerman went further on Israel's Channel 2 TV referencing North Korea's nuclear activity and adding: "what Iran is about to do could be much worse, much more frightening and much more dangerous." This language practically demands an attack on Iran to destroy its presumed "nuclear threat" even though Iran is no threat to any country and the real threat is a growing likelihood of an Israeli and/or US attack on Iran or any other country in the region targeted as an enemy.

The US and Israel are allowed to get away with these kinds of outrageously stark and provocative statements even though the only pretext either country can fabricate is the baseless claim that Iran's legitimate right to enrich uranium for commercial use means the country has embarked on a nuclear weapons program that will threaten Israel. In fact, Iran is a signatory to the Nuclear Non-Proliferation Treaty (NPT), and, from all the evidence uncovered from years of monitoring by the UN International Atomic Energy Agency (IAEA), is in full compliance with it. It has every legal right to pursue its commercial nuclear program and nuclear enrichment for it. Israel, on the other hand, never signed the treaty, is known to have two to three hundred or more sophisticated nuclear weapons and launching systems for them, has stated its intention to use them if it chooses to, and is a nuclear outlaw - but one with an important ally the Iranians lack.

Today the debate in Israel is only over the method and timing of attacking Iran. Petras explains the Israelis have been pushing the US to do it for over a decade with the power of the Jewish Lobby in full support claiming the Islamic Republic threatens Israel's security and its dominance in the region. It doesn't matter that Iran never attacked its neighbors and isn't likely to undertake a military action except in self-defense as it did against Iraq in the 1980s. Further, it's an Israeli and made-in-America agitprop fabrication that Iranian President Ahmadinejad threatened "to wipe Israel off the map." The president said a number of things including…."this regime that is occupying Jerusalem must vanish from the page of time" meaning an illegal racist colonial one, but he didn't say or mean it should be removed by force or that Jews should be expelled from Israel.

Further proof of Iran's intentions came from Grand Ayatollah Khamenei's public pledge never to attack another country. He also condemned the development and use of nuclear weapons as being against Islam. The Western media was careful to suppress Khamenei's pledge and instead published false reports that he threatened the US to heighten the tension between the two countries. It's all part of the scheme to get full US support for Israel's intended war plans and the long held desire of both countries for regime change in Iran.

Petras lays out a dire scenario if a US, Israeli or joint attack is launched. It will be especially bad if the US does it using so-called "mini-nuke robust earth penetrator bunker-buster" munitions which are weapons that can be made to any desired potency and are likely to be from one-third to two-thirds as powerful as the Hiroshima bomb. In other words, there's nothing "mini" about them. Aside from the catastrophic level of immediate and long-term casualties from nuclear annihilation and radiation in Iran and beyond, Petras explains such an attack will only be a "pyrrhic victory." If Israel does it alone, it may set off a chain "political conflagration (to) unseat the rulers of Jordan, Egypt, Syria and Saudi Arabia." If the US attacks, it "would be even worse: major oil wells burning, US troops in Iraq surrounded (with the catastrophic consequences of far greater loss of life on both sides), long-term relations with Arab regimes undermined and increased oil prices (possibly high enough to cause a worldwide economic calamity) and supplies disrupted." It's almost certain this would inflame or enrage public opinion in the US and Israel that could lead to the ouster of the ruling parties in both countries.

It would also likely undermine Big Oil's existing and desired major oil exploration projects and cause the Israelis to crack down harder on the Palestinians and make them face forced massive ethnic cleansing expulsion from their homeland. Further, it would almost certainly get a response from Hezbollah or other resistance in South Lebanon, reignite the conflict there, unleash the Israeli killing machine all over again and cause more mass displacement and reoccupation by the IDF as the UN Blue Helmets and Lebanese forces evacuate the conflict zone. And it would lead to a growing threat of retaliatory terror attacks in the US, other Western countries and in Israel and would likely strengthen the resolve of other nations feeling potentially threatened by a hostile US, Israel and the West to seek defensive economic and military alliances in a structure like the Shanghai Cooperation Organization (SCO) that was formed in 2001 for political, diplomatic, economic and security reasons to act as a counterweight to NATO which the US dominates.

Still, with all the hazards of attacking Iran clearly in the minds of US policy makers, the momentum for it is moving ahead. It's happening in spite of serious high-level dispute in Washington about undertaking it. The Pentagon has war plans for it to include NATO, Israel and Canada, and it currently has a major US naval strike group deployment in the Persian Gulf and Eastern Mediterranean. Part of it is permanently stationed in the region, and in early October, The powerful Eisenhower Carrier Strike Group got "prepare to deploy" orders, headed there on October 3 and is now in place for whatever action may be intended. It joins the Enterprise and Iwo Jima Expeditionary Strike Groups making a total of three US naval task forces in position opposite Iran for whatever purpose may be planned and will shortly be joined by a fourth Boxer Expeditionary Strike Group that left Singapore on October 16 for the region. Naval forces already there have been engaged in what the Iranian foreign ministry calls "dangerous and suspicious" exercises in the Gulf practicing intercepting and searching ships for potential WMDs and missiles.

This all may be just a saber-rattling bluff, but if it's more than that it could unfold as a late October or early November "surprise" ahead of the November 7 congressional elections now only days away and be initiated in response to a manufactured incident on the order of the August, 1964 Gulf of Tonkin one or the blowing up of the USS Maine in February, 1898 in Havana Harbor. It's never hard for an aggressor to find reasons for war if it wants one and just needs a convenient excuse to start it.

The Bush administration and Israelis may get their wish if the Navy goes ahead with its reported plans to blockade Iranian oil ports. This action will be an act of war if it's done that Iran will have a legal right to respond to in self-defense under Article 51 of the UN Charter but will surely be met with a "shock and awe" counterattack against about 400 Iranian target sites already designated as ones to destroy in the event of hostilities. None of this guarantees an attack is imminent, but it shows a real possibility one may be coming. It also shows the power of the Jewish Lobby in the US that supports Israel's long-term aim to attack Iran no matter how grim the fallout from it may be. There's so much open speculation about this, it's gotten saner military, political and economic analysts here to believe this would be an act of insanity with the kind of potentially catastrophic consequences Petras outlined above. Will it happen? We can only hold our breathe waiting to find out, but it may not be long before we do.

Part III - Experts on Terror or Terrorist Experts

In this part of his book, Petras goes head-to-head with the so-called self-styled "terrorist experts" (TE) and clearly comes out ahead with his incisive dissection of them explaining why they're prominently featured in the major media. He calls them the "set-up" people – there to play a role to "motivate the colonial and imperial conquerors and reinforce their idea that the terrorists are not worthy of ruling or being ruled," so we have to get rid of them. It doesn't matter that the so-called "war on terrorism" is a shameless overused but very effective ruse scare tactic. It's always used because the public never catches on no matter how many times before supposed threats turned out to be another scam to get them to go along with whatever schemes our government had in mind to undertake. It never ceases to amaze how short an attention span the public has, but it's clear the power of the corporate-run media has a lot to do with it. It led author Studs Terkel to refer to a national Alzheimer's disease and author and political critic Gore Vidal to subtitle his 2004 book Imperial America - Reflections on the United States of Amnesia.

It gives the whole propaganda apparatus and the TE an open field to manipulate the public mind and get it to believe most anything. Petras calls these people "verbal assassins" who can't or won't understand that people pummeled by "shock and awe" attacks, their countries plundered in the name of "liberation," their people mass-murdered, raped, arrested and tortured might be desperate and motivated enough to strike back in retaliatory self-defense. It follows logically from Newton's law that for every action there's a corresponding reaction. In 1954, the CIA understood this and invented a term for it (no self-respecting TE will touch). The agency called it "blowback" referring to the unintended consequences from US hostile acts abroad like overthrowing legitimate or otherwise constituted governments as it did against Mohammed Mossadegh in Iran in 1953 ushering in the 25 year terror reign of the Shah. It finally led to the "blowback" 1979 revolution, and it causes other instances of retaliation now ongoing in Iraq and Afghanistan and for nearly six decades in Palestine.

But prominent TE featured in the major media have a different diagnosis of resistance fighters. They call them "incurable psychopaths (who are) extremely dangerous when at large (so we must flush them out to) capture, confine, torture or kill (them)." A convenient division of labor is then arranged to do it and the TE play their assigned role along with the military, recruited satraps, prison commandants, interrogators, guards and assorted other functionaries. They're team member hegemon-devil's disciples turning "victims into executioners and the executioners into victims." They do it by dehumanizing the legitimate resistance they label Islamo-fascists, Islamic fundamentalists, terrorists or other invented designations of inferiority or implied threat that must be destroyed.

It's incomprehensible to the TE that almost any act of retaliatory self-defense might be justifiable resistance given the level of state-directed violence used against them mercilessly. In Israel, and now in Iraq and Afghanistan it led to the phenomenon of suicide bombings which Petras calls "a form of individual sacrifice, of individual resistance taken in the name of the collective." He explains further that in the West individual sacrifice is rewarded with medals, but in the Middle East and specifically in the case of suicide bombers the reward is martyrdom for giving their lives in the cause of national liberation against a superior hostile force. This is a phenomenon common throughout history when a people face an overpowering conqueror and occupier. Petras explains "there have always been and always will be self-sacrificing individuals or (whole populations).... prepared to defend nation and home...and to use (their) body as a missile or weapon (to do it)."

Petras also explains there are different forms of imperial conquest and subjugation, and the one the US uses in Iraq and Afghanistan and that Israel uses against the Palestinians is a cruel and dehumanizing "process of destruction, degradation, and exploitation followed by efforts to 'reconstruct' a colonized military, police, and political structure willing and able to repress and contain anti-colonial resistance." It's a doctrine of "total war" against target nations too weak to fight back except by asymmetrical guerilla warfare means that include tactics like car and suicide bombings. Petras calls this practice "one of the ultimate forms of rejection of tryanny" that will only end when "total war" does. And that will only happen when the "colonial revivalist strand of imperialism in....its US, European and Israel variants" are defeated....Peace and reconciliation is only possible if justice is meted to the architects and practitioners of total war and human degradation." A long and painful struggle for liberation may be ahead before that goal is ever achieved.

Part IV - Noam Chomsky and the Pro-Israel Lobby

In the book's final part, Petras challenges a man who may best be described as an iconic figure on the Left, an anti-war activist, and much more but not one unused to being challenged and sometimes harshly. Petras points out that Chomsky has been a sharp critic of Israeli policies through the years and has been strongly attacked for his views by pro-Israeli organizations and the major media on the rare times his name is even allowed in it. Still he defends the existence of the Zionist state and has a different view than Petras on the power and influence of the Jewish Lobby in shaping US policy toward Israel. Petras lists what he calls Chomsky's fifteen erroneous theses reflecting his long-held belief that the Lobby isn't as potent as the strong case Petras makes in this book that it is. Not wishing to take sides with two distinguished men this writer holds in high esteem, the points of disagreement will only be listed so the reader can decide who makes the better case.

Petras begins by listing what he calls Chomsky's eight "dubious propositions:"

1. The pro-Israel Lobby is like any other one.

2. The Lobby's backers have no more power than other pressure groups.

3. The Lobby succeeds because its interests coincide with those of the US.

4. Israel is a tool of the US empire and used as needed.

5. "Big Oil" and the "military-industrial complex" are the major forces shaping Middle East policy.

6. US and Israeli interests usually coincide.

7. The Iraq war and threats to Iran and Syria stem from the "oil interests" and "military-industrial complex."

8. US behavior in the Middle East is the same as what it practices worldwide.

Petras then uses the above list to discuss what he calls Chomsky's 15 theses and uses the persuasive evidence presented in his book to take issue with them, one by one. He sums up his case stating he's done this because of Chomsky's enormous stature making whatever his views are stand out prominently. It's a matter of consequence when a man like Noam Chomsky believes the Jewish Lobby is like all others which in Petras' view gives a "free ride to the principal authors, architects and lobbyists in favor of the (Iraq) war (and is an) obstacle to achieving clarity about whom we are fighting and why. To ignore the pro-Israel Lobby is (also) to allow it a free hand in pushing for the invasion of Iran and Syria (and any other regime in the region Israel may wish to remove)." Petras sums up by saying that "the peace and justice movements, at home and abroad, are bigger than any individual or intellectual - no matter what their past credentials." In this battle of noted titans on the Left, it's for the reader to decide who's right.

Summation - Confronting Zionism and Reclaiming American Middle East Policy

Petras has written a powerful and important new book that needs broad exposure and resonance. But he'll never get its content past the corporate gatekeepers controlling the major media because of his courage to reveal what others fear to do - confront Zionism, its agenda of aggressive wars and colonization, and the power of the Jewish Lobby to assure Israel gets the full and unconditional support of every US administration regardless of whether what it does serves the interests of this country. That Lobby power reached its apogee and full fruition with the ascent of the Bush administration neocons that effectively pledge their fealty to the rulers of the Israeli state and prove Ariel Sharon may have been right when he once arrogantly boasted about his relationship with George Bush saying: "We have the US under our control."

The result has been disastrous for this country and the sacred principles on which it was founded. In partnership with Israel, the US began tearing apart the Middle East and Central Asia by attacking and occupying Iraq and Afghanistan. It now threatens to inflame the whole region enough to make it explode if we go ahead with plans to attack Iran, do it with nuclear weapons, and then move on to Syria and even Saudi Arabia while continuing to hold Lebanon hostage and under siege in a state of interregnum awaiting the next inevitable trigger igniting the whole ugly business there all over again. The Bush administration "long war" against Islam enraged 1.8 billion Muslims worldwide growing in unity against us. It's also destroying our freedom and democracy at home in the process threatening everyone with the emerging power of a national security police state that spells tyranny with an out-of-control president usurping the dictatorial power of a "unitary executive" claiming the right to go around the law of the land and its international obligations to govern as he pleases.

Petras sounds the alarm and asks how did we get into this debacle, and who's responsible for it. He stresses the need for a full-scale Congressional investigation to find out, but laments it's not likely to happen as long as the Bush neocons have their way. The central thesis of his book is that the Jewish Lobby serves the interests of Zionism and acts as agents for the state of Israel. It co-opted the Bush administration, all others preceding it, and the key centers of power and influence in the country leading us to the disaster we now face because of our misguided Middle East adventurism.

Petras equates our actions in league with Israel to the Nazi war crimes committed in WW II, saying "These are the highest crimes against humanity." Referring to the crime of aggression, the Nuremberg Tribunal called it the "supreme international crime," and those Nazis found guilty of it were hanged. Petras explains that the "worst crimes are committed by those who claim to be a divinely chosen people, a people with 'righteous' claims of supreme victimhood." He goes on to say: "Righteous victimology, linked to ethno-religious loyalties and directed by fanatical civilian militarists with advanced weaponry, is the greatest threat to world peace and humanity."

Petras makes an impassioned plea for progressives (really all people of conscience) to reject the imperial agenda of all nations, and in the case of Israel, to stand firm against inevitably being labeled anti-Semitic. Scurrilous name-calling is another refuge of scoundrels that shouldn't be tolerated or allowed to deter our committed assault against the forces of darkness that will destroy us unless we stand firmly against them. Petras tells us it won't be easy, and we can expect forceful ideological attacks against us premised on the notion that Israel is the embodiment of "democracy, liberty and justice" and those daring to criticize the Jewish state will be called supporters of "Arab dictatorships, repression, injustice and terrorism."

The stakes are much too high to let them get away with it using scurrilous name-calling in defense of it. In Petras' words: "Israel and its overseas network in the US....(threatens) not only the oppressed people of Palestine (and Iraq, Iran, Lebanon, Syria and any other state Israel takes aim at) but the rights of people throughout the world." He stresses we have mass public opinion on our side nearly everywhere outside the US, and it's gaining resonance here as well. It sees Israel and our actions in support of the Israeli state as the greatest of all threats to world peace and stability. Petras ends his book with one final impassioned call to arms: "Let's move ahead and de-colonize our country, our minds and politics as a first step in reconstituting a democratic republic, free of entangling colonial and neo-imperial alliances." Wise thoughts from a wise and courageous man. We can't ignore them lest we pay the supreme price of the loss of our freedom (and maybe our lives) because we didn't know it was being taken from us until it was too late to act to save it.

Stephen Lendman is a widely published specialist on Middle East affairs and is a frequent contributor to Global Research.org where this article first appeared. He lives in Chicago and can be reached at lendmanstephen@sbcglobal.net. Also visit his blog site at www.sjlendman.blogspot.com.

Purim Special
From Esther to AIPAC

by Gilad Atzmon

"In certain contexts, memory can be subversive; in others, memory can shield the status quo. When individuals and communities become vested with memory as a form of identity and special-ness, then other suffering threatens to displace the centrality of our experience. Instead of a bridge of solidarity to others who are suffering in the present, suffering in the past can become a badge of honor, protecting us from the challenges that are before us. Then our witness, originally powerful, opening questions about God and power, becomes diluted, can be seen as fake, contrived, even willfully so. An industry grows up around you, honors you, and at the same time uses your witness for other reasons. In the end a confusion results, externally and internally, until the witness himself can no longer differentiate between the world of interpretation he helped articulate and the world that now speaks in his name. Is this what happened to [Elie] Wiesel, or is [Norman] Finkelstein's more acerbic analysis accurate?"[1]

Jewishness is a rather broad term. It refers to a culture with many faces, varied distinctive groups, different beliefs, opposing political camps, different classes and diversified ethnicity. Nevertheless, the connection between those very many people who happen to identify themselves as Jews is rather intriguing. In the paragraphs that follow, I will try to further the search into the notion of Jewishness. I will make an attempt to trace the intellectual, spiritual and mythological collective bond that makes Jewishness into a powerful identity.

Clearly, Jewishness is neither a racial nor an ethnic category. Though Jewish identity is racially and ethnically orientated, the Jewish people do not form a homogenous group. There is no racial or ethnic continuum. Jewishness may be seen by some as a continuation of Judaism. I would maintain that this is not necessarily the case either. Though Jewishness borrows some fundamental Judaic elements, Jewishness is not Judaism and it is even categorically different from Judaism. Furthermore, as we know, more than a few of those who proudly define themselves as Jews have very little knowledge of Judaism, many of them are atheists, non-religious and even overtly oppose Judaism or any other religion. Many of those Jews who happen to oppose Judaism happen to maintain their Jewish identity and to be extremely proud about it[2]. This opposition to Judaism obviously includes Zionism (at least the early version) but it also is the basis of much of Jewish socialist anti-Zionism.

Though Jewishness is different from Judaism one may still wonder just what constitutes Jewishness: whether it is a new form of religion an ideology or if it is just a 'state of mind'.

If Jewishness is indeed a religion, the next questions that have to be asked are, "what kind of religion is it? What does this religion entail? What do its followers believe in?" If it is a religion, one may wonder whether it is possible to divorce from it as much as it is possible to step out of Judaism, Christianity or Islam.

If Jewishness is an ideology, then the right questions to ask are, "what does this ideology stand for? Does it form a discourse? Is it a monolithic discourse? Does it portray a new world order? Is it aiming for peace or violence? Does it carry a universal message to humanity or is it just another manifestation of some tribal precepts?"

If Jewishness is a state of mind, then the question to raise is whether it is rational or irrational. Is it within the expressible or rather within the inexpressible?

At this point I may suggest to consider the remote possibility that Jewishness may be a strange hybrid, it can be all of those things at once i.e., a religion, an ideology and a state of mind.

The Holocaust Religion

"Yeshayahu Leibowitz, the philosopher who was an observant orthodox Jew, told me once: "The Jewish religion died 200 years ago. Now there is nothing that unifies the Jews around the world apart from the Holocaust." –Uri Avnery[3]

Philosopher Yeshayahu Leibowitz, the German born Hebrew University professor, was probably the first to suggest that the Holocaust has become the new Jewish religion. 'The Holocaust' is far more than historical narrative, it indeed contains most of the essential religious elements: it has its priests (Simon Wiesenthal, Elie Wiesel, Deborah Lipstadt, etc.) and prophets (Shimon Peres, Benjamin Netanyahu and those who warn about the Iranian Judeocide to come). It has its commandments and dogmas ('never again', 'six million', etc.). It has its rituals (memorial days, Pilgrimage to Auschwitz etc.). It establishes an esoteric symbolic order (kapo, gas chambers, chimneys, dust, Musselmann, etc.). It has its shrines and temples (Yad Vashem, the Holocaust Museum and now the UN). If this is not enough, the Holocaust religion is also maintained by a massive economic network and global financial infrastructures (Holocaust industry *a la* Norman Finkelstein). Most interestingly, the Holocaust religion is coherent enough to define the new 'antichrists' (the Deniers) and it is powerful enough to persecute them (Holocaust denial laws).

Critical scholars who dispute the notion of 'Holocaust religion' suggest that though the new emerging religion retains many characteristics of an organized religion, it doesn't establish an external God figure to point at, to worship or to love. I myself cannot agree less. I insist that the Holocaust religion embodies the essence of the liberal democratic worldview. It is there to offer a new form of worshiping. It made self-loving into a dogmatic belief in which the observant follower worships himself. In the new religion it is 'the Jew' whom the

Jews worship. It is all about 'me', the subject of endless suffering who makes it into redemption.

However, more than a few Jewish scholars in Israel and abroad happen to accept Leibowitz's observation. Amongst them is Marc Ellis, the prominent Jewish theologian who suggests a revealing insight into the dialectic of the new religion. "Holocaust theology," says Ellis, "yields three themes that exist in dialectical tension: suffering and empowerment, innocence and redemption, special-ness and normalization."[4]

Though Holocaust religion didn't replace Judaism, it gave Jewishness a new meaning. It sets a modern Jewish narrative allocating the Jewish subject within a Jewish project. It allocates the Jew a central role within his own self-centered universe. The 'sufferer' and the 'innocent' are marching towards 'redemption' and 'empowerment'. God is obviously out of the game, he is fired, he has failed in his historic mission, He wasn't there to save the Jews. Within the new religion the Jew becomes 'the Jews' new God', it is all about the Jew who redeems himself.

The Jewish follower of the Holocaust religion idealizes the condition of his existence. He then sets a framework of a future struggle towards recognition. For the Zionist follower of the new religion, the implications seem to be relatively durable. He is there to *'schlep'* the entirety of world Jewry to Zion at the expense of the indigenous Palestinian people. For the Socialist Jew, the project is slightly more complicated. For him redemption means setting a new world order, namely a socialist haven. A world dominated by dogmatic working class politics in which Jews happen to be no more than just one minority amongst many. For the humanist observant, Holocaust religion means that Jews must locate themselves at the forefront of the struggle against racism, oppression and evil in general. Though it sounds promising, it happens to be problematic because of obvious reasons. In our current world order it is Israel and America that happen to be amongst the leading oppressive evils. Expecting Jews to be in the forefront of humanist struggle sets Jews in a fight against their brethren and their supportive single superpower. However, it is rather clear that all three Holocaust churches assign the Jews a major project with some global implications.

* * *

As we can see, the Holocaust functions as an ideological interface. It provides its follower with a *logos*. On the level of consciousness, it suggests a purely analytical vision of the past and present, yet, it doesn't stop just there, it also defines the struggle to come. It defines a vision of a Jewish future. Nevertheless, as a consequence it fills the Jewish subject's unconsciousness with the ultimate anxiety: the destruction of the 'I'.

Needless to say, a faith that stimulates the consciousness (Ideology) and steers the unconsciousness (Spirit) is a very good recipe for a winning religion. This structural bond of ideology and spirit is fundamental to the Judaic tradition. The bond between the legal clarity of the *halacah* (ideology) and the mysteriousness of Jehovah or even *Kabala* (spirit) makes Judaism into a totality, a universe in itself. Bolshevism, the mass movement rather than the political theory, is built upon the same structure, the lucidity of pseudo-scientific materialism together with the fear of the capitalistic appetite. Neoconservative's politics of fear is again all about locking the subject in the chasm between the alleged forensic lucidity of WMDs and the inexpressible fright of 'terror to come'.

This very bond between consciousness and unconsciousness brings to mind the Lacanian notion of the 'real'. The 'real' is that which cannot be symbolized i.e., expressed in words. The real is the 'inexpressible', the inaccessible. In Zizek's words, 'the real is impossible'; 'the real is the trauma'. Nevertheless, it is this trauma that shapes the symbolic order. It is the trauma that forms our reality.

The Holocaust religion fits nicely into the Lacanian model. Its spiritual core is rooted deeply within the domain of the inexpressible. Its preaching teaches us to see a threat in everything. It is the ultimate conjunction between the ideology and the spirit that has materialized into sheer pragmatism.

Interestingly enough, the Holocaust religion extends far beyond the internal Jewish discourse. In fact the new religion operates as a mission. It sets shrines in far lands. As we can see, the emerging religion is already becoming a new world order. It is the Holocaust that is now used as an alibi to nuke Iran[5]. Clearly, Holocaust religion serves the Jewish political discourse both on the right and left but it appeals to the Goyim as well, especially those who are engaged in merciless killing 'in the name of freedom'[6]. To a certain extent we are all subject to this religion, some of us are worshipers, others are just subject to its power. Interestingly enough, those who deny the Holocaust are themselves subject to abuse by the high priests of this religion. Holocaust religion constitutes the Western 'Real'. We are not allowed to touch it or to look into it. Very much like the Israelites who are entitled to obey their God but never to question him.

* * *

The Scholars who are engaged in the study of the Holocaust religion (theology, ideology and historicity), are engaged mainly with structural formulations, its meanings, its rhetoric and its historical interpretation. Some happen to search for the theological dialectic (Marc Ellis), others formulate the commandments (Adi Ofir), some learn its historical evolution (Lenni Brenner), and others expose its financial infrastructure (Finkelstein). Interestingly enough, most scholars who are engaged in the subject of Holocaust religion are engaged with a list of events that happened between 1933–1945. Most of the scholars are themselves orthodox observants. Though they may be critical of different aspects of the exploitation of the Holocaust, they all accept the validity of the Nazi Judeocide and its mainstream interpretations and implications. Most of the scholars, if not all of them, do not challenge the Zionist narrative, namely Nazi Judeocide, yet, more than a few are critical of the way Jewish and Zionist institutes employ the Holocaust. Though some may dispute the numbers (Shraga Elam), and others question the validity of memory (Ellis, Finkelstein), no one goes as far as revisionism, not a single Holocaust religion scholar dares engage in a dialogue with the so-called 'deniers' to discuss their vision of the events or any other revisionist scholarship.

Far more interesting is the fact that none of the Holocaust religion scholars have spent any energy studying the role of the Holocaust within the long-standing Jewish continuum. From this point onward, I will maintain that Holocaust religion was well established a long time before the Final Solution (1942), well before the Kristalnacht (1938), well before the Nuremberg Laws (1936), well before the first anti-Jewish law was announced by Nazi Germany, well before the American Jewish Congress declared a financial war against Nazi Germany (1933) and even well before Hitler was born (1889). The Holocaust religion is probably as old as the Jews.

Jewish Archetypes

In a previous paper I have defined the notion of 'Pre-Traumatic Stress Disorder' (Pre-TSD)[7]. Within the condition of the Pre-TSD, the stress is the outcome of a phantasmic imaginary episode set in the future, an event that has never taken place. Unlike the Post-Traumatic Stress Disorder, in which stress is realized as the direct reaction to an event that (may) have taken place in the past, within the state of Pre-TSD, the stress is formed as the outcome of an imaginary potential event. Within the Pre-TSD an illusion pre-empts the conditions in which the fantasy of future terror is shaping the present reality.

As it seems, the dialectic of fear dominates the Jewish existence as well as mindset far longer than we are ready to admit. Though fright is exploited politically by Jewish ethnic leaders since the early days of emancipation, the dialectic of fear is far older than modern Jewish history. In fact it is the heritage of the Tanach (the Hebrew Bible) that is there to set the Jew in a pre-traumatic state. It is the Hebrew Bible that sets a binary framework of Innocence/Suffering and Persecution/Empowerment. More particularly, the fear of Judeocide is entangled with Jewish spirit, culture and literature.

I would argue here that the Holocaust religion was there to transform the ancient Israelites into Jews.

The American anthropologist Glenn Bowman who specialized in the study of exilic identities offers a crucial insight into the subject of fear and its contribution to the subject of Identity politics. "Antagonism," says Bowman, "is fundamental to process of fetishization underlying identity, because one tends precisely to talk about who one is or what one is at a moment in which that being seems threatened. I begin to call myself such and such a person, or such and such a representative of an imagined community, at the moment something seems to threaten to disallow the being the name I speak stands in for. Identity terms come into usage at precisely the moment in which for some reason one comes to feel them signifying a being or entity one has to fight to defend."[8]

In short, Bowman stresses that it is the fear that crystallizes the notion of identity. However, once the fear is matured into a state of a collective pre-traumatic stress then identity re-forms itself. When it comes to the Jewish people, it is the Bible that is there to set the Jews within a state of Pre-TSD. It is the Bible that initiates the fear of Judeocide.

* * *

More and more Bible scholars are now disputing the historicity of the Bible. Niels Lechme in 'The Canaanites and Their Land' argues that the Bible is for the most part "written after the Babylonian Exile and that those writings rework (and in large part invent) previous Israelite history so that it reflects and reiterates the experiences of those returning from the Babylonian exile."[9]

In other words, being written by home-comers, the Bible incorporates some hardcore exilic ideology into an historic narrative. Very much like in the case of the early Zionist ideologist who regarded assimilation as a death threat, "The communities which aggregated under the leadership of the Yahwehist priesthood (at the time of the Babylonian exile) saw assimilation and apostasy not only as social death for themselves as Judeans but also as attempted deicide. They resolved to maintain an absolute and exclusive commitment to Yahweh who they were sure would lead them back to the land from which they had been expelled. The prescribed blood purity as a means of maintaining the borders of the national community thus proscribed inter-marriage with those surrounding them. They also established a series of exclusivist rituals that set themselves off from their neighbors, and these not only included a surrogate form of temple worship but also a distinct calendar which ritualistically enabled them to exist in a different time frame than the communities with which they shared space. All of these diacritical devices served to mark and maintain difference, but did not prevent them from trading with and thus being able to sustain themselves amongst the Babylonians."

Looking into Bowman and Lechme's spectacular reading of the Bible and the Judaic narrative as a manifestation of exilic and marginal identity may explain the fact that Jewishness flourishes in exile but rather loses its impetus once it becomes a domestic adventure. If Jewishness is indeed centered around an émigré collective survival ideology, than its followers will prosper in Exile. However, that which maintains the Jewish collective identity is fear. Similar to the case of Holocaust religion, Jewishness sets the fear of Judeocide at the core of the Jewish psyche, yet, it also offers the spiritual, ideological and pragmatic measures to deal with this fear.

Book of Esther

The Book of Esther is a biblical story that is the basis for the celebration of Purim, probably the most joyous Jewish festival. The book tells the story of an attempted Judeocide but it also tells a story in which Jews manage to change their fate. In the book the Jews do manage to rescue themselves and even to mete revenge.

It is set in the third year of Ahasuerus, and the ruler is a king of Persia usually identified with Xerxes I. It is a story of a palace, conspiracy, an attempted Judeocide and a brave and beautiful Jewish queen (Esther) who manages to save the Jewish people at the very last minute.

In the story, King Ahasuerus is married to Vashti, whom he repudiates after she rejects his offer to 'visit' him during a feast. Esther was selected from the candidates to be Ahasuerus's new wife. As the story progresses, Ahasuerus's prime minister Haman plots to have the king kill all the Jews without knowing that Esther is actually Jewish. In the story, Esther together with her cousin Mordechai saves the day for their people. At the risk of endangering her own safety, Esther warns Ahasuerus of Haman's murderous anti-Jewish plot. Haman and his sons are hanged on the fifty cubit gallows he had originally built for cousin Mordecai. As it happens, Mordecai takes Haman's place, he becomes the prime minister. Ahasuerus's edict decreeing the murder of the Jews cannot be rescinded, so he issues another edict allowing the Jews to take up arms and kill their enemies, which they do.

The moral of the story is rather clear. If Jews want to survive, they better find infiltrates into the corridors of power. With Esther, Mordechai and Purim in mind, AIPAC and the notion of 'Jewish power' looks like an embodiment of a deep Biblical and cultural ideology.

However, here is the interesting twist. Though the story is presented as an historic tale, the historical accuracy of the *Book of Esther* is largely disputed by most modern Bible Scholars. It is largely the lack of clear corroboration of any of the details of the story of the Book of Esther with what is known of Persian History from classical sources that led scholars to come to a conclusion that the story is mostly or even totally fictional.

In other words, though the moral is clear, the attempted genocide is fictional. Seemingly, the Book of Esther set its followers into a collective Pre-Traumatic Stress Disorder. It makes a fantasy of destruction into an ideology of survival. And indeed, some read the story as an allegory of quintessentially assimilated Jews who discover that they are targets of anti-Semitism, but are also in a position to save themselves and their fellow Jews.

Keeping Bowman in mind may throw some light here. The Book of Esther is there to form the exilic identity. It is there to implant the existential stress, it introduces the Holocaust religion. It sets the conditions that turn the Holocaust into reality.

Interestingly enough, the Book of Esther (in the Hebrew version) is one of only two books of the Bible that do not directly mention God (the other is Song of Songs). In the Book of Esther it is the Jews who believe in themselves, in their own power, in their uniqueness, in their sophistication, in their ability to conspire, in their ability to take over kingdoms, in their ability to save themselves. The Book of Esther is all about empowerment and the Jews who believe in their powers.

From Purim to Birkenau

In an article named "A Purim Lesson: Lobbying Against Genocide, Then and Now"[10], Dr. Rafael Medoff shares with his readers what he regards as the lesson inherited to the Jews by the Book of Esther. If to be more precise, it is the art of lobbying which Esther and Mordechai are there to teach us. "The holiday of Purim" says Medoff, "celebrates the successful effort by prominent Jews in the capitol of ancient Persia to prevent genocide against the Jewish people." But Medoff doesn't stop just there. This specific exercise of what some call 'Jewish power' has been carried forward and performed by modern emancipated Jews: "What is not well known is that a comparable lobbying effort took place in modern times – in Washington, D.C., at the peak of the Holocaust."

In the article Medoff explores the similarities between Esther's lobbying in Persia and her modern brothers lobbying within the FDR's administration at the start of WWII. "The Esther in 1940s Washington was Henry Morgenthau Jr." says Medoff, "a wealthy, assimilated Jew of German descent who (as his son later put it) was anxious to be regarded as 'one hundred percent American.' Downplaying his Jewishness, Morgenthau gradually rose from being FDR's friend and adviser to his Treasury Secretary."

Clearly, Medoff spotted a modern Mordechai as well, "a young Zionist emissary from Jerusalem, Peter Bergson (real name: Hillel Kook) who led a series of protest campaigns to bring about U.S. rescue of Jews from Hitler. The Bergson group's newspaper ads and public rallies roused public awareness of the Holocaust – particularly when it organized over 400 rabbis to march to the front gate of the White House just before Yom Kippur in 1943."

Medoff's reading of the Book of Esther provides us with a glaring insight into the internal code of Jewish collective survival dynamics in which the assimilated (Esther) and the observant (Mordechai) are joining forces with clear Judeo centric interests in their minds.

According to Medoff the similarities are indeed shocking. "Mordechai's pressure finally convinced Esther to go to the king; the pressure of Morgenthau's aides finally convinced him to go to the president, armed with a stinging 18-page report that they titled 'Report to the Secretary on the Acquiescence of This Government in the Murder of the Jews.'"

Dr. Medoff is rather ready to draw his historical conclusions. "Esther's lobbying succeeded. Ahasuerus cancelled the genocide decree and executed Haman and his henchmen. Morgenthau's lobbying also succeeded. A Bergson-initiated Congressional resolution calling for U.S. rescue action quickly passed the Senate Foreign Relations Committee – enabling Morgenthau to tell FDR that 'you have either got to move very fast, or the Congress of the United States will do it for you.' Ten months before Election Day, the last thing FDR wanted was an embarrassing public scandal over the refugee issue. Within days, Roosevelt did what the Congressional resolution sought – he issued an executive order creating the War Refugee Board, a U.S. government agency to rescue refugees from Hitler."

It is clear beyond doubt that Medoff sees the Book of Esther as a general guideline for a healthy Jewish future. Medoff ends his paper saying: "the claim that nothing could be done to help Europe's Jews had been demolished by Jews who shook off their fears and spoke up for their people – in ancient Persia and in modern Washington." In other words, Jews can do and should do for themselves. This is indeed the moral of the Book of Esther as well as the Holocaust religion.

What Jews should do for themselves is indeed an open question. Different Jews have different ideas. The Neocon believes in dragging America and the West into an endless war against Islam. Emmanuel Levinas, on the contrary, believes that Jews should actually position themselves at the forefront of the struggle against oppression and injustice. Indeed, Jewish empowerment is just one answer among many. Yet, it is a very powerful not to say a dangerous one. It is especially dangerous when the American Jewish Committee (AJC) acts as a modern-day Mordechai and publicly engages in an extensive lobbying effort for a war against Iran.

When analyzing the work and influence of American Israel Public Affairs Committee (AIPAC) within American politics it is the Book of Esther that we should bear in mind. AIPAC is more than a mere political lobby. AIPAC is a modern-day Mordechai, the AJC is modern -day Mordechai. Both AIPAC and AJC are inherently in line with the Hebrew Biblical school of thought. However, while the Mordechais are relatively easy to spot, the Esthers, those who act for Israel behind the scenes, are slightly more difficult to trace.

I believe that once we learn to look at Israeli lobbying in the parameters that are drawn by the Book of Esther/Holocaust-religion, we are then entitled to regard [Iranian President] Ahmadinejad as the current Haman/Hitler figure. The AJC is Mordechai, Bush is obviously Ahasuerus, yet Esther can be almost anyone, from the last Neocon to Cheney and beyond.

Brenner and Prinz

In the opening paragraph of this essay I ask what Jewishness stands for. Though I accept the complexity of the notion of Jewishness, I tend to additionally accept Leibowitz's contribution to the subject: Holocaust is the new Jewish religion. However, within the paper I took the liberty of extending the notion of the Holocaust. Rather than referring merely to the Shoah, i.e., the Nazi Judeocide, I argue here that the Holocaust is actually engraved within the Jewish discourse and spirit. The Holocaust is the essence of the collective

Jewish Pre-Traumatic stress disorder and it predates the Shoah. To
be a Jew is to see the 'other' as a threat rather than as a brother.
To be a Jew is to be on a constant alert. To be a Jew is to internal-
ize the message of the Book of Esther. It is to aim towards the most
influential junctions of hegemony. To be a Jew is to collaborate with
power.

The American Marxist historian Lenni Brenner is fascinated by
the collaboration between Zionists and Nazism. In his book *Zionism
In The Age of Dictators* he presents an extract from Rabbi Joachim
Prinz's book published in 1937 after Rabbi Prinz left Germany for
America.

"Everyone in Germany knew that only the Zionists could responsi-
bly represent the Jews in dealings with the Nazi government. We all
felt sure that one day the government would arrange a round table
conference with the Jews, at which after the riots and atrocities of
the revolution had passed the new status of German Jewry could be
considered. The government announced very solemnly that there
was no country in the world which tried to solve the Jewish problem as seriously as did Germany. Solution of the Jewish question? It
was our Zionist dream! We never denied the existence of the Jewish
question! Dissimilation? It was our own appeal! ... In a statement
notable for its pride and dignity, we called for a conference."[11]

Brenner then brings in extracts from a Memorandum that was sent
to the Nazi Party by the German Zionist federation (ZVfD) on 21
June 1933:

"Zionism has no illusions about the difficulty of the Jewish condition, which consists above all in an abnormal occupational pattern
and in the fault of an intellectual and moral posture not rooted in
one's own tradition ... On the foundation of the new state, which
has established the principle of race, we wish so to fit our community into the total structure so that for us too, in the sphere assigned
to us, fruitful activity for the Fatherland is possible. ... Our acknowl-
edgement of Jewish nationality provides for a clear and sincere
relationship to the German people and its national and racial reali-

ties. Precisely because we do not wish to falsify these fundamentals, because we, too, are against mixed marriage and are for maintaining the purity of the Jewish group ... We believe in the possibility of an honest relationship of loyalty between a group-conscious Jewry and the German state ... "[12]

Brenner doesn't approve either of Prinz's take nor the Zionist initiative. Filled with loathing he says, "This document, a treason to the Jews of Germany, was written in standard Zionist clichés: 'abnormal occupational pattern', 'rootless intellectuals greatly in need of moral regeneration', etc. In it the German Zionists offered calculated collaboration between Zionism and Nazism, hallowed by the goal of a Jewish state: we shall wage no battle against thee, only against those that would resist thee."

Brenner fails to see the obvious. Rabbi Prinz and the ZVfD were not traitors, they were actually genuine Jews. They followed their very Jewish cultural code. They followed the Book of Esther, they took the role of Mordechai. They tried to find a way to collaborate with what they correctly identified as a prominent emerging power. In 1969, Rabbi Prinz confessed that ever "since the assassination of Walther Rathenau in 1922, there was no doubt in our minds that the German development would be toward an anti-Semitic totalitarian regime. When Hitler began to arouse, and as he put it 'awaken' the German nation to racial consciousness and racial superiority, we had no doubt that this man would sooner or later become the leader of the German nation."[13]

Whether Brenner or anyone else likes it or not, Rabbi Prinz proves to be an authentic Jewish leader. He proves to possess some highly developed survival radar mechanism that fit perfectly well with the exilic ideology. In 1981 Lenni Brenner interviewed Rabbi Prinz. Here is what he had to say about the collaborator Rabbi:

"(Prinz) dramatically evolved in the 44 years since he was expelled from Germany. He told me, off tape, that he soon realized that nothing he said there made sense in the U.S. He became an American liberal. Eventually, as head of the American Jewish Congress, he was asked to march with Martin Luther King and he did so."

Once again, Brenner fails to see the obvious. Prinz didn't change at all. Prinz didn't evolve in those 44 years. He was and remained a genuine authentic Jew, and an extremely clever one. A man who internalized the essence of Jewish émigré philosophy: In Germany be a German, and in America be American. Be flexible, fit in and adopt relativistic ethical thinking. Prinz, being a devoted follower of Mordechai, realized that whatever is good for the Jews is simply good.

I went back and listened to the invaluable Brenner interviews with Rabbi Prinz that are now available online[14]. I was rather shocked to find out that actually Prinz presents his position eloquently. It is Prinz rather than Brenner who provides us a glimpse into Jewish ideology and its interaction with the surrounding reality. It is Prinz rather than Brenner who happens to understand the German *volk* and their aspirations. Prinz presents his past moves as a proud Jew. From his point of view, collaborating with Hitler was indeed the right thing to do. He was following Mordechai, he was probably searching for an Esther to come. Thus, it is only natural that Rabbi Prinz later became the President of the American Jewish Congress. He became a prominent American leader In spite of his 'collaboration with Hitler'. Simply because of the obvious reason: from a Jewish ideological point of view, he did the right thing.

Final Words About Zionism

Once we learn to look at Jewishness as an exilic culture, as the embodiment of the 'ultimate other' we can then understand Jewishness as a collective continuum grounded on a fantasy of horror. Jewishness is the materialization of politics of fear into a pragmatic agenda. This is what Holocaust religion is all about and it is indeed as old as the Jews. Rabbi Prinz could foresee the Holocaust. Both Prinz and the ZVfD could anticipate a Judeocide. Thus, from a Jewish ideological point of view they acted appropriately. They were committed to their esoteric ethics within an esoteric cultural discourse.

Zionism was indeed a great promise, it was there to convert the Jews into Israelites. It was going to make the Jews into people like other peoples. Zionism was there to identify and fight the *Galut* (Diaspora), the exilic characteristic of the Jewish people and their culture. But Zionism was doomed to failure. The reason is obvious: within a culture that is metaphysically grounded upon exilic ideology the last thing you can expect is a successful homecoming. In order to live for its promise Zionism had to liberate itself of the Jewish exilic ideology, Zionism had to liberate itself of the Holocaust religion. But this is exactly what it fails to do. Being exilic to the bone, Zionism had to turn to antagonizing the indigenous Palestinians in order to maintain its fetish of Jewish identity.

Since Zionism failed to divorce itself from the Jewish émigré ideology, it lost the opportunity to evolve into any form of domestic culture. Consequently, Israeli culture and politics is a strange amalgam of indecisiveness; a mixture of colonial empowerment together with *Galut's* victim mentality. Zionism is a secular product of exilic culture that cannot mature into authentic homegrown perception.

Gilad Atzmon is the author of two novels: *A Guide to the Perplexed* and the recently released *My One and Only Love*. He is also one of the most accomplished jazz saxophonists in Europe. Atzmon's recent CD, Exile, was named in 2003 as the year's best jazz CD by the BBC. Atzmon was born in Israel and served in the Israeli military. He now lives in London and can be reached at: atz@onetel.net.uk

Notes

1. Marc Ellis, Marc Ellis on Finkelstein

2. http://www.counterpunch.org/

3. http://www.ramallahonline.com

4. Marc H. Ellis, *Beyond Innocence & Redemption - Confronting The Holocaust And Israeli Power, Creating a Moral Future for the Jewish People* (San Francisco: Harper & Row, 1990).

5. http://peacepalestine.blogspot.com/

6. http://www.amin.org/

7. http://www.imemc.org/article/21744

8. Glenn Bowman-Migrant Labour: Constructing Homeland in the Exilic Imagination, Anthropological Theory II:4. December 2002 pp 447–468.

9. Ibid

10. http://www.wymaninstitute.org/articles/2004–03-purim.php

11. http://www.marxists.de/middleast/brenner/ch05.htm

12. Ibid

13. http://www.marxists.de/middleast/brenner/ch03.htm

14. http://cosmos.ucc.ie/cs1064/jabowen/IPSC/php/clip.php?cid=512

Will Fundamentalist Christians and Jews Ignite Apocalypse?

by Margot Patterson

National Catholic Reporter, October 11, 2002

In September, thousands of Christian Zionists met in Jerusalem for the Jewish holiday of Sukkot to cheer on Israeli Prime Minister Ariel Sharon and to declare their unconditional support for the State of Israel. Organized by the International Christian Embassy, the meeting appeared to be a love-in as much as a rally. "Walking here, I heard many times, and many people said, 'We love you, we love Israel,' " Sharon said. "May I tell you we love you. We love all of you."

On the face of it, the love affair between conservative Christians and Israel's hawkish head of state seems unlikely, but mutual interests notoriously make for strange bedfellows. Many fundamentalist Christians embrace the state of Israel because of its role in their own end-of-time theology. For its part, the right wing in Israel welcomes the economic and political support it receives from conservative Christians around the world and particularly in the United States.

Religion and politics. It's an incendiary combination anywhere, and particularly in the Middle East where Christian fundamentalists, often working in tandem with Jewish Messianic settlers, promote the formation of a Greater Israel that they believe will usher in Armageddon itself. Many of this country's most ardent Christian supporters of Israel welcome that prospect. Others who don't subscribe to the end-of-time theology of "dispensational premillennialism" worry that the agenda pushed by the tactical alliance between Jewish and Christian fundamentalists will transform the Israeli-Palestinian conflict from a battle between two nationalities into a war of civilizations that will engulf the world.

"It's a very tragic situation in which Christian fundamentalists, certain groups of them that focus on Armageddon and the Rapture and the role of a war between Muslims and Jews in bringing about the Second Coming, are involved in a *folie à deux* with extremist Jews," said Ian Lustick, a professor of political science at the University of Pennsylvania, a consultant on the Middle East to the last four presidential administrations and the author of the book *For the Land and the Lord: Jewish Fundamentalism in Israel.*

Whether the Bush administration is reflecting the views of the Christian right or responding to them is difficult to say, but some Mideast analysts are convinced they are seeing their effect played out in U.S. support for Sharon's hard-line policies. "I think in general it's safe to say Christian fundamentalism has an influence on the administration and specifically with regard to the Israeli-Palestinian conflict," said Kathleen Christison, a former CIA political analyst and the author of *Perceptions of Palestine: Their Influence on U.S. Middle East Policy.*

"There is a group of people in the Defense Department and in the vice president's office who are very, very pro-Israeli and very pro the Likud Party in Israel," said Christison, who named Deputy Defense Secretary Paul Wolfowitz; Undersecretary of Policy in the Defense Department Douglas Feith; adviser to the Defense Department Richard Perle; Vice President Cheney's chief of staff Lewis Libby Jr.; and Elliot Abrams on the National Security Council staff.

The United States' current and exclusive focus on Islamic fundamentalism is a case of what some argue is selective blindness.

"We pay a lot of attention to Islamic extremism, but we don't pay a lot of attention to Christian extremism or the extremism in the Jewish religion that is being used to justify what is going on today," said James Zogby, founder and president of the Arab American Institute in Washington, speaking about the turmoil in the Middle East. Zogby argues that despite disclaimers to the contrary the United States is waging a war on Islam at home and abroad even as it tacitly supports extremist settlers in the occupied territories Israel controls.

Since Sept. 11, suspected Muslim charities have been shut down by the U.S. government without the government offering any evidence that these charities have links to terrorists, Zogby said. At the same time, a known terrorist organization such as the Jewish Defense League is not placed on the government's list of terrorist organizations, he said.

"Without question, we are subsidizing those settlements. Money is money," said Zogby, noting that Israel is not only the largest recipient of U.S. foreign aid but the only country that receives its foreign aid in cash without going through the Agency For International Development and without being held accountable to the General Accounting Office for what it does with U.S. aid.

"We say settlements are unhelpful or counterproductive, but every single effort to sanction Israel for building settlements or to take international steps to stop Israel from building settlements, we block," Zogby said. "We're massive enablers of Israel's bad practices."

Ordinary people

Gershom Gorenberg, author of *The End of Days: Fundamentalism and the Struggle for the Temple Mount,* remarks that depictions of those who believe they are living in history's final days are often cartoonish, drawing too rigid a separation between mainstream religion and beliefs that are relegated to doomsday cult status. An American-born Israeli journalist who is an associate at the Center for Millennial Studies at Boston University, Gorenberg has studied the spectrum of Messianic belief both in Israel and in the United States.

"The fact is that millions of quite rational men and women, belonging to established religious movements around the globe, look forward to history's conclusion, to be followed by the establishment of a perfected era. They draw support from ideas deeply embedded in Western religion and culture. You don't need to go to central Africa to find them; they live in American suburbs; they work in insurance offices and high-tech startups. Some are influential leaders of America's Christian right," Gorenberg writes.

An article in the May 23 issue of *The Wall Street Journal* headlined, "How Israel Became a Favorite Cause of Christian Right," discusses the effects on U.S. foreign policy of the alliance between the Christian right and traditional supporters of Israel. "More than any other single factor, it explains why there has been so little pressure from a Republican White House on Israel to curb its crackdown on Palestinians," write *Wall Street Journal* reporters Tom Hamburger and Jim VandeHei.

In describing the transformation of the Republican Party by religious conservatives during the past 20 years, the two reporters detail how conservative Christian Republicans once suspected of intolerance and even anti-Semitism have become some of the staunchest supporters of Israel.

Ralph Reed, Pat Robertson, Jerry Falwell and a host of other conservative Christian leaders now lobby on behalf of Israel and support the most hard-line Israeli positions. Many fundamentalist Christian groups finance efforts to resettle Russian Jews in Israel, often in settlements in the occupied territories that offer settlers special tax breaks and financial inducements to move there.

"You have a number of very conservative Christian groups that support settlements because they see this as a way of strengthening Jewish hold on the land of Israel because in their mind this is important for end-of-time theology and part of hastening the Second Coming and the conversion of Jews that would be entailed in some of the theology. One would think that would be a good reason for conservative Jewish groups not to be involved with these groups, but they have made a pact to focus on political goals. They leave the proselytizing at the door when they entered into joint activity," said Lewis Roth, president of Americans for Peace Now, a U.S. branch of the Israeli movement Peace Now.

Esther Levens, president of the National Unity Coalition for Israel, an alliance of Christian and Jewish organizations founded in 1993–94 to support Israel, said the coalition has a hard-and-fast rule against members proselytizing. Beyond that, Levens said she doesn't probe too deeply into the reasons why many Christian groups have chosen to partner with the coalition.

But end-of-time theology is an important motive to many. For biblical literalists, particularly those who subscribe to dispensational premillennialism, a theology articulated by British preacher John Darby in the 19th century and popularized today by such books as Hal Lindsay's *The Late, Great Planet Earth or the Left Behind* books by the Rev. Tim LaHaye and Jerry B. Jenkins, the Rapture is near at hand in which Christ's faithful will be caught up in the clouds and given new, immortal bodies while the rest of the population faces the horrors of the last seven years of human history. Israel plays a key role in this theology, which posits that the Second Coming requires Israel to be reconstituted and the Jewish Temple, destroyed in 70 A.D., rebuilt. According to the script many Christian fundamentalists read from, the Antichrist will desecrate the rebuilt Temple, which will be followed by a period of tribulation when earthquakes, plagues and all the other furies outlined in the Book of Revelation will come to pass. This in turn will be followed by Jesus' return to earth. At that time, according to some Christians, those Jews who accept Jesus will enter the kingdom along with faithful Christians. Others will perish violently.

Jews have their own Messianic reading of the future. No apocalypse. No mass conversion of the Jews. No second coming of Jesus. For fundamentalist Jews, the establishment of the state of Israel and the extension of its sovereignty to the West Bank, Gaza and even further, is part of the process of world redemption. Eventually, Jewish rule will extend beyond the borders of the present state of Israel to the entire land of Israel described in the Hebrew Scriptures, the Temple will be rebuilt, and the Messiah will arrive, ushering in the redemption of the world.

For both fundamentalist Christians and Jews, an end to human history as we know it is connected to a transcendent imperative that necessitates actions that others see as risky, provocative and aggressive. For both groups, Israeli settlers are the vanguard troops in a campaign of action rooted in believers' reading of the Bible.

"Certainly Jewish messianism inspires this sort of affinity and sense of entitlement to these territories and to the land of Israel itself," said Geoffrey Aronson of the Foundation for Middle East Peace, a nonprofit organization in Washington that tracks the growth of settlements in the occupied territories. "That idea, that the Bible has some sort of contemporary relevance to Israel's territorial breadth and extent, is reality. It affects the entire political spectrum that one of the basic presumptions of the Israeli Jewish community is that they live and claim title to the state of Israel and perhaps areas beyond it by right, and it's a right that's recognized in the Bible. Ultimately, this sort of idea has been a very important motivator of the Jewish community in Palestine for the past hundred years," said Aronson.

The Bible as property deed

While the notion of biblical entitlement to the land of Israel was latent in the founding of the state of Israel, religious claims were soft-pedaled by early Zionist leaders. Opposed by many Orthodox Jews who believed it violated the rabbinic injunction to avoid human efforts to bring redemption, Zionism was a predominantly secular movement that appealed to Jews and non-Jews alike by arguing that providing Jews a homeland of their own would end Jews' condition as a persecuted minority and make Jews into a people like any other.

If arguably a streak of secular Messianism underlay the Zionist enterprise, it was the Six Day War in 1967 and the swift and surprising victory Israel achieved in that war, doubling in less than a week the amount of territory it controlled, including the prized city of old Jerusalem, that provided the impetus for the settler movement and the development of a Jewish fundamentalism that had been largely dormant for 18 centuries.

Even secular Israelis regarded the victory as a kind of miracle while for others, especially religious Zionists, the conquest of the West Bank was proof of a divine plan at work. "As never before, Messianism became a respected ideology, powering the movement that settled Jews across the West Bank," Gorenberg writes. He adds that Israel's victory became part of another story, too: the resurgence of Christian fundamentalism in the last third of the 20th century.

"The Jewish conquest of Jerusalem provided 'proof' of premillennial doctrine. It amplified hopes for the Second Coming; it spurred some people to predict just when the great event would take place. …

"Christian millennialists eagerly watched the Middle East for more signs. In time, some moved from being onlookers to being participants, offering support to Israel – or to the Israelis deemed most likely to make prophecy come true," Gorenberg writes.

Now some conservative Christians not only raise money for Israel, they meet in breakfasts and monthly briefings organized by the Israeli Embassy and participate in schemes to build the third Temple in Jerusalem. In 1998, for instance, the Canaan Land Restoration Inc. of Israel was established by Clyde Lott, an American cattleman and a Pentecostal minister.

Responding to verses in the Book of Numbers that say only the ashes of an unblemished red heifer that has never been yoked can purify a priest to enter the Temple, Lott joined forces with Rabbi Chaim Richman in Israel in an effort to raise red cattle suitable for Old Testament sacrifices. An Internet page for the Canaan Land Restoration, Inc., solicited tax-deductible contributions that would cover the costs of shipping red cows from the United States to Israel. Lott's project is now idle because of internal problems and fear of an impending war, but Dean Hubbard, the vice president of the now-bankrupt organization, said the idea is to regroup and refocus when they can. "It's staggering to see how it's all on schedule," Dean Hubbard said of the pace of world events.

The Web site of one Christian Zionist organization states that "Today, tens of millions of Protestant Christians in the United States and more around the world support Israel with an uncritical fervor, exceeding even Jewish support."

"There are a lot of forces at work here," said Jim Besser, a writer for *The New York Jewish Week* and *The Baltimore Jewish Times*. "There are evangelical Christians who support Israel simply because they believe it is biblically mandated for them to do so. There are also those who support the right wing in Israel because of their views of the end-time prophecies. They believe Israel will play a central role just by view of getting destroyed. These are not necessarily distinctive groups. There are different motivations. The third element of the equation is that a lot of political conservatives are increasingly supporting the right wing in Israel because of purely geopolitical reasons. They see Israel as the front line in the battle against terrorism and Islamic fundamentalism," Besser said.

Not all evangelical Christians are unqualified supporters of Israel, of course. A letter sent to President Bush from 40 evangelical Christian leaders this past summer called upon him to employ an even-handed policy toward Israeli and Palestinian leadership and noted that the "American evangelical community is not a monolithic bloc in full and firm support of present Israeli policy."

Still, many of the most prominent names in the evangelical world support Israel unconditionally and are opposed to Israel negotiating a peace agreement with the Palestinians.

"The feeling among evangelicals is that any effort to create peace in the Middle East is ultimately a trick," Besser said. "If you pick up any of Hal Lindsay's books or Pat Robertson's books, it's all laid out there in quite a lot of detail by many of these popular evangelical authors. The demands of these prophecies are very much in the minds of many of these evangelicals who are so vocal in their support of Israel right now."

The intransigence of certain Christian fundamentalists mirrors that of many right-wing Israelis, notably the ultra-nationalist religious settlers on the West Bank who view the conquest of the West Bank as part of a plan for divine redemption and who oppose a peace settlement that would involve Israel ceding any inch of territory it controls. For many of these settlers, rebuilding the Temple, an activity that would almost inevitably involve the destruction of the Dome of the Rock, Islam's third-holiest site, which is believed to lie on the ruins of the old Temple, has become a rallying cry.

A little-known force

In his book *For the Land and the Lord,* Ian Lustick writes that Americans and Israelis alike share a dangerous ignorance of the animating beliefs of Jewish fundamentalists despite the importance fundamentalists have assumed on the Israeli political scene since 1967.

Haim Dov Beliak seconds that statement. A rabbi in California, Beliak studied at the Merkaz Harav yeshiva in Israel. Headed by the messianic Rabbi Tzvi Yehudah Kook, the yeshiva was at the ideological center of the settler movement in the 1970s when Beliak attended it. According to Beliak, neither the Jewish community in the United States nor the American public at large knows much about the settlers. "There is a profound lack of curiosity about them," Beliak said. "They are very problematic because they are going to cause World War III. They are not dealing with a normal political reality. There's a complete denial of any rights that the Arabs might have."

"Many of these settlers simply want to come in where Palestinians are living and say a Jew lived here 75 years ago so they should be living here now, or that 1,500 years ago Jews controlled the land so Jews now should control the land. There's an attempt to use the Bible as a land deed claim," said Beliak.

If Christian scenarios of the end of time involving the anti-Christ and Armageddon sometimes seem outlandish or bizarre, fundamentalist Jewish schemes for redemption can appear no less so. Beliak reported efforts underway by some Zionist groups to track down the Ten Lost Tribes of Israel, who disappeared in 276 B.C. when they were carried off into captivity. Scouts are looking for the descendents of these tribes in Africa and Asia, and a group of people in Burma and another in Peru are being seriously investigated.

"The lengths of this search is almost comical," Beliak said. "The hope is that these people will discover their Jewishness, reconvert to Judaism and therefore they will need a place to live and then it will be legitimate to displace the Arabs who are living [in the occupied territories.] …

"It is fantastic the lengths of religious nationalistic jingoism these people are prepared to go to," said Beliak.

Beliak and others distinguish between those settlers who move to the West Bank and Gaza for ideological reasons and those who are drawn by the economic inducements offered them and who would resettle if similar opportunities were provided elsewhere. It's the first and smaller group that forms the core of the settler movement: Israelis who because of fundamentalist religious views or extreme nationalism believe all of the occupied territories should be incorporated into the state of Israel, despite the Arab population living there.

Practically speaking, there is no distinction between the settler movement and the current Israeli government headed by Prime Minister Ariel Sharon, Beliak said.

"Sharon is the architect of the settler movement, and he's the practical engineer of the idea that there is no room for the Arabs to live between the Jordan River and the Mediterranean Sea in their own political entity," Beliak said. "They can live there as laborers and choppers of wood and drawers of water but only if they eschew any political aspirations."

According to Peace Now, since February 2001 when Prime Minister Ariel Sharon took office, 34 new settlements have been established in the occupied territories. Close to 400,000 settlers now live in East Jerusalem, the West Bank, and Gaza, and their presence poses what many analysts call the biggest obstacle to peace between Israelis and Palestinians.

The growth and entrenchment of the settlers, whose population has doubled since the 1993 Oslo Peace Accords were signed, have proved to be Jewish fundamentalists' greatest success. But Ian Lustick said fundamentalists in Israel have experienced reverses, too, notably the peace accords themselves and the 1995 assassination of Yitzhak Rabin.

"The peace process showed they actually had to assassinate an Israeli leader to stop a Palestinian state from emerging," Lustick said. "The need to rely on spectacular violence is something they wanted to avoid relying on. They wanted to naturalize Israeli rule over the whole of Greater Israel and to trivialize the question of the Arabs. The intifada, the first and second one, has made it impossible for Israelis to not see the Arabs, to see the West Bank and Gaza as just extensions of Israel."

Lustick called settlements the main reason for the failure of the Camp David negotiations.

"Barak was proposing at Camp David that all settlements and all roads leading to them would remain under Israeli sovereignty. That was the achievement of the settlers' movement, that even a dovish prime minister would begin a peace conference with such a hawkish and unworkable proposal, therefore leading to the second intifada and the current disastrous circumstances we see today," Lustick said.

A worldwide phenomenon

Reading the Bible as a set of predictions about the future sends chills through many mainstream theologians. "No reputable Catholic theologian or certainly no reputable mainline Protestant theologian would look at the Bible this way," said Jesuit Fr. John R. Sachs, who teaches at Weston Jesuit School of Theology near Boston. Americans' growing interest in the apocalypse forms part of a worldwide phenomenon, said Sachs, with conservative, literalistic, fundamentalistic movements in religion taking place in vast areas of the world today.

Decrying Christian fundamentalist theology and its influence on U.S. Mideast policy strikes Baylor University professor Marc Ellis as hypocritical, even though Ellis acknowledges he would like to see the political sway of fundamentalists curtailed.

"Most of the Christian and Jewish support for the state of Israel has come from liberal sources. Now liberal Christians are beginning to understand that something is wrong with those policies, but those policies have already had their effect," said Ellis.

A professor of American and Jewish studies at Baylor, Ellis points out that if some fundamentalist Christians promote the state of Israel, so too in the past did prominent liberal theologians such as Reinhold Niebuhr and other Christians, if for different reasons.

"Liberal Christians supported Israel out of guilt over the Holocaust. Fundamentalist Christians have supported Israel because of biblical eschatology," said Ellis.

"Jews were the vehicle through which Christians renewed their own theology after the Holocaust: the recovery of the Hebrew Bible that had been so denigrated in Christian theology, the recovery of the prophets, the Jewishness of Jesus. Jews were seen as carriers of those values that Christians needed to embrace," Ellis said. "It's about how Christianity renewed itself in the face of atrocities it was responsible for. Jews were elevated where once they were demeaned."

What Ellis called "the political naiveté" of liberal Christians who saw Jews only as innocents has played a large role in contributing to a steady deterioration in the conditions Palestinians live in that he said threatens to get worse still if the United States invades Iraq.

"It's been getting worse from the beginning, since 1948, and it's been getting worse since 1993 when Oslo was signed. Everything that has been gained since 1993 has been wiped out in the last two years. Now there are three million Palestinians on the West Bank who are in virtual prison, or worse. They are under closure. No one delivers their food. You have an entire population in prison but without the perks of prison," said Ellis.

Margot Patterson is senior writer at the National Catholic Reporter. Her e-mail address is mpatterson@natcath.org

(Can we talk?)
Jewish Power

by Paul Eisen

The crime against the Palestinian people is being committed by a Jewish state with Jewish soldiers using weapons displaying Jewish religious symbols, and with the full support and complicity of the overwhelming mass of organised Jews world-wide. But to name Jews as responsible for this crime seems impossible to do.

The future is always open and nothing can ever be ruled out; but, for now, it's hard to see how Israel can be stopped. After over fifty years, it is clear that Israel will only relinquish its eliminationist attitude to Palestinians and Palestinian life when it has to. This need not be through military action but it is hard to see how anything else will do. The conventional wisdom – that if America turned off the tap, Israel would be brought to its knees – is far from proven. First, it's not going to happen. Second, those who believe it, may well be underestimating both the cohesiveness of Israeli society and the force of Jewish history which permeates it. Even more unlikely is the military option. The only force on earth which could possibly confront Israel is the American military, and, again, that is not going to happen.

Palestinian resistance has been astonishing. After over fifty years of brutal assault by what may well one day be seen as one of the most ruthless and irrational powers of modern times, and with just about every power on earth ranged against them, Palestinians are still with us, still steadfast, still knowing who they are and where they come from. Nonetheless, for the time being effective resistance may be over (though the possibility of organised non-violent resistance can never be ruled out), and, for now, the only strategy open may be no more than one for survival.

For us it is so much easier to deny this reality than to accept it, and doubtless the struggle will continue. How fruitful this will be no one can say. Although the present seems hopeless, survival is still vital and no-one knows when new opportunities may arise. Anyway, to struggle against injustice is always worth doing. But what if the struggle becomes so delusional that it inhibits rather than advances resistance? What if the struggle becomes a way of avoiding rather than confronting reality? Those slogans "End the Occupation!" and "Two States for Two Peoples!" are now joined by a new slogan, "*The One-State Solution!*" This is every bit as fantastic as its predecessors because, just as there never was going to be an end to the occupation, nor a real Palestinian state, so, for now, there is no possibility of any "one state" other than the state of Israel which now stretches from the Mediterranean Sea to the Jordan River, and the only "solution" is a final solution and even that cannot be ruled out.

"Zionism is not Judaism; Judaism is not Zionism...."

The crime against the Palestinian people is being committed by a Jewish state with Jewish soldiers using weapons with Jewish religious symbols all over them, and with the full support and complicity of the overwhelming mass of organised Jews worldwide. But to name Jews as responsible for this crime seems impossible to do. The past is just too terrible. All of us know of the hatred and violence to which accusations against Jews have led in the past. Also, if we were to examine critically the role of Jews in this conflict, what would become of us and of our struggle? Would we be labelled anti-Semites and lose much of the support that we have worked so hard to gain?

The present, too, is full of ambiguities. *Zionism is not Judaism; Judaism is not Zionism* has become an article of faith, endlessly repeated, as is the assertion that Zionism is a secular ideology opposed, for much of its history, by the bulk of religious Jews and even now still opposed by true Torah Jews such as Neturei Karta. But Zionism is now at the heart of Jewish life with religious Jews amongst the most virulent of Zionists and Neturei Karta, despite their impeccable anti-Zionism, their beautiful words and the enthusiasm with which they are welcomed at solidarity rallies, etc., may well be a million miles from the reality of Jewish life.

And even if Zionism can still be disentangled from Judaism, can it be distinguished from a broader Jewish identity or *Jewishness?* So often Zionism is proclaimed to be a modern add-on to Jewish identity, another, albeit anachronistic, settler-colonial ideology simply adopted by Jews in response to their predicament. But, could it be that our need to avoid the accusation of anti-Semitism and our own conflicted perceptions and feelings, our insistence that Zionism and Jewishness are separate, has led us seriously to misunderstand the situation? Has our refusal to look squarely at the very *Jewishness* of Zionism and its crimes caused us to fail to understand exactly what we are up against?

Jews, Judaism and Zionism

Jews are complex; Jewish identity is complex and the relationship between Judaism the religion, and a broader, often secular, Jewish identity or Jewishness is very complex indeed. Jewishness may be experienced a long way from synagogue, *yeshiva* or any other formal aspect of Jewish religious life, yet is often still inextricably bound to Judaism. That is why secular Jews are able to proclaim their secularity every bit as loudly as they proclaim their Jewishness. Marc Ellis, a religious Jew, says that when you look at those Jews who are in solidarity with Palestinians, the overwhelming majority of them are secular – but, from a religious point of view, the Covenant is with *them*. For Ellis, these secular Jews unknowingly and even unwillingly may be carrying with them the future of Jewish life.

Jewish identity, connecting Jews to other Jews, comes from deep within Jewish history. This is a shared history, both real and imagined, in that it is both literal and theological. Many Jews in the west share a real history of living together as a distinct people in Eastern, Central and then Western Europe and America. Others share a real history of settlement in Spain followed by expulsion and then settlement all over the world, particularly in Arab and Islamic lands. But this may not be what binds *all* Jews, because for *all* Jews it is not a real, but maybe a theological, history that is shared. Most Palestinians today probably have more Hebrew blood in their little fingers then most western Jews have in their whole bodies. And yet, the story of the Exodus from Egypt is as real to many of them, and most importantly was as real to them when they were children, as if they, along with all Jews, had stood with Moses at the foot of Mount Sinai.

And histories like that don't stop at the present. Even for secular Jews, though unacknowledged and even unrealized, there is a sense, not only of a shared history, but also of a shared destiny. Central to Jewish identity both religious and non-religious is the sense of mission centered on exile and return. How else to explain the extraordinary devotion of so many Jews, religious and secular, to the "return" to a land with which, in real terms, they have very little connection at all?

For many Jews, this history confers a 'specialness'. This is not unique to Jews – after all, who in their heart of hearts does not feel a little bit special? But for Jews this specialness is at the centre of their self-identification and much of the world seems to concur. For religious Jews, the specialness comes from the supposed covenant with God. But for secular Jews, the specialness comes from a special history. In either case this can be a good, even a beautiful, thing. In much of Jewish religious tradition this specialness is no more than a special moral obligation, a special responsibility to offer an example to the world, and for so many secular Jews it has led them to struggle for justice in many places around the world.

At the heart of this Jewish specialness is Jewish suffering and victim-hood. Like the shared history itself, this suffering may, but need not, correspond to reality. Jews have certainly suffered but their suffer-ing remains unexamined and unexplained. The Holocaust, now the paradigm of Jewish suffering, has long ceased to be a piece of his-tory, and is now treated by religious and secular alike, as a piece of theology – a sacred text almost – and therefore beyond scrutiny. And the suffering never ends. No matter how much Jews have suffered they are certainly not suffering now, but for many Jews their history of suffering is not just an unchallengeable past but also a possible future. So, no matter how safe Jews may be, many feel just a hair's-breadth away from Auschwitz.

Zionism is at the heart of this. Zionism is also complex and also comes from deep within Jewish history with the same sense of ex-ile and return. Zionism also confirms that Jews are special in their suffering and is explicit that Jews should 'return' to a land given to them, and only them – by God if they are religious, or by history if they are not – because they simply are not safe anywhere else on earth.

But so what? If Jews think that they are a people with a religious link to a land and have a deep wish to 'return', why should we care, so long as the land is not already populated by Palestinians? And if Jews feel that they are special and that God has made some kind of special arrangement with them, so what, so long as this does not lead them to demand preferential treatment and to discriminate against others? And if Jews feel that they have suffered like no-one else on the face of the earth, fine, so long as they do not use this suffering to justify the imposition of suffering on others and to blackmail morally the whole world into quiescent silence.

This is the problem with Zionism. It expresses Jewish identity but also empowers it. It tells Jews (and many others too) that Jews can do what Jews have always dreamed of doing. It takes the perfectly acceptable religious feelings of Jews, or if you prefer, the perfectly harmless delusions of Jews, and tries to turn them into a terrible reality. Jewish notions of specialness, choseness and even supremacism, are fine for a small, wandering people, but, when empowered with a state, an army and F16s become a concern for us all.

Zionism as Jewish empowerment in statehood changes everything. Israel is not just any state, it is a Jewish state and this means more than just a state for Jews. This Jewish state is built on traditions and modes of thought that have evolved amongst Jews for centuries – amongst which are the notions that Jews are special and that their suffering is special. By their own reckoning, Jews are "a nation that dwells alone" it is "us and them" and, in many cases, "us *or* them". And these tendencies are translated into the modern state of Israel. This is a state that knows no boundaries. It is a state that both believes, and uses as justification for its own aggression, the notion that its very survival is always at stake, so anything is justified to ensure that survival. Israel is a state that manifestly believes that the rules of both law and humanity, applicable to all other states, do not apply to it.

Their Own Worst Nightmare

It is a terrible irony that this empowerment of Jews has come to most resemble those empowerments under which Jews have suffered the most. Empowered Christianity, also a marriage of faith and power, enforced its ideology and pursued its dissidents and enemies with no greater fervor than has empowered Judaism. In its zeal and self-belief, Zionism has come to resemble the most brutal and relentless of modern ideologies. But unlike the brutal rationality of Stalinism, willing to sacrifice millions for political and economic revolution, this Jewish ideology, in its zealotry and irrationality, resembles more the National Socialism which condemned millions for the attainment of a nonsensical racial and ethnic supremacy.

Of course there are differences but there are also similarities. National Socialism, like Zionism, another blend of mysticism and power, gained credibility as a means to right wrongs done to a victimized people. National Socialism, like Zionism, also sought to maintain the racial/ethnic purity of one group and to maintain the rights of that ethnic group over others, and National Socialism, like Zionism, also proposed an almost mystical attachment of that group to a land. Also, both National Socialism and Zionism shared a common interest – to separate Jews from non-Jews, in this case to remove Jews from Europe – and actively co-operated in the attainment of this aim. And if the similarity between these two ideologies is simply too great and too bitter to accept, one may ask what National Socialism with its uniforms, flags and mobilized youth must have looked like to those Germans, desperate after Versailles and the ravages of post-First World War Germany. Perhaps not so different from how the uniforms, flags and marching youth of pre- and post-state Zionism must have looked to Jews after their history of suffering, and particularly after the Holocaust.

This is, for Jews, their own worst nightmare: the thing they love the most has become the thing they hate the most. And for those Jews and others, who shrink from the comparison, let them ask themselves this: What would an average German, an enthusiastic Nazi even, have said in, say, 1938 had they been confronted with the possibility of an Auschwitz? They would have thought that you were stark, staring mad.

American Jews and Jewish America

At the heart of the conflict is the relationship between Israel and America. The statistics – billions in aid and loans, UN vetoes, etc., etc. need not be repeated here – American support for Israel seems limitless. But what is the nature of this support? For many, perhaps most, the answer is relatively simple. Israel is a client state of America, serving American interests or, more particularly, the interests of its power elites. This view is underpinned by the obvious importance of oil, the huge strategic importance of the region and the fact that, if Israel did not further the interests of those who control America, then we can be sure America would not support Israel. Also, there is no doubt that, in the IDF, America has found a marvellously flexible and effective force, easily aroused and let loose whenever any group of Arabs get a little above themselves.

But is this the whole story? Does Israel really serve America's interests and is their relationship wholly based on the sharing of these interests? Consider how much in terms of goodwill from other nations America *loses* by its support for Israel, and consider the power and influence of the "Jewish", "Zionist" or "pro-Israel" lobby, as when many an otherwise responsible lawmaker, faced with the prospect of an intervention in their re-election campaign from the Jewish lobby, seems happy to put his or her re-election prospects way in front of what is good for America.

The details of the workings of AIPAC and others, and the mechanics by which these groups exert pressure on America's lawmakers and governors, have been dealt with elsewhere; we need only note that this interest group is undoubtedly extraordinarily effective and successful. Not just a small group of Jews supporting Israel, as its supporters would have us believe, these are powerful and committed ideologues: billionaires, media magnates, politicians, activists and religious leaders. In any event, the power of the Jewish lobby to make or break pretty well any public figure is legendary – not for nothing is it often referred to simply as "The Lobby".

But again, there may be far more to the Israel/U.S. relationship than just a commonality of interest and the effectiveness of certain interest groups. That support for Israel must be in the interests of those who control America is certainly true, but who controls America? Perhaps the real relationship is not between Israel and America but between Jews and America.

The overwhelming majority of Jews in America live their lives just like any other Americans. They've done well and are undoubtedly pleased that America supports their fellow Jews in Israel but that's as far as it goes. Nonetheless, an awful lot of Jews certainly do control an awful lot of America – not the industrial muscle of America – the steel, transport, etc., nor the oil and arms industries, those traditional money-spinners. No, if Jews have influence anywhere in America, it's not over its muscle and sinew but over its blood and its brain. It is in finance and the media that we find a great many Jews in very influential positions. Lists abound (though you have to go to some pretty unpopular websites to find them) of Jews, prominent in financial and cultural life: Jews in banks; Jews in Forbes Magazine's Richest Americans; Jews in Hollywood; Jews in TV; Jewish journalists, writers, critics, etc.,

Nor have Jews been slow in exploiting their position. Jews have not hesitated to use whatever resources they have to advance their interests as they see them. Nor does one need to subscribe to any conspiracy theory to note how natural it is for Jews in the media to promote Jews and their values as positive and worthy of emulation. When did anyone last see a Jew portrayed in anything other than a favourable light? Jews are clever, moral, interesting, intense, warm, witty, complex, ethical, contradictory, prophetic, infuriating, sometimes irritating, but always utterly engaging. Nor is it any wonder that Jews in influential positions are inclined to promote what they see as Jewish collective interests. Is it really all that incredible that Jewish advisers around the Presidency bear Israel's interests at heart when they advise the President on foreign affairs?

But so what? So there are a lot of Jews with a lot of money, and a lot of Jews with a lot to say and the means to say it. If Jews by virtue of their ability and use of resources (as honestly gained as by anyone else) promote what they perceive as their own collective interest, what's wrong with that? First, with some notable exceptions, the vast majority of Jews can, in good faith, lay hands on hearts and swear that they never take decisions or actions with collective Jewish interests in mind, certainly not consciously. And even if they did, they are acting no differently from anyone else. With a few exceptions, Jews have earned their advantageous positions. They came with nothing, played according to the rules and, if they use their influence to further what they perceive as Jewish interests, what's so special about that? Do not the Poles, the Ukrainians, the Gun lobby, the Christian Evangelicals also not work to further their group interests?

The difference between Jews and other groups is that they probably do it better. Jews are, by pretty well any criteria, easily the most successful ethnic group in America and, for whatever reason, have been extraordinarily successful in promoting themselves both individually and collectively. And there would probably be nothing wrong with this were it not for the fact that these same people who exert so much control and influence over American life also seem to refuse to be held accountable. It is the surreptitiousness with which Jews are perceived to have achieved their success that arouses suspicion. Jews certainly seem cagey about the influence they have. Just breathe the words "Jewish power" and wait for the reaction. They claim it's because this charge has so often been used as a precursor to discrimination and violence against them, but never consider the possibility that their own reluctance to discuss the power they wield arouses suspicion and even hostility.

But there is another claim, subtler and more worrying. This is that *it doesn't exist;* that Jews do not wield power, that there is no Jewish lobby; that Jews in America do not exert power and influence to advance Jewish interests, even *that there are no such things as Jewish interests!* There are no Jewish interests in the war in Iraq, there are no Jewish interests in America; most amazing, there are no Jewish interests even in Israel and Palestine. There is no Jewish collective. Jews do not act together to advance their aims. They even say that the pro-Israeli lobby has actually not all that much to do with Jews, that the Jewishness of Israel is irrelevant and the Public Affairs Committees (PACs) which lobby so hard for Israel are in fact doing no more than supporting an ally and thus looking after America's best interests even to the extent of concealing their true purpose behind names such as "American for Better Citizenship", "Citizen's Organised PAC" or the "National PAC" – none of which make one reference in their titles to Israel, Zionism or Jews. Similarly, Jews and Jewish organisations are said to be not so much furthering Jewish interests and values as American, or, even, universal interests and values. So, the major Holocaust Museum, styled as a "Museum of Tolerance", focuses not only on anti-Semitism, but on every kind of intolerance known to mankind (except that shown by Jews to non-Jews in Israel and Palestine). Similarly, the Anti-Defamation League is but an organisation for the promotion of universal principles of tolerance and justice, not just for Jews but for everyone.

This conflation of Jewish interests with American interests is no-where more stark than in present American foreign policy. If ever an image was reminiscent of a Jewish world conspiracy, the spectacle of the Jewish neo-cons gathered around the current presidency and directing policy in the Middle East, this must be it. But we are told that the fact that the Jewish neo-cons, many with links with right wing political groups within Israel, are in the forefront of urging a pro-Israel policy, is but a coincidence, and any suggestion that these figures might be influenced by their Jewishness and their links with Israel is immediately marginalised as reviving old anti-Semitic myths about Jewish dual loyalty. The idea that American intervention in Iraq, the one viable military counterweight to Israeli hegemony in the Middle East and therefore an inspiration to Arab and Palestinian resistance, primarily serves Israeli rather than American interests has also been consigned to the nether world of mediaeval anti-Semitic myth. The suggestion that those Jews around the president act from motives other than those to promote the interests of all Americans is just anti-Semitic raving. And maybe they're right. Perhaps those who promote Jewish interests are in fact promoting American interests because, for now at least, they appear to be one and the same.

Jewish America

In Washington, D.C. is a memorial to a terrible tragedy. Not a memorial to a tragedy visited on Americans by a foreign power as at Pearl Harbour or 9/11, nor to a tragedy visited by Americans on Americans such the sacking of Atlanta. Nor is it a memorial of contrition to a tragedy inflicted by Americans onto another people, such as to slavery or to the history of racial injustice in America. It is to none of these. The Holocaust memorial is to a tragedy inflicted *on* people who were not Americans, *by* people who were not Americans, and *in* a place a very long way from America. And the co-religionists or, even, if you like, the co-nationals, of the people on whom the tragedy was visited and to whom the memorial is built make up around two percent of the American population. How is it that a group of people who make up such a tiny percentage of the overall American population can command such respect and regard that a memorial to them is built in the symbolic heart of American national life?

The Jewish narrative is now at the centre of American life, certainly that of its cultural and political elites. There is, anyway, much in the way that Americans choose to see themselves and their history which is quite naturally compatible with the way Jews see themselves and their history. What more fitting paradigm for a country founded on immigration, than the story of the mass immigration of Jews at the end of the nineteenth and early twentieth centuries? For many Americans, the story of those Jews who came to their Goldenes Medina, their Golden Land, with nothing and, through hard work and perseverance, made it to the very top of American society, is also their story. And what could be more inspirational for a country, if not officially but still viscerally, deeply Christian than the story of the Jews, Jesus' own people and God's chosen people, returning to their ancient homeland and transforming it into a modern state. And for a nation which sees itself as a beacon of democracy in the world, what better international soul-mate than the state of Israel, widely held to be "the only democracy in the Middle-East"? Finally what greater validation for a country itself founded on a narrative of conquest and ethnic cleansing than the Biblical narrative of the conquest and ethnic cleansing of the Promised Land with the addition of the equally violent settlement of modern Palestine with its own ethnic cleansing and then "making the desert bloom"?

Most resonant, of course, is the notion of Jews as a suffering people. The fact that this "suffering people" is now enjoying a success beyond the dreams of any other ethnic group in America seems irrelevant. Also ignored is how American Jews have made it to the very top of American society whilst, every step of the way, complaining about how much they're being discriminated against. Nonetheless, to America, Jews have an enduring and ongoing history of suffering and victimhood. But this history has rarely been examined or even discussed.

A Suffering People

That Jews have suffered is undeniable, but Jewish suffering is claimed to have been so enduring, so intense and so particular that it is to be treated differently from other sufferings. The issue is complex and cannot be fully debated or decided here but the following points may stimulate thought and discussion.

- During even the most terrible times of Jewish suffering such as the Crusades or the Chmielnitzky massacres of seventeenth century Ukraine, and even more so at other times in history, it has been said that the average peasant would have given his eye-teeth to be a Jew. The meaning is clear: generally speaking, and throughout most of their history, the condition of Jews was often far superior to the mass of the population.

- The above-mentioned Ukrainian massacres took place in the context of a peasant uprising against the oppression of the Ukrainian peasantry by their Polish overlords. As has often been the case, Jews were seen as occupying a traditional position of being in alliance with the ruling class in their oppression of the peasantry. Chmielnitzky, the leader of this popular uprising, is today a Ukrainian national hero, not for his assaults on Jews (there are even references to his having offered poor Jews to join the uprising against their exploitative co-religionists – the Jews declined) but for his championing of the rights of the oppressed Ukrainians. Again, the inference is plain: outbreaks of anti-Semitic violence, though never justified, have often been responses to Jewish behaviour both real and imaginary.

- In the Holocaust three million Polish Jews died, but so did three million non-Jewish Poles. Jews were targeted but so were Gypsies, homosexuals, Slavs and Poles. Similarly, the Church burned Jews for their dissenting beliefs but then the church burned everyone for their dissenting beliefs. So again, the question must be asked: what's so special about Jewish suffering?

The Holocaust, the paradigm for all anti-Semitism and all Jewish suffering, is treated as being beyond examination and scrutiny. Questioning the Holocaust narrative is, at best, socially unacceptable, leading often to social exclusion and discrimination, and, at worst, in some places is illegal and subject to severe penalty. Holocaust revisionist scholars, named Holocaust deniers by their opponents, have challenged this. They do not deny a brutal and extensive assault on Jews by the Nazi regime but they do deny the Holocaust narrative as framed by present day establishments and elites. Specifically, their denial is limited to three main areas. First, they deny that there ever was an official plan on the part of Hitler or any other part of the Nazi regime systematically and physically to eliminate every Jew in Europe; second, they deny that there ever existed homicidal gas-chambers; third, they claim that the numbers of Jewish victims of the Nazi assault have been greatly exaggerated.

But none of this is the point. Whether those who question the Holocaust narrative are revisionist scholars striving to find the truth and shamelessly persecuted for opposing a powerful faction, or whether they are crazy Jew-haters denying a tragedy and defaming its victims, the fact is that one may question the Armenian genocide, one may freely discuss the Slave Trade, one can say that the murder of millions of Ibos, Kampucheans and Rwandans never took place and that the moon is but a piece of green cheese floating in space, but one may not question the Jewish Holocaust. Why? Because, like the rest of the Jewish history of suffering, the Holocaust underpins the narrative of Jewish innocence which is used to bewilder and befuddle any attempt to see and to comprehend Jewish power and responsibility in Israel/Palestine and elsewhere in the world.

Jewish Power

What is a Jew? Israel Shamir, the Russian-born Israeli writer, advocates the right of all people, whatever their ethnicity or religion, to live together in complete equality between the Mediterranean and the Jordan River. Shamir condemns the behaviour of Israel and of Diaspora Jews and calls for an end to their preferential treatment, but he also proposes an opposition to Judaism itself for which he stands accused of being anti-Jewish – a charge he does not deny but actually embraces.

Shamir proposes the existence of a Jewish ideology, or "Jewish paradigm" as he puts it, and proposes that it is the voluntary adherence to this "spirit" which makes a Jew into a Jew. For him, Jewishness is neither race nor ethnicity – there is, for Shamir, no such thing as a Jewish 'tribe' or 'family' – no biological or ethnic body from which there can be no escape. Further, this ideology, based on notions of choseness, exclusivity and even supremacism is, at least when empowered, incompatible with peace, equality and justice in Palestine or anywhere else for that matter.

No-one wants to oppose any Jews simply for being Jews, or even for what they believe, but only because of what they do. The problem is that since, according to Shamir, what Jews believe and even do is precisely what makes them into Jews, so opposition to Jewishness as an ideology surely comes dangerously close to opposition to Jews simply for being Jews. But for Shamir, Jews are Jews because they choose to be Jews. Someone may be born of Jews and raised as a Jew but they can if they wish reject their Jewish upbringing and become a non-Jew. And many have done just that including such famous escapees as Karl Marx, St. Paul, Leon Trotsky (and Shamir himself), etc. Opposition to Jews is not, therefore, like opposition to Blacks or to Asians or to other common racist attitudes since the object of the opposition is perfectly able to relinquish the ideology in question.

Shamir has never in any way called for any harm to be done to Jews or anyone else, nor for Jews or anyone else to be discriminated against in any way. Adherence to this Jewish ideology is, for Shamir, regrettable, but not, in itself, a matter for active opposition. Nor does this mean that Shamir is opposed to any individual Jew just because he or she is a Jew. What Shamir actively opposes is not "Jews" but "Jewry". Analogous to say, the Catholic Church, Jewry consists of those organised Jews and their leaders who actively promote corrosive Jewish interests and values, particularly now in the oppression of the Palestinians

One doesn't have to be in complete agreement with Shamir to understand what he is talking about. Why should Jews not have a "spirit"; after all, such a concept has been discussed with regard to other nations?

"It is dangerous, wrong, to speak about the "Germans," or any other people, as of a single undifferentiated entity, and include all individuals in one judgement. And yet I don't think I would deny that there exists a spirit of each people (otherwise it would not be a people) a Deutschtum, an italianita, an hispanidad: they are the sums of traditions, customs, history, language, and culture. Whoever does not feel within himself this spirit, which is national in the best sense of the word, not only does not entirely belong to his own people but is not part of human civilization. Therefore, while I consider insensate the syllogism, "All Italians are passionate; you are Italian; therefore you are passionate," I do however believe it legitimate, within certain limits, to expect from Italians taken as a whole, or from Germans, etc., one specific, collective behavior rather than another. There will certainly be individual exceptions, but a prudent, probabilistic forecast is in my opinion possible." –Primo Levi

And for Jews it is, perhaps, even more appropriate. The place of Judaism as an ideology at the centre for all Jewish identity may be debated, but few would dispute that Judaism is at least at the historic heart of Jewishness and, whatever else may bind Jews together, it is certainly true that religion plays an important part. Second, for a group of people who have retained such a strong collective identity with no shared occupation of any land, language, nor even, in many cases, a culture, it is hard to see what else there could be that makes Jews into Jews. Surely for Jews, in the absence of other, more obvious factors, it is precisely such a spirit that has enabled them to retain their distinctive identity for so long and in the face of such opposition.

But if there is some kind of Jewish spirit or ideology, what is it? As far as Judaism, the religion, goes it seems fairly clear that there is an ideology based on the election of Israel by God, the special relationship Jews are supposed to have with God and the special mission allocated to Jews by God. So for observant Jews there is a special quality intrinsic to the covenant and to Judaism itself, though not all of them find it entirely appealing:

"There is a strain in Jewish thought that says there is a special Godly something or other that is passed down in a certain genetic line which confers a special quality on people and Jewishness is a special quality. I call that metaphysical racism." –Rabbi Mark Solomon

But whilst easy to see such a common spirit in religious Jews – after all it is precisely that which makes them religious – it is so much harder to define it in secular Jews, those Jews who reject, often quite vociferously, all aspects of Jewish faith. They often claim that they don't have an ideology, or that their ideology is one of, say, the left: not only not Jewish, but opposed to all religions including Judaism. Yet seemingly so free of all such ignorant superstition, these same people still call themselves Jews, still more often than not marry other Jews and still turn up to solidarity rallies only with other Jews and under Jewish banners. What is their ideology?

For my money it is much the same sense of specialness found in religious Jews but with a special reference to victimhood. "Yes, but only in the Hitlerian sense", answered philosopher Maxime Rodinson when asked if he still considered himself a Jew. For many of these Jews it is their identity as a threatened and victimized people that makes them Jews. "Hitler said I was a Jew, so I may as well be a Jew" is one response or "To be a Jew somehow denies all those who ever persecuted Jews a victory – so I'm a Jew". For these Jews, albeit estranged from Jewish religious and often community life as well, Emil Fackenheim's famous post-Holocaust 614th commandment (to add to the other 613): *Thou shall survive!* is an absolute imperative. But whatever the motive, this self-identity runs very deep indeed. Amongst these Jews, no matter how left or progressive they may be, one may criticize Israel to the nth degree, poke fun at the Jewish establishment and even shamefully denigrate Judaism as a religion, but depart one iota from the approved text on anti-Semitism and Jewish suffering, and you are in deep trouble. For these rational folk, Jewish suffering and anti-Semitism is every bit as inexplicable, mysterious and therefore, unchallengeable as for any religious Jew.

Jewish secularism is often offered as evidence that there is no such thing as a Jewish identity gathered around any shared ideology. After all, if all Jews subscribe to the same basic ideology, then how come so many Jews so obviously don't? And if all Jews essentially support the same interests, how come so many Jews so obviously don't? But is it that obvious? Not only do secular Jews very often seem to subscribe to Jewish notions of specialness and victimhood, but also, in their attitudes to non-Jews in general, and Palestinians in particular, they are by no means all that different from religious Jews.

It is often quoted how many Jews are in solidarity movements with Palestinians and how many of these are secular. And it's true: there are many Jews in sympathy with the Palestinians and the overwhelming majority are secular, and the main thrust of post-1967 virulent Zionism has come to be associated with the religious right. But this secular Jewish tradition, in fact, has been at the forefront of Zionism's assault on the Palestinians. It was secular Labour Zionists who created the Zionist ideology and the pre-state Jewish-only society. It was secular Zionists–good, humanistic, left-wing kibbutzniks–who directed and carried out the ethnic cleansing of 750,000 Palestinians, and the destruction of their towns and villages. It was secular Zionists who established the present state with all its discriminatory practices; and it was a largely secular Labour government that held the Palestinian citizens of Israel under military government in their own land for eighteen years. Finally, it was a secular, Labour government which conquered the West Bank and Gaza, and first built the settlements, and embarked on the Oslo peace process, coolly designed to deceive the Palestinians into surrendering their rights.

And even those secular Jews who do support Palestinian rights, on so many occasions, the solidarity they offer is limited by self-interest. That these people, at least as much as anyone else, act out of their highest motives may be true. Many have been lifelong activists for many causes and many find their activism springs, consciously or unconsciously, from what they see as the highest ideals of their Jewishness. But nonetheless for many of them, solidarity with Palestinians means above all, the protection of Jews. They call for a Palestinian state on 22 per cent of the Palestinian homeland, but only to keep and protect the 'Jewishness' of the Jewish state. The Palestinian state they call for would inevitably be weak, dominated by the Israeli economy and under the guns of the Israeli military – surely they must know what this would mean!

At rally after rally, in speeches and on leaflets and banners, these Jews denounce the occupation: "Down with the occupation…down with the occupation…down with the occupation…" but not a word of the inherent injustice of a state for Jews only; perhaps a mention of the ill-gotten gains of 1948, but nothing of the right of return of the refugees, no restitution merely 'a just solution' taking account, of course, of Israel's 'demographic concerns'. "We are with you….we are with you….we are with you" they say "……*but..*" Whether it be condemnation of some form of Palestinian resistance of which they disapprove, or some real or perceived occurrence of anti-Semitism, for these Jews there is always a *"but."*

They should take a leaf from Henry Herskovitz. He is part of an organization called Jewish Witnesses for Peace, which holds silent vigils outside synagogues on shabbat. Of course, all the other Jewish activists are shrieking at him that you mustn't target Jews for protest, that you must draw a distinction between Jews, Israelis and Zionists, that you'll only alienate the people we want to engage…. but he doesn't care. He knows that support from the Jewish mainstream, as Tony Cliff the Trotskyite used to say, "….is like honey on your elbow - you can see it, you can smell it but you can never quite taste it!" Henry also knows that to say that Jews in America individually and in their religious and community organizations should not be held accountable for what is happening is a lie and discredits all Jews before the non-Jewish world.

So these secular Jews often end up being just another round of Michael Neuman's "veritable shell game" of Jewish identity. "Look! We're a religion! No! a race! No! a cultural entity! Sorry – a religion!" Because this is the key to maintaining Jewish power – if it's indefinable, it's invisible. Like a Stealth Bomber (you can't see it on your radar but you sure know when you've been hit) Jewish power, with its blurred outlines and changing forms, becomes invisible. And if you can't see it you can't fight it. Meanwhile the assault on the Palestinians continues.

"The Jews"

The phrase is itself terrifying because of its past association with discrimination and violence against Jews, but Jews themselves have no problem with it. The notion of a Jewish People is at the centre of Jewish faith with Jews of all or no degrees of religious adherence over and over again affirming its existence. It is also at the heart of Zionism even in its most secular forms and is written into the foundational texts of the state of Israel. The concept even received international legal approval when the Jewish people were declared, by the West German state, to be the post-war residual heirs of intestate Jews. And yet it is an absolute article of faith for everyone, including those in the solidarity movement, that while we may criticize and confront Israel and Israelis, we may not criticize and confront the Jewish people and Jews. Unlike Israel and any other state, the Jewish People has no common policy and any attack on the Jewish people is, therefore, aimed at what they are and not at what they do.

But is speaking of the Jews doing this or doing that any more or less acceptable than speaking of, say, the Americans? If the American military lays waste a third world country, it is done by order of the government (a small group) with the full support of the ruling elites (another small group), the tacit support of a substantial segment of the population (a larger group), the silent denial of probably the majority of the population (a very large group) and the opposition of a tiny minority (a small group). Is it all that different with Jews?

It may be. Unlike the United States, 'the Jews' are not a legally constituted body and they do not have an obvious and defined common policy. 'The Jews' do not have an officially designated leadership, nor do they inhabit one area of land, nor do they speak a common language or even share a common culture. Theoretically at least there seem to be so many differences as to render any comparison untenable. In practice this may not be the whole story.

It is true that 'the Jews' do not constitute a legally recognized body, but Zionism, with its claim to represent all Jews, has increasingly confused the issue. It is also true that the Zionists do not represent all Jews but they do represent the views of very many Jews indeed, and certainly the most powerful and influential Jews. And there is no doubt that the overwhelming majority of organized Jews are fully behind the Zionist project. That 'the Jews' do not have a formally designated leadership does not mean that they have no leadership - bodies again to which the overwhelming majority of organized Jews owe allegiance: the Israeli Government, the World Zionist Organization; numerous large and powerful Jewish organizations such as the Anti-Defamation League and The Conference of Presidents of Major American Jewish Organizations, The Simon Wiesenthal Centre; lesser bodies such as the Board of Deputies of British Jews and similar organizations in every country in which Jews reside. Then there is the extensive network of Jewish bodies often linked, through synagogues to the whole spectrum of mainstream Jewish religious and community life. All these bodies with their vast and interconnected network do provide leadership; they do have clearly defined policies and they are all four-square behind Zionism and Israel in its assault on the Palestinians.

Does this constitute a definable Jewish collective engaged in advancing Jewish interests? Officially, perhaps not, but, effectively, when one notes the remarkable unanimity of intent of all these bodies, the answer may well be yes. They do not of course represent all Jews nor are all individual Jews responsible for their actions, but nonetheless 'the Jews' - organized, active and effective Jews – are as responsible for the pursuit of Jewish interests in Palestine and elsewhere as 'the Americans' in Vietnam, 'the French' in Algeria, and 'the British' in India.

So why should our response be different? Why should 'the Jews' not be as accountable as 'the Americans' and even ordinary Jews as accountable as ordinary Americans? Why do we not picket the offices of the Anti-Defamation League or The Conference of Presidents or the offices or even the homes of Abe Foxman, Edgar Bronfman and Mort Zuckerman in the U.S. and Neville Nagler in the U.K.? Why do we not heckle Alan Dershowitz in the U.S. and Melanie Phillips in the U.K.? What about the U.K. Chief Rabbi who in his time has had lots to say about Israel and Palestine? Why do we not take the struggle to every synagogue and Jewish community centre in the world? After all, every Shabbat a prayer is said for the state of Israel in every mainstream synagogue in the land, most of which are focal points for Zionist propagandizing and fundraising, so why should these Jews who choose to combine their prayers and their politics be immune while at prayer from our legitimate protests at their politics? And for those few Jews who are really prepared to stand up and be counted for their solidarity with Palestinians, why can we not still give to them due honor and regard as we did to those few Americans who opposed American imperialism and those white South Africans who opposed apartheid?

The answer is that we are frightened. Even knowing that Jews are responsible and should be held accountable, still we are frightened. We are frightened because criticism of Jews with its woeful history of violence and discrimination seems just too dangerous a position to take – it may open the flood-gates to a burst of Jew hatred. We are frightened that if we were to discuss the role of Jews in this conflict and in other areas and begin to hold Jews accountable, we might be labelled anti-Semites and lose support. And, perhaps most of all, we are frightened of the conflicted inner passions that confound us all whenever we come to look at these things.

Does speaking the truth about Jewish identity, power and history lead to Jews being led to concentration camps and ovens? Of course it doesn't! It is hatred, fear and the suppression of free thought and speech which leads to these things – whether the hatred, fear and suppression is directed against Jews *or by Jews*. Anyway, despite efforts to convince us to the contrary, we do not live in the thirteenth century. Californians are unlikely to pour out of their cinemas showing Mel Gibson's 'Passion' chanting "Death to the Jews!" And, at a time when Jews in Israel/Palestine, overwhelmingly backed by Jewish organizations in the west, are desecrating churches and mosques wholesale and brutally oppressing entire Christian and Muslim populations, we may be forgiven for finding it hard to get excited about graffiti daubed on some synagogue somewhere.

If we were to begin to engage with the role of Jews in this conflict, we may well be labelled anti-Semites and we may well, initially at least, lose support. The anti-Semite curse has long served as a frightener to silence all criticism of Jews, Israel and Zionism, and undoubtedly will be used to discredit our cause. But so what? They call us anti-Semites anyway so what's to lose? Edward Said spent a lifetime picking his way through the Israel/Zionism/Judaism minefield and never once criticised Jews, and he was called an anti-Semite his whole life, right up to and even after his death. As a movement we have probably spent as much time being nice to Jews as we have speaking up for Palestinians, and for what? Where has it got us? We are not racists and we are not anti-Semites, so let them do their worst. We shall speak our minds.

For so long now Jews have told the world that black is white and not only that, but also if anyone should dare to deny that black is white they will be denounced as anti-Semites with all the attendant penalties. We are held in a moral and intellectual lock, the intention of which has been to silence all criticism of Israeli and Jewish power. In saying the unsayable we may set ourselves and others free. And think how it will feel the next time you are called an anti-Semite to say "Well, I don't know about that, but I do have some very strong but legitimate criticisms to make of Jews and the way they are behaving....and I intend to speak out"?

And you never know; we may be pleasantly surprised. Israel Shamir, who has no trouble whatsoever in calling a Jew a Jew, was cheered spontaneously recently when he introduced himself from the floor at a London solidarity meeting. I saw it with my own eyes. His first English-language book has just been published; he corresponds freely and reciprocally with many highly respected figures and is on the boards of advisers of The Association for One Democratic State in Palestine and of Deir Yassin Remembered. Perhaps it's all just a case of the Emperor's new clothes. Perhaps we're all just waiting for some innocent child to blow the whistle.

The situation facing the Palestinian people is truly terrible. Old political strategies have got us nowhere. We need a new and widened debate. It may be that a new and credible discourse which puts Jews and Jewishness at the critical centre of our discussions is part of that.

And one final point: In a previous piece, paraphrasing Marc Ellis I wrote:

"To the Christian and to the entire non-Jewish world, Jews say this: 'You will apologise for Jewish suffering again and again and again. And, when you have done apologising, you will then apologise some more. When you have apologised sufficiently we will forgive you … provided that you let us do what we want in Palestine."

Shamir took me to task, "Eisen is too optimistic", he said, "Palestine is not the ultimate goal of the Jews….the world is."

Well, I don't know about that, but, if as now seems likely, the conquest of Palestine is complete and the state of Israel stretches from Tel-Aviv to the Jordan River, what can we expect? Will the Jews of Israel, supported by Jews outside of Israel, now obey the law, live peaceably behind their borders and enjoy the fruits of their victory, or will they want more?

Paul Eisen is a writer and Director of **Deir Yassin Remembered**. He can be reached at: paul@eisen.demon.co.uk

Philo - prefix
loving, having an attraction to, or affinity for

Philo-Semitic Attacks On The Rise

by Joh Domingo

A non-existent, unpublished and undocumented report which substantiates the incidence of attacks committed by philo-Semites reveals a disturbing pattern: philo-Semites are victimizing more and more people, and philo-Semitic activity is officially sanctioned by States in Europe and North America.

Even in geographically removed continents such as Australia, a state-sanctioned campaign is being waged against non-Jews that find themselves at odds with Jews and other philo-Semites. This represents a disturbing trend towards assimilating and subordinating non-Jewish cultures into a facsimile of unwarranted hatred of others that is found among extremist elements of religious and secular Judaism. More and more self-hating non-Jews find it necessary to proclaim their philo-Semitism, or worse, to indulge themselves in a generous helping of goy-bashing.

Though philo-Semitic attacks are often verbal and presented on the opinion pages of the Philo-Semitic mass media. But these incidents represent the tip of the iceberg in a rising wave of philo-Semitism which has its roots in the European conflicts, Middle-East wars and even the events of 9/11. More worrying is the growing list of fatalities arising from these campaigns. The twelve-month period ending Dec. 2004 reveals that more people died from philo-Semitic attacks in Palestine and Iraq than died in the massive tsunami that engulfed coastal Asia that same year. That such incredible and ongoing casualties attributable to rising philo-Semitism would go unacknowledged and unreported, except in the most marginal of forums, is a matter of grave concern.

While philo-Semitism is often described by adherents as an aversion to bigotry against Jews, it often veils an irrational hatred of non-Jews. Yet even some non-Jews become infected. This manifests itself as an irrational self-hatred highlighted by extreme guilt and aggressive outbreaks of philo-Semitism. Side effects include finding and identifying thoughts and utterances that can be construed as being anti-philo-Semitic. Soon, this becomes an obsession for those affected, and discovering new enemies becomes a cult-like past time. No excuse is left unturned to justify the errant behavior of Jewish Supremacists, and no lopsided equivalence is considered beyond the pale, since Jewish security concerns exceed the value of non-Jewish life. Shame and remorse do not come into play.

It is not surprising that philo-Semitic attacks are ignored by the mass media, since philo-Semitism is considered normal and unremarkable. Being commonplace, outbreaks of philo-Semitism are not considered newsworthy, even when it's lethal for others. Empathy for victims of philo-Semitism is not considered a normal activity for residents of philo-Semitic countries. Sure, a few compatriots suffer its consequences, but they are mostly dissidents: an Ernest Zundel here, a nameless Muslim there – not of much consequence to its upright citizenry.

Such apathy however led to mass-slaughter during the first half of the last century, as philo-Semites rampaged their way across Central Europe slaughtering non-Jews in vast numbers. Today, philo-Semites are poised and capable of wiping out huge numbers of people in countries they consider recalcitrant malcontents or "threatening". Philo-Semitism starts small, protesting hatred against Jews. Soon, they are calling for nuclear bombs to be dropped on the heads of anti-philo-Semites.

This shows up in the research done by dissidents. First, people complain; then they are denounced as anti-Semites, even though they possess the right of free speech. Eventually, thousands are quietly incarcerated and the prisons overflow. This is not a prediction. It is already happening. In some circumstances, few know of the actual arrest except for a small circle of friends and family. In the wake of 911, it was presumed that those arrested were being held for activities that were criminal and that there was sufficient cause. But years later, only trickles of detainees were being released. It became apparent that they were held on suspicion of being dissidents against judeophilia. This crime is often associated with the practice of the Islamic religion.

Being a practicing Muslim is an occupational hazard in philo-Semitic countries. Your congregational services are recorded, your mosques monitored, religious leaders are harassed or arrested, and the contents of the collection plates confiscated. Yet we are only supposed to notice these problems when a mosque is firebombed by a lunatic. But most attacks are more sophisticated than that. The funds of any charity with the word 'Islamic' in its name is now considered to be under State control and subject to damage claims from philo-Semites. While the arrests of non-Muslim dissidents are occasionally subject to at least some protest, the detention of Muslims is accompanied by silence. Muslims are all Palestinians now.

Australia's Mamdouh Habib is one such victim of philo-Semitism. He was picked up in Pakistan a month after 9-11 on the basis that he was a trained al-Queda operative. After being transferred to Pakistan via Egypt, he's been held incommunicado at Guatanomo Bay. The philo-Semitic Australian government has always presumed that Habib was guilty and made little effort to provide him the protections that Australian citizenship guarantees. Then, after three years of imprisonment, the US released him without ever filing charges. But the Australian Government is annoyed. They are not upset that an innocent man was incarcerated; they are upset that an innocent man has been set free. They are upset also that the myth that one is innocent until proven guilty has been exposed as a sham. The philo-Semitic authorities have decided that Habib will be subject to home detention until they can figure out what it is they can charge him with. Philo-Semites often work this way. They determine the desired outcome, then conjure up a series of circumstances that will provide them with that result.

Almost unnoticed around the world are the thousands of families who are indirect victims of these philo-Semitic assaults, since the 'rendition' of a vital breadwinner will often impoverish an entire household. It is also becoming increasingly apparent that the vast majority of these detainees are being subjected to crude tortures based on pseudo-psychological theories about breaking the will of individuals. Yet these processes appear to be yielding little useful or concrete evidence against those arrested. So far only an embarrassingly few have been charged, and amongst them, some of the convicted have had their convictions overturned after discovering that evidence had been fabricated.

How does this begin? Sometimes uttering words offensive to philo-Semites initiates the process. This provides them with justification for conducting an investigating until improprieties are discovered. After that, you can be 'disappeared' into the legal black hole of the anti-terror Patriot Act. Legislation of this kind has been enacted by Judeophile governments worldwide. Often, after a few years, the prisoner is released due to "lack of evidence". Many philo-Semites consider this a mere legal technicality and are upset. What's happened though is that your life and the lives of your family have been devastated.

This is the democratic process that philo-Semitic governments are waging wars over. But what if the unwashed masses of the third world don't want this? Much of the third world has progressed to living under 'benevolent dictatorships; and for them, this may be a more appealing prospect than what is being offered at gunpoint by the Western world. Some believe that they have a better future to look forward to if they can just avoid the clutches of the rapacious Judeophile elite that have subjugated these 'free societies'.

Minor resistance against judeophilia is magnified to appear to be a tidal wave of anti-Semitism, while the genuine trappings of a true holocaust are being hidden from view. In what appears to be a fantastic delusion, judeophiles believe that hundreds of thousands of people a month were incinerated in ovens at Auschwitz. The reality is that judeophiles today possess the means to instantly incinerate millions. This is not a fantastic theory. It is a real possibility. The rising tide of philo-Semitism almost guarantees it.

Joh Domingo *is a writer and South African born Muslim with roots in the full spectrum of the varied racial mix that makes up the South African milieu. His background traverses the divide between his traditional African tribal kin and the rich cultural influences of colonial East Asia. His maternal grandfather was the sibling of a Methodist Scottish priest and his paternal grandfather was an indentured Indian sugar cane worker from Madras, India.*

His email: *johd7894@hotmail.com*

The Deadly Embrace Zion-power and War: From Iraq to Iran

by James Petras

November 6th, 2007

Introduction

Why, in 2003, did the United States launch a preemptive war against Iraq? Explanations range from military-political pretexts to accounts focusing on geopolitical and economic interests.

The original official explanation was the now discredited claim that Saddam Hussein possessed chemical, biological and other weapons of mass destructions (WMD), which threatened the US, Israel and the Middle East. Subsequent to the US military occupation, when no WMD were discovered, Washington justified the invasion and occupation by citing the removal of a dictator and the establishment of a prosperous democracy in the Arab world. The imposition of a colonial puppet regime, propped up by an imperial occupation force of over 200,000 troops and irregular death squads, which have killed close to a million Iraqi civilians, forced over 4 million into exile and impoverished over 95% of the population, puts the lie to that line of argument.

The latest line of justification revolves around the notion that the US occupation is necessary to 'prevent a civil war'. Most Iraqis and military experts think the presence of the US colonial occupation army is the cause of violent conflict, particularly the US military's devastating attacks on civilians, their financing of rival tribal leaders and Kurdish mercenaries and their contracting of local police-military to repress the population. Since most Americans (not to speak of the rest of the world) are not convinced by these specious arguments, the Washington regime rationalizes its continued war and occupation by citing the need for a colonial military victory to maintain its world and regional status as a super-power, and to assure its Middle East client regimes that Washington can defend their ruling cliques and their hegemonic ally, Israel. The Bush White House and pro-Israel Congressional leaders claim a victory in Iraq will bolster Washington's image as a successful global 'anti-terrorist' (anti-insurgent) regime. These post-facto justifications have lost credibility as the war drags on, popular resistance grows in Iraq, Afghanistan, Palestine, Lebanon, Somalia, Thailand, Philippines, Pakistan and elsewhere. The longer the war continues, the greater the economic cost and the demoralization and depletion of military personnel, the more difficult the task of sustaining the capacity to intervene in defense of the empire.

If the official political and military justifications for the US colonial wars in Iraq and Afghanistan ring hollow and convince few, what of the other economic explanations for the war put forth *mostly but not exclusively* by critics of the Bush administration?

The major focus of the economic determinists of the war centers on the issue of oil, as in 'war for oil'. These explanations in turn break down into several variants: The first and most popular is that the big US oil companies were behind the war, that Bush and Cheney were pressured by their Big Oil handlers into launching the war so that US oil companies could seize the nationally-owned Iraqi oil fields and refineries. A second, slightly modified, version argued that the White House was not pressured by Big Oil but acted on their behalf as a reflex action. (This is put forth to explain why the spokesmen for Big Oil multinationals were so conspicuously absent from the media and halls of Congress in the lead-up to the war.)

A third version argued that the US went to war to secure oil for US national security interests threatened by Saddam Hussein. This explanation cites the danger of Saddam Hussein closing down the Strait of Hormuz, invading the Gulf States, inciting revolts in Saudi Arabia and/or reducing the flow of Middle East oil to the US and its allies. In other words, the 'geopolitics' of the Middle East dictated that a non-client regime was a threat to US, European and Japanese access to oil. This is apparently the latest argument put forth by [former Federal Reserve Chairman] Alan Greenspan, a former proponent of the WMD propaganda.

The major advocates of the 'war for oil' (WFO) argument fail several empirical tests: Namely that the oil companies were not actively supporting the war via propaganda, congressional lobbying or through any other policy vehicle. Secondly the proponents of WFO fail to explain the efforts by major oil companies to develop economic ties with Iraq prior to the invasion and were in fact, working through clandestine third parties to trade in Iraqi oil. Thirdly, all the major oil companies operating in the Middle East were mainly concerned with political stability, the liberalization of the economic policies of the region and the opening of oil services for foreign investors. The big oil companies' strategies were to advance their global interests through the on-going liberalization process in the Middle East and conquering new markets and oil resources through their formidable market power – investments and technology. The onset of the US invasion of Iraq was viewed with anxiety and concern as a military action, which would destabilize the region, increase hostility to their interests throughout the Gulf and slow down the liberalization process. Not a single CEO from the entire petroleum industry viewed the US invasion as a positive 'national security' measure, because they understood that Saddam Hussein, after over a decade of economic and military sanctions and frequent bombing of his military installations and infrastructure throughout the Clinton years, was not in a position to launch any acts of aggression against Gulf oil companies or states. Moreover the oil companies had several real prospects of developing lucrative service and commercial oil contracts with Saddam Hussein's regime in the lead-up to the war. It was the US government pressured by the Zionist Power Configuration (ZPC), which pushed legislation blocking (through sanctions) Big Oil from consummating these economic agreements with Iraq.

The argument that Big Oil promoted the war for its own benefit fails the empirical test. A corollary to that is that Big Oil has failed to benefit from the US occupation because of the heightened conflict, continuous sabotage, the predictable resistance of the Iraqi oil workers to privatization and the general insecurity, instability and hostility of the Iraqi people.

The American Left jumped on Alan Greenspan's declaration that the Iraq war was about oil, as some kind of confirmation in the absence of any evidence. Yet everyday that has transpired since the beginning of the war five years ago, demonstrates that 'Big Oil' not only did not promote the invasion, but has failed to secure a single oil field, despite the presence of 160,000 US troops, thirty thousand Pentagon/State Department paid mercenaries and a corrupt puppet regime. As of September 19, 2007 the *Financial Times* of London featured an article on the conspicuous absence of the 'Oil Majors' in Iraq: "Big Oil Plays a Waiting Game over Iraq's Reserves' (September 19, 2007). Only a few small companies ('oil minnows') have contracts in Northern Iraq ('Kurdistan'), which has only 3% of Iraq's reserves. 'Big Oil' did not start the Iraq war, nor has 'Big Oil' benefited from the war. The reason why 'Big Oil' did not support the war is the same reason they haven't invested after the occupation: "The level of violence is still unacceptably high…if anything the prospects of agreement appears to be receding as tensions between parties grow." (ibid) 'Big Oil's' worst nightmares leading up to the Zionist-influenced war have all been utterly confirmed. Whereas 'Big Oil's' negotiations and third party deals with pre-war Iraq provided a stable and consistent flow of oil and revenue, the war has not only reduced these revenues to zero, but has all but eliminated any new options for the next decade.

Despite the war, liberalization elsewhere in the region has proceeded and US oil and financial interests have advanced despite the increased obstacles and hostilities, which have grown out of the US slaughter of Muslims.

Big Oil, Texas billionaires, even big contributors to the Bush family political campaigns were no match for the ZPC when it came to Middle East war policy. They lacked the inside and outside power, the disciplined grass roots organization of Jewish community organizations to overcome the Zionist warmongering power over Congress, their position in strategic executive offices and their army of academic scribes from Harvard, Yale and Hopkins churning out bellicose propaganda in the US media. What is striking about the position papers and op-ed reprints in the principle propaganda sheet (*Daily Alert*) of the Presidents of the Major American Jewish Organizations (PMAJO) is their total absence of any deviation from official Israeli pro-war positions: Whether it is killing children in Jenin, bombing population centers in Lebanon, shelling Arab families relaxing at the beach in Gaza, the Daily Alert simply echoes the official Israeli line and blatant lies about human shields, accidents, gunmen among school children, self-induced atrocities. Never in the entire period analyzed is there a single critical article questioning Israel's massive displacement of hundreds of thousands of Palestinians. No crime against humanity is too great for the Presidents of the Leading American Jewish Organizations to defend. It is this slavish obedience to the official Israeli policy that marks out the Zionist Power Configuration as something much more than just another lobby as its 'left' apologists and even Walt and Mearsheimer claim.

The ZPC is much more sinister both as a transmission belt for the policies and interests of a colonial power hell-bent on domination in the Middle East and as the most serious authoritarian threat to our democratic freedoms: no single individual who dares criticize can escape the long hand of the pro-Israel authoritarians. Book sellers are picketed, editors are intimidated, university presses and distributors are threatened, university presidents are blackmailed, local and national candidates are browbeaten and smeared, meetings are cancelled and venues are pressured, faculty are fired or denied promotion, corporations are blacklisted, union pension funds are raided, theater performances and concerts are cancelled. And the list of repressive actions taken by these authoritarian Zionist organizations at the national and local levels runs on, arousing fear among some, anger among many more and a slowly burning resentment and growing awareness among the silent majority. The second geo-political version of 'oil for war' focuses on the national security issues. After the First Gulf War in 1991 and eleven years of economic sanctions and military disarmament, Iraq was an impoverished, weak nation partially dismembered by the US backed Kurdish enclave in the north and constant US bombing and over flights. Iraq was severely bombed several times during the Clinton regimes and over 1 million of its citizens, including an estimated 500,000 children, died prematurely from conditions related to the US imposed deprivation of food and essential medical and water treatment supplies.

Before the invasion in 2003, Iraq did not even control its shorelines, airspace or even a third of its national territory. As the US invasion demonstrated, Saddam's military lacked the most elementary capacity to mount any defense in a conventional war, not even a single fighter plane presented a threat to any offshore US client or to the Strait of Hormuz. The stiff resistance to the US came later in the form of irregular forces engaged in guerrilla warfare, not from any organized force established by the Baathist regime. In other words no matter how far the concept of 'national security' is stretched to include US military bases, oil installations, client rulers and transport and shipping lanes in the Middle East, Saddam Hussein was clearly not a threat. If however the concept of 'national security' is re-defined to mean the physical elimination of any potential opponent of US and Israeli domination in the region, then Saddam Hussein could be labeled a national security threat. But that takes the discussion of the explanation for the US war against Iraq to another terrain and a discussion of the political forces who manipulated the phony WMD and 'War for Oil' propaganda to justify a war for US and Israeli hegemony in the Middle East. Even more important, the disinformation campaign about who was responsible for the US invasion and occupation of Iraq is highly relevant to the current propaganda blitz driving us toward a war with Iran.

From the Iraq War Cover-up on to Iran War Propaganda

The pro-Israel power configuration beats the war drums for an assault on Iran with greater insistency and successfully induces the Democratic Congress and Presidential hopefuls as well as the Republican White House to "put the military option on the table." Parallel to overt war propaganda, a number of liberal critics of the Iraq war have published articles arguing that Israel "really opposed the Iraq war." Writers as diverse as Gareth Porter, ex-CIA analyst Ray McGovern, Colonel Wilkerson (Colin Powell's Aide), ultra Zion-Con Michael Ledeen and others claim that Israel opposed the war because they wanted the US to target Iran. Others argue that Israel had advised the US that an invasion of Iraq would have dire consequences for the Middle East, tipping the balance toward Iran and which they now claim to have predicted. These Israel-exonerators point to other culprits, namely Bush-Cheney-Rumsfeld or the American Neo-Cons (better known as the Zion-Cons) who, they insist, have acted independently of Israel or ignored Israeli priorities in the region.

There is an alternative view which argues that Israel promoted the US attack on Iraq, did all in its power through its US pro-Israel followers to design, propagandize and plan the war. This alternative view sustains that at no point did the Zion-Cons act contrary to Israeli state interests. In fact, Israeli officials worked on a daily basis with its US agents inside the government, particularly the Pentagon's Office of Special Plans to provide disinformation to justify the military attack. If, as we will show, Israel was deeply involved in pushing the US to attack Iraq and is behind the current disinformation campaign to provoke a US war against Iran, then anti-war forces and US public opinion must openly confront the 'Israel factor'.

We will argue that the exoneration of Israel is mainly an attempt to deflect US public hostility away from those Israel Firsters who manipulated us into this costly, bloody unending war. Exoneration of Israeli responsibility for the US invasion of Iraq allows the Jewish state and its US agents to escape any blame for the degradation of US forces in Iraq and provides them a 'clean moral slate' for launching a new bloody US attack against Iran. Rather than seeing Israel as giving us a double dose of an incurable colonial disease, exoneration allows Israel and its agents to follow the same Iraq invasion pattern of manipulation and duplicity in leading us to war with Iran. The White House and Democratic Congress, echoing Israel, are using inflated threats of nuclear attack, demonizing Iran's leaders, financing low intensity warfare through the training and funding of violent Iranian exile-based clients, economic sanctions and 'failed' diplomatic maneuvers . . . to lead up to a new war. Taking advantage of their liberal (Zion-lib)-led exoneration for their role in the invasion of Iraq, the Zionist Power Configuration, through such loyal mouthpieces as Senator Joseph Lieberman, blame the Iranians for the deaths of US soldiers in Iraq. It is not the Zionist pro-war officials in and out of the government who sent young American soldiers to die in Iraq at the behest of the Israeli state to whom the US public should direct its anger, but rather the Iranians who are accused of arming and training Iraqi resistance fighters. Leaving Israel out and bringing Iran into the debacle in Iraq serves the Israeli purpose of covering their backsides while inciting Americans into a new military adventure against the much larger and better-armed Iranians.

The exonerators of Israel are not homogeneous in their political background or goals. Some liberals, fearful of arousing a powerful Zionist backlash, seek to whitewash Israel's lobby operatives in the US as a way of gaining sympathy among pro-Israel Congressional Democrats and financial backing from wealthy Jewish liberals critical of the Iraq war. Democratic Party Chairman Howard Dean, following the new Israeli script declared during a visit to Tel Aviv in 2006 that the "the US invaded the wrong country!"

The price of the 'exonerate Israel' strategy is to overlook the powerful role that the Israel First lobby is playing in bringing us to a new war with Iran as part of a sequence of invasions promoted by Israeli strategists. These clever ploys are backfiring. Playing to the prejudices of the liberal pro-Israel crowd in the Democratic Party has led to the current absence of any significant anti-war movement against the Zionist-led propaganda and war-mongering blitz against Iran.

There is no question that some anti-war Zion-Libs are trying to put some distance from the Zion-Con/Israeli policymakers who promoted the invasion of Iraq. But this does not come from any opposition to another new and more dangerous military commitment. On the contrary, the Zion-Libs criticize the discredited Bush-Cheney-Iraq policy in favor of a new more aggressive war policy toward Iran. By exonerating Israel and its transmission belt of organized local and national Jewish and fundamentalist Christian organizations, the liberals have not found allies for peace – they have revived the powerful influence of Israel and its US apparatus which was being increasingly rejected by the US public and elements in the US military. By putting the blame for the debacle in Iraq exclusively on Bush/Cheney and their allies in 'Big Oil' and excluding the role of Israel, the ZPC and their toadies among the Democrats in Congress, the liberal exonerators, open the way for a new cycle of war in the Middle East. To prevent a future Zionist and Israeli-orchestrated US attack against Iran, we must be perfectly clear about who maneuvered the US into attacking Iraq.

Israel, the ZPC and the Run-up to the Invasion of Iraq

Analytically, the differences between Israeli state policy and the leading US Zionist organizations are, with very rare exceptions, indistinguishable. The run-up to the US attack on Iraq is a case in point. From the late 1980's, through the first Gulf War, the Clinton Administration's sanctions, daily bombings and territorial separation of northern Iraq, 'Kurdistan', from the rest of the country, to the 2003 US invasion of Iraq, the Israeli government pressured US Congresspeople and senior policy makers toward bellicose policies toward Israel's 'enemies'. Israeli state policy urging further US degradation of Iraq was transmitted through the major Zionist organizations and key Zionist officials in the Clinton and later Bush administrations. Dennis Ross, Martin Indyk, Madeleine Albright, Richard Holbrook,

Sandy Berger, William Cohen and others were the most important foreign policy-makers toward the Middle East in the Clinton Administration and they produced and implemented the sanctions, bombings and territorial dismemberment of Iraq. Following their term of office, key Clinton Zionists went to work at pro-Israeli think tanks in Washington. Following the attacks of September 11, 2001, the Zion-Cons in top level positions in the Bush Administration (Ari Fleischer, Paul Wolfowitz, David Frum, Richard Perle, Douglas Feith, Eliott Abrams, Irving (Scooter) Libby, David Wurmser and others) and key Zionist Congress-members like Senator Joseph Lieberman, called for the US to attack Iraq, as part of a series of sequential wars, to include Syria and Iran. They echoed the policies of the Israeli state and in particular Prime Minister Ariel Sharon.

Israeli state officials, at no point expressed any reservations or differences with the bellicose efforts of its highly placed liaison agents in the Bush Government, nor with its servile lobby, AIPAC, nor with the pro-Israel Op-Ed writers of the major newspapers and broadcast media. Zionist ideologues prevailed everywhere berating the US military officials for their timid caution. Israel, consistent with its policies since the late 1980's, encouraged the Bush Administration toward an invasion and occupation of Iraq in all of its top level meetings with Rumsfeld, Powell, Rice and Bush. The Israeli media, with rare exceptions, demonized Saddam, played up his 'threat' to the Middle East and Israel's security, conflated Palestinian suicide bombings with Iraqi support for the Palestinian people's national aspirations, and energized their fundamentalist Christian allies in the US to follow suit in calling for an invasion of Iraq.

An analysis of the relationship between the Israeli state and highly placed Zionist officials in the Bush Administration reveals first and foremost that Tel Aviv laid out the strategic policies of eliminating Middle East regimes opposed to its ethnic cleansing of the occupied territories and unlimited expansion of colonial settlements in Occupied Palestine and the consolidation of Israeli hegemony in the Middle East. The Zionist elite in the Bush regime invented the pretext and the propaganda for war and most important, successfully designed and operationalized the US invasion of Iraq. This 'division of labor' included the Zion-Cons in the executive branch, backed by the Presidents of the Major Jewish American Organizations (including AIPAC), the regional, state and local Jewish federations through their influence over Congress.

Testimony by former Pentagon analyst, retired U.S. Air Force Lt. Colonel Karen Kwiatkowski confirms that throughout the period leading to the Iraq war, Israeli military officials, intelligence officers and other high ranking functionaries had daily access with top Zionist Pentagon officials like Undersecretary of Defense Douglas Feith. Frequent consultation, intelligence coordination and joint planning between top Zion-Cons in the Pentagon and top Israeli military operatives in the US indicates that there was close agreement in directing the US to invade Iraq. There was Zion-Con/Israeli agreement, confirmed in the immediate aftermath of the initial 'successful' occupation, that Iraq was the first of a series of invasions in the Middle East, to be followed by attacks against Iran and Syria. The Israeli joke current at the time was: 'Anyone can take Baghdad, real men go for Tehran.' In November 2002, Ariel Sharon, in an interview with the *Times* of London, called for the bombing of Iran "the day after the US invades Iraq".

The Zion-Con/Israeli blueprint for sequential wars was explicitly stated in the policy paper "Project for a New American Century', a kind of American-Israeli *Mein Kampf* of US world domination in which Israel would be a co-benefactor of American military might and treasure. Most of the Zion-Con designers and executers of US war policy in the Middle East were listed as authors or sponsors of the 'New American Project'. Many were also contributors to the policy paper for Likud leader, Benyamin Netanyahu, which specifically called for the dismemberment of Iraq into manageable ethnic enclaves.

Israeli intelligence disinformation about Saddam Hussein's 'threat' to the region was embellished and adapted to the propaganda needs of the White House. While Israeli propaganda pounded away at Saddam Hussein as the modern Hitler, Zionist propaganda chief and Bush speechwriter, David Frum, repeated the same theme in the infamous 'Axis of Evil' speech in which Bush pronounced before the world his intention to attack other nations preemptively. Given the Israeli regime's pro-war propaganda it is understandable that Israeli public opinion was overwhelmingly in favor of the war as were all the leaders of the major American Jewish organization, but not the majority of American Jews, especially young Jews and those who were not members of any of the Zionist (Israel First) front organizations.

Israeli advisers and Zion-Cons in the US government were highly influential in the dismantling of the entire civilian and military administrative structures in Iraq – the so-called De-Baathification campaign – in order to decisively weaken any attempt to reconstruct Iraq as a modern secular republic opposed to Israeli regional hegemony. The Israeli policy, pursued by the Zion-Cons, was to fragment the Iraqi state and society into pre-modern ethno-religious entities run by pro-Israeli Iraqi exiles (like Ahmed Chalabi who had business ties with Douglas Feith), incapable of ever challenging Israeli policy in the Middle East.

Israeli Zion-Con policy succeeded insofar as it secured the US destruction of the Iraqi state; but it failed to secure a rapid victory on the road to the second phase of invading Iran, because of the massive armed resistance by the Iraqis. In their blind racism against Arabs, the Israeli officials and their American agents discounted any possibility of Iraqis mounting a people's war against the destruction of their society. As the Iraqi resistance gained momentum and US military and economic losses multiplied, US public opinion turned against the war and began to ask who was responsible for the military debacle. In the face of this potentially dangerous question Zionist propaganda shifted gears in order to cover their tracks. Top Zionist officials who framed the war quickly left the scene, beginning with the most obvious war perpetrators: Paul Wolfowitz, Douglas Feith and Abram Shumsky in the Pentagon and David Frum and Ari Fleischer in the White House. The hardliners with less overt profiles in the State Department stayed on for a while longer– Elliot Abrams, Scooter Libby, David Wurmser. Libby later was convicted of a felony for his role in exposing the CIA operative married to

Ambassador Joseph Wilson in retaliation for his exposing his Zionist cohorts' fabrication of 'intelligence' in the lead up to the war.

War with Iran: The Highest Priority for the ZPC (and Israel)

Israel's campaign for the destruction of Iran has already led to two acts of war. In June 2006 Israel assaulted Lebanon, aiming, unsuccessfully, to destroy the Shiite political-military organization Hezbollah, an ally of Iran. A little more than a year later (Sept 6, 2007) Israel engaged in an even more provocative act, an unprovoked bombing mission over Syrian territory, destroying a military installation. Since Syria and Iran have a mutual defense pact, the Israeli action was designed to test the willingness of Iran and Syria to respond to a surprise (sneak) military attack.

The propaganda arm of the Israeli intelligence services prepared a piece of disinformation comparable to their earlier weapons of mass destruction lie: They claimed that they bombed a nuclear site which North Korea was constructing and supplying with nuclear material. Israeli disinformation was immediately reproduced verbatim in the leading US newspapers, *Los Angeles Times, Washington Post, Wall Street Journal* and the *New York Times* and all the major television networks. Pro-Israeli propaganda experts justified the attack and were in turn quoted in the *Washington Post* (Sept 20, 2007). The *Post* quoted Bruce Riedel, formerly an intelligence 'expert' at the pro-Israel Saban Center for Middle East Policy (housed in the now discredited Brookings Institute): "There is no question it was a major raid. It was an extremely important target. It came at a time the Israelis were very concerned about war with Syria and wanted to dampen down the prospects of war (sic). The decision was taken despite their concerns it could produce a war (sic). The decision reflects how important this target was to Israeli military planners." In other words, Israel is "concerned about war" so it engages in an unprovoked act of war in which the propagandists don't even know the nature of the target!

On September 21, 2007, the *Daily Alert* then reproduced the pro-war propaganda cycled through the *Washington Post* and sent it out to all top officials and Congressmen in Washington and across the country and activated its lobbyists in AIPAC to ensure US support for the blatant Israeli act of war. True to its deceptive propaganda function, the *Daily Alert* published a highly misleading excerpt from an article in the *Financial Times* (September 21, 2007 p.4), which combines the Israeli propaganda line of a 'potential' Syria-North Korea nuclear tie without including several paragraphs debunking the Israeli-Zionist disinformation campaign. The *Financial Times* article quotes Joseph Circcione, Director of Nuclear Policy at the Center for American Progress: "It is highly unlikely that the Israeli attack had anything to do with significant Syrian-North Korean nuclear cooperation. The basic, well-documented fact is that the 40-year-old Syrian nuclear research program is too basic to support any weapons capability. Universities have larger nuclear facilities than Syria," (*Financial Times*, September 21, 2007, p.4). A former senior Asian adviser to President Bush and expert on North Korea, now at the Center for Strategic and International Studies, also debunked the Israeli-Zionist nuclear weapon ploy: "I would be very, very surprised if the North Koreans were dumb enough to transfer fissile material to Syria or were trying to do work outside of North Korea in a place like Syria", (ibid). Equally damaging to the Israeli-Zionist war propaganda, the Bush Administration never raised North Korea's supposed involvement with Syria during the entire series of meetings during 2007, despite the fact that it was greatly hostile to Syria and looking for any excuse to attack it. In contrast to previous Israeli provocations in which the Bush Administration rushed to vouch for Israel's pretexts, Bush declined to comment on the Israeli attacks against Syria, likely advised by his intelligence chiefs that it was an Israeli act of provocation hoping to draw in the United States.

The Israeli act of war against Syria and its defense and promotion by the US Zionist Power Configuration is the latest step in bringing the US into a joint war against Iran and Syria. A survey of the *Daily Alert* (the house organ of the Presidents of the Major American Jewish Organizations) from January to September 2007 (180 issues) reveals that there is an average of three articles in each issue calling on the US to engage in acts of war, impose strict economic sanctions and a naval blockade and prepare for a widespread confrontation with Iran. There is not a single voice or article that questions Israel's pro-war posture. Every issue of the *Daily Alert* parrots the Israeli line, even when it involves supporting the brutal cutting of electricity, gas and drinking water to over a million trapped civilians in Gaza – a war crime under international law. In the words of the Daily Alert, Israeli murders of unarmed teenage Palestinian boys and girls are labeled 'militants' or 'gunmen'. And the *Daily Alert* describes Israeli 'peace negotiations' as being carried out in 'good faith' – despite continued land grabs and assassinations of scores of Palestinians, including young kids. "In the time between George W. Bush, US President announcing the (Annapolis) peace meeting on July 16, 2007 and October 15, 2007, the Israeli military had killed 104 Palestinians including 12 children." (*Financial Times*, October 18, 2007 p.4)

After the November 2006 Democratic Party Congressional victory thanks to the increasingly angry anti-Iraq war voters, Israeli Foreign Minister Tzipi Levi attended the AIPAC meeting in Washington to urge the thousands of Zionist activists and a large contingent of US Democratic and Republican congressmen to continue to support the Bush Administration's occupation of Iraq and incited them toward another war against Iran. In a highly charged screed, she ejaculated on the non-existent "existential threat" of Iranian nuclear capability. The entire Jewish Lobby picked up the line and went into action.

The scope, depth and centralized structure of the Zionist Power Configuration far exceed anything, which can be properly conceived of as a 'lobby'. In that sense Mearsheimer and Walt in the study of the Israel Lobby underestimate the power and political influence of the pro-Israeli forces. Secondly the measure of the ZPC power must take account of several factors. These include its direct and indirect power. ZPC power is exercised directly on political, academic and cultural decision makers to make sure their policies back pro-Israel, pro-Zionist interests. An even more direct expression of power is when Zionists occupy top decision-making positions and make policies on behalf of Israeli military and economic interests. Elliot Abrams, President Bush's key Middle East advisor on the National Security Council is one of many examples as is the Director of Homeland Security, Michael Chertoff, who allocates over three-quarters of available funds for the 'security' of private Jewish organizations.

Equally formidable is the ZPC exercise of indirect power through several mechanisms.

One is by parlaying influence over a small group of Congressmen into a large majority. For example, AIPAC wrote up the bill, presented by Senator Lieberman and co-signed by Senator Kyl, labeling the Iranian Revolutionary Guards as 'terrorists', which paves the way for Bush to launch an attack. It was passed by 80% of Congress.

Cumulative power is the convergence of different sectors of the ZPC on a single issue. For example, pro-Israel writers and Jewish leaders from all major organizations and spheres of its media from Left to far Right, joined to denounce Mearsheimer and Walt's essay and subsequent book, most resorting to either *ad hominem* attacks ('anti-Semites') or illogical and convoluted arguments ignoring the empirical data.

Propaganda of the deed is a favorite power tool of the ZPC. This involves publicizing the successful punishment of critics of Israel and the ZPC in order to intimidate current or future policymakers. An example is how Zion-fascist Professor Alan Dershowitz of the Harvard Law School successfully campaigned, with backing from the ZPC, to oust Professor Norman Finkelstein from his university post, thus serving as 'exemplary punishment' to any future academic critics of Israel. Dershowitz's campaign went so far as to slander Professor Finkelstein's deceased mother, a survivor of the Nazi death camps, as a Jewish 'kapo' or Nazi collaborator.

The ZPC has multiple resources that are mutually re-enforcing in both the private, and public spheres. Large-scale, long-term party and electoral financing buy Congressional influence. This in turn increases the power of the large minority of Zionist Congressmen in gaining control over party nominations and committee assignments in Congress. This in turn feeds back into greater influence for the

ZPC in shaping US-Middle East foreign policy and facilitating access of pro-Israeli writers to the Op-Ed pages of the major dailies, weeklies and other branches of the corporate media.

Zionist power is also the result of a long-standing, pervasive and totally one-sided propaganda campaign that demonizes Israel's Arab, especially Palestinian critics, and paints Israel (the world's fourth largest and Middle East's only nuclear power) as a democratic fortress, surrounded by hostile authoritarian governments. Through its access and partial control over most of the major media, the Zionist Power Configuration provides heavily biased reports on events such as the Israeli terror bombings of population centers in Lebanon, Gaza and elsewhere. Reputational power projected by the ZPC in the US counteracts reality in the Middle East to the extent that Palestinian victims of all ages and genders, suffering 40 years of Israeli military rule, land expropriation and constant violent assaults are made into aggressors and the Israeli executioners are portrayed as virtuous, peaceful victims.

Israel Lobby or 'Zionist Power Configuration'?

Mearsheimer and Walt describe the pro-Israel power configuration as a "lobby, just like any other US lobby", a "loose collection of individuals and groups" outside of government, acting on behalf of Israel. Nothing could be further from the truth. The power of Israel in the United States is manifested through a multiplicity of highly organized, well-financed and centrally directed structures throughout the United States. The ZPC include several score political action committees with innocuous names, at least a dozen propaganda mills ('think tanks') employing scores of former highly connected top policymakers mostly in Washington and the East Coast, and the 52 major American Jewish Organizations grouped under the umbrella listing 'Conference of Presidents of Major American Jewish Organizations' (CPMAJO). AIPAC and other national organizations (ADL, AJC etc.) are important influences at the national Executive-Congressional lobbying levels. But equally or even more important in censoring and purging critics, controlling local media and shaping opinion

throughout cities, towns and villages are the local Jewish community federations and organizations which browbeat local cultural
programmers, editors, bookstores, universities, churches and civic
groups to deny public platforms to speakers, writers, artists, religious
spokespeople and other public figures critical of Israel and its Zionist disciples.

The power base of the ZPC is found in the local activist doctors,
dentists, lawyers, real estate brokers and landlords who preside over
the local confederations and their several hundred thousand affiliates. It is they who harass, badger, browbeat, raise money and
organize propaganda junkets for elected officials and ensure their
support for Israeli wars and increases in the US multi-billion dollar
aid packages to Israel. The local Zionist power structure organizes
successful campaigns forcing state pension funds to purchase billions
of dollars in underperforming Israel state bonds and to disinvest in
companies engaged in economic transactions with Israel's self-described 'state terrorists adversaries'. It is the Jewish based pro-Israel
student organizations which spy on US professors, who may or may
not be critical of Israel and smear them in local and national newsletters and pressure administrations to fire them. Even where less
than 1% of the local population is Jewish, Zionist zealots are able
to pressure small private Christian colleges to ban a Nobel Peace
Prize winning theologian, like Bishop Desmond Tutu, from speaking on their campus. The Zionist octopus has extended its tentacles
far beyond the traditional centers of big city power and national
politics, reaching into remote towns and cultural spheres. Not even
the American small town obituary pages are exempt: When a Connecticut newspaper published a memorial of a prominent Palestinian grandmother and community leader from Hebron (May 2003)
the 61 year old Shadeen abu Hijleh, who was shot in her home by Israelis soldiers, members of the local Jewish confederation expressed
outrage at the exposure of Israeli military crimes – thus censoring a
moving obituary page tribute written by her American friends and
relatives.

Centralized structures – coordinated policy, targets, quotas, fund
raising, large-scale special campaigns, black lists ('anti-Semites' and

'self-hating Jews'), and networks all are integral parts of the ZPC. Mearsheimer and Walt have failed to analyze the organizational relations between the head office, regional staff and local organizations of the major pro-Israel Jewish organizations and how quickly they can be mobilized to stigmatize, censor or support a given speaker, activity or fund raiser in favor of Israeli interests.

Throughout the country the newsletters of local Jewish Community Relations Councils have parroted the line or reprinted libelous canards of their national offices denouncing Mearsheimer and Walt's book *The Israel Lobby* – and from their rather ill-informed caricatures of M and W's discussion it is clear they have barely even read the book's cover.

One thing is clear from the largely emotional ejaculations from the predominantly Jewish intellectuals' attacks against the book, the intellectual level of contemporary Jewish intellectuals has seriously deteriorated to the point that envy, communal spite and partisan vitriol has gotten the better of a reasoned review of data and logic. The literary efforts by Abraham Foxman of the ADL to answer M and W are reminiscent of the Stalinist diatribes featured during the Moscow show trials of the 1930's (our Jewish version of Andrei Vishinsky). What accounts for the influence of these intellectual mediocrities is neither the evil vapors emanating from their venomous writing, nor their appeal to reason – though some pretense to reasoned debate is made by Zionist progressives – if such exist – but the fact that their repetitious message circulate throughout their mass media outlets uncontested.

The ZPC, having organized the war through falsified data, via the top two officials in the Pentagon (Wolfowitz and Douglas Feith), the Vice Presidents office (Wurmser and Irving Scooter Libby) and the National Security Council (Elliot Abrams) organized the President's office (Ari Fleischer) and written Bush's pre-emptive war speech (David Frum) are now fearful they will face the anger of the American people who have suffered the loss of thousands of soldiers – to an extent not experienced by the authors and implementers of this war for Israel. To avoid identification with this disastrous war,

Zionist Power Configuration War planners and propagandists have resorted to lies (denial of the crucial role of Israel in bringing the US to war) and the somewhat more clever operators like Alan Greenspan have joined the mindless American left to drag out the old canard of 'War for Oil'.

War: For Oil or For Israel? The Public Record War

Zionist Power Configuration support for the Iraq War was an open, relentless, propaganda campaign by well-known writers, publicists, and community leaders as well as by the 52 leading Jewish organizations. There was 'no conspiracy' or 'cabal' – the Zionist campaign was brazenly public, aggressive and reiterative.

A systematic review of the major propaganda organ of the Presidents of the Major American Jewish Organization's newsletter, *Daily Alert*, from 2002 to September 2007 – 1,760 issues – provides us with a scientific sample of ZPC opinion. On average, each issue contained 5 articles in favor of the war or moves toward war with Iraq and/or Iran. The *Daily Alert* featured op-ed articles by the major liberal, conservative and Zion-fascist writers and academics that regularly appeared in the *Washington Post, Wall Street Journal, the New York Sun,* and *the New York and Los Angeles Times,* the *Daily Telegraph* and *Times of London, YNet* and others. In other words, in the crucial pre-war to post-invasion period, the leading pro-Israel Jewish organizations produced approximately 8,800 pieces of pro-Iraq war propaganda and circulated it to all its member organizations, every Congressman, every leading member of the executive branch with follow-ups by local activists and an army of Washington lobbyists (150 from AIPAC alone) plus several hundred full-time activists from local and regional offices.

In a comparable survey of the leading Anglo-American business and financial newspaper, the *Financial Times* between 2002 and September 2007, regarding Big Oil's policy toward war with Iraq and now Iran is just as revealing. I reviewed the opinion, editorial and letter pages of 1,872 issues of the *Financial Times* and there is not a single article or letter by any spokesperson or representative of a major (or minor) oil company calling for the invasion and occupation of Iraq or the bombing of Iran. There was no oil lobby or grass roots organization demanding Congress or the Bush Administration to go to war in defense of US oil interests. But the ZPC was active, promoting the lie that disarmed and embargoed Iraq represented an 'existential threat' to the nuclear armed Israel.

A similar comparison of Zionist and Big Oil regarding propaganda for a US military confrontation with Iran reinforces the argument of the centrality of the major Jewish organizations in promoting United States involvement in Middle East wars for Israel. Between 2004 and September 2007 (three years and nine months) the Zionist propaganda sheet, the *Daily Alert*, published 960 issues in which an average of 6 articles argued for an immediate or near future US or Israeli preemptive military attack on Iran, tougher economic sanctions than the Security Council was willing to support, organized disinvestment and boycotts of Iran. A survey of the *Financial Times* during the same period, 1,053 issues, (the *FT* prints six times a week, the *Daily Alert* five times), fails to produce a single letter or op-ed article by any representative or spokesperson of Big Oil supporting war against Iran. On the contrary, as was the case with Iraq, major oil leaders expressed anxiety and fear that an [Israeli instigated] war would destabilize the entire area and lead to the destruction of vital oil installations, undermine transport routes and shipping lanes and cancel lucrative service contracts. Contrary to the latest Zionist propaganda, Big Oil wants the US to lift its sanctions against investment in Iran, since it has lost lucrative deals to competitors.

In complete contradiction to the 'leftist' Trotskyist-Zionist finger pointing at Big Oil as the main push for war, big Texas oil was working profitably with Saddam Hussein's Iraq, signing hundreds of millions of dollars in illegal contracts with the now executed ruler. Oscar Wyatt, a Texas oil billionaire, recently convicted for paying bribes to Saddam Hussein, was one of many big oil dealers involved in the lucrative pre-war oil trade with Iraq (*Financial Times*, Oct. 2, 2007, p.2).

James Petras

Zionist Warmongering: Fear and Venom

As the pressure from Israel for a US-backed military attack on Iran mounts, and as top US military officials and the general public grow increasingly hostile to Zionist arm-twisting and gross manipulation of policy makers, the ZPC turns aggressively authoritarian in its effort to silence opposition which exposes its role as a disloyal actor for a foreign power. In the past, agents for a foreign power, once detected, usually received severe sanction or worse. Today, numerous Zionist insiders know they are playing an increasingly risky game as the perceived costs of a new war with Iran rise and their Israeli 'handlers' press them to promote an attack Iran at the top of their agenda.

Ultimately, the Zionist Power Configuration, despite their wealth and current dominance over US Middle East policy, know that they represent less than 1% of the population; they are an elite without a mass base. They have power only as long as the other 99% of the population is inactive, manipulated or intimidated to serve Israel's interests. But as the growing flow of books, articles and speeches begin to call attention to the Israeli-directed ZPC and their destructive war-mongering activities, their self-promoted images of their members as brilliant professionals, successful leaders in the world of business and finance and compassionate politicians serving the best interests of the USA, begins to erode. The ugly side of their servile loyalty to Israel, an arrogant, racist colonial power provoking wars via the US to establish itself as an unchallenged regional power has entered into the American public debate.

The ZPC is at or near the peak of its political power – in Congress, the Executive, the Office of Homeland Security and prospective Attorney General, in 'culture' and the mass media propaganda. But paradoxically, as the ZPC peaks, it also exposes more of itself – much more than it wants to be seen by the American public.

Even the brash and impudent Zionist polemicists who hole up in the prestigious universities and 'think tank-propaganda mills' are beginning to feel public anxiety, even perhaps private worries. As they do so, they back track, trying to cover their fingerprints on all the war plans and propaganda leading to the now-massively unpopular invasion of Iraq. They resort to outright lies in the form of denials or complicity or 'warmongering'. Outrageous denials abound! For the more aggressive die-hard Zion-Cons, exposure of the disloyal role of the ZPC and their complicity evokes savage rejoinders, academic screeds in the gutter language of *ad hominem* abuse which reflects poorly on their vaunted academic positions. The ZPC, its scribes, operatives and power brokers are vulnerable – they have committed great crimes against the interests of the American people. Their actions have led to the death and maiming of tens of thousands of US soldiers, 99.9% of whom have no 'loyalties' to the interest of greater Israel or its US agents who have their own children pursuing lucrative civilian careers. Recent estimates found less than 0.2% of US soldiers serving on the ground in Iraq are American Jews, some of whom were Jewish immigrants from the former Soviet Union. This despite the strong Zionist pressure to invade and destroy Iraq and Iran. The manipulations of the ZPC in pushing the Bush Administration into invading and occupying Iraq has led the US military into an unprecedented state of disgrace and demoralization, with thousands of officers tendering their early retirement, thousands of troops going AWOL and facing court-martial, and an increasing number of retired senior officers expressing outrage. It is no surprise that Secretary of Defense Robert Gates secured the support of top military officers in the Middle East in opposing an immediate invasion of Iran.

Zionist vituperation against their critics expresses fears of exposure and unmasking of their double discourse, their false amalgamation of Israeli colonial policies with the democratic values of the American people. Nothing else can explain the shrill verbal personal assaults – aimed at killing the messenger rather than facing unpleasant realities and working to rectify a disastrous situation. While the state of Israel has placed its American promoters in an uncomfortable position as the occupation of Iraq crumbles and Americans resist shrill calls for attacking Iran, nevertheless Israel has turned out to be the real winner, in the short term, having achieved the destruction of the unified, secular republic of Iraq.

James Petras

From a Scratch to Gangrene: The Transition from Zionism to Zion-Fascism

The 'mainstream' Zionist conservatives early on demonstrated their authoritarian politics through their whole-hearted and un-problematical support for Israel's brutal campaigns driving hundreds of thousands of Palestinians from their homes and lands. Subsequently, the Zion-Cons fully and un-questioningly endorsed the killing and jailing of thousands of Palestinian civilians protesting the Israeli military occupation and conversion of the occupied West Bank and Gaza into 'open air' concentration camps, with over 500 military outposts and roads blocks. More recently the entire leadership of the major Jewish organizations, comprising both Zion-Cons and Zion-Libs, defended Israel's building of a massive 30 meter wall, effectively corralling the entire Palestinian population in ghettos resembling the walls constructed around the huge Jewish population in Warsaw by the Nazis. The wall and the military outposts strangle trade, movement of food and people from the occupied territories to markets, schools and hospitals and prevent farmers from even tilling their lands.

On October 10, 2007 the *Jerusalem Post* quoted Aron Soffer, head of research and lecturer at the Israeli Defense Forces (IDF) National Defense College. The 71-year old father of 4 and grandfather of 8 had said on May 21, 2004: "When 2.5 million people live in a closed off Gaza, it's going to be a human catastrophe. Those people will become even bigger animals than they are today, with the aid of an insane fundamentalist Islam. The pressure at the border will be awful. It's going to be a terrible war. So if we want to remain alive, we will have to kill and kill and kill. All day . . . every day."

This is the literal message of murder taught to Israeli officers at their most advanced military school by eminent Zion-Fascist lecturers. This helps us understand the naked brutality and homicidal behavior of Israeli soldiers in the occupied territories.

A recent Israeli study by two prominent psychologists illustrates the deep strain of sadism and racism inculcated by Israel's military academies and backed by Israel's top politicians, including the

Prime Minister's Office. According to *Haaretz* on September 21, 2007, two Israeli psychologists interviewed 21 Israeli soldiers, who expressed "their innermost emotions about the horrendous crimes, in which they took part: murder, breaking the bones of Palestinian children, acts of humiliation, destruction of property, robbery and theft." One of the Israeli psychologists was "shocked to find that the soldiers enjoyed the 'intoxication of power' and had pleasure from using violence." She said, "Most of my interviewees enjoyed their own instigated violence during the occupation." (*Haaretz*, September 21, 2007) Absolute colonial domination brings out the psychopathic tendencies in an occupation army. Soldier C testified, "If I didn't enter Rafah (Palestinian City in Gaza) to put down some rebellion – at least once a week I'd go beserk." Like previous colonial occupiers, the Israeli soldiers adopt a totalitarian 'super-race complex'. Soldier D testified, "What is great is that you don't follow any law or rule. You feel that YOU ARE THE LAW. Once you go into the Occupied Territory YOU ARE GOD!." The soldiers' internalization of the powerful Zion-fascist ideology provides a self-justification in the eyes of the interviewees for castrating a man, bashing in the face of a woman protester, shooting an innocuous pedestrian, breaking the arm of a four-year old child and other 'gratuitous' acts of random violence.

The Presidents of the Major American Jewish Organizations never ever mention, let along criticize, the daily psychopathic behavior of the IDF. Major Jewish billionaire philanthropists contribute hundreds of millions in support of the IDF's violent occupation and repression of Palestinian civilians, described with cruel pleasure by the soldier-subjects of the Israeli study. In fact, the biggest Zionist contributor to the Democratic Party, Haim Saban ($12.3 million dollars in 2002 alone), has a 'soft spot for Israeli combat soldiers.' According to *Haaretz* (September 12, 2006), Saban declared, "I can't handle combat soldiers, whenever I have any interaction with them . . . I cry." There is a powerful emotional bond that links Israeli Zion-fascism to its US counterparts. Saban arrogantly points to the primacy of his loyalty to Israel, "I strut around like a peacock in America and say I am an Israeli-American. What you hear… an Israeli-American." (*Haaretz*, October 14, 2007). The formerly respectable Brooking's Institute now houses the 'Saban Center', financed by Haim Saban, turning Brookings into just another of a dozen propaganda mills churning out apologetics for the totalitarian practices of the IDF – their leading research directors and their Prime Minister. The deadly sentimentality of the Israeli-American billionaires toward the psychopaths in the IDF does not extend to the young Americans serving Israel's interests as US soldiers in Iraq and who are suffering the burdens of a war to extend Israel's regional power. Saban, like the great majority of the top leaders of the most influential Zionist organization are pushing for another war – this time with Iran. According to Saban, "I would try other things first, but if they don't work, then attack...In Iran you go in and wipe out their infrastructure completely. Plunge them into darkness. Cut off their water." (*Haaretz,* October 14, 2007). These are not the homicidal ranting of a fanatical Jewish settler beating a pre-adolescent Palestinian shepherd. Saban is a major leader in AIPAC, family friend and political broker of the Clintons and the entire current Israeli leadership. His $2.8 billion dollars buys the fawning attention of all major US presidential "candidates courting Jewish support" (MSNBC, October 14, 2007).

The Zionist Power Configuration has buried 3 top-level political initiatives designed to reach a settlement of the Israeli colonial occupation of Palestine. A statement to President Bush and Secretary of State Rice sent by former top political officials of both political parties, including Zbigniev Brzezinski, Lee Hamilton, Brent Scowcroft and others calling for Israel to abide by UN Security Council Resolution 242 and 338 and other initiatives, was totally dismissed by the Democratic Congress and the Republican White House, after the ZPC intervened and labeled Brzezinski as 'hostile to Israel' – following the Israeli state's complete dismissal of the statement. Tony Blair's efforts as head of the 'Quartet Peace-Making Mission' has been a total failure in resolving even the humanitarian plight of the Palestinians, in the face of Israeli intransigence and rejection of any but the most banal conversations with the now subdued (formerly so frenetic) ex-British Prime Minister (*Guardian,* October 13, 2007). Secretary Rice's efforts to organize a Middle East peace conference for late November in Annapolis, Maryland were diluted to the point of pointlessness by Israeli pronouncements. Israel rejects any substantive agreements on borders, timetables, Jerusalem, settlements, territory etc. They insist the conference focus on meaningless general agreements that commit them to nothing. In action designed to further humiliate US Secretary of State Rice, the Israeli government illegally seized several hundred acres of Palestinian lands – a clear example of extending the settlements (*Aljazeera*, October 14, 2007). While trying to appear stylish in a dunce cap, Secretary Rice responded that the new Israeli confiscation of Palestinian land might 'erode confidence in the parties' commitment to a two state solution' (BBC, October 14, 2007).

Recognizing that the ZPC has completely tied up her negotiation position, and that she cannot demand anything substantive from Israel, Secretary Rice signaled the futility of the Annapolis meeting by calling for 'lower expectations'; that is, no agreements of substance. There is good reason to believe that Israel and its Fifth Column have effectively scuttled Bush's own Annapolis initiative. Even US clients like Egypt, Saudi Arabia, Jordan and even the Palestinian puppet Abbas have expressed doubts since there are no substantive agreements on state boundaries, which are anathema to Israel and the ZPC. Whether the conference is 'postponed' or actually takes place, the event promises to be another inconsequential gesture, another US Middle East defeat, another victory for Israel's colonial status quo and another reason for increased Arab resistance in the Middle East.

What is more ominous, Israel and the ZPC will find that their successful sabotage of the White House Annapolis Peace Conference is likely to encourage them to press ahead with further violent seizures in the Occupied Territories, new more deadly incursions in Lebanon and Syria and heightened pressure for war with Iran. Zion-fascism feeds into the sense of irresistible power over US Middle East policy against any major US institutional force, which fails to follow the Israeli line.

Along with the right-wing radicalization of Zion-Con ideology with regard to Israel's push toward totalitarian solutions, came overt manifestations of racist anti-Islamic, anti-Arab and anti-Persian practices and speeches from leading Zion-Con spokespeople and especially academic propagandists in the United States.

War propaganda and military solutions dominate Zion-Con rhetoric: first against Palestine, then Afghanistan, Iraq, Lebanon, Syria, Somalia and Sudan. Accompanying the radicalization of Zion-con rhetoric is a growing number of repressive acts within US society.

The ZPC and Holocaust Denial: At the Service of Israel

Leading Zionist Democrats following Israeli directives played a major role in undermining a Congressional resolution condemning as genocide the Turkish murder of 1.5 million Armenians. For many years the state of Israel and its academic specialists both in Israel as well as in the US have denied Turkish-led Genocide against the Armenians in their ancient homeland between 1915–1917 despite the voluminous documentary record complied by scholars throughout the world. One reason is that the Jewish Holocaust industry insists on the exclusive franchise on 20th century genocide, in order to push its fundraising and propaganda efforts. An even more important contemporary reason for Israeli and US Zionist holocaust denial is the close military collaboration between Israel and Turkey and more recently the heavy presence of Israeli military advisers and secret police (Mossad) operations in Kurdish-controlled Northern Iraq, dubbed Kurdistan.

Former member of the Israeli armed services, 'US' Congressman Rahm Emanuel, Chairman of the House Democratic Caucus, opposed the resolution from the start and convinced a group of senior House Democrats to demand the Democratic Congressional leadership drop plans for a vote on the measure. Deeply implicated with the interests of Israel, Emanuel has both feet in the terrain of an Israeli-defined Middle East reality. Congressman Emanuel cynically rationalized his service for the state of Israel in a convoluted statement: "This vote (on the Armenian genocide) came face to face with the reality on the ground in that region of the world." (*NY Times,* October 16, 2007) The Israeli fifth column in the US Congress has extended the scope of its control beyond narrow focus on the contemporary Middle East and Israel's quest for regional dominance to encompass historical issues involving non-Arab, non-Muslim people who indirectly affect Israeli strategic interests. Israeli strategists see the Congressional resolution on the Armenian genocide as provoking Turkish hostility to the US, and increasing the likelihood of an invasion against the US and Israeli-backed 'Kurdistan' in Northern Iraq. Israeli officials have been training and arming Kurdish commandos to engage in terrorist activities in Iran and elsewhere on the Turkish, Iranian and Syrian border. A Turkish land invasion and aerial attack would, at a minimum, destroy or disarticulate these terrorist bases and more likely lead to a generalized Kurdish mobilization in defense of the Kurdish irregulars. The Kurds are loyal clients and their Peshmerga militias play an integral role in ethnic cleansing of non-Kurds in Northern Iraq and savage repression in Central Iraq as US-led mercenary forces against the Iraq Arab resistance. A Turkish invasion is likely to result in the transfer of the Kurdish military toward their Turkish frontier, undermining US control in Iraq and weakening their assaults on Iran. The Israelis will have to choose between its alliance with Turkey, its only consequential ally in the Middle East, by withdrawing its operative and arms sales from 'Kurdish' Northern Iraq or its support for Kurdish separatists.

The entire ZPC was on maximum alert to block or defeat the Armenian resolution in the US Congress in order to show the Turkish Prime Minister Erdogan that Israel is using its power over the US Congress on Turkey's behalf. In this conflict between, on the one hand, millions of Americans who abhor genocide – wherever it occurs and whoever is victimized – and the influential Armenian lobby, and, on the other hand, a few dozen highly placed 'Israel First' Congress members and their billionaire Zionist political contributors, the latter won out. Even on an issue as palpable as genocide, the ZPC has no fear or shame in opposing a symbolic resolution recognizing a historic 'world crime'.

The Zionist Congressional victory on the Armenian resolution illustrates in the most graphic manner the way Israeli interests degrades our institutions and values. The fact that many Congress-members, including the majority of Democrats, were initially convinced of the justice of passing the resolution, and later under the pressure of the Zionist Congressional leadership, withdrew their support, is indicative of just how far Congress has degenerated into a Zionist colonized institution. Not only does Congress ignore its electorate, the values of the people who elected them, but also they surrender their own values and conscience, for what Seymour Hersh aptly refers to as "New York Jewish money".

The Israeli effort to head off a Turkish attack on their Kurdish clients is closely related to their efforts to undermine Iranian defenses and gain intelligence via terrorist 'commando operations' by Kurdish irregulars.

The centerpiece of activity for all the major national, state and local pro-Israeli Jewish organizations is to isolate and destroy Iran, by economic sanctions and a massive military attack by the US. There is absolutely no consideration of the millions of Iranians who would be killed, injured or made homeless by a US or Israeli effort to 'wipe Iran off the map.'

The major recipient of 'New York (and Los Angeles, Miami and Chicago) Jewish money' is Hillary Clinton, the most hawkish Democratic war monger in the 2008 president race – in fact the most hawkish Democratic candidate since the Vietnam era. Clinton, in a recent article in *Foreign Affairs*, has all but written the date and weapons with which the US will strike Iran. She argues that 'Iran poses a long-term strategic challenge to America and its allies and that it must not be permitted to build or acquire nuclear weapons..." If Iran does not comply, all options must remain on the table. (Guardian, October 15, 2007).

Israel keeps a box score on how servile US presidential candidates are to Israeli state interests and obedient to the dictates of the Israel lobby. Clinton, by far, is the Zionist choice among Democratic presidential candidates. They have forgiven her for kissing Suha Arafat over a decade ago, because she has kissed both cheeks of each and all male and female Zionist lobbyists and Israeli officials in Washington and applauded the repression of Palestinians. Clinton aroused the passion and pleasure of the pro-Israel Presidents of the Major American Jewish Organization by being the only Democratic presidential candidate to support the Senate resolution calling on the US government to declare the Iranian government's 'Revolutionary Guards', an elite division of Teheran's military, to be a 'terrorist entity', thus providing the Bush administration with a justification for a massive pre-emptive attack against Iran and its infrastructure.

Both in terms of financing war resolutions and sanctions campaigns against Iran, in terms of lobby authored legislation and Congressional speeches, of hours campaigning for an attack on Iran, of op-ed columns published and media pundits comments, the Zionist Power Configuration exceeds by a multiple of ten any other group in pushing for a war with Iran. Not only does the Zionist monopolize the 'attack Iran' propaganda, but they lead all other authoritarian groups in silencing US critics of this aggressive military option.

Let us be perfectly clear that the ZPC, the Presidents of the Major American Jewish Organizations, the Rahm Emanuels (Israeli-Americans) controlling the Democratic caucus agenda...do not always and everywhere speak for the majority of American Jews, especially on the denial of the Turkish genocide of the Armenians. Pugnacious ADL President Abraham Foxman found out in Watham, Massachusetts that both the local Armenian-American community and their Jewish-American compatriots and neighbors do not tolerate the denial of genocide – even by the ADL. Substantial sectors of American Jews object to Clinton's warmongering and find her servile truckling to Israeli officials offensive, even obscene. Zionist polls reveal the majority of educated young American Jews are less and less interested in Israel and its local Fifth Column – much to the chagrin of the self-styled 'leaders' of the community. Saying that a Jewish minority speaks in the name of an unwilling majority, however, does not lessen its power and stranglehold over US political institutions and public opinion with regard to policy or appropriations touching on the Middle East or Israeli-defined interests.

'Jew-haters' became the agitation slogan animating the Zion-con purge of public forums and a call for mass direct action by hundreds of local Jewish notables and 'community' councils. Even Presbyterian elders were browbeaten by Jewish Zionists because of their tepid stand in favor of divesting from US companies involved in oppressing Palestinians.

There is no transcendent event, which defines the moment in which Zion-conservation became Zion-Fascism. The transition was an evolutionary process, during which racism, militarism and authoritarianism developed a mass community base and took hold over time and became the definitive modus operandi of the ZPC.

Like earlier fascist movements, Zion-fascism subscribes to racialist doctrines of knowledge: According to Zionist epistemology only Jews can (if they dare) criticize Jews as knowledge of Jewry is monopolized by a closed communally defined people. This Zion-fascist theory of knowledge is buttressed by the frequent utterances of progressive or leftist Zionists who frequently dismiss or warn non-Jewish writers that they enter the 'Jewish' debate at their peril.

Zion-fascism is not merely an ideological expression of a marginal group of unbalanced extremists – its ideology and practice, in full or part, has been taken over by mainstream Jewish organizations.

Zionist Authoritarianism on the March

Grassroots Zionist-led authoritarianism, practicing coercion, repression and financial blackmail in defense of Israel and the ZPC is occurring in every region of the country, in every sphere of social, cultural and academic life at an accelerating pace. Below we cite a small sample of cases which have gotten national and even international attention and which illustrate a far more extensive pattern. We lack a comprehensive data bank to cover the hundreds of incidents of Zionist intimidation and thought control which occur on a weekly basis and go unreported by their victims for fear of retaliation or because they would not receive sympathetic public attention given the media bias. In informal interviews, writers and journalists have reported to me 'visits' by local Jewish 'notables' and members of the Jewish Community Councils to local newspaper editors to demand the firing of columnists who dared to criticize, for example, Israel's horrific invasion of Lebanon. After one such 'visit' and 'talk', a local columnist never ventured to criticize or even write about the Middle East. This is not a matter confined to the United States. In 2004, after I wrote an article for the Mexico City daily *La Jornada* critical of Israel's savage repression of Palestinians in Jena and the US Zionist apology for mass killings, the Israeli Ambassador in Mexico visited the editors to demand they discontinue publishing my articles. The editor refused to accede at that time, but immediately afterwards they published several vicious personal attacks by their regular columnists (one a Trotskyist and the other a Jewish dentist) labeling my critiques as 'Nazi' propaganda in line with the 'Protocols of Zion'. This was in a reputed independent progressive daily newspaper.

'Private visits', abusive phone calls by Zionist zealots, including death threats are not uncommon practices among 'respectable' Zion-fascists. One incident involved a local doctor who received a visit to her office by a fanatical Zionist 'colleague' complaining of her letter to the local newspaper criticizing the role of the Zionists in financing the electoral defeat of Georgia Congresswoman, Cynthia McKinney because of her criticism of Israeli policy. She was warned that it was anti-Semitic to criticize the activities of organized Jewry in destroying politicians, especially black politicians, for their support of Palestinian civil rights. African Americans, she was told, were increasingly ungrateful to American Jews, who had lead and financed the civil rights struggle, and therefore had to be taught a history lesson. A local 'group' of notables had chosen her Harvard-educated Zionist colleague to deliver this message. When he declared himself a "Jew and a Zionist", she countered that she was an "anti-fascist and an anti-Zionist" and pointed to the door; but not before asking him how an educated man of high professional standing could stomach such a degrading task of trying to censor a colleague. These types of 'visits' from 'respectable' Zionists intimidate others with less standing and intestinal fortitude.

When presented with the manuscript of my book, *The Power of Israel in the United States*, many of my previous editors informed me that it would make a great book… but… they didn't want to face the backlash, threats and vituperation that they expected from the ZPC, Jewish academics, writers on contract and publishers. Even the publisher and editor who finally agreed to publish my MS expressed real fear of Zionist hostility – and eventually a dozen or so Jewish academics cancelled book orders for their classes.

A sample of the most publicized cases of Zionist efforts to silence and purge American society of critics of Israel and the Zionist Power Configuration includes the case of over one thousand Zionist alumni of Barnard College campaigning to deny tenure to Professor Nadia Abu el-Haj for publishing Facts on the Ground, her groundbreaking critique on Israeli archeologists efforts to erase centuries of continued Palestinian presence in the Holy Lands (Chronicle of Higher Education, August 5, 2007).

More recently there was the public campaign to rescind Colombia University's invitation to Iranian Prime Minister Mahmoud Ahmadinejad resulting in an unprecedented insulting introductory address by the President of Colombia University.

Banning the successful British play, 'My Name is Rachel Corrie' based on the writings of the murdered American activist from scheduled performances in Miami, Toronto and nearly New York caused consternation among theater goers and actors on both sides of the Atlantic. The Israeli soldier who murdered the young woman was exonerated in Israel while Rachel's words were nearly banned from the cultural capital of her own country.

Even more recently, the Chicago Council of Global Affairs bowed to pressure from the Zionist lobby and cancelled a lecture by the respected professors of political science, John Mearsheimer and Stephan Walt, because of their critical study The Israel Lobby.

The list goes on to include the cancellation of a concert by Marcel Khalife in San Diego, California, and the cancellation of an invitation to Nobel Peace Prize winner, South African Bishop Desmond

Tutu, because of his criticism of Israeli apartheid policies in the occupied territories.

There was a successful campaign to prevent author Susan Abulhawa from presenting her gripping novel, *The Scar of David,* at a Barnes and Noble Bookstore in Bayside, New York. This was followed by a cyberspace attack on the author to undermine a scheduled speaking tour. This pro-Israel attack was led by 14 rabbis and the President of the Queens Jewish Community Council.

The University of Michigan Press was pressured to withdraw distribution of Joel Kovel's *Overcoming Zionism,* violating a contract with his publisher, Pluto Press. The University Press then threatened to stop distribution of all books published by Pluto Press.

The recent Congressional Hearings of a blue ribbon committee, which finally got around to investigating the Israeli military attack on the USS Liberty (after 40 years of successfully preventing an official investigation through the pressure of the Israel lobby) found Israel guilty of the deliberate killing and maiming of over 100 US service personnel. Its explosive findings, published in the Congressional Record, almost never even appeared in the print and broadcast media.

In violation of United Nations resolutions, Israel's military aggression against Lebanon, Syria and Palestine, were rewarded by the US Congress with an additional $30 billion dollars in military aid over the next 10 years, making the US annual 'tribute to Israel' in excess of $6 Billion dollars a year (*NY Times,* August 16, 2007). At a time of record US deficits and cuts in domestic health programs for poor children and educational services, the vote to give Israel an additional $30 billion dollars passed with virtually no opposition or even discussion.

Australian journalist and documentary maker, John Pilger produced a searing critique of Israel entitled *Palestine is Still the Issue* which has been viewed all over the world. Its scheduled showing on the public educational channel in San Francisco was blocked by a campaign led by the Jewish Community Relations Council.

The bilingual Arabic-English public middle school in New York City named after the Lebanese Christian poet, Kahil Gibran, was attacked by the ZPC (*NY Times*, August 11, 2007) leading to the firing of its Arab American Principal. Her 'crime' was accurately translating the Arabic word 'intifada' into 'shaking off' instead of ranting against the Palestinian rights movement in the Occupied Territories. The Zionist-controlled United Federation of Teachers actively backed the blatant purge of one of its own members for her thought crimes.

At San Francisco State College there was a campaign led by the executive director of the Jewish Community Relations Council of San Francisco to ban a mural depicting a famous Palestinian cartoon character, a little boy defiant before Israeli occupiers. The subject in question was a child holding a key in his hand, which, according to the local Jewish leadership represented a "veiled reference to Palestinian right of return to Israel" (*Jewish Forum*, August 10, 2007).

One of the most bitter and successful Zionist Purge campaigns was to deny tenure to highly respected scholar, Professor Norman Finkelstein of De Paul University in Chicago. The purge, led by Harvard Law Professor Alan Dershowitz, was a direct response to Finkelstein's numerous scholarly studies critical of Israel and the exploitation of the Holocaust to further the aims of the Zionist Power Configuration.

Despite the recommendations of three academic committees at Yale University, Zionist millionaire philanthropists were able to block the appointment of renowned Middle East specialist, Professor Juan Cole. The millionaires threatened to withdraw contributions and several Zionist professors prepared a scurrilous attack on Professor Cole (June 1, 2006).

A campaign was mounted to pressure several state pension funds to divest funds from any company doing business with Iran and pushing the funds to invest in Israel bonds. This has so far succeeded in Texas, Florida, New York, and New Jersey. Several state governors were 'persuaded' while on Zionist-paid junkets to Israel (see *Houston Chronicle*, July 18, 2007). During one of these junkets, the now disgraced New Jersey Governor McGreevy met an Israeli operative with whom he formed a homosexual relation and later had him installed as 'Homeland Security' Chief for the State of New Jersey; that is, until the FBI intervened. McGreevy resigned from office after denouncing the Israeli, Golan Cipal, for blackmail.

Pro-Israel transmission belt operatives in the Anti Defamation League forced the only Muslim Congressman, Keith Ellison, to recant and humiliate himself for daring to compare the tactics of the Bush Administration to the Nazis (*Jewish Telegraph Agency*, July 20, 2007). As in the case of Congresswoman McKinney, Zionist 'punishment' against African-American politicians is particularly vehement.

The major Zionist organizations led by the American Jewish Committee successfully mobilized the major US trade union bureaucrats to denounce the United Kingdom's militant trade union's boycotts of Israel (*Jerusalem Post*, July 22, 2007). The AFL-CIO unions are under the thumb of the ZPC and have purchased over $5 billion dollars of their members pension funds in Israel bonds which consistently under-perform market indexes, thus costing their 12 million members hundreds of millions of investment returns each year.

The dean of religion, Barry Levin, a pro-Israel activist at McGill University recently fired Professor Norman Cornelt after 15 years of teaching for his support of Palestinian human rights (Montreal Gazette, June 2, 2007).

Every major newspaper published editorials and scurrilous book reviews attacking former US President Jimmy Carter's critical study, *Palestine: Peace Not Apartheid*. This was part of a high-priority propaganda campaign coordinated by major Zionist organizations and prominently included Professor Alan Dershowitz (*Washington Report on Middle East Affairs*, April 2007).

The prominent Jewish writer, Professor Tony Judt of New York University, was dis-invited from a scheduled talk at the Polish Consulate because of Zionist opposition to his criticism of Israeli policy.

B'nai Brith of Vancouver, Canada attacked a Canadian web site called 'Peace, Earth and Justice' forcing the removal of 18 articles critical of Israel.

In early 2007, the ZPC intervened in the US Civil Rights Commission and introduced a section equating anti-Zionism with anti-Semitism and slandered dozens of academic Middle Eastern studies programs as centers of campus 'anti-Semitism'. The Middle East Studies Association of North America, the major academic group, wrote a reasoned refutation on June 11, 2007.

Plans to construct a mosque for the Muslim community in Roxbury, Massachusetts were attacked in a campaign by the 'David Project', a Zionist front group affiliated with the Jewish Community Council of Greater Boston.

On the basis of secret testimony by Israeli intelligence agents and backed by the ZPC, 'terrorism' charges were made against 16 members of a US Islamic charity. A Texas court convicted them of 'crimes' against Israel, even though many of the accused were US citizens and had no access to challenge their hooded accusers, who were Israeli secret agents operating in the US. The lead defendant, Dr. Rafil Dhofer received a sentence of 22 years for an 'Israeli' crime – although he was never convicted of any crime committed in the US. The defendants and their attorneys were never allowed to question the secret foreign 'witnesses'.

Campus Zion-fascist organizations run by their 'little fuehrer' David Horowitz, routinely bait blacks, Latinos and Arab Americans by praising the 'benefits' of the African slave trade and defend the use of torture and assassination by Israelis and their US counterparts in Iraq and Guantanamo. They also smear professors not sufficiently favorable to Zionism, spy on instructors, disrupt classes, bring lawsuits for 'anti-Zionist' bias against teachers, other students and college administrators throughout the US.

Despite the Zionist turn to fascist tactics and embrace of authoritarian-coercive measures, the fact of the matter is they still have only partial control over civil society and political power. Some of the Zion-fascist power plays were, at least temporarily, defeated in specific circumstances. The play, *My Name is Rachel Corrie,* played to packed houses in London, Seattle and other cities even as it was banned in Toronto, Miami, and nearly New York.

Norman Finkelstein was fired, but he got powerful support throughout the academic world and was able to negotiate monetary compensation for De Paul University's cowardly betrayal of one of its faculty. Above all, Professor Finkelstein is fighting back courageously.

The University of Michigan was forced to distribute Kovel's book even as they threatened to cancel their contract with his publisher, Pluto Press.

The lesson is clear: the rise of Judeo-fascism (JF) represents a clear and present danger to our democratic freedoms in the United States. They do not come with black shirts and stiff-arm salutes. The public face is a clean-shaved, necktied, pink-jowled attorney, real estate philanthropist or Ivy League professor. They work hard to send the family members of non-Zionists to fight wars in the Middle East in the interest of Greater Israel. And they tells us to keep quiet or face slander, ostracism in our communities, loss of jobs or worse… And it is the exemplary punishment of the many small voices, which keeps the number of vocal critics low…until recently. There is rising anger and hostility in America against the ZPC, and against its arrogant authoritarian communal attacks on our democratic values. Sooner or later there will be a major backlash – and it ill behooves those who, through vocation or conviction, engaged in the firings, censoring and intimidation campaigns against the American majority. The American people will not remember their cries of 'anti-Semitism' they will recall their role in sending thousands of American soldiers to their death in the Middle East in the interests of Israel.

Let us hope that those who seek justice will not use the same authoritarian laws like the Patriot Act, nor the harsh interrogation techniques of degradation (torture) and anti-Arab/Muslim practices promoted by the Zionists in the Pentagon, Congress, Justice

Department and Homeland Security. Those who oppose Zionism need to abide solidly by higher moral standards.

James Petras, a former Professor of Sociology at Binghamton University, New York, owns a 50-year membership in the class struggle, is an adviser to the land-less and jobless in Brazil and Argentina, and is co-author of Globalization Unmasked *(Zed Books). His latest book is* The Power of Israel in the United States *(Clarity Press, 2006). His forthcoming book is* Rulers and Ruled (Bankers, Zionists and Militants *(Clarity Press, Atlanta). He can be reached at: jpetras@binghamton.edu or http://petras.lahaine.org/*

For Fear of the Jews

by Joseph Sobran

The news that I would be addressing the Institute of Historical Review [IHR] came to some people as, well… news. It was mentioned in the Jewish newspaper *Forward* [June 14] and on the Zionist *Wall Street Journal* Online. The editors of two conservative magazines called and wrote me to express their concern that I might damage my reputation, such as it is, by speaking to "Holocaust deniers."

I'm not sure why this should matter. Even positing that I was speaking to a disreputable audience, I expect to be judged by what I say, not whom I say it to. I note that my enemies have written a great deal about me, yet they rarely quote me directly.

Why not? If I am so disreputable myself, I must at least occasionally say disreputable things. Is it possible that what I say is more cogent than they like to admit?

My enemies are always are welcome to quote anything I say, if they dare. I would say the same things to them, and they may consider my remarks to the IHR as addressed to them too. I wasn't just speaking to "Holocaust deniers," but also to Holocaust believers.

Because I've endured smears and ostracism for my criticism of Israel and its American lobby, some people credit me with courage. I'm

279

flattered, of course, but this compliment, whether or not I deserve it, implies that it's professionally dangerous for a journalist to criticize Israel. That tells you a lot.

But if I'm "courageous," what do you call Mark Weber and the Institute for Historical Review? They have been smeared far worse than I have; moreover, they have been seriously threatened with death. Their offices have been firebombed. Do they at least get credit for courage? Not at all. They remain almost universally vilified.

When I met Mark, many years ago, I expected to meet a raving Jew-hating fanatic, such being the generic reputation of "Holocaust deniers." I was immediately and subsequently impressed to find that he was just the opposite: a mild-mannered, good-humored, witty, scholarly man who habitually spoke with restraint and measure, even about enemies who would love to see him dead. The same is true of other members of the Institute. In my many years of acquaintance with them, I have never heard any of them say anything that would strike an unprejudiced listener as unreasonable or bigoted.

It was their enemies who were raving, hate-filled fanatics, unable to discuss "Holocaust deniers" in measured language, without wild hyperbole, loose accusation, and outright lies. I began to wonder: if they can't tell the truth about "Holocaust deniers," how can they tell the truth about the Holocaust itself?

Even if the Holocaust had really happened, as I assumed, maybe it should be studied with a critical rationality most of its believers obviously lacked. After all, even Stalin's crimes might be exaggerated, quite understandably, by his victims. As Milton puts it, "Let truth and falsehood grapple; who ever knew truth put to the worse in a free and open encounter?" Even those in error might have something to say, some marginal clarification to offer. Why stop our ears against them?

Why on earth is it "anti-Jewish" to conclude from the evidence that the standard numbers of Jews murdered are inaccurate, or that the Hitler regime, bad as it was in many ways, was not, in fact, intent on racial extermination? Surely these are controversial conclusions;

but if so, let the controversy rage. There is no danger in permitting it to proceed. It might be different if denying the Holocaust could somehow affect the course of events, as the denial of Stalin's crimes by the New York Times in the 1930s helped him to continue committing them. Why is the Institute for Historical Review notorious, while the Times, despite its active support of Stalin at the height of his power, remains a pillar of respectability?

The Holocaust has never been a consuming interest of mine. But as I read the Journal of Historical Review over the years, I found in it the same calm virtue of critical rationality I'd found in Mark himself. And it was applied to many other subjects besides the question of whether Hitler had tried to exterminate the Jews. An article it carried about Abraham Lincoln some years ago caused me to revise my entire view of Lincoln and stimulated me to write a book about him. [Robert Morgan, "Abraham Lincoln and the Issue of Race," The Journal of Historical Review, Sept.-Oct. 1993.]

The IHR's mission can't be fairly summed up as "Holocaust denial." Its real mission is criticism of the suffocating progressive ideology that has infected and distorted the telling of history in our time. But of course its specific skepticism of the standard Holocaust story is regarded as blasphemy, and has earned it the dreaded epithet of anti-Semitism.

Not long ago the only label more lethal to one's reputation was that of child molester, but, as many men of the cloth are now discovering, there is this difference: a child molester may hope for a second chance.

There is also another difference. We have a pretty clear idea what child molestation is. Nobody really knows what "anti-Semitism" is. My old boss Bill Buckley wrote an entire book called *In Search of Anti-Semitism* without bothering to define anti-Semitism.

At the time I thought this was an oversight. I was wrong. The word would lose its utility if it were defined. As I observed in my own small contribution to the book, an "anti-Semite" used to mean a man who hated Jews. Now it means a man who is hated by Jews.

Joseph Sobran

I doubt, in fact I can't imagine, that anyone associated with the IHR has ever done harm to another human being because he was Jewish. In fact the IHR has never been accused of anything but thought-crimes.

The same is true of me. Nobody has ever accused me of the slightest personal indecency to a Jew. My chief offense, it appears, has been to insist that the state of Israel has been a costly and treacherous "ally" to the United States. As of last September 11, I should think that is undeniable. But I have yet to receive a single apology for having been correct.

If I were to hate Jews en masse, without distinction, I would be guilty of many things. Obviously I'd be guilty of injustice and uncharity to Jews as human beings. I would also be guilty of willful stupidity. More personally, I'd be guilty of ingratitude to my benefactors -- which Dante, in his Inferno, ranks the worst of all sins -- since many of my benefactors, in large ways and small, have been Jewish.

Moreover, I would be becoming exactly the man my Zionist enemies would like me to be; a man like them, in whom ethnic hostilities take priority over all other values and considerations. I would justify them in treating me as an enemy. In fact I'd go so far as to say that I would be helping to justify the state of Israel. I consider that if I fight these people on their terms, they have already won.

What, exactly, is "anti-Semitism"? One standard dictionary definition is "hostility toward or discrimination against Jews as a religious or racial group." How this applies to me has never been explained. My "hostility" toward Israel is a desire not for war, but for neutrality -- out of a sense of betrayal, waste, and shame. Our venal politicians have aligned us with a foreign country that behaves dishonorably. Most alleged "anti-Semites" would wince if Jews anywhere were treated as Israel treats its Arab subjects. Moreover, Israel has repeatedly betrayed its only benefactor, the United States. I have already alluded to the place Dante reserves for those who betray their benefactors.

These are obvious moral facts. Yet it's not only politicians who are afraid to point them out; so are most journalists -- the people who

282

are supposed to be independent enough to say the things politicians can't afford to say. In my thirty years in journalism, nothing has amazed me more than the prevalent fear in the profession of offending Jews, especially Zionist Jews.

The fear of the label anti-Semitic is a fear of the power that is believed to lie behind it: Jewish power. Yet this is still pretty much unmentionable in journalism. It's rather as if sportswriters covering pro basketball were prohibited from mentioning that the Los Angeles Lakers were in first place.

There has been a qualitative change that is downright eerie in American conservatism generally. The "fear of the Jews," to use the phrase so often repeated in the Gospel according to John, seems to have wrought a reorientation of the tone, the very principles, of today's conservatism. The hardy skepticism, critical intelligence, and healthy irony of men like James Burnham, Willmoore Kendall, and the young Buckley have given way to the uncritical philo-Semitism of George Will, Cal Thomas, Rush Limbaugh, and of course the later Buckley -- men who will go to any lengths, even absurd and dishonorable lengths, to avoid the terrorizing label anti-Semite.

It was once considered "anti-Semitic" to impute "dual loyalty" to Jews -- that is, to assert that most American Jews divide their loyalty between the United States and Israel. This is now passé. Today most politicians assume, as a matter of course, that Israel commands the primary loyalty of Jewish voters. Are they accused of "anti-Semitism" for doing so? Does this assumption cost them Jewish votes? Not at all! Dual loyalty nothing! Dual loyalty would be an improvement!

Once again, it's a practical necessity to know what it would be professional suicide to say. No politician in his right mind would accuse Jews of giving their primary loyalty to Israel; but most politicians act as if this were the case. And they succeed.

You can read Jewish publications like *Commentary* for years, and you'll read interminable discussions about what's good for Israel, but you'll never encounter the slightest suggestion that what's good for Israel might not be good for America. The possibility simply never comes up. The only discernible duty of Jews, it seems, is to look out for Israel. They never have to choose between Israel and the United States. So much for the "canard" of dual loyalty.

I've often noticed how eager and desperate mainstream conservatives are to avoid Jewish wrath. Again, they don't just speak favorably of Israel: they refuse to acknowledge any cost to American interests in the U.S.-Israel alliance. They treat the two countries' interests as identical; when they scold either government, it's always -- always -- the U.S. Government for failing to support our "reliable ally." They are in headlong flight from reality. They have none of the realism of James Burnham, whose writings and style of thought would be wholly unwelcome in today's conservative movement.

They are frightened. You can sense this in their bluster, in the vicarious jingoism with which they address Israel. Their fear produces a peculiar intellectual thinness that pervades all their thinking on foreign policy. Individualists have been replaced by apparatchiks. Zionism has infiltrated conservatism in much the same way Communism once infiltrated liberalism.

Here I should lay my own cards on the table. I am not, heaven forbid, a "Holocaust denier." I lack the scholarly competence to be one. I don't read German, so I can't assess the documentary evidence; I don't know chemistry, so I can't discuss Zyklon-B; I don't understand the logistics of exterminating millions of people in small spaces. Besides, "Holocaust denial" is illegal in many countries I may want to visit someday. For me, that's proof enough. One Israeli writer has expressed his amazement at the idea of criminalizing opinions about historical fact, and I find it puzzling too; but the state has spoken.

Of course those who affirm the Holocaust need know nothing about the German language, chemistry, and other pertinent subjects; they need only repeat what they have been told by the authorities. In every controversy, most people care much less for what the truth is than for which side it's safer and more respectable to take. They shy away from taking a position that is likely to get them into trouble. Just as only people on the Axis side were accused of war crimes after

World War II, only people critical of Jewish interests are accused of thought-crimes in today's mainstream press.

So, life being as short as it is, I shy away from this controversy. Of course I'm also incompetent to judge whether the Holocaust did happen; so I've become what might be called a "Holocaust stipulator." Like a lawyer who doesn't want to get bogged down debating a secondary point, I stipulate that the standard account of the Holocaust is true. What is undisputed -- the massive violation of human rights in Hitler's Germany -- is bad enough.

What interests me is the growth of what Norman Finkelstein has called "the Holocaust Industry." True or not, the Holocaust story has been put to many uses, some of them mischievous. It is currently being used to extort reparations and to blacken reputations, for example. Daniel Goldhagen is soon to publish a book ["Hitler's Willing Executioners"] blaming the Holocaust on the central teachings of the Catholic Church. This is only the most ambitious project of a school of thought, largely but not exclusively Jewish, that sees Christianity as the source of all "anti-Semitism."

So if you want to avoid being called "anti-Semitic," the safest course is to renounce Christianity. Whether this is a safe course for your immortal soul is a question Goldhagen doesn't address. The important thing is to avoid Jewish censure. Obviously this sort of thinking presupposes Christian fear of the Jews. Jews themselves are not unaware of Jewish power; some of them have rather exaggerated confidence in it.

But the chief use of the Holocaust story is to undergird the legitimacy of the state of Israel. According to this view, the Holocaust proves that Jewish existence is always in danger, unless the Jews have their own state in their own homeland. The Holocaust stands as the historical objectification of all the world's gentiles' eternal "anti-Semitism." Jewish life is an endless emergency, requiring endless emergency measures arid justifying everything done in the name of "defense." Jews and Israel can't be judged by in normal standards, at least until Israel is absolutely safe -- if even then. Their circumstances are forever abnormal.

But the daily news reports suggest that Israel may not really be the safest place for Jews. Theodore Herzl's original dream was of a Jewish state where Jews could at last live the normal lives they were denied in the Diaspora. Yet today it's Diaspora Jews who live relatively normal lives, at least in the West, while they must worry about the very survival of Israel. And far from being the independent state Herzl hoped for, Israel depends heavily on the support not only of Diaspora Jews but of foreign gentiles, especially Americans.

Israel insists that its "right to exist" is nothing more than the right of every nation on earth to be left in peace. This right is allegedly threatened by fanatical Arabs who want to "drive the Jews into the sea," as witness the recent wave of Palestinian terror. But in truth, Israel's claimed "right to exist" is much more than it seems at first sight. It means a right to rule as Jews, enjoying rights denied to native Palestinians.

We are told incessantly that Israel is a "democracy," and therefore the natural ally of the United States, whose "democratic values" it shares. This is a very dubious claim. To Americans, democracy means majority rule, but with equal rights for minorities. In Israel and the occupied territories, equal rights for the minority are simply out of the question.

Majority rule itself has taken a peculiar form in Israel. The original Arab majority was driven out of their homes and their native land, and kept out. Meanwhile, a Jewish "majority" was artificially imported. Not only the first immigrants from Eastern Europe, but every Jew on earth was granted a "right of return" -- that is, "return" to a "homeland" most have never lived in, and in which none of their ancestors has ever lived. A Jew from Brooklyn (whose grandfather came from Poland) can fly to Israel and immediately claim rights denied to an Arab whose people have always lived in Palestine. In recent years Israel has been augmenting its Jewish majority by vigorously encouraging Jewish immigration, especially from Russia. Ariel Sharon has told a group of American senators that Israel needs a million more Jewish immigrants.

Israel rejects demands for a "right of return" for Palestinians exiled since 1948. Its reason? This would mean "the end of the Jewish state." An Arab majority would surely vote down Jewish ethnic privileges. If Israel remained democratic, it wouldn't long remain Jewish. It must be the only "democracy" whose existence depends on inequality.

American gentiles, bemused by the propaganda claim that a beleaguered little democracy is fighting for its very right to exist, still haven't figured out that Israeli "democracy" is essentially and radically different from -- even repugnant to -- what they understand as democracy. Put otherwise, Zionism is a denial of the "self-evident truths" of the Declaration of Independence. To acknowledge those truths, and to put them into practice, would mean the end of Israel as a Jewish state. Again, honest and rigorous Zionists have always seen and said this.

With the verbal sleight-of-hand at which they are masters, the Israelis always appeal to the Holocaust. Maybe they have nuclear weapons, but their existence is threatened -- once more! -- by rock-throwing Arab boys. The Arabs are the new Nazis, repeating and perpetuating the eternal peril of the Jews. Israel is determined to prevent another Holocaust and must crush the Arab threat by any means necessary, including harsh measures.

Israel without the Holocaust is hard to imagine. But let's try to imagine it.

Suppose the Holocaust had never occurred, had never been alleged, had never been called "the Holocaust." Imagine that no great persecution had provided the Jewish state with a special excuse for oppressive emergency measures. In other words, imagine that Israel were forced to justify itself like any other state.

In that case, Israel's treatment of its Arab minorities would appear to the world in a very different light. Its denial of equal or even basic rights to those minorities would lack the excuse of a past or prospective "Holocaust." Civilized people would expect it to treat those it ruled with impartial justice. Special privileges for Jews would appear as outrageous discrimination, no different from insulting legal discrimination against Jews. The sense -- and excuse -- of perpetual crisis would be absent. Israel might be forced or pressured, possibly against its will, to be "normal." If it chose to be democratic, its Jews would have to take their chance of being outnumbered, just like majorities in other democracies. Nobody would suppose that losing elections would mean their annihilation.

In short, the Holocaust has become a device for exempting Jews from normal human obligations. It has authorized them to bully and blackmail, to extort and oppress. This is all quite irrational, because even if six million Jews were murdered during World War II, the survivors are not entitled to commit the slightest injustice. If your father was stabbed in the street, that's a pity, but it's not an excuse for picking someone else's pocket.

In a peculiar way, the Holocaust story has promoted not only pity, but actual fear of the Jews. It has removed them from the universe of normal moral discourse. It has made them victims with nukes. It has made them even more dangerous than their enemies have always charged. It has given the world an Israel ruled by Ariel Sharon.

Benjamin Netanyahu has written that Israel is "an integral part of the West." I think it would be truer to say that Israel has become a deformed limb of the West.

Joseph Sobran is an author, lecturer and syndicated columnist. For 21 years he wrote for National Review magazine, including 18 years as a senior editor. He is editor of the monthly newsletter Sobran's (P.O. Box 1383, Vienna, VA 22183), or see http://www.sobran.com/

This article is adapted from his address at the 14th IHR Conference, June 22, 2002, in Irvine, California. It was published in the August 2002 issue of Sobran's newsletter, and in the May–August 2002 issue of the IHR's Journal of Historical Review.

A most interesting document and a first-hand witness: our friend, the Chairman of Deir Yassin Remembered, Prof Dan McGowan visited and comforted the German political prisoner of Zion, Ernst Zündel. Visiting prisoners is a great mitzvah, a good deed which is counted twice, on earth and on heaven, and the Lord is blessed as "matir asurim", He Who Releases Prisoners. Whoever visits and comforts a prisoner is like one who comforts Christ, and he will be comforted. By spreading the news of his visit, we participate in McGowan's good deed and benefit of his virtue. – **Israel Shamir**

A Visit in Prison with Ernst Zundel

by Prof. Daniel McGowan

December, 28, 2006

During the recent conference in Iran (Review of the Holocaust: Global Vision) I was in prison in Mannheim, Germany interviewing Ernst Zundel. Labelled a "Holocaust denier," Ernst has been in jail for almost four years without being charged with a violent crime or without even being convicted of a non-violent one. He is 67 year old.

As a six-year old Ernst witnessed the Allied firebombing of Pforzheim in which ten to twenty thousand German civilians were killed. As a teenager he became a pacifist; at age 19 he moved to Canada to avoid serving in the post-war German army. In Canada he worked as a graphic artist and publisher specializing in 20th century

German history. Many of the books he republished questioned the Holocaust, such as the underground booklet Did Six Million Really Die? by Richard Harwood. Others he merely distributed, like The Rudolf Report by Germar Rudolf, An Eye for an Eye: The Untold Story of Jewish Revenge Against Germans in 1945 by John Sack, and Jewish Supremacism: My Awakening to the Jewish Question by David Duke. He also sold books on UFOs and alternative medicines.

Ernst's interest in history and revisionism led him to dispute and challenge specific "facts" about the Holocaust. He claimed

1. that Hitler's "Final Solution" was intended to be ethnic cleansing, not extermination

2. that there were no homicidal gas chambers used by the Third Reich. (He did not deny that there were gas chambers used for disinfection.)

3. there were fewer than 6 million Jews killed of the alleged 55 million who died in WWII

Over the years such firmly held beliefs expressed in writing and later on his wife's Internet site (<http://www.zundelsite.org/>) caused him to be charged with incitement. He was tried twice in Canada. In the middle of the second trial in 1988, Ernst sent the first forensic team to Auschwitz. It was this "Leuchter Expedition" and the subsequent Leuchter Report that he believed revolutionized Holocaust revisionism, taking it beyond the "he said, she said…" testimonies and into the realm of solid forensic science.

Such endeavours made him the target of those who protect the standard Holocaust narrative. He survived three assassination attempts, including by arson and pipe bomb, and although he lived in Canada for 42 years, he was never able to gain Canadian citizenship even though immigration officials had described his application as "flawless."

While some consider his views to border on heresy, freedom of speech in both the United States and Canada protected his right to publish and distribute the truth as he sees it. But neither our Bill of Rights nor the pleadings of his lawyers could prevent his being rendered by the United States, forced back to Canada, and then on to Germany where denying or revising certain aspects of the Holocaust is a crime.

The Latest Incarceration

On February 5, 2003, Ernst was arrested at his home in the mountain region of eastern Tennessee. He was seized on the pretext that he had violated immigration regulations, or had missed an interview date with US immigration authorities, even though he had entered the US legally, was married to an American citizen, had been checked out by the FBI, had been given a health check, a work permit, and a social security number, had no criminal record, and was trying to secure status as a permanent legal resident.

After being held for two weeks, he was deported to Canada. For the next two years – from mid-February 2003 to March 1, 2005 – he was held in solitary confinement in the Toronto West Detention Centre, on the charge that he was a threat to national security. Like others who suffer rendition, there was no bail, no public trial, and no appeal. His mail was censored and the lights in his cell were kept on day and night.

On March 1, 2005 Ernst was put in handcuffs and leg irons on a private jet and deported from Canada to Germany where he has been held as an Untersuchungsgefangener or a prisoner under investigation. As in Canada, bail was again denied. On June 29, 2005, the state's prosecutor, Mr. Grossman, formally charged him with inciting "hatred" by having written or distributed texts that "approve, deny or play down" genocidal actions carried out by Germany's wartime regime, and which "denigrate the memory of the [Jewish] dead."

The trial began on November 8, 2005, eight months after he arrived in Germany.

Ernst is confined to his cell 22 ¾ hours per day. He has no access to phone or Internet and he may not communicate anything about the trial. He is able to receive two 30-minute visits per month, but all conversations must be in German or must be conducted through a prison-approved translator.

Still Ernst remains upbeat and convinced that he has made a contribution to the truth surrounding WWII and the Holocaust. He does not deny that millions of people suffered at the hands of the Nazis, including millions of Jews, who were worked to death and suffered from disease (especially typhus) and who were often deliberately murdered both inside and outside of concentration camps. But he does not regard Jewish suffering as unique. He considers his efforts to tell the truth about the Holocaust as ground breaking and is satisfied to let others continue the research.

Ernst believes that Zionists treat the Holocaust as a sword and a shield to deflect criticism of their racist quest to build a Jewish state in Palestine, a state in which over half the people today are not Jewish, "the state" being defined as all the land currently controlled by Israel, including West Bank, Gaza, and the Golan Heights. He regards himself as a political prisoner of Zionists who try to erase his contributions and punish him with defamation and imprisonment.

A Day in Court

An admirer once described Ernst Zundel as "an outgoing, good-humoured man who is blessed with a rare combination of unflagging optimism and practical ability. He maintains this infectious spirit even under very trying conditions. He is an unusually alert and sensitive individual with a keen understanding of human nature. He inspires confidence, loyalty and affection." On December 7, 2006 I witnessed his trial in Mannheim and found this description to be uncannily accurate.

A VISIT IN PRISON WITH ERNST ZUNDEL

On that particular day those in the courtroom included Ernst, three judges, three jurors, a court reporter, three defense attorneys, four armed guards, twenty-four spectators, and one prosecutor, Mr. Grossman. Ernst wore an old blue suit with a red tie; he was attentive; he often smiled approvingly when something was said with which he agreed. The guards were friendly but disinterested. Facing the court, all the participants sat on the left hand side, except the state prosecutor who sat all by himself at a table on the right side. The jurors and the court reporter sat in line with the judges on an elevated platform along the front and the spectators sat in rows along the back wall. No media were present.

The spectators were clearly there for Ernst. Most were German men in their late 60s or 70s; there were also a couple of younger women. Several men commented that they were proud of having been to every court session with Ernst over the past 21 months. Although they had not met him personally, they were following his trial closely and were supportive of him. They were helpful to my American Jewish colleague and me and guided us through the security outside the courtroom and made sure we got front row seats so that we could fully appreciate the courtroom experience. Many spoke English and had sons and daughters in America. Most were retired but one younger man had taken time off from work to witness this day of the trial.

Ernst and his attorneys have not been allowed to discuss or challenge the veracity of the facts about the Holocaust, including facts that Ernst disputes and about which he would like to submit scientific evidence and expert-witness testimony. Offenkundigkeit, the German version of judicial notice, precludes it. The court is only allowed to consider if Ernst denied these particular facts and if so, when and where and how. During our visit, one of Ernst's attorneys, 84-year old Dr. Herbert Schaller[1], read a lengthy and impassioned statement saying that he believed in the same facts of the Holocaust as does Ernst and by so stating this he too is guilty. He ended by saying that in over 53 years of practicing law he had until now never been guilty of the same crime as the man he was charged to defend. The head judge, Ulrich Meinerzhagen, appeared tired, agitated, and ready to explode.

Visiting Ernst in prison

It is not easy to visit Ernst Zundel. He is allowed only two 30-minute visits per month, one hour if the visitor travels more than 100 km. Though I wrote and faxed the prison a dozen times beginning in February 2006, the answer was always the same, no answer. But through his wife, Ingrid, Ernst knew that a colleague and I wished to visit him and he asked the judge to grant us permission to do so. Finally on September 23rd Judge Meinerzhagen told Ernst to tell his wife to tell me to fax him and formally request a visit. We were to each include a copy of our résumés and a copy of our passports.

Another month passed before we received the visitation permission. Once we had that document, stamped and signed by the judge, we were able to make an appointment at the prison in Mannheim.

On arrival the guards filled out a long form on each of us. They took our passports and had us put everything else in a locker. Then we were searched, warned against speaking English, and told to cross the courtyard to the visitation rooms. There we sat on one side of a table with a plastic shield in the middle; they brought Ernst from the other side and allowed him to sit across from us while a guard sat at the end to monitor both parties. We asked if it was permissible to shake hands and the guard smiled and said that would be all right.

Ernst began by asking us to contact his wife and tell her that he looked well and that he missed her. He had not been in contact with her for several weeks and he was worried that she would be worried about him. Then he asked if my colleague's family had discouraged him from making this trip. My friend understood what Ernst was asking, but he was unable to answer in German, so I had to tell Ernst that indeed pressure had been put on us both not to have anything to do with a Holocaust "denier."

We asked Ernst about life in prison and his relationship with guards and other prisoners. He described a typical day and told us that he had only limited contact with other prisoners, but that they were friendly towards him. So too were the guards, especially because he followed the rules and was a threat to no one. He often asked the man monitoring our visit to corroborate what he was saying, almost as if to include him in the conversation.

He talked about history and philosophy and about recent books he had read. He praised the prison library, which he said was markedly better than the one in the US jail in Tennessee, which had "only Tom Clancy novels and one old book on the US Presidents." I had been forced to leave my notes outside and though I had many questions, I was not allowed to ask him anything about the trial, not even the names of his attorneys.

The hour passed quickly and the guard soon told us we would have to go. When we stood we looked questioningly at the guard and he nodded to us. We shook hands with Ernst, slowly, he taking each of our hands in both of his. They were big, soft, and warm; although Ernst is only six years older than I, he reminded me of my father saying goodbye when we last parted.

Holocaust Denial

Contrary to the warning given to people who currently tour Auschwitz, "Holocaust denial" is not infectious. In many ways the term is used as an epithet to discredit and demean those who question facts surrounding the Holocaust. Nor is Holocaust denial anti-Semitic; there are many Jews who question facts about the Holocaust and many more who object to its being used to elevate Jewish suffering above that of others.[2] Treating those who question the Holocaust as heretics reveals the degree to which the Holocaust itself has become a religion, a faith to be accepted and worshiped with spectacular memorials, best-selling books, and mandatory curricula for school children.

Ernst believes that Jewish groups have wanted him jailed for promoting views that the Jewish-Zionist lobby considers harmful to its interests. He claims that the only sustained and institutionalized efforts to imprison him have come from this lobby, which includes the Simon Wiesenthal Center, the Canadian Jewish Congress, the Canadian Holocaust Remembrance Association, and the League for Human Rights of B'nai B'rith (with the Anti-Defamation League, its counterpart in the US). It is noteworthy that even the ACLU refused to defend his right of free speech. [3]

Ernst Zundel is neither a monster nor a heretic. He is a man with strong convictions and the courage to express them. He views himself not as a Holocaust "denier," but rather as a Holocaust revisionist. For that he has been rendered by the United States, which otherwise professes to protect the right of free speech and the writ of habeas corpus, and by Canada, both countries in which he broke no law. To force him back to his birth country to be tried for a "crime" which he never committed in Germany is unjust. Those who would incarcerate revisionists like Ernst Zundel and hold them, without bail, for years on end to drain them of their resources and to silence them as "Prisoners of Zion" could well be labelled as "justice deniers."

Daniel McGowan, Professor Emeritus, Hobart and William Smith Colleges. He can be reached at: mcgowan@hws.edu

Postscript: On Feb. 15, 2007, a German court sentenced Ernst Zundel to five years in prison for crimes associated with 'Holocaust Denial'. His defense attorney, Sylvia Stolz, was later arrested and sentenced to three and one half years in prison for remarks she made during her courtroom defense of Ernst Zundel that also questioned the Holocaust.-mg

Notes

1. Upon his release from prison in Austria on December 21, 2006, the English historian David Irving said, "I have the fine oratory of my 84-year-old defense lawyer Dr. Herbert Schaller to thank

for the unexpected victory in the appeal court. I spent over 400 days in solitary confinement in Austria's oldest prison, sentenced in February to three years' jail for an opinion I expressed in two talks seventeen years ago."

2. Of the 63 participants at the recent conference in Tehran, six were Orthodox rabbis.

3. Perhaps Benjamin Ginsburg is correct when he infers that the ACLU is an organization, which promotes Jewish interests. "In the realm of lobbying and litigation, Jews ... play leadership roles in such important public interest groups as the American Civil Liberties Union and Common Cause.... Their role in American economic, social, and political institutions has enabled Jews to wield considerable influence in the nation's public life." ("The Fatal Embrace: Jews and the State," p. 1)

The Fascinating Warnings and Recollections of Benjamin Freedman

Introduction: *Benjamin H. Freedman* (1890–1984) was one of the most intriguing and amazing individuals of the 20th century.

Mr. Freedman, born in 1890, was a successful Jewish businessman of New York City who was at one time the principal owner of the Woodbury Soap Company. He broke with organized Jewry after the Judeo-Communist victory of 1945, and spent the remainder of his life and the great preponderance of his considerable fortune exposing the soft tyranny which has enveloped the United States.

Mr. Freedman knew what he was talking about because he had been an insider at the highest levels of Jewish organizations and personally witnessed the machinations which contributed to the extraordinary rise of Jewish political power during the first half of the twentieth century. Mr. Freedman was personally acquainted with Bernard Baruch, Samuel Untermyer, Woodrow Wilson, Franklin Roosevelt, Joseph Kennedy, and John F. Kennedy, and many more movers and shakers of our times.

This speech was given in 1961 at the Willard Hotel in Washington, D.C., on behalf of Conde McGinley's patriotic newspaper of that time, 'Common Sense'. Though in some minor ways this wide-ranging and extemporaneous speech has become dated,

Mr. Freedman's essential message to us – his warning to the West – is more urgent than ever before. – K.A.S.

~~~~~~~~~~~~~~~~~~~~~~~~~~~~~~~

Benjamin Freedman: "What I intend to tell you tonight is something that you have never been able to learn from any other source, and what I tell you now concerns not only you, but your children and the survival of this country and Christianity. I'm not here just to dish up a few facts to send up your blood pressure, but I'm here to tell you things that will help you preserve what you consider the most sacred things in the world: the liberty, and the freedom, and the right to live as Christians, where you have a little dignity, and a little right to pursue the things that your conscience tells you are the right things, as Christians.

Now, first of all, I'd like to tell you that on August 25th 1960 – that was shortly before elections – Senator Kennedy, who is now the President of the United States, went to New York, and delivered an address to the Zionist Organization of America. In that address, to reduce it to its briefest form, he stated that he would use the armed forces of the United States to preserve the existence of the regime set up in Palestine by the Zionists who are now in occupation of that area.

In other words, Christian boys are going to be yanked out of their homes, away from their families, and sent abroad to fight in Palestine against the Christian and Moslem Arabs who merely want to return to their homes. And these Christian boys are going to be asked to shoot to kill these innocent [Arab Palestinians] people who only want to follow out fifteen resolutions passed by the United Nations in the last twelve years calling upon the Zionists to allow these people to return to their homes.

Now, when United States troops appear in the Middle East to fight with the Zionists as their allies to prevent the return of these people who were evicted from their homes in the 1948 armed insurrection by the Zionists who were transplanted there from Eastern Europe… when that happens, the United States will trigger World War III.

You say, when will that take place? The answer is, as soon as the difficulty between France and Algeria has been settled, that will take place. As soon as France and Algeria have been settled, that will take place. As soon as France and Algeria have settled their difficulty, and the Arab world, or the Moslem world, has no more war on their hands with France, they are going to move these people back into their homes, and when they do that and President Kennedy sends your sons to fight over there to help the crooks hold on to what they stole from innocent men, women and children, we will trigger World War III; and when that starts you can be sure we cannot emerge from that war a victor. We are going to lose that war because there is not one nation in the world that will let one of their sons fight with us for such a cause.

I know and speak to these ambassadors in Washington and the United Nations – and of the ninety-nine nations there, I've consulted with maybe seventy of them – and when we go to war in Palestine to help the thieves retain possession of what they have stolen from these innocent people we're not going to have a man there to fight with us as our ally.

And who *will* these people have supporting them, you ask. Well, four days after President Kennedy – or he was then Senator Kennedy – made that statement on August 28, 1960, the Arab nations called a meeting in Lebanon and there they decided to resurrect, or reactivate, the government of Palestine, which has been dormant more or less, since the 1948 armed insurrection by the Zionists.

Not only that… they ordered the creation of the Palestine Army, and they are now drilling maybe a half a million soldiers in that area of the world to lead these people back to **their** homeland. With them, they have as their allies all the nations of what is termed the Bandung Conference Group. That includes the Soviet Union and every Soviet Union satellite. It includes Red China; it includes every independent country in Asia and Africa; or eighty percent of the world's total population. Eighty percent of the world's population. Four out of five human beings on the face of the earth will be our enemies at war with us. And not alone are they four out of five human beings now on the face of this earth, but they are the non-Christian population of the world and they are the non-Caucasians... the non-white nations of the world, and that's what we face.

And what is the reason? The reason is that here in the United States, the Zionists and their co-religionists have complete control of our government. For many reasons too many and too complex to go into here at this – time I'll be glad to answer questions, however, to support that statement – the Zionists and their co-religionists rule this United States as though they were the absolute monarchs of this country.

Now, you say, 'well, that's a very broad statement to make', but let me show what happened while you were – I don't want to wear that out – let me show what happened while *WE* were all asleep. I'm including myself with you. We were all asleep. What happened?

World War I broke out in the summer of 1914. Nineteen-hundred and fourteen was the year in which World War One broke out. There are few people here my age who remember that. Now that war was waged on one side by Great Britain, France, and Russia; and on the other side by Germany, Austria-Hungary, and Turkey. What happened?

Within two years Germany had won that war: not alone won it nominally, but won it actually. The German submarines, which were a surprise to the world, had swept all the convoys from the Atlantic Ocean, and Great Britain stood there without ammunition for her soldiers, stood there with one week's food supply facing her – and after that, starvation.

At that time, the French army had mutinied. They lost 600,000 of the flower of French youth in the defense of Verdun on the Somme. The Russian army was defecting. They were picking up their toys and going home, they didn't want to play war anymore, they didn't like the Czar. And the Italian army had collapsed.

Now Germany – not a shot had been fired on the German soil. Not an enemy soldier had crossed the border into Germany. And yet, here was Germany offering England peace terms. They offered England a negotiated peace on what the lawyers call a status quo ante basis. That means: "Let's call the war off, and let everything be as it was before the war started."

Well, England, in the summer of 1916 was considering that. Seriously! They had no choice. It was either accepting this negotiated peace that Germany was magnanimously offering them, or going on with the war and being totally defeated.

While that was going on, the Zionists in Germany, who represented the Zionists from Eastern Europe, went to the British War Cabinet and – I am going to be brief because this is a long story, but I have all the documents to prove any statement that I make if anyone here is curious, or doesn't believe what I'm saying is at all possible – the Zionists in London went to the British war cabinet and they said: "Look here. You can yet win this war. You don't have to give up. You don't have to accept the negotiated peace offered to you now by Germany. You can win this war if the United States will come in as your ally."

The United States was not in the war at that time. We were fresh; we were young; we were rich; we were powerful. They [Zionists] told England: "We will guarantee to bring the United States into the war as your ally, to fight with you on your side, if you will promise us Palestine after you win the war."

In other words, they made this deal: "We will get the United States into this war as your ally. The price you must pay us is Palestine after you have won the war and defeated Germany, Austria-Hungary, and Turkey."

Now England had as much right to promise Palestine to anybody, as the United States would have to promise Japan to Ireland for any reason whatsoever. It's absolutely absurd that Great Britain – that never had any connection or any interest or any right in what is known as Palestine – should offer it as coin of the realm to pay the Zionists for bringing the United States into the war.

Benjamin Freedman

However, they made that promise, in October of 1916. October, nineteen hundred and sixteen. And shortly after that – I don't know how many here remember it – the United States, which was almost totally pro-German – totally pro-German – because the newspapers here were controlled by Jews, the bankers were Jews, all the media of mass communications in this country were controlled by Jews, and they were pro-German because their people, in the majority of cases came from Germany, and they wanted to see Germany lick the Czar.

The Jews didn't like the Czar, and they didn't want Russia to win this war. So the German bankers – the German-Jews – Kuhn Loeb and the other big banking firms in the United States refused to finance France or England to the extent of one dollar. They stood aside and they said: "As long as France and England are tied up with Russia, not one cent!" But they poured money into Germany, they fought with Germany against Russia, trying to lick the Czarist regime.

Now those same Jews, when they saw the possibility of getting Palestine, they went to England and they made this deal. At that time, everything changed, like the traffic light that changes from red to green. Where the newspapers had been all pro-German, where they'd been telling the people of the difficulties that Germany was having fighting Great Britain commercially and in other respects, all of a sudden the Germans were no good. They were villains. They were Huns. They were shooting Red Cross nurses. They were cutting off babies' hands. And they were no good.

Well, shortly after that, Mr. Wilson declared war on Germany.

The Zionists in London sent these cables to the United States, to Justice Brandeis: "Go to work on President Wilson. We're getting from England what we want. Now you go to work, and you go to work on President Wilson and get the United States into the war." And that did happen. That's how the United States got into the war. We had no more interest in it; we had no more right to be in it than we have to be on the moon tonight instead of in this room.

Now the war – World War One – in which the United States participated had absolutely no reason to be our war. We went in there – we were railroaded into it – if I can be vulgar, we were suckered into – that war merely so that the Zionists of the world could obtain Palestine. Now, that is something that the people in the United States have never been told. They never knew why we went into World War One. Now, what happened?

After we got into the war, the Zionists went to Great Britain and they said: "Well, we performed our part of the agreement. Let's have something in writing that shows that you are going to keep your bargain and give us Palestine after you win the war." Because they didn't know whether the war would last another year or another ten years. So they started to work out a receipt. The receipt took the form of a letter, and it was worded in very cryptic language so that the world at large wouldn't know what it was all about. And that was called the Balfour Declaration.

The Balfour Declaration was merely Great Britain's promise to pay the Zionists what they had agreed upon as a consideration for getting the United States into the war. So this great Balfour Declaration, that you hear so much about, is just as phony as a three dollar bill. And I don't think I could make it more emphatic than that.

Now, that is where all the trouble started. The United States went in the war. The United States crushed Germany. We went in there, and it's history. You know what happened. Now, when the war was ended, and the Germans went to Paris, to the Paris Peace Conference in 1919, there were 117 Jews there, as a delegation representing the Jews, headed by Bernard Baruch. I was there. I ought to know. Now what happened?

The Jews at that peace conference, when they were cutting up Germany and parceling out Europe to all these nations that claimed a right to a certain part of European territory, the Jews said, "How about Palestine for us?" And they produced, for the first time to the knowledge of the Germans, this Balfour Declaration. So the Germans, for the first time realized, "Oh, that was the game! That's why the United States came into the war." And the Germans for the first time realized that they were defeated, they suffered this terrific reparation that was slapped onto them, because the Zionists wanted Palestine and they were determined to get it at any cost.

Now, that brings us to another very interesting point. When the Germans realized this, they naturally resented it. Up to that time, the Jews had never been better off in any country in the world than they had been in Germany.

You had Mr. Rathenau there, who was maybe 100 times as important in industry and finance as is Bernard Baruch in this country. You had Mr. Balin, who owned the two big steamship lines, the North German Lloyd's and the Hamburg-American Lines. You had Mr. Bleichroder, who was the banker for the Hohenzollern family. You had the Warburgs in Hamburg, who were the big merchant bankers – the biggest in the world. The Jews were doing very well in Germany. No question about that. Now, the Germans felt: "Well, that was quite a sellout."

It was a sellout that I can best compare – suppose the United States was at war today with the Soviet Union. And we were winning. And we told the Soviet Union: "Well, let's quit. We offer you peace terms. Let's forget the whole thing." And all of a sudden Red China came into the war as an ally of the Soviet Union. And throwing them into the war brought about our defeat. A crushing defeat, with reparations the likes of which man's imagination cannot encompass.

Imagine, then, after that defeat, if we found out that it was the Chinese in this country, our Chinese citizens, who all the time we thought they were loyal citizens working with us, were selling us out to the Soviet Union and that it was through them that Red China was brought into the war against us. How would we feel, in the United States against Chinese? I don't think that one of them would dare show his face on any street. There wouldn't be lampposts enough, convenient, to take care of them. Imagine how we would feel.

Well, that's how the Germans felt towards these Jews. "We've been so nice to them"; and from 1905 on, when the first Communist revolution in Russia failed, and the Jews had to scramble out of Russia, they all went to Germany. And Germany gave them refuge. And they were treated very nicely. And here they sold Germany down the river for no reason at all other than they wanted Palestine as a so-called "Jewish commonwealth."

Now, Nahum Sokolow — all the great leaders, the big names that you read about in connection with Zionism today — they, in 1919, 1920, '21, '22, and '23, they wrote in all their papers — and the press was filled with their statements — that "the feeling against the Jews in Germany is due to the fact that they realized that this great defeat was brought about by our intercession and bringing the United States into the war against them."

The Jews themselves admitted that. It wasn't that the Germans in 1919 discovered that a glass of Jewish blood tasted better than Coca-Cola or Muenschner Beer. There was no religious feeling. There was no sentiment against those people merely on account of their religious belief. It was all political. It was economic. It was anything but religious.

Nobody cared in Germany whether a Jew went home and pulled down the shades and said "Shema' Yisrael" or "Our Father." No one cared in Germany any more than they do in the United States. Now this feeling that developed later in Germany was due to one thing: that the Germans held the Jews responsible for their crushing defeat, for no reason at all, because World War One was started against Germany for no reason for which they [Germans] were responsible. They were guilty of nothing. Only of being successful. They built up a big navy. They built up world trade.

You must remember, Germany, at the time of Napoleon, at the time of the French Revolution, what was the German Reich consisted of 300 — three hundred! — small city-states, principalities, dukedoms, and so forth. Three hundred little separate political entities. And between that time, between the period of. . . between Napoleon and Bismarck, they were consolidated into one state. And within 50 years after that time they became one of the world's great powers. Their navy was rivaling Great Britain's, they were doing business all over the world, they could undersell anybody and make better products. And what happened? What happened as a result of that?

There was a conspiracy between England, France, and Russia that: "We must slap down Germany", because there isn't one historian in the world that can find a valid reason why those three countries decided to wipe Germany off the map politically. Now, what happened after that?

When Germany realized that the Jews were responsible for her defeat, they naturally resented it. But not a hair on the head of any Jew was harmed. Not a single hair. Professor Tansill, of Georgetown University, who had access to all the secret papers of the State Department, wrote in his book, and quoted from a State Department document written by Hugo Schoenfelt, a Jew who Cordell Hull sent to Europe in 1933 to investigate the so-called camps of political prisoners. And he wrote back that he found them in very fine condition.

They were in excellent shape; everybody treated well. And they were filled with Communists. Well, a lot of them were Jews, because the Jews happened to be maybe 98 per cent of the Communists in Europe at that time. And there were some priests there, and ministers, and labor leaders, Masons, and others who had international affiliations.

Now, the Jews sort of tried to keep the lid on this fact. They didn't want the world to really understand that they had sold out Germany, and that the Germans resented that.

So they did take appropriate action against them [against the Jews]. They. . . shall I say, discriminated against them wherever they could? They shunned them. The same as we would the Chinese, or the Negroes, or the Catholics, or anyone in this country who had sold us out to an enemy and brought about our defeat.

Now, after a while, the Jews of the world didn't know what to do, so they called a meeting in Amsterdam. Jews from every country in the world attended in July 1933. And they said to Germany: "You fire

Hitler! And you put every Jew back into his former position, whether he was a Communist, no matter what he was. You can't treat us that way! And we, the Jews of the world, are calling upon you, and serving this ultimatum upon you." Well, the Germans told them. . . you can imagine. So what did they [the Jews] do?

They broke up, and Samuel Untermyer, if the name means anything to people here. . . (You want to ask a question? – - Uh, there were no Communists in Germany at that time… they were called 'Social Democrats.)

Well, I don't want to go by what they were *called*. We're now using English words, and what they were called in Germany is not very material. . . but they were Communists, because in 1917, the Communists took over Germany for a few days. Rosa Luxembourg and Karl Liebknecht, and a group of Jews in Germany took over the government for three days. In fact, when the Kaiser ended the war, he fled to Holland because he thought the Communists were going to take over Germany as they did Russia, and that he was going to meet the same fate that the Czar did in Russia. So he left and went to Holland for safety and for security.

Now, at that time, when the Communist threat in Germany was quashed, it was quiet, the Jews were working, still trying to get back into their former – their status – and the Germans fought them in every way they could, without hurting a hair on anyone's head. The same as one group, the Prohibitionists, fought the people who were interested in liquor, and they didn't fight one another with pistols, they did it every way they could.

Well, that's the way they were fighting the Jews in Germany. And, at that time, mind you, there were 80 to 90 million Germans and there were only 460,000 Jews. . . less than one half of one percent of Germany were Jews. And yet, they controlled all of the press, they controlled most of the economy, because they had come in and with cheap money – you know the way the Mark was devalued – they bought up practically everything.

Well, in 1933 when Germany refused to surrender, mind you, to the World Conference of Jews in Amsterdam, they broke up and Mr. Untermeyer came back to the United States – who was the head of the American delegation and the president of the whole conference – and he went from the steamer to ABC and made a radio broadcast throughout the United States in which he said:

"The Jews of the world now declare a Holy War against Germany. We are now engaged in a sacred conflict against the Germans. And we are going to starve them into surrender. We are going to use a world-wide boycott against them, that will destroy them because they are dependent upon their export business."

And it is a fact that two thirds of Germany's food supply had to be imported, and it could only be imported with the proceeds of what they exported. So if Germany could not export, two thirds of Germany's population would have to starve. There just was not enough food for more than one third of the population.

Now in this declaration, which I have here, it was printed on page – a whole page – in the New York Times on August 7, 1933, Mr. Samuel Untermyer boldly stated that: "this economic boycott is our means of self-defense. President Roosevelt has advocated its use in the NRA" . [National Recovery Administration] – which some of you may remember, where everybody was to be boycotted unless they followed the rules laid down by the New Deal, which of course was declared unconstitutional by the Supreme Court at that time.

Nevertheless, the Jews of the world declared a boycott against Germany, and it was so effective that you couldn't find one thing in any store anywhere in the world with the words "made in Germany" on it.

In fact, an executive of the Woolworth Company told me that they had to dump millions of dollars worth of crockery and dishes into the river; that their stores were boycotted. If anyone came in and found a dish marked "made in Germany," they were picketed with signs: "Hitler", "murderer", and so forth, and like – something like these sit-ins that are taking place in the South.

R. H. Macy, which is controlled by a family called Strauss who also happen to be Jews...a woman found stockings there which came from Chemnitz, marked "made in Germany". Well, they were cotton stockings. They may have been there 20 years, because since I've been observing women's legs in the last twenty years, I haven't seen a pair with cotton stockings on them. So Macy! I saw Macy boycotted, with hundreds of people walking around with signs saying "MURDERS" and "HITLERITES", and so forth.

Now up to that time, not one hair on the head of any Jew had been hurt in Germany. There was no suffering, there was no starvation, there was no murder, there was nothing.

Now, **that**...naturally, the Germans said, "Why, who are these people to declare a boycott against us and throw all our people out of work, and our industries come to a standstill? Who are they to do that to us?" They naturally resented it. Certainly they painted swastikas on stores owned by Jews.

Why should a German go in and give their money to a storekeeper who was part of a boycott who was going to starve Germany into surrender into the Jews of the world, who were going to dictate who their premier or chancellor was to be? Well, it was ridiculous.

That continued for some time, and it wasn't until [Nov. 7] 1938, when a young Jew from Poland [Herschel Grynszpan], walked into the German embassy in Paris and shot one of the officials [Ernst vom Rath] that the Germans really started to get rough with the Jews in Germany. And you found them then breaking windows and having street fights and so forth ["Kristallnacht"].

Now, for anyone to say that – I don't like to use the word 'anti-Semitism' because it's meaningless, but it means something to you still, so I'll have to use it – the only reason that there was any feeling in Germany against Jews was that they were responsible: number one, for World War One; number two, for this world-wide boycott, and number three – did I say for World War One, they were responsible? For the boycott – and also for World War II, because after this thing got out of hand, it was absolutely necessary for the Jews and Germany to lock horns in a war to see which one was going to survive.

In the meanwhile, I had lived in Germany, and I knew that the Germans had decided [that] Europe is going to be Christian or Communist: there is no in between. It's going to be Christian or it's going to be Communist. And the Germans decided: "We're going to keep it Christian if possible". And they started to re-arm.

And there intention was – by that time the United States had recognized the Soviet Union, which they did in November, 1933 – the Soviet Union was becoming very powerful, and Germany realized: "Well, our turn is going to come soon, unless we are strong." The same as we in this country are saying today, "Our turn is going to come soon, unless we are strong."

And our government is spending 83 or 84 billion dollars of your money for defense, they say. Defense against whom? Defense against 40,000 little Jews in Moscow that took over Russia, and then, in their devious ways, took over control of many other governments of the world.

Now, for this country to now be on the verge of a Third World War, from which we cannot emerge a victor, is something that staggers my imagination. I know that nuclear bombs are measured in terms of megatons. A megaton is a term used to describe one million tons of TNT. One million tons of TNT is a megaton. Now, our nuclear bombs have a capacity of 10 megatons, or 10 million tons of TNT. That was when they were first developed five or six years ago. Now, the nuclear bombs that are being developed have a capacity of 200 megatons, and God knows how many megatons the nuclear bombs of the Soviet Union have.

So, what do we face now? If we trigger a world war that may develop into a nuclear war, humanity is finished. And why will it take place? It will take place because Act III...the curtain goes up on Act III. Act I was World War I. Act II was World War II. Act III is going to be World War III.

The Jews of the world, the Zionists and their co-religionists every-where, are determined that they are going to again use the United States to help them permanently retain Palestine as their foothold for their world government. Now, that is just as true as I am standing here, because not alone have I read it, but many here have read it, and it's known all over the world.

Now, what are we going to do? The life you save may be your son's. Your boys may be on their way to that war tonight; and you, you don't know it any more than you knew that in 1916 in London the Zionists made a deal with the British War Cabinet to send your sons to war in Europe. Did you know it at that time? Not a person in the United States knew it. You weren't permitted to know it.

Who knew it? President Wilson knew it. Colonel House knew it. Others knew it. Did I know it? I had a pretty good idea of what was going on: I was liaison to Henry Morgenthau, Sr., in the 1912 cam-paign when President Wilson was elected, and there was talk around the office there.

I was 'confidential man' to Henry Morgenthau, Sr., who was chair-man of the Finance Committee, and I was liaison between him and Rollo Wells, the treasurer. So I sat in these meetings with President Wilson at the head of the table, and all the others, and I heard them drum into President Wilson's brain the graduated income tax and what has become the Federal Reserve, and also indoctrinate him with the Zionist movement.

Justice Brandeis and President Wilson were just as close as the two fingers on this hand, and President Woodrow Wilson was just as in-competent when it came to determining what was going on as a newborn baby. And that's how they got us into World War I, while we all slept.

Now, at this moment...at this moment they may be planning this World War III, in which we don't stand a chance even if they don't use nuclear bombs. How can the United States – about five percent of the world – go out and fight eighty to ninety percent of the world on their home ground? How can we do it...send our boys over there to be slaughtered? For what? So the Jews can have Palestine as their 'commonwealth'? They've fooled you so much that you don't know whether you're coming or going.

Now any judge, when he charges a jury, says, "Gentlemen, any witness that you find has told a single lie, you can disregard **all** his testimony." That is correct. I don't know from what state you come, but in New York state that is the way a judge addresses a jury. If that witness said one lie, disregard his testimony.

Now, what are the facts about the Jews?

The Jews – I call them Jews to you, because they are known as Jews. I don't call them Jews. I refer to them as so-called Jews, because I know what they are. If Jesus was a Jew, there isn't a Jew in the world today, and if those people are Jews, certainly our Lord and Savior was not one of them, and I can prove that.

Now what happened? The eastern European Jews, who form 92 per cent of the world's population of those people who call themselves Jews, were originally Khazars.

They were a warlike tribe that lived deep in the heart of Asia. And they were so warlike that even the Asiatics drove them out of Asia into Eastern Europe – and to reduce this so you don't get too confused about the history of Eastern Europe – they set up this big Khazar kingdom: 800,000 square miles. Only, there was no Russia, there were no other countries, and the Khazar kingdom was the biggest country in all Europe – so big and so powerful that when the other monarchs wanted to go to war, the Khazars would lend them 40,000 soldiers. That's how big and powerful they were.

Now, they were phallic worshippers, which is filthy. I don't want to go into the details of that now. It was their religion the way it was the religion of many other Pagans or Barbarians elsewhere in the world.

Now, the [Khazar] king became so disgusted with the degeneracy of his kingdom that he decided to adopt a so-called monotheistic faith – either Christianity, Islam – the Moslem faith – or what is known today as Judaism – really Talmudism. So, like spinning a top and calling out "eeny, meeny, miney, moe," he picked out so-called Judaism. And that became the state religion.

He sent down to the Talmudic schools of Pumbedita and Sura and brought up thousands of these rabbis with their teachings, and opened up synagogues and schools in his kingdom of 800,000 people – 800,000 thousand square miles – and maybe ten to twenty million people; and they became what we call Jews. There wasn't one of them that had an ancestor that ever put a toe in the Holy Land, not only in Old Testament history, but back to the beginning of time. Not one of them! And yet they come to the Christians and they ask us to support their armed insurrection in Palestine by saying:

"Well, you want to certainly help repatriate God's chosen people to their Promised Land, their ancestral homeland; it's your Christian duty. We gave you one of our boys as your Lord and Savior. You now go to church on Sunday, and kneel and you worship a Jew, and we're Jews."

Well, they were pagan Khazars who were converted just the same as the Irish [were converted]. And it's just as ridiculous to call them "people of the Holy Land," as it would be…there are 54 million Chinese Moslems. Fifty four million! And, Mohammed only died in 620 A.D., so in that time, 54 million Chinese have accepted Islam as their religious belief.

Now imagine, in China, 2,000 miles away from Arabia, where the city of Mecca is located, where Mohammed was born…imagine if the 54 million Chinese called themselves 'Arabs'. Imagine! Why, you'd say they're lunatics. Anyone who believes that those 54 million Chinese are Arabs must be crazy. All they did was adopt as a religious faith; a belief that had its origin in Mecca, in Arabia.

The same as the Irish. When the Irish became Christians, nobody dumped them in the ocean and imported from the Holy Land a new crop of inhabitants that were Christians. They weren't different people. They were the same people, but they had accepted Christianity as a religious faith.

315

Now, these Pagans, these Asiatics, these Turko-Finns. . . they were a Mongoloid race who were forced out of Asia into eastern Europe. They likewise, because their king took the faith – Talmudic faith – they had no choice. Just the same as in Spain: If the king was Catholic, everybody had to be a Catholic. If not, you had to get out of Spain. So everybody – they lived on the land just like the trees and the bushes; a human being belonged to the land under their feudal system – so they [Khazars] all became what we call today, Jews!

Now imagine how silly it was for the Christians. . . for the great Christian countries of the world to say, "We're going to use our power, our prestige to repatriate God's chosen people to their ancestral homeland, their Promised Land."

Now, could there be a bigger lie than that? Could there be a bigger lie than that?

And because they control the newspapers, the magazines, the radio, the television, the book publishing business, they have the ministers in the pulpit, they have the politicians on the soap boxes talking the same language . . . so naturally you'd believe black is white if you heard it often enough. You wouldn't call black 'black' anymore – you'd start to call black white. And nobody could blame you.

Now, that is one of the great lies. . . that is the foundation of all the misery that has befallen the world. Because after two wars fought in Europe – World War I and World War II – if it wasn't possible for them to live in peace and harmony with the people in Europe, like their brethren are living in the United States, what were the two wars fought for? Did they have to – like you flush the toilet – because they couldn't get along, did they have to say, "Well, we're going back to our homeland and you Christians can help us"?

I can't understand yet how the Christians in Europe could have been that dumb because every theologian, every history teacher, knew the things that I'm telling you. But, they naturally bribed them, shut them up with money, stuffed their mouths with money, and now. . . I don't care whether you know all this or not. It doesn't make any difference to me whether you know all these facts or not, but it does make a difference to me. I've got, in my family, boys that will have to be in the next war, and I don't want them to go and fight and die… like they died in Korea. Like they died in Japan. Like they've died all over the world. For what?

To help crooks hold on to what they stole from innocent people who had been in peaceful possession of that land, those farms, those homes for hundreds and maybe thousands of years? Is that why the United States must go to war? Because the Democratic Party wants New York State – the electoral vote? Illinois, the electoral vote? And Pennsylvania, the electoral vote?… which are controlled by the Zionists and their co-religionists?. . . the balance of power?

In New York City there are 400,000 members of the liberal party, all Zionists and their co-religionists. And New York State went for Kennedy by 400,000 votes. Now, I don't blame Mr. Kennedy. I'm fond of Mr. Kennedy. I think he's a great man. I think he can really pull us out of this trouble if we get the facts to him. And I believe he knows a great deal more than his appointments indicate he knows. He's playing with the enemy. Like when you go fishing, you've got to play with the fish. Let 'em out and pull 'em in. Let 'em out and pull 'em in. But knowing Mr. Kennedy's father, and how well informed he is on this whole subject, and how close Kennedy is to his father, I don't think Mr. Kennedy is totally in the dark.

But I do think that it is the duty of every mother, every loyal Christian , every person that regards the defense of this country as a sacred right, that they communicate – not with their congressman, not with their senator, but with President Kennedy. And tell him, "I do not think you should send my boy, or our boys, wearing the uniform of the United States of America, and under the flag that you see here, our red, white and blue, to fight there to help keep in the hands of these that which they have stolen". I think everyone should not alone write once, but keep writing and get your friends to write.

Now, I could go on endlessly, and tell you these things to support what I have just asked you to do. But I don't think it's necessary to do that. You're above the average group in intelligence and I don't think it's necessary to impress this any more.

But. . . I want to tell you one more thing. You talk about… "Oh, the Jews. Why the Jews? Christianity. Why, we got Christianity from the Jews and the Jews gave us Jesus, and the Jews gave us our religion". But do you know that on the day of atonement that you think is so sacred to them, that on that day… and I was one of them! This is not hearsay. I'm not here to be a rabble-rouser. I'm here to give you facts.

When, on the Day of Atonement, you walk into a synagogue, the very first prayer that you recite, you stand – and it's the only prayer for which you stand – and you repeat three times a short prayer: The Kol Nidre. In that prayer, you enter into an agreement with God Almighty that any oath, vow, or pledge that you may make during the next twelve months – any oath, vow or pledge that you may take during the next twelve months **shall be null and void.**

The oath shall not be an oath; the vow shall not be a vow; the pledge shall not be a pledge. They shall have no force and effect, and so forth and so on.

And further than that, the Talmud teaches: "Don't forget – whenever you take an oath, vow, and pledge – remember the Kol Nidre prayer that you recited on the Day of Atonement, and that exempts you from fulfilling that".

How much can you depend on their loyalty? You can depend upon their loyalty as much as the Germans depended upon it in 1916.

And we're going to suffer the same fate as Germany suffered, and for the same reason. You can't depend upon something as insecure as the leadership that is not obliged to respect an oath, vow or pledge. Now I could go on and recite many other things to you, but I would have a little respect for your time, and you want to really, uh, get through with all of this. Tomorrow's going to be a long day.

Now I want to say one thing. You ask me. . . well, you think to yourself: "well how did this fellow get mixed up in this the way he got mixed up in it." Well, I opened my mouth in 1945, and I took big pages in newspapers and tried to tell the American people what I'm telling you. And one newspaper after another refused the advertisement. And when I couldn't find a newspaper to take them — I paid cash, not credit — what happened? My lawyer told me, "There's an editor over in Jersey with a paper who will take your announcement". So, I was brought together with Mr. McGinley, and that's how I met him.

So somebody told me the lawyer who introduced me, who was the son of the Dean of the Methodist Bishop, he said: "Well, I think he's a little anti-Semitic.

I don't know whether I can get him over here. So he brought him over to my apartment and we hit it off wonderfully, and have since then.

Now, I say this, and I say it without any qualifications. I say it without any reservations. And I say it without any hesitation. . . if it wasn't for the work that Mr. Conley McGinley did with "Common Sense" — he's been sending out from 1,800,000 to 2,000,000 every year — if it wasn't for the work he's been doing sending those out for fifteen years now, we would already be a communist country. Nobody has done what he did to light fires. Many of the other active persons in this fight learned all about if for the first time through "Common Sense".

Now, I have been very active in helping him all I could. I'm not as flush as I was. I cannot go on spending the money. . . I'm not going to take up a collection. Don't worry. I see five people getting up to leave. (laughter)

I haven't got the money that I used to spend. I used to print a quarter of a million of them out of my own pocket and send them out. Mr. McGinley, when I first met him, had maybe 5,000 printed and circulated them locally. So I said, "With what you know and what I know, we can really do a good job". So I started printing in outside shops of big newspaper companies, a quarter of a million, and paid for them. Well, there's always a bottom to the barrel. I suppose we've all reached that at times.

I'm not so poor that I can't live without working and that's what worries the Anti-Defamation League. I can just get by without going and asking for a job or getting on the bread line. But Mr. McGinley is working. He's sick and he's going at this stronger than ever. And all I want to say is that they want to close up "Common Sense" more than any other single thing in the whole world, as a death-blow to the fight Christians are making to survive.

So I just want to tell you this. All they do is circulate rumors: "Mr. Benjamin H. Freedman is the wealthy backer of 'Common Sense'." The reason they do that is to discourage the people in the United States: don't send any money to Common Sense. They don't need it. They've got the wealthy Mr. Freedman as a backer. That's [been their] strategy. They don't want to advertise me so that people that have real estate or securities to sell will come and call on me. They just want people to lay off "Common Sense". And all I'm telling you is, I do try to help him, but I haven't been able to. And I will be very honest. One thing I won't do is lie. In the last year I've had so much sickness in my family that I could not give him one dollar.

How he's managed to survive, I don't know. God alone knows. And he must be in God's care because how he's pulled through his sickness and with his financial troubles, I don't know. But that press is working. . . and every two weeks about a hundred or a hundred-fifty-thousand of "Common Sense" go out with a new message. And if that information could be multiplied. . . if people that now get it could buy ten or twenty five, or fifty, give them around. Plow that field. Sow those seeds, you don't know which will take root, but for God's sake, this is our last chance".

(Benjamin Freedman then discusses the importance of people forgoing unnecessary purchases to 'buy more stuff', play golf, etc., and use the money to keep "Common Sense" going. He explains that the paper is going in debt; could be closed down and he (Freedman) no longer has the funds, having spent some $2,400,000 in his attempt to bring the information to the American public and elected officials. He then asks for questions from the audience.)

~~~~~~~~~~~~~~~~~~~~~~~~~~~~~~~~

{Question inaudible]

Freedman: All right, I'll comment on that. This is rather deep, but you all have a very high degree of intelligence, so I'm going to make an attempt. In the time of Bible history, there was a geographic area known as Judea. Judea was a province of the Roman Empire. Now, a person who lived in Judea was known as a Judean, and in Latin it was Judaeus; in Greek it was Judaius. Those are the two words, in Greek and Latin, for a Judean.

Now, in Latin and Greek there is no such letter as 'j', and the first syllable of Judaeus and Judaius starts 'ghu'. Now, when the Bible was written, it was first written in Greek, Latin, Panantic, Syriac, Aramaic… all those languages. Never Was the word Jew in any of them because the word didn't exist. Judea was the country, and the people were Judeans, and Jesus was referred to only as a Judean. I've seen those early… the earliest scripts available.

In 1345, a man by the name of Wycliffe in England thought that it was time to translate the Bible into English. There was no English edition of the Bible because who the Devil could read? It was only the educated church people who could read Latin and Greek, Syriac, Aramaic and the other languages. Anyhow, Wycliffe translated the Bible into English. But in it, he had to look around for some words for Judaeas and Judaius.

There was no English word because Judea had passed out of existence. There was no Judea. People had long ago forgotten that. So in the first translation he used the word, in referring to Jesus, as 'gyu', "jew". At the time, there was no printing press.

Then, between 1345 and the 17th century, when the press came into use, that word passed through so many changes… I have them all here. If you want I can read them to you. I will. That word 'gyu' which was in the Wycliffe Bible became. . . first it was 'gyu' , then 'giu', then 'iu' (because the 'i' in Latin is pronounced like the 'j'. Julius Caesar is 'Iul' because there is no 'j' in Latin) then 'iuw', then 'ieuu', then 'ieuy', then 'iwe', then 'iow', then 'iewe', all in Bibles as time went on. Then 'ieue', then 'iue', then 'ive', and then 'ivw', and finally in the 18th century… 'jew'. Jew.

All the corrupt and contracted forms for Judaius, and Judaeas in Latin. Now, there was no such thing as 'Jew', and any theologian – I've lectured in maybe 20 of the most prominent theological seminaries in this country, and two in Europe – there was no such word as Jew. There only was Judea, and Jesus was a Judean and the first English use of a word in an English bible to describe him was 'gyu' – Jew. A contracted and shortened form of Judaeus, just the same as we call a laboratory a 'lab', and gasoline 'gas'… a tendency to short up.

So, in England there were no public schools; people didn't know how to read; it looked like a scrambled alphabet so they made a short word out of it. Now for a theologian to say that you can't harm the Jews, is just ridiculous. I'd like to know where in the scriptures it says that. I'd like to know the text.

Look at what happened to Germany for touching Jews. What would you, as a citizen of the United States, do to people who did to you what the so-called Jews – the Pollacks and Litvaks and Litzianers – they weren't Jews, as I just explained to you. They were Eastern Europeans who'd been converted to Talmudism. There was no such thing as Judaism. Judaism was a name given in recent years to this religion known in Bible history as Torah [inaudible]. No Jew or no educated person ever heard of Judaism. It didn't exist. They pulled it out of the air. . . a meaningless word.

Just like 'anti-Semitic'. The Arab is a Semite. And the Christians talk about people who don't like Jews as anti-Semites, and they call all the Arabs anti-Semites. The only Semites in the world are the Arabs. There isn't one Jew who's a Semite. They're all Turkothean Mongoloids. The Eastern European Jews. So, they brainwashed the public, and if you will invite me to meet this reverend who told you these things, I'll convince him and it'll be one step in the right direction. I'll go wherever I have to go to meet him.

~~~~~~~~~~~~~~~~~~~~

Question from audience member: (inaudible)

Freedman: Yes, ma'am. Well... I can answer that. First of all, your first premise is wrong. Your first premise that all the Jews are loyal to each other is wrong. Because, the Eastern European Jews outnumber all the rest by so many that they create the impression that they are the Jewish 'race'; that they are the Jewish nation; that they are the Jewish people. . . and the Christians swallow it like a cream puff.

But in 1844 the German rabbis called a conference of rabbis from all over the world for the purpose of abolishing the Kol Nidre from the Day of Atonement religious ceremony. In Brunswick, Germany, where that conference was held in 1844, there was almost a terrific riot. A civil war.

The Eastern Europeans said, "What the hell. We should give up Kol Nidre? That gives us our grip on our people. We give them a franchise so they can tell the Christians, 'Go to hell. We'll make any deal you want', but they don't have to carry it out. That gives us our grip on our people". So, they're not so united, and if you knew the feeling that exists. . .

Now, I'll also show you from an official document by the man responsible for. . . uh, who baptized this race. Here is a paper that we obtained from the archives of the Zionist organization in New York City, and in it is the manuscript by Sir James A. Malcolm, who – on behalf of the British Cabinet – negotiated the deal with these Zionists.

And in here he says that all the Jews in England were against it. The Jews who had been there for years, the [inaudible – probably Sephardim], those who had Portuguese and Spanish and Dutch ancestry... who were monotheists and believed in that religious belief. That was while the Eastern European Jews were still running around in the heart of Asia and then came into Europe. But they had no more to do with them than. . . can we talk about a Christian 'race'? or a Christian religion?... or are the Christians united?

So the same disunity is among the Jews. And I'll show you in this same document that when they went to France to try and get the French government to back that Zionist venture, there was only one Jew in France who was for it. That was Rothschild, and they did it because they were interested in the oil and the Suez Canal.

~~~~~~~~~~~~~~~~~~~

[Question inaudible] Freedman: You know why? Because if they don't, they're decked up. They come around and they tell you how much you must give, and if you don't . . . oh, you're anti-Semitic. Then none of their friends will have anything to do with them, and they start a smear campaign. . . and you have got to give.

In New York City, in the garment center, there are twelve manufacturers in the building. And when the drive is on to sell Israel Bonds, the United Jewish Drive, they put a big scoreboard with the names of the firms and opposite them, as you make the amount they put you down for, they put a gold star after the name. Then, the buyers are told, "When you come into that building to call on someone and they haven't got a gold star, tell them that you won't buy from them until they have the gold star". BLACKMAIL. I don't know what else you can call it.

Then what do they do? They tell you it's for 'humanitarian purposes' and they send maybe $8 billion dollars to Israel, tax exempt, tax deductible. So if they hadn't sent that eight billion dollars to Israel, seven billion of it would have gone into the U.S. Treasury as income tax. So what happens? That seven billion dollars deficit – that air pocket – the gullible Christians have to make up.

They put a bigger tax on gas or bread or corporation tax. Somebody has to pay the housekeeping expenses for the government. So why do you let these people send their money over there to buy guns to drive people out of their ancient homeland? And you say, "Oh, well. The poor Jews. They have no place to go and they've been persecuted all their lives". They've never been persecuted for their religion. And I wish I had two rows of Rabbis here to challenge me.

Never once, in all of history, have they been persecuted for their religion.

Do you know why the Jews were driven out of England? King Edward the First in 1285 drove them out, and they never came back until the Cromwell Revolution which was financed by the Rothschilds. For four-hundred years there wasn't a Jew. But do you know why they were driven out? Because in the Christian faith and the Moslem faith it's a sin to charge 'rent' for the use of money. In other words – what we call interest [usury] is a sin.

So the Jews had a monopoly in England and they charged so much interest, and when the Lords and Dukes couldn't pay, they [Jews] foreclosed. And they were creating so much trouble that the king of England finally made himself their partner, because when they came to foreclose, some of these dukes bumped off the Jews. . . the money-lenders. So the king finally said – and this is all in history, look up Tianson [Tennyson?] or Rourke, the History of the Jews in England; two books you can [not] find in your library. When the king found out what the trouble was all about, and how much money they were making, he declared himself a fifty-percent partner of the money lenders. Edward the First. And for many years, one-third of the revenues of the British Treasury came from the fifty-percent interest in money-lending by the Jews.

But it got worse and worse. So much worse that when the Lords and Dukes kept killing the money-lenders, the King then said, "I declare myself the heir of all the money-lenders. If they're killed you have to pay me, because I'm his sole heir". That made so much trouble, because the King had to go out and collect the money with an army, so he told the Jews to get out. There were 15,000 of them, and they had to get out, and they went across to Ireland, and that's how Ireland got to be part of the United Kingdom.

When King Edward found out what they were doing, he decided to take Ireland for himself before someone else did. He sent Robert Southgard with a mercenary army and conquered Ireland. So, show me one time where a Jew was persecuted in any country because of his religion. It has never happened. It's always their impact on the political, social, or economic customs and traditions of the community in which they settle.

~~~~~~~~~~~~~~~~~~~

[Question inaudible] Freedman: Yes, sir. Well, they say most of those things themselves. It was unnecessary for Benjamin Franklin to say it. Most of those things they say themselves. But Benjamin Franklin observed, and by hearsay understood, what was happening in Europe.

When Russia, in 920 was formed, and gradually surrounded the Khazar Kingdom, and absorbed them, most of the well-to-do Khazars fled to Western Europe and brought with them the very things to which you object and I object and a lot of other people object. The customs, the habits, the instincts with which they were endowed.

When Benjamin Franklin referred to them as Jews because that's the name that they went by, and when the Christians first heard that these people who were fleeing from Russia – who they were – that they had practiced this Talmudic faith – the Christians in Western Europe said, "They must be the remnants of the lost ten tribes!"

And Mr. Grutz, the greatest historian amongst the Jews, said that – and he's probably as good an authority on that subject as there is. So when Ben Franklin came to Europe in the 18th century, he already saw the results of what these people had done after they left their homeland. And every word of it is true... they say it themselves. I can give you half a dozen books they've written in which they say the same thing: When they have money they become tyrants. And when they become defeated, they become ruthless. They're only barbarians. They're the descendants of Asiatic Mongols and they will do anything to accomplish their purpose.

What right did they have to take over Russia the way they did? The Czar had abdicated nine or ten months before that. There was no need for them. . . they were going to have a constitutional monarchy. But they didn't want that. When the constitutional monarchy was to assemble in November, they mowed them all down and established the Soviet Union.

There was no need for that. But they thought, "Now is the time", and if you you will look in the Encyclopedia Britannica under the word 'Bolshevism', you'll find the five laws there that Lenin put down for a successful revolution. One of them is, "Wait for the right time, and then give them everything you've got". It would pay you to read that.

You'd also find that Mr. Harold Blacktree, who wrote the article for the Encyclopedia Britannica states that the Jews conceived and created and cultivated the Communist movement. And that their energy made them the spearhead of the movement. Harold Blacktree wrote it and no one knew more about Communism than he. And the Encyclopedia Britannica for 25 years has been printing it".

~~~~~~~~~~~~~~~~~~~

[Question inaudible]

Freedman: Well, I can't advocate that you do anything that's criminal, but I can tell you this. You can start what I call an endless chain. If you can get your friends to write, objectively, here is the statement: Mr. Kennedy's office gave me this himself. Mr. Smith, who succeeded Mr. Kennedy, took over his office – was in his office – and gave me this. He delivered this on the 25th, and it says here:

"For release to AM (that means morning papers), August 25th". "Israel is here to stay. It is a national commitment, special obligation of the Democratic Party. The White House must take the lead. American intervention. We will act promptly and decisively against any nation in the Middle East which attacks its neighbor. I propose that we make clear to both Israel and the Arab states our guarantee that we will act with whatever force and speed are necessary to halt any aggression by any nation".

Well, do you call the return of people to their homeland [the Arab Palestinians] aggression? Is Mr. Kennedy going to do that? Suppose three million Mexicans came into Texas and drove the six million Texans into the deserts of Arizona and New Mexico. Suppose these Mexicans were slipped in there armed – the Texans were disarmed

– and one night they drove them all out of Texas and declared themselves the Republic of the Alamo. What would the United States say?

Would we say it's aggression for these Texans to try to get their homes back from the Mexican thieves? Suppose the Negroes in Alabama were secretly armed by the Soviets and overnight they rose up and drove all the whites into the swamps of Mississippi and Georgia and Florida. . . drove them out completely, and declared themselves the Republic of Ham, or the Republic of something-or-other. Would we call it aggression if these people, the whites of Alabama, tried to go back to their homes?

Would we. . . what would we think if the soviet Union said, "No, those Negroes now occupy them! Leave them there!", or "No, those Mexicans are in Texas. they declared themselves a sovereign state. Leave them there. You have plenty of room in Utah and Nevada. Settle somewhere else".

Would we call it aggression if the Alabama whites or the Texans wanted to go back to their homes? So now, you've got to write to President Kennedy and say, "We do not consider it aggression in the sense that you use the word, if these people want to return to their homes as the United Nations – fifteen times in the last twelve years – called upon the Zionists in occupation of Palestine to allow the Arab Palestinians to return to their former homes and farms".

[End of transcript of Benjamin Freedman speech, given in 1961 at the Willard Hotel in Washington, D.C., on behalf of Conde McGinley's newspaper of that time, *Common Sense.*]

Transcript source:
http://www.sweetliberty.org/issues/israel/freedman.htm

Update: 'Balfour Declaration' Author was Secretly Jewish

The historic Balfour Declaration of 1917, which officially sanctioned the nascent Zionist movement under the imprimatur of British authority, was famously written in the name of British Foreign Secretary Arthur Balfour.

But it was Leopold Amery, Assistant Secretary to the British War Cabinet, who actually wrote the text. Balfour merely reviewed and signed it.

In 1999, William Rubenstein, professor of modern history at the University of Wales, published research which indicated that Amery disguised his family background, changed his name, and deliberately hid the fact that his mother was Jewish. But this did not lessen his desire to advance Jewish-Zionist interests at the height of WWI.

"This case is possibly the most remarkable example of concealment of identity in 20th Century British political history," commented Professor Rubenstein in 'History Today' Magazine. -mg

The Jewish Declaration of War on Nazi Germany

The Economic Boycott of 1933

Article from *The Barnes Review*, Jan./Feb. 2001, pp. 41–45.

by M. Raphael Johnson, Ph.D.

Few people today know about the singular event that helped spark what ultimately became known as World War II.

Only months after Adolf Hitler came to power in 1933, and well before any official German government sanctions or reprisals against Jews were carried out, there was an international Jewish 'declaration of war' on Germany. The March 24, 1933, issue of *The Daily Express* of London (previous page) described how Jewish leaders, in alliance with powerful international financial institutions, launched a boycott of Germany for the express purpose of crippling that nation's fragile economy. This was at a time when the U.S. government as well as many Jews in Germany and elsewhere was urging caution in dealing with the new Hitler regime.

The Jewish boycott and other provocations not only sparked reprisals by the German government but also set the stage for a little-known economic and political alliance between the Hitler government and the leaders of the nascent Zionist movement. Some of the early proponents for a Jewish State in Palestine hoped that the tension between the Nazi government and Germany's Jews would lead to massive Jewish influx into Palestine. In short, a tactical alliance emerged between the Nazis and the founders of the modern-day state of Israel – a fact that many today would prefer be forgotten.

To this day, it is generally (although incorrectly) believed that when Adolf Hitler was appointed German chancellor in January of 1933, the German government began policies to suppress the Jews of Germany, including rounding up of Jews and putting them in concentration camps and launching campaigns of terror and violence against the domestic Jewish population.

While there were sporadic eruptions of violence against Jews in Germany after Hitler came to power, this was not officially sanctioned. And the truth is that anti-Jewish sentiments in Germany (or elsewhere in Europe) were actually nothing new. As all Jewish historians attest with much fervor, anti-Semitic uprisings of various degrees had been ever-present in European history.

In any case, in early 1933, Hitler was not the undisputed leader of Germany, nor did he have full command of the armed forces. Hitler was a major figure in a coalition government, but he was far from being the government himself. Hitler's eventual dictatorship was the result of a process of consolidation that evolved later.

Indeed, even Germany's Jewish Central Association, known as the *Verein,* disputed the suggestion (made mostly by Jewish leaders outside of Germany) that the new government was deliberately provoking anti-Jewish sentiments.

The *Verein* issued a statement that "the responsible government authorities [i.e. the Hitler regime] are unaware of the threatening situation," saying, "we do not believe our German fellow citizens will let themselves be carried away into committing excesses against the Jews." Jewish leaders in the United States and Britain however advanced a different tactic.

On March 12, 1933, the American Jewish Congress announced a massive protest at New York's Madison Square Garden for March 27. At that time, the commander in chief of the Jewish War Veterans called for an American boycott of German goods. Some 20,000 Jews protested at New York's City Hall on March 23 as rallies were staged outside the North German Lloyd and Hamburg-American shipping lines and boycotts were mounted against German goods throughout shops and businesses in New York City.

According to *The Daily Express* of London of March 24, 1933, Jewish leaders had already launched their boycott against Germany and her elected government. The headline read "Judea Declares War on Germany - Jews of All the World Unite - Boycott of German Goods - Mass Demonstrations." The article described a forthcoming "holy war" and went on to implore Jews everywhere to boycott German goods and engage in mass demonstrations against German economic interests. According to the *Express*:

> *"The whole of Israel throughout the world is uniting to declare an economic and financial war on Germany. The appearance of the Swastika as the symbol of the new Germany has revived the old war symbol of Judas to new life. Fourteen million Jews scattered over the entire world are tight to each other as if one man, in order to declare war against the German persecutors of their fellow believers.*
>
> *The Jewish wholesaler will quit his house, the banker his stock exchange, the merchant his business, and the beggar his humble hut, in order to join the holy war against Hitler's people".*

The *Express* said that Germany was "now confronted with an international boycott of its trade, its finances, and its industry…. In London, New York, Paris and Warsaw, Jewish businessmen are united to go on an economic crusade."

In a similar vein, the Jewish newspaper *Natscha Retsch* wrote:

> *"The war against Germany will be waged by all Jewish communities, conferences, congresses… by every individual Jew. Thereby the war against Germany will ideologically enliven and promote our interests, which require that Germany be wholly destroyed.*
>
> *The danger for us Jews lies in the whole German people, in Germany as a whole as well as individually. It must be rendered harmless for all time…. In this war we Jews have to participate, and this with all the strength and might we have at our disposal".*

Many Jews however rejected these draconian measures. The Zionist Association of Germany put out a telegram on the 26th of March rejecting many of the allegations made against the [German] National Socialists as "propaganda," "mendacious" and "sensational."

In fact, the Zionist faction had many reasons to support the permanence of National Socialist ideology in Germany. Klaus Polkehn, writing in the *Journal of Palestine Studies* ("The Secret Contacts: Zionism and Nazi Germany, 1933–1941"; JPS v. 3/4, spring/summer 1976), claims that the moderate attitude of the Zionists was due to their vested interest in forcing [Jewish] immigration to Palestine. This little-known factor would ultimately come to play a pivotal part in the relationship between Nazi Germany and Zionist Jews.

In the meantime, German Foreign Minister Konstantin von Neurath complained of the "vilification campaign" adding:

> *"As concerns Jews, I can only say that their propagandists abroad are rendering their co-religionists in Germany no service by giving the German public, through their distorted and untruthful news about persecution and torture of Jews, the impression that they actually halt at nothing, not even at lies and calumny, to fight the present German government".*

The fledgling Hitler government itself was clearly trying to contain the growing tension – both within Germany and without. In the United States, even U.S. Secretary of State Cordell Hull wired

Rabbi Stephen Wise of the American Jewish Congress and urged caution:

> *"Whereas there was for a short time considerable physical mistreat-ment of Jews, this phase may be considered virtually terminated.... A stabilization appears to have been reached in the field of personal mistreatment.... I feel hopeful that the situation which has caused such widespread concern throughout this country will soon revert to normal".*

Despite these cautionary pronouncements, the leaders of the Jewish community declined to relent. On March 27, 1933, there were simultaneous protest rallies at Madison Square Garden, in Chicago, Boston, Philadelphia, Baltimore, Cleveland and 70 other locations. The New York rally was broadcast worldwide. The "New Germany" was declared to be an enemy of the Jewish people and was targeted for economic strangulation.

This international boycott *preceded* Hitler's decision to embargo Jewish economic concerns.

NY Daily News (March 28, 1933): 40000 ROAR PROTEST HERE AGAINST HITLER

Despite some undersized efforts on both sides to alleviate political tensions, the anti-German rally was held in Madison Square Garden on March 27, 1933. Similar rallies and protest marches were also held in other cities at around the same time. The intensity of the campaign against Germany was such that the Hitler government vowed that if the boycott did not stop, there would be a one-day boycott throughout Germany of Jewish-owned stores, which did occur on April 1.

M. Raphael Johnson

German Propaganda Minister Dr. Joseph Goebbels announced that if, after the one-day boycott, there were no further provocations against Germany, the boycott would be stopped. Hitler himself responded to the Jewish boycott and the threats in a speech on March 28, four days after the original Jewish declaration of war, saying:

> "Now that the domestic enemies of the nation have been eliminated by the Volk itself, what we have long been waiting for will not come to pass.
>
> The Communist and Marxist criminals and their Jewish-intellectual instigators, who, having made off with their capital stocks across the border in the nick of time, are now unfolding an unscrupulous, treasonous campaign of agitation against the German Volk as a whole from there....
>
> Lies and slander of positively hair-raising perversity are being launched about Germany. Horror stories of dismembered Jewish corpses, gouged out eyes and hacked off hands are circulating for the purpose of defaming the German Volk in the world for the second time, just as they had succeeded in doing once before in 1914".

Hitler's boycott order on March 28, 1933, though incendiary, was retaliatory. It was a clear response to economic privations launched four days earlier by international Jewry. Yet today, Hitler's boycott order is widely marketed as *unprovoked* aggression, even within the most ponderous and detailed 'histories' of World War II.

Not even Saul Friedlander, in his otherwise comprehensive overview of German policies during that era, *Nazi Germany and the Jews*, mentions the Jewish 'declaration of war' edict that preceded Hitler's "anti-Semitic" speech of March 28, 1933. Discerning readers would be wise to ask why Friedlander considered this historic event to be so irrelevant.

To understand Germany's reaction to the international Jewish boycott, it is important to remember the critical state of the German economy in 1933. That year, some three million Germans were on public assistance with a total of 6 million unemployed. Hyperinflation had ravaged the economic vitality of the German nation. Furthermore, the anti-German propaganda pouring out of the global press strengthened the resolve of Germany's enemies, especially the Poles and their hawkish military high command. In addition, Germany's humiliating defeat in World War I remained a fresh and festering wound in their national psyche. The widely perceived sense of injustice (held by Germans) for the Treaty of Versailles—which shifted most of the blame and reparations for the Great War upon Germany – was also viewed as a moral and political outrage. The German people were deeply resentful, but the boycott was imposed anyway.

As a result of the boycott, Jewish scholars such as Edwin Black reported that German exports were cut by ten percent, and that many Jewish leaders were demanding the seizure of German assets in foreign countries (Edwin Black, *The Transfer Agreement - The Untold Story of the Secret Pact between the Third Reich and Jewish Palestine*, New York, 1984).

Indeed, the economic and diplomatic assault on Germany did not cease. An International Jewish Boycott Conference was soon held in Amsterdam to coordinate the ongoing campaign. It was held under the auspices of the self-styled 'World Jewish Economic Federation'. New York City attorney and longtime political power broker, Samuel Untermyer, was elected its President. In the wake of the conference, Untermyer delivered a confrontational speech over WABC Radio (New York), of which a transcript was printed in *The New York Times* on August 7, 1933.

Untermyer's called for a "sacred war" against Germany, charging that Germany was engaged in a plan to "exterminate the Jews." Among his comments:

> *"...Germany [has] been converted from a nation of culture into a veritable hell of cruel and savage beasts.*
>
> *We owe it not only to our persecuted brethren but to the entire world to now strike in self-defense a blow that will free humanity from a repetition of this incredible outrage....*

Now or never must all the nations of the earth make common cause against the... slaughter, starvation and annihilation... fiendish torture, cruelty and persecution that are being inflicted day by day upon these men, women and children....

When the tale is told... the world will confront a picture so fearful in its barbarous cruelty that the hell of war and the alleged Belgian atrocities pale into insignificance as compared to this devilishly, deliberately, cold-bloodedly planned and already partially executed campaign for the extermination of a proud, gentle, loyal, law-abiding people...

The Jews are the aristocrats of the world. From time immemorial they have been persecuted and have seen their persecutors come and go. They alone have survived. And so will history repeat itself, but that furnishes no reason why we should permit this reversion of a once great nation to the Dark Ages or fail to rescue these 600,000 human souls from the tortures of hell....

...What we are proposing and have already gone far toward doing, is to prosecute a purely defensive economic boycott that will undermine the Hitler regime and bring the German people to their senses by destroying their export trade on which their very existence depends.

...We propose to and are organizing world opinion to express itself in the only way Germany can be made to understand...."

Untermyer then proceeded to provide his listeners with a one-sided account about events that lead to the German boycott. He also reiterated the claim that the Germans were bent on a plan to "exterminate the Jews":

"The Hitler regime originated and are fiendishly prosecuting their boycott to exterminate the Jews by placarding Jewish shops, warning Germans against dealing with them, by imprisoning Jewish shopkeepers and parading them through the streets by the hundreds under guard of Nazi troops for the sole crime of being Jews, by ejecting them from the learned professions in which many of them had at-

tained eminence, by excluding their children from the schools, their men from the labor unions, closing against them every avenue of live- lihood, locking them in vile concentration camps and starving and torturing them without cause and resorting to every other conceivable form of torture, inhuman beyond conception, until suicide has become their only means of escape, and all solely because they are or their remote ancestors were Jews, and all with the avowed object of exter- minating them".

Untermyer concluded his polemic by declaring that with the support of "Christian friends... we will drive the last nail in the coffin of bigotry and fanaticism....".

During this same period however there were some unusual develop- ments at work. The spring of 1933 also witnessed the beginning of a period of private cooperation between the German government and the Jewish Zionist movement in Germany and Palestine (and actu- ally worldwide) to increase the flow of German-Jewish immigrants and capital to an as yet *non-established* Jewish homeland.

This was the genesis of the 'Transfer Agreement', the pact between Zionist Jews and Germany's National Socialist regime to transfer German Jews to Palestine.

While most chroniclers have managed to keep this Nazi-Zionist ac- cord under wraps, the facts about this remarkable chapter have be- gun to emerge. Jewish historian Lenni Brenner's *Zionism In the Age of the Dictators* as well as *51 Documents* are among the first major endeav- ors in this realm.

Zionist apologists have tended to explain the Nazi-Zionist collabo- ration as a tactic undertaken solely to save the lives of Jews, but the fact is there was no state-sanctioned persecution of Jews in Germa- ny at this time. Indeed, contrary to popular myth, Jews did remain somewhat free inside Germany – albeit subject to laws (beginning in 1935) which did restrict many of their freedoms and privileges—up until the outbreak of World War II in 1939.

According to Jewish historian Walter Laqueur however, German Jews were far from convinced that immigration to Palestine was the answer to domestic mistreatment. Furthermore, although the majority of German Jews refused to consider the Zionists as their political leaders, it is evident that Hitler protected and cooperated with the Zionists for the purposes of implementing the final solution: the mass transfer of Jews to the Middle East.

Edwin Black, in his massive tome *The Transfer Agreement* (Macmillan, 1984), stated that although most Jews did not want to flee to Palestine, due in part to the Zionist movement's influence within Nazi Germany the Transfer Agreement mandated that German-Jewish capital could go only to Palestine.

Thus, with the help of Zionists, a Jew could leave Germany only if he went to the [Middle East] Levant.

The primary difficulty with the Transfer Agreement (or even the idea of such an agreement) was that the English were demanding, as a condition of immigration, that each immigrant pay 1,000 pounds sterling upon arrival in Haifa or elsewhere. The difficulty was that such hard currency was nearly impossible to come by in a cash-strapped and radically inflationary Germany.

The relationship between Zionists and National Socialists in Germany in the 1930s was not one merely of mutual interest and political favoritism on the part of Hitler, but a close financial relationship with German banking families and financial institutions as well. Black writes:

> *"It was one thing for the Zionists to subvert the anti-Nazi boycott. Zionism needed to transfer out the capital of German Jews, and merchandise was the only available medium. But soon Zionist leaders understood that the success of the future Jewish Palestinian economy would be inextricably bound up with the survival of the Nazi economy. So the Zionist leadership was compelled to go further. The German economy would have to be safeguarded, stabilized, and if necessary reinforced. Hence, the Nazi party and the Zionist organizers shared a common stake in the recovery of Germany".*

Thus, one sees a radical fissure in world Jewry around 1933 and beyond. First, there were the non-Zionist Jews (manifested by the newly-founded World Jewish Congress), which, on the one hand, advocated the boycott and obliteration of Germany. But on the other hand, there were the minority Zionists. Laqueur states that "the Zionists became motivated not to jeopardize the German economy or currency." As a result, Zionists largely boycotted the boycott.

Another significant (though 'forgotten') occurrence in the build-up to WWII was the pledge made by Chaim Weizmann, who was among the most prominent Jews in the world. Weizmann was president of both the international "Jewish Agency" and of the World Zionist Organization. He later became Israel's first president. On September 6, 1939, the London Times published a letter he sent to British Prime Minister Neville Chamberlain. Among Weizmann's vows:

> *"I wish to confirm, in the most explicit manner, the declarations which I and my colleagues have made during the last month, and especially in the last week, that the Jews [worldwide] stand by Great Britain and will fight on the side of the democracies. Our urgent desire is to give effect to these declarations [against Germany].*
>
> *We wish to do so in a way entirely consonant with the general scheme of British action, and therefore would place ourselves, in matters big and small, under the coordinating direction of His Majesty's Government. The Jewish Agency is ready to enter into immediate arrangements for utilizing Jewish manpower, technical ability, resources, etc."*

Thus, in addition to launching and sustaining, six year long economic boycott, countless diplomatic rows and efforts to induce war between the U.S. and Germany, there was a public vow by one of the world's most influential Jews to bring the full weight and power of international Jewry down against Hitler's Germany. As a consequence, the German authorities deemed all Jews to be potential enemy agents.

Ironically, Germany's National Socialist policies (themselves a reflection of Zionist values) were probably vital to the Zionist movement, since they 'proved' that German (and European) anti-Semitism was irredeemable. Thus, Zionism came to represent the interests of world Jewry through no small amount of trickery, provocation and cooperation with none other than Adolf Hitler.

The misrepresentation of these historic details continues.

The Barnes Review, 645 Pennsylvania Ave SE, Suite 100, Washington D.C. 20003, USA. By M. Raphael Johnson, Ph.D., assistant editor of The Barnes Review.

Published here with kind permission from The Barnes Review.

Additional photo source: http://en.wikipedia.org/wiki/Image:DailyExpress_March1933_judeafrontpage.jpg

Zionism and the Third Reich

by Mark Weber

Early in 1935, a passenger ship bound for Haifa in Palestine left the German port of Bremerhaven. Its stern bore the Hebrew letters for its name, "Tel Aviv," while a swastika banner fluttered from the mast. And although the ship was Zionist-owned, its captain was a National Socialist Party member. Many years later a traveler aboard the ship recalled this symbolic combination as a "metaphysical absurdity."1 Absurd or not, this is but one vignette from a little-known chapter of history: the wide-ranging collaboration between Zionism and Hitler's Third Reich.

Common Aims

Over the years, people in many different countries have wrestled with the "Jewish question": that is, what is the proper role of Jews in non-Jewish society? During the 1930s, Jewish Zionists and German National Socialists shared similar views on how to deal with this perplexing issue. They agreed that Jews and Germans were distinctly different nationalities, and that Jews did not belong in Germany. Jews living in the Reich were therefore to be regarded not as

"Germans of the Jewish faith," but rather as members of a separate national community. Zionism (Jewish nationalism) also implied an obligation by Zionist Jews to resettle in Palestine, the "Jewish homeland." They could hardly regard themselves as sincere Zionists and simultaneously claim equal rights in Germany or any other "foreign" country.

Theodor Herzl (1860–1904), the founder of modern Zionism, maintained that anti-Semitism is not an aberration, but a natural and understandable response by non-Jews to alien Jewish behavior and attitudes. The only solution, he argued, is for Jews to recognize reality and live in a separate state of their own. "The Jewish question exists wherever Jews live in noticeable numbers," he wrote in his most influential work, *The Jewish State*. "Where it does not exist, it is brought in by arriving Jews ... I believe I understand anti-Semitism, which is a very complex phenomenon. I consider this development as a Jew, without hate or fear." The Jewish question, he maintained, is not social or religious. "It is a national question. To solve it we must, above all, make it an international political issue ..." Regardless of their citizenship, Herzl insisted, Jews constitute not merely a religious community, but a nationality, a people, a Volk. 2 Zionism, wrote Herzl, offered the world a welcome "final solution of the Jewish question."3

Six months after Hitler came to power, the Zionist Federation of Germany (by far the largest Zionist group in the country) submitted a detailed memorandum to the new government that reviewed German-Jewish relations and formally offered Zionist support in "solving" the vexing "Jewish question." The first step, it suggested, had to be a frank recognition of fundamental national differences: 4

"Zionism has no illusions about the difficulty of the Jewish condition, which consists above all in an abnormal occupational pattern and in the fault of an intellectual and moral posture not rooted in one's own tradition. Zionism recognized decades ago that as a result of the assimilationist trend, symptoms of deterioration were bound to appear ....

"Zionism believes that the rebirth of the national life of a people, which is now occurring in Germany through the emphasis on its Christian and national charac-

ter, must also come about in the Jewish national group. For the Jewish people, too, national origin, religion, common destiny and a sense of its uniqueness must be of decisive importance in the shaping of its existence. This means that the egotistical individualism of the liberal era must be overcome and replaced with a sense of community and collective responsibility. ...

"We believe it is precisely the new [National Socialist] Germany that can, through bold resoluteness in the handling of the Jewish question, take a decisive step toward overcoming a problem which, in truth, will have to be dealt with by most European peoples ....

"Our acknowledgment of Jewish nationality provides for a clear and sincere relationship to the German people and its national and racial realities. Precisely because we do not wish to falsify these fundamentals, because we, too, are against mixed marriage and are for maintaining the purity of the Jewish group and reject any trespasses in the cultural domain, we – having been brought up in the German language and German culture – can show an interest in the works and values of German culture with admiration and internal sympathy ....

"For its practical aims, Zionism hopes to be able to win the collaboration of even a government fundamentally hostile to Jews, because in dealing with the Jewish question not sentimentalities are involved but a real problem whose solution interests all peoples and at the present moment especially the German people ...

Boycott propaganda – such as is currently being carried on against Germany in many ways – is in essence un-Zionist, because Zionism wants not to do battle but to convince and to build ....

We are not blind to the fact that a Jewish question exists and will continue to exist. From the abnormal situation of the Jews severe disadvantages result for them, but also scarcely tolerable conditions for other peoples".

The Federation's paper, the *Jüdische Rundschau* ("Jewish Review"), proclaimed the same message: "Zionism recognizes the existence of a Jewish problem and desires a far-reaching and constructive solution. For this purpose Zionism wishes to obtain the assistance of all peoples, whether pro- or anti-Jewish, because, in its view, we are dealing here with a concrete rather than a sentimental problem, the solution of which all peoples are interested."[5] A young Berlin rabbi,

Joachim Prinz, who later settled in the United States and became head of the American Jewish Congress, wrote in his 1934 book, *Wir Juden* ("We Jews"), that the National Socialist revolution in Germany meant "Jewry for the Jews." He explained: "No subterfuge can save us now. In place of assimilation we desire a new concept: recognition of the Jewish nation and Jewish race."[6]

Active Collaboration

On this basis of their similar ideologies about ethnicity and nation-hood, National Socialists and Zionists worked together for what each group believed was in its own national interest. As a result, the Hitler government vigorously supported Zionism and Jewish emigration to Palestine from 1933 until 1940–1941, when the Second World War prevented continued collaboration.

Even as the Third Reich became more entrenched, many German Jews, probably a majority, continued to regard themselves, often with considerable pride, as Germans first. Few were enthusiastic about pulling up roots to begin a new life in far-away Palestine. Neverthe-less, more and more German Jews turned to Zionism during this pe-riod. Until late 1938, the Zionist movement flourished in Germany under Hitler. The circulation of the Zionist Federation's bi-weekly *Jüdische Rundschau* grew enormously. Numerous Zionist books were published. "Zionist work was in full swing" in Germany during those years, the Encyclopaedia Judaica notes. A Zionist convention held in Berlin in 1936 reflected "in its composition the vigorous party life of German Zionists." 7

The German SS was very supportive of Zionism. An internal June 1934 SS position paper urged active and wide-ranging support for Zionism by the government and the Party as the best way to en-courage emigration of Germany's Jews to Palestine. This would re-quire increased Jewish self-awareness. Jewish schools, Jewish sports leagues, Jewish cultural organizations – in short, everything that would encourage this new consciousness and self-awareness - should be promoted, the paper recommended.[8]

SS officer Leopold von Mildenstein and Zionist Federation official Kurt Tuchler toured Palestine together for six months to assess Zionist development there. Based on his firsthand observations, von Mildenstein wrote a series of twelve illustrated articles for the important Berlin daily *Der Angriff* that appeared in late 1934 under the heading "A Nazi Travels to Palestine." The series expressed great admiration for the pioneering spirit and achievements of the Jewish settlers. Zionist self-development, von Mildenstein wrote, had produced a new kind of Jew. He praised Zionism as a great benefit for both the Jewish people and the entire world. A Jewish homeland in Palestine, he wrote in his concluding article, "pointed the way to curing a centuries-long wound on the body of the world: the Jewish question." *Der Angriff* issued a special medal, with a Swastika on one side and a Star of David on the other, to commemorate the joint SS-Zionist visit. A few months after the articles appeared, von Mildenstein was promoted to head the Jewish affairs department of the SS security service in order to support Zionist migration and development more effectively. 9

The official SS newspaper, *Das Schwarze Korps*, proclaimed its support for Zionism in a May 1935 front-page editorial: "The time may not be too far off when Palestine will again be able to receive its sons who have been lost to it for more than a thousand years. Our good wishes, together with official goodwill, go with them."[10] Four months later, a similar article appeared in the SS paper:[11]

"The recognition of Jewry as a racial community based on blood and not on religion leads the German government to guarantee without reservation the racial separateness of this community. The government finds itself in complete agreement with the great spiritual movement within Jewry, the so-called Zionism, with its recognition of the solidarity of Jewry around the world and its rejection of all assimilationist notions. On this basis, Germany undertakes measures that will surely play a significant role in the future in the handling of the Jewish problem around the world".

A leading German shipping line began direct passenger liner service from Hamburg to Haifa, Palestine, in October 1933 providing "strictly kosher food on its ships, under the supervision of the Hamburg rabbinate."[12]

With official backing, Zionists worked tirelessly to "reeducate" Germany's Jews. As American historian Francis Nicosia put it in his 1985 survey, The Third Reich and the Palestine Question: "Zionists were encouraged to take their message to the Jewish community, to collect money, to show films on Palestine and generally to educate German Jews about Palestine. There was considerable pressure to teach Jews in Germany to cease identifying themselves as Germans and to awaken a new Jewish national identity in them."[13]

In an interview after the war, the former head of the Zionist Federation of Germany, Dr. Hans Friedenthal, summed up the situation: "The Gestapo did everything in those days to promote emigration, particularly to Palestine. We often received their help when we required anything from other authorities regarding preparations for emigration."[14]

At the September 1935 National Socialist Party Congress, the Reichstag adopted the so-called "Nuremberg laws" that prohibited marriages and sexual relations between Jews and Germans and, in effect, proclaimed the Jews an alien minority nationality. A few days later the Zionist *Jüdische Rundschau* editorially welcomed the new measures:[15]

"Germany ... is meeting the demands of the World Zionist Congress when it declares the Jews now living in Germany to be a national minority. Once the Jews have been stamped a national minority it is again possible to establish normal relations between the German nation and Jewry. The new laws give the Jewish minority in Germany its own cultural life, its own national life. In future it will be able to shape its own schools, its own theatre, and its own sports associations. In short, it can create its own future in all aspects of national life ...

"Germany has given the Jewish minority the opportunity to live for itself, and is offering state protection for this separate life of the Jewish minority: Jewry's process of growth into a nation will thereby be encouraged and a contribution will be made to the establishment of more tolerable relations between the two nations".

Georg Kareski, the head of both the 'Revisionist' Zionist State Organization and the Jewish Cultural League, and former head of the Berlin Jewish Community, declared in an interview with the Berlin daily *Der Angriff* at the end of 1935:[16]

"For many years I have regarded a complete separation of the cultural affairs of the two peoples [Jews and Germans] as a pre-condition for living together without conflict... I have long supported such a separation, provided it is founded on respect for the alien nationality. The Nuremberg Laws ... seem to me, apart from their legal provisions, to conform entirely with this desire for a separate life based on mutual respect... This interruption of the process of dissolution in many Jewish communities, which had been promoted through mixed marriages, is therefore, from a Jewish point of view, entirely welcome".

Zionist leaders in other countries echoed these views. Stephen S. Wise, president of the American Jewish Congress and the World Jewish Congress, told a New York rally in June 1938: "I am not an American citizen of the Jewish faith, I am a Jew... Hitler was right in one thing. He calls the Jewish people a race and we are a race."[17]

The Interior Ministry's Jewish affairs specialist, Dr. Bernhard Lösener, expressed support for Zionism in an article that appeared in a November 1935 issue of the official *Reichsverwaltungsblatt:*[18]

"If the Jews already had their own state in which the majority of them were settled, then the Jewish question could be regarded as completely resolved today, also for the Jews themselves. The least amount of opposition to the ideas underlying the Nuremberg Laws have been shown by the Zionists, because they realize at once that these laws represent the only correct solution for the Jewish people as well. For each nation must have its own state as the outward expression of its particular nationhood".

In cooperation with the German authorities, Zionist groups organized a network of some forty camps and agricultural centers throughout Germany where prospective settlers were trained for their new lives in Palestine. Although the Nuremberg Laws forbid Jews from displaying the German flag, Jews were specifically guaranteed the right to display the blue and white Jewish national banner.

The flag that would one day be adopted by Israel was flown at the Zionist camps and centers in Hitler's Germany.[19]

Himmler's security service cooperated with the *Haganah*, the Zionist underground military organization in Palestine. The SS agency paid *Haganah* official Feivel Polkes for information about the situation in Palestine and for help in directing Jewish emigration to that country. Meanwhile, the *Haganah* was kept well informed about German plans by a spy it managed to plant in the Berlin headquarters of the SS.[20] *Haganah*-SS collaboration even included secret deliveries of German weapons to Jewish settlers for use in clashes with Palestinian Arabs.[21]

In the aftermath of the November 1938 "Kristallnacht" outburst of violence and destruction, the SS quickly helped the Zionist organization to get back on its feet and continue its work in Germany, although now under considerably much more restricted supervision. [22]

Official Reservations

German support for Zionism was obviously not unlimited. Government and Party officials were very mindful of the continuing campaign by powerful Jewish communities in the United States, Britain and other countries to mobilize "their" governments and fellow citizens against Germany. As long as world Jewry remained implacably hostile toward National Socialist Germany, and as long as the great majority of Jews around the world showed little eagerness to resettle in the Zionist 'promised land', a sovereign Jewish state in Palestine would not really solve the international Jewish question. Instead, German officials reasoned, it would immeasurably strengthen this dangerous anti-German campaign. German backing for Zionism therefore became limited to support for a Jewish homeland in Palestine under British control, not a sovereign Jewish state.[23]

A Jewish state in Palestine, the Foreign Minister informed diplomats in June 1937, would not be in Germany's interest because it would not be able to absorb all Jews around the world, but would only serve as an additional power base for international Jewry, in much the same way as Moscow served as a base for international Communism. 24 Reflecting something of a shift in official policy, the German press expressed much greater sympathy in 1937 for Palestinian Arab resistance to Zionist ambitions, at a time when tension and conflict between Jews and Arabs in Palestine was sharply increasing.[25]

A Foreign Office circular bulletin of June 22, 1937, cautioned that in spite of support for Jewish settlement in Palestine, "it would nevertheless be a mistake to assume that Germany supports the formation of a state structure in Palestine under some form of Jewish control. In view of the anti-German agitation of international Jewry, Germany cannot agree that the formation of a Palestine Jewish state would help the peaceful development of the nations of the world."[26] "The proclamation of a Jewish state or a Jewish-administered Palestine," warned an internal memorandum by the Jewish affairs section of the SS, "would create for Germany a new enemy, one that would have a deep influence on developments in the Near East." Another SS agency predicted that a Jewish state "would work to bring special minority protection to Jews in every country, therefore giving legal protection to the exploitation activity of world Jewry."[27] In January 1939, Hitler's new Foreign Minister, Joachim von Ribbentrop, likewise warned in another circular bulletin that "Germany must regard the formation of a Jewish state as dangerous" because it "would bring an international increase in power to world Jewry."[28]

Hitler himself personally reviewed this entire issue in early 1938 and, in spite of his long-standing skepticism of Zionist ambitions and misgivings that his policies might contribute to the formation of a Jewish state, decided to support Jewish migration to Palestine even more vigorously. The prospect of ridding Germany of its Jews, he concluded, outweighed the possible dangers.[29]

Meanwhile, the British government imposed ever more drastic restrictions on Jewish immigration into Palestine in 1937, 1938 and 1939. In response, the SS security service concluded a secret alliance with the clandestine Zionist agency *Mossad le-Aliya Bet* to smuggle Jews illegally into Palestine. As a result of this intensive collaboration, several convoys of ships succeeded in reaching Palestine past

British gunboats. Jewish migration, both legal and illegal, from Germany (including Austria) to Palestine increased dramatically in 1938 and 1939. Another 10,000 Jews were scheduled to depart in October 1939, but the outbreak of war in September brought the effort to an end. All the same, German authorities continued to promote indirect Jewish emigration to Palestine during 1940 and 1941.[30] Even as late as March 1942, at least one officially authorized Zionist "kibbutz" training camp for potential emigrants continued to operate in Hitler's Germany.[31]

The Transfer Agreement

The centerpiece of German-Zionist cooperation during the Hitler era was the Transfer Agreement, a pact that enabled tens of thousands of German Jews to migrate to Palestine with their wealth intact. The Agreement, also known as the Haavara (Hebrew for "transfer"), was concluded in August 1933 following talks between German officials and Chaim Arlosoroff, Political Secretary of the Jewish Agency, the Palestine center of the World Zionist Organization.[32]

Through this unusual arrangement, each Jew bound for Palestine deposited money in a special account in Germany. The money was used to purchase German-made agricultural tools, building materials, pumps, fertilizer, and so forth, which were exported to Palestine and sold there by the Jewish-owned Haavara company in Tel-Aviv. Money from the sales was given to the Jewish emigrant upon his arrival in Palestine in an amount corresponding to his deposit in Germany. German goods poured into Palestine through the Haavara, which was supplemented a short time later with a barter agreement by which Palestine oranges were exchanged for German timber, automobiles, agricultural machinery, and other goods. The Agreement thus served the Zionist aim of bringing Jewish settlers and development capital to Palestine, while simultaneously serving the German goal of freeing the country of an unwanted alien group.

Delegates at the 1933 Zionist Congress in Prague vigorously debated the merits of the Agreement. Some feared that the pact would undermine the international Jewish economic boycott against Germany. But Zionist officials reassured the Congress. Sam Cohen, a key figure behind the Haavara arrangement, stressed that the Agreement was not economically advantageous to Germany. Arthur Ruppin, a Zionist Organization emigration specialist who had helped negotiate the pact, pointed out that "the Transfer Agreement in no way interfered with the boycott movement, since no new currency will flow into Germany as a result of the agreement..."[33] The 1935 Zionist Congress, meeting in Switzerland, overwhelmingly endorsed the pact. In 1936, the *Jewish Agency* (the Zionist "shadow government" in Palestine) took over direct control of the Haavara, which remained in effect until the Second World War forced its abandonment.

Some German officials also opposed the arrangement. Germany's Consul General in Jerusalem, Hans Döhle, for example, sharply criticized the Agreement on several occasions during 1937. He pointed out that it cost Germany the foreign exchange that the products exported to Palestine through the pact would bring if sold elsewhere. The Haavara monopoly sale of German goods to Palestine through a Jewish agency naturally angered German businessmen and Arabs there. Official German support for Zionism could lead to a loss of German markets throughout the Arab world. The British government also resented the arrangement.[34] A June 1937 German Foreign Office internal bulletin referred to the "foreign exchange sacrifices" that resulted from the Haavara.[35]

A December 1937 internal memorandum by the German Interior Ministry reviewed the impact of the Transfer Agreement: "There is no doubt that the Haavara arrangement has contributed most significantly to the very rapid development of Palestine since 1933. The Agreement provided not only the largest source of money (from Germany!), but also the most intelligent group of immigrants, and finally it brought to the country the machines and industrial products essential for development."

The main advantage of the pact, the memo reported, was the emigration of large numbers of Jews to Palestine, the most desirable target country as far as Germany was concerned. But the paper also noted the important drawbacks pointed out by Consul Döhle and others. The Interior Minister, it went on, had concluded that the disadvantages of the agreement now outweighed the advantages and that, therefore, it should be terminated.[36]

Only one man could resolve the controversy. Hitler personally reviewed the policy in July and September 1937, and again in January 1938, and each time decided to maintain the Haavara arrangement. The goal of removing Jews from Germany, he concluded, justified the drawbacks.[37]

The Reich Economics Ministry helped to organize another transfer company, the International Trade and Investment Agency, or Intria, through which Jews in foreign countries could help German Jews emigrate to Palestine. Almost $900,000 was eventually channeled through the Intria to German Jews in Palestine.[38] Other European countries eager to encourage Jewish emigration concluded agreements with the Zionists modeled after the Haavara. In 1937 Poland authorized the *Halifin* (Hebrew for "exchange") transfer company. By late summer 1939, Czechoslovakia, Romania, Hungary and Italy had signed similar arrangements. The outbreak of war in September 1939, however, prevented large-scale implementation of these agreements.[39]

Achievements of Haavara

Between 1933 and 1941, some 60,000 German Jews imigrated to Palestine through the Haavara and other German-Zionist arrangements, or about ten percent of Germany's 1933 Jewish population. (These German Jews made up about 15 percent of Palestine's 1939 Jewish population.) Some Haavara emigrants transferred considerable personal wealth from Germany to Palestine. As Jewish historian Edwin Black has noted: "Many of these people, especially in the late

1930s, were allowed to transfer actual replicas of their homes and factories – indeed rough replicas of their very existence."[40]

The total amount transferred from Germany to Palestine through the Haavara between August 1933 and the end of 1939 was 8.1 million pounds or 139.57 million German marks (then equivalent to more than $40 million). This amount included 33.9 million German marks ($13.8 million) provided by the *Reichsbank* in connection with the Agreement.[41]

Historian Black has estimated that an additional $70 million may have flowed into Palestine through corollary German commercial agreements and special international banking transactions. The German funds had a major impact on a country as underdeveloped as Palestine was in the 1930s, he pointed out. Several major industrial enterprises were built with the capital from Germany, including the Mekoroth waterworks and the Lodzia textile firm. The influx of Haavara goods and capital, concluded Black, "produced an economic explosion in Jewish Palestine" and was "an indispensable factor in the creation of the State of Israel."[42]

The Haavara agreement greatly contributed to Jewish development in Palestine and thus, indirectly, to the foundation of the Israeli state. A January 1939 German Foreign Office circular bulletin reported, with some misgivings, that "the transfer of Jewish property out of Germany [through the Haavara agreement] contributed to no small extent to the building of a Jewish state in Palestine."[43]

Former officials of the Haavara company in Palestine confirmed this view in a detailed study of the Transfer Agreement published in 1972: "The economic activity made possible by the influx German capital and the Haavara transfers to the private and public sectors were of greatest importance for the country's development. Many new industries and commercial enterprises were established in Jewish Palestine, and numerous companies that are enormously important even today in the economy of the State of Israel owe their existence to the Haavara."[44] Dr. Ludwig Pinner, a Haavara company official in Tel Aviv during the 1930s, later commented that the exceptionally competent Haavara immigrants "decisively contributed" to the economic, social, cultural and educational development of Palestine's Jewish community.[45]

The Transfer Agreement was the most far-reaching example of cooperation between Hitler's Germany and international Zionism. Through this pact, Hitler's Third Reich did more than any other government during the 1930s to support Jewish emigration and development in Palestine.

Zionists Offer a Military Alliance With Hitler

In early January 1941 a small but important Zionist organization submitted a formal proposal to German diplomats in Beirut for a military-political alliance with wartime Germany. The offer was made by the radical underground "Fighters for the Freedom of Israel," better known as the Lehi or Stern Gang. Its leader, Avraham Stern, had recently broken with the radical nationalist "National Military Organization" *(Irgun Zvai Leumi)* over the group's attitude toward Britain, which had effectively banned further Jewish settlement of Palestine. Stern regarded Britain as the main enemy of Zionism.

This remarkable Zionist proposal "for the solution of the Jewish question in Europe and the active participation of the NMO [Lehi] in the war on the side of Germany" is worth quoting at some length:[46]

"In their speeches and statements, the leading statesmen of National Socialist Germany have often emphasized that a New Order in Europe requires as a prerequisite a radical solution of the Jewish question by evacuation. ("Jew-free Europe")

"The evacuation of the Jewish masses from Europe is a precondition for solving the Jewish question. However, the only way this can be totally achieved is through settlement of these masses in the homeland of the Jewish people, Palestine, and by the establishment of a Jewish state in its historical boundaries.

"The goal of the political activity and the years of struggle by the Israel Freedom Movement, the National Military Organization in Palestine (Irgun Zvai

Leumi), is to solve the Jewish problem in this way and thus completely liberate the Jewish people forever.

"The NMO, which is very familiar with the good will of the German Reich government and its officials towards Zionist activities within Germany and the Zionist emigration program, takes that view that:

1. *Common interests can exist between a European New Order based on the German concept and the true national aspirations of the Jewish people as embodied by the NMO.*

2. *Cooperation is possible between the New Germany and a renewed, folkish-national Jewry [Hebr_ertum].*

3. *The establishment of the historical Jewish state on a national and to-talitarian basis, and bound by treaty with the German Reich, would be in the interest of maintaining and strengthening the future German position of power in the Near East.*

"On the basis of these considerations, and upon the condition that the German Reich government recognize the national aspirations of the Israel Freedom Movement mentioned above, the NMO in Palestine offers to actively take part in the war on the side of Germany.

"This offer by the NMO could include military, political and informational activity within Palestine and, after certain organizational measures, outside as well. Along with this the Jewish men of Europe would be militarily trained and organized in military units under the leadership and command of the NMO. They would take part in combat operations for the purpose of conquering Palestine, should such a front by formed.

"The indirect participation of the Israel Freedom Movement in the New Order of Europe, already in the preparatory stage, combined with a positive-radical solution of the European Jewish problem on the basis of the national aspirations of the Jewish people mentioned above, would greatly strengthen the moral foundation of the New Order in the eyes of all humanity.

"The cooperation of the Israel Freedom Movement would also be consistent with a recent speech by the German Reich Chancellor, in which Hitler stressed that

he would utilize any combination and coalition in order to isolate and defeat England".

There is no record of any German response. Acceptance was very unlikely anyway because by this time German policy was decisively pro-Arab.[47] Remarkably, Stern's group sought to conclude a pact with the Third Reich at a time when stories that Hitler was bent on exterminating Jews were already in wide circulation. Stern apparently either did not believe the stories or he was willing to collaborate with the mortal enemy of his people to help bring about a Jewish state.[48]

An important Lehi member at the time the group made this offer was Yitzhak Shamir, who later served as Israel's Foreign Minister and then, during much of the 1980s and until June 1992, as Prime Minister. As Lehi operations chief following Stern's death in 1942, Shamir organized numerous acts of terror, including the November 1944 assassination of British Middle East Minister Lord Moyne and the September 1948 slaying of Swedish United Nations mediator Count Bernadotte. Years later, when Shamir was asked about the 1941 offer, he confirmed that he was aware of his organization's proposed alliance with wartime Germany.[49]

Conclusion

In spite of the basic hostility between the Hitler regime and international Jewry, for several years Jewish Zionist and German National Socialist interests coincided. In collaborating with the Zionists for a mutually desirable and humane solution to a complex problem, the Third Reich was willing to make foreign exchange sacrifices, impair relations with Britain and anger the Arabs. Indeed, during the 1930s no nation did more to substantively further Jewish-Zionist goals than Hitler's Germany.

Notes

1. W. Martini, "Hebr_isch unterm Hakenkreuz," Die Welt (Hamburg), Jan. 10, 1975. Cited in: Klaus Polken, "The Secret Contacts: Zionism and Nazi Germany, 1933–1941," Journal of Palestine Studies, Spring-Summer 1976, p. 65.

2. Quoted in: Ingrid Weckert, Feuerzeichen: Die "Reichskristallnacht" (Tübingen: Grabert, 1981), p. 212. See also: Th. Herzl, The Jewish State (New York: Herzl Press, 1970), pp. 33, 35, 36, and, Edwin Black, The Transfer Agreement (New York: Macmillan, 1984), p. 73.

3. Th. Herzl, "Der Kongress," Welt, June 4, 1897. Reprinted in: Theodor Herzls zionistische Schriften (Leon Kellner, ed.), erster Teil, Berlin: Jüdischer Verlag, 1920, p. 190 (and p. 139).

4. Memo of June 21, 1933, in: L. Dawidowicz, A Holocaust Reader (New York: Behrman, 1976), pp. 150–155, and (in part) in: Francis R. Nicosia, The Third Reich and the Palestine Question (Austin: Univ. of Texas, 1985), p. 42.; On Zionism in Germany before Hitler's assumption of power, see: Donald L. Niewyk, The Jews in Weimar Germany (Baton Rouge: 1980), pp. 94–95, 126–131, 140–143.; F. Nicosia, Third Reich (Austin: 1985), pp. 1–15.

5. Jüdische Rundschau (Berlin), June 13, 1933. Quoted in: Heinz H_hne, The Order of the Death's Head (New York: Ballantine, pb., 1971, 1984), pp. 376–377.

6. Heinz Höhne, The Order of the Death's Head (Ballantine, 1971, 1984), p. 376.

7. "Berlin," Encyclopaedia Judaica (New York and Jerusalem: 1971), Vol. 5, p. 648. For a look at one aspect of this "vigorous life," see: J.-C. Horak, "Zionist Film Propaganda in Nazi Germany," Historical Journal of Film, Radio and Television, Vol. 4, No. 1, 1984, pp. 49–58.

8. Francis R. Nicosia, The Third Reich and the Palestine Question (1985), pp. 54–55.; Karl A. Schleunes, The Twisted Road to Auschwitz (Urbana: Univ. of Illinois, 1970, 1990), pp. 178–181.

9. Jacob Boas, "A Nazi Travels to Palestine," History Today (London), January 1980, pp. 33–38.

10. Facsimile reprint of front page of Das Schwarze Korps, May 15, 1935, in: Janusz Piekalkiewicz, Israels Langer Arm (Frankfurt: Goverts, 1975), pp. 66-67. Also quoted in: Heinz H_hne, The Order of the Death's Head (Ballantine, 1971, 1984), p. 377. See also: Erich Kern, ed., Verheimlichte Dokumente (Munich: FZ-Verlag, 1988), p. 184.

11. Das Schwarze Korps, Sept. 26, 1935. Quoted in: F. Nicosia, The Third Reich and the Palestine Question (1985), pp. 56–57.

12. Lenni Brenner, Zionism in the Age of the Dictators (1983), p. 83.

13. F. Nicosia, The Third Reich and the Palestine Question (1985), p. 60. See also: F. Nicosia, "The Yishuv and the Holocaust," The Journal of Modern History (Chicago), Vol. 64, No. 3, Sept. 1992, pp. 533–540.

14. F. Nicosia, The Third Reich and the Palestine Question (1985), p. 57.

15. Jüdische Rundschau, Sept. 17, 1935. Quoted in: Yitzhak Arad, with Y. Gutman and A. Margaliot, eds., Documents on the Holocaust (Jerusalem: Yad Vashem, 1981), pp. 82–83.

16. Der Angriff, Dec. 23, 1935, in: E. Kern, ed., Verheimlichte Dokumente (Munich: 1988), p. 148.; F. Nicosia, Third Reich (1985), p. 56.; L. Brenner, Zionism in the Age of the Dictators (1983), p. 138.; A. Margaliot, "The Reaction...," Yad Vashem Studies (Jerusalem), vol. 12, 1977, pp. 90–91.; On Kareski's remarkable career, see: H. Levine, "A Jewish Collaborator in Nazi Germany," Central European History (Atlanta), Sept. 1975, pp. 251–281.

17. "Dr. Wise Urges Jews to Declare Selves as Such," New York Herald Tribune, June 13, 1938, p. 12.

18. F. Nicosia, The Third Reich (1985), p. 53.

19. Lucy Dawidowicz, The War Against the Jews, 1933-1945 (New York: Bantam, pb., 1976), pp. 253–254.; Max Nussbaum, "Zionism Under Hitler," Congress Weekly (New York: American Jewish Congress), Sept. 11, 1942.; F. Nicosia, The Third Reich (1985), pp. 58–60, 217.; Edwin Black, The Transfer Agreement (1984), p. 175.

20. H. H_hne, The Order of the Death's Head (Ballantine, pb., 1984), pp. 380–382.; K. Schleunes, Twisted Road (1970, 1990), p. 226.; Secret internal SS intelligence report about F. Polkes, June 17, 1937, in: John Mendelsohn, ed., The Holocaust (New York: Garland, 1982), vol. 5, pp. 62–64.

21. F. Nicosia, Third Reich (1985), pp. 63–64, 105, 219–220.

22. F. Nicosia, Third Reich (1985), p. 160.

23. This distinction is also implicit in the "Balfour Declaration" of November 1917, in which the British government expressed support for "a national home for the Jewish people" in Palestine, while carefully avoiding any mention of a Jewish state. Referring to the majority Arab population there, the Declaration went on to caution, "...it being clearly understood that nothing shall be done which may prejudice the civil and religious rights of existing non-Jewish communities in Palestine." The complete text of the Declaration is reproduced in facsimile in: Robert John, Behind the Balfour Declaration (IHR, 1988), p. 32.

24. F. Nicosia, Third Reich (1985), p. 121.

25. F. Nicosia, Third Reich (1985), p. 124.

26. David Yisraeli, The Palestine Problem in German Politics 1889-1945 (Bar-Ilan University, Israel, 1974), p. 300.; Also in:

Documents on German Foreign Policy, Series D, Vol. 5. Doc. No. 564 or 567.

27. K. Schleunes, The Twisted Road (1970, 1990), p. 209.

28. Circular of January 25, 1939. Nuremberg document 3358-PS. International Military Tribunal, Trial of the Major War Criminals Before the International Military Tribunal (Nuremberg: 1947–1949), vol. 32, pp. 242–243. Nazi Conspiracy and Aggression (Washington, DC: 1946-1948), vol. 6, pp. 92-93.

29. F. Nicosia, Third Reich (1985), pp. 141–144.; On Hitler's critical view of Zionism in Mein Kampf, see esp. Vol. 1, Chap. 11. Quoted in: Robert Wistrich, Hitler's Apocalypse (London: 1985), p. 155.; See also: F. Nicosia, Third Reich (1985), pp. 26–28.; Hitler told his army adjutant in 1939 and again in 1941 that he had asked the British in 1937 about transferring all of Germany's Jews to Palestine or Egypt. The British rejected the proposal, he said, because it would cause further disorder. See: H. v. Kotze, ed., Heeresadjutant bei Hitler (Stuttgart: 1974), pp. 65, 95.

30. F. Nicosia, Third Reich (1985), pp. 156, 160–164, 166–167.; H. H_hne, The Order of the Death's Head (Ballantine, pb., 1984), pp. 392–394.; Jon and David Kimche, The Secret Roads (London: Secker and Warburg, 1955), pp. 39-43. See also: David Yisraeli, "The Third Reich and Palestine," Middle Eastern Studies, October 1971, p. 347.; Bernard Wasserstein, Britain and the Jews of Europe, 1939–1945 (1979), pp. 43, 49, 52, 60.; T. Kelly, "Man who fooled Nazis," Washington Times, April 28, 1987, pp. 1B, 4B. Based on interview with Willy Perl, author of The Holocaust Conspiracy.

31. Y. Arad, et al., eds., Documents On the Holocaust (1981), p. 155. (The training kibbutz was at Neuendorf, and may have functioned even after March 1942.)

32. On the Agreement in general, see: Werner Feilchenfeld, et al., Haavara-Transfer nach Palaestina (Tübingen: Mohr/Sie-

beck, 1972).; David Yisraeli, "The Third Reich and the Transfer Agreement," Journal of Contemporary History (London), No. 2, 1971, pp. 129-148.; "Haavara," Encyclopaedia Judaica (1971), vol. 7, pp. 1012-1013.; F. Nicosia, The Third Reich and the Palestine Question (Austin: 1985), pp. 44–49.; Raul Hilberg, The Destruction of the European Jews (New York: Holmes and Meier, 1985), pp. 140–141.; The Transfer Agreement, by Edwin Black, is detailed and useful. However, it contains numerous inaccuracies and wildly erroneous conclusions. See, for example, the review by Richard S. Levy in Commentary, Sept. 1984, pp. 68–71.

33. E. Black, The Transfer Agreement (1984), pp. 328, 337.

34. On opposition to the Haavara in official German circles, see: W. Feilchenfeld, et al., Haavara-Transfer nach Palaestina (1972), pp. 31–33.; D. Yisraeli, "The Third Reich," Journal of Contemporary History, 1971, pp. 136–139.; F. Nicosia, The Third Reich and the Palestine Question, pp. 126–139.; I. Weckert, Feuerzeichen (1981), pp. 226–227.; Rolf Vogel, Ein Stempel hat gefehlt (Munich: Droemer Knaur, 1977), pp. 110 ff.

35. W. Feilchenfeld, et al., Haavara-Transfer (1972), p. 31. Entire text in: David Yisraeli, The Palestine Problem in German Politics 1889–1945 (Israel: 1974), pp. 298–300.

36. Interior Ministry internal memo (signed by State Secretary W. Stuckart), Dec. 17, 1937, in: Helmut Eschwege, ed., Kennzeichen J (Berlin: 1966), pp. 132-136.

37. W. Feilchenfeld, et al, Haavara-Transfer (1972), p. 32.

38. E. Black, Transfer Agreement, pp. 376–377.

39. E. Black, Transfer Agreement (1984), pp. 376, 378.; F. Nicosia, Third Reich (1985), pp. 238-239 (n. 91).

40. E. Black, Transfer Agreement, p. 379.; F. Nicosia, Third Reich, pp. 212, 255 (n. 66).

41. W. Feilchenfeld, et al., Haavara-Transfer, p. 75.; "Haavara," Encyclopaedia Judaica, (1971), Vol. 7, p. 1013.

42. E. Black, Transfer Agreement, pp. 379, 373, 382.

43. Circular of January 25, 1939. Nuremberg document 3358-PS. International Military Tribunal, Trial of the Major War Criminals Before the International Military Tribunal (Nuremberg: 1947–1949), Vol. 32, pp. 242–243.

44. Werner Feilchenfeld, et al., Haavara-Transfer nach Palaestina (Tübingen: Mohr/Siebeck, 1972). Quoted in: Ingrid Weckert, Feuerzeichen (Tübingen: Grabert, 1981), pp. 222–223.

45. W. Feilchenfeld, et al., Haavara-Transfer nach Palaestina (1972). Quoted in: I. Weckert, Feuerzeichen (1981), p. 224.

46. Original document in German Ausw_rtiges Amt Archiv, Bestand 47–59, E 224152 and E 234155–58. (Photocopy in author's possession).; Complete original German text published in: David Yisraeli, The Palestine Problem in German Politics 1889-1945 (Israel: 1974), pp. 315–317. See also: Klaus Polkhen, "The Secret Contacts," Journal of Palestine Studies, Spring-Summer 1976, pp. 78-80.; (At the time this offer was made, Stern's Lehi group still regarded itself as the true Irgun/NMO.)

47. Arab nationalists opposed Britain, which then dominated much of the Arab world, including Egypt, Iraq and Palestine. Because Britain and Germany were at war, Germany cultivated Arab support. The leader of Palestine's Arabs, the Grand Mufti of Jerusalem, Haj Amin el-Husseini, worked closely with Germany during the war years. After escaping from Palestine, he spoke to the Arab world over German radio and helped raise Muslim recruits in Bosnia for the Waffen SS.

48. Israel Shahak, "Yitzhak Shamir, Then and Now," Middle East Policy (Washington, DC), Vol. 1, No. 1, (Whole No. 39), 1992, pp. 27–38.; Yehoshafat Harkabi, Israel's Fateful Hour (New York: Harper and Row, 1988), pp. 213–214. Quoted in: Andrew J. Hurley, Israel and the New World Order (Santa Barbara, Ca-

lif.: 1991), pp. 93, 208–209.; Avishai Margalit, "The Violent Life of Yitzhak Shamir," New York Review of Books, May 14, 1992, pp. 18-24.; Lenni Brenner, Zionism in the Age of the Dictators (1983), pp. 266–269.; L. Brenner, Jews in America Today (1986), pp. 175–177.; L. Brenner, "Yitzhak Shamir: On Hitler's Side," Arab Perspectives (League of Arab States), March 1984, pp. 11–13.

49. Avishai Margalit, "The Violent Life of Yitzhak Shamir," New York Review of Books, May 14, 1992, pp. 18–24.; Lenni Brenner, Zionism in the Age of the Dictators (1983), pp. 266-269.; L. Brenner, Jews in America Today (1986), pp. 175–177.; L. Brenner, "Skeletons in Shamir's Cupboard," Middle East International, Sept. 30, 1983, pp. 15-16.; Sol Stern, L. Rapoport, "Israel's Man of the Shadows," Village Voice (New York), July 3, 1984, pp. 13 ff.

From *The Journal of Historical Review*, July-August 1993 (Vol. 13, No. 4), pages 29–37.

Mark Weber studied history at the University of Illinois (Chicago), the University of Munich, Portland State University and Indiana University (M.A., 1977). In March 1988 he testified for five days in Toronto District Court as a recognized expert witness on Germany's wartime Jewish policy and the Holocaust Issue. He is Director of the Institute for Historical Review in Newport Beach, California.

The Fraud of
Neoconservative
"Anti-Communism"

by Max Shpak

Neoconservatives and their apologists would have the public believe that the neocons were former Leftists who saw the light and came to reject liberal or Marxist ideology as a matter of conviction and principle. Regrettably, this official line has come to be conventional wisdom, no doubt reflecting neocon efforts to hide the fact that their transformation was neither sincerely motivated nor sincerely enacted. To understand the real agenda that drove and continues to drive much of neoconservatism, one needs to look back to the origins of the movement and the cultural backgrounds of those who lead it.

It is a well-established fact that many of the early luminaries of neoconservatism (most famously Irving Kristol in the 1940's, a more recent famous example being David Horowitz) came from Marxist backgrounds, and that neoconservatism (like Marxism itself) began and continues to be a largely a phenomenon of Jewish intellectualism.

In the early part of the 20th century, Marxism attracted a disproportionate pool of Jewish recruits for a number of obvious reasons. There are a number of complex psychological and social reasons for the attraction, all of which largely stem from the fact that Marxist internationalism is an ideology which by its very nature finds disciples among a rootless, anti-religious urban intelligentsia.

More important for the purposes of this analysis, however, are the practical reasons for Jewish sympathy with Bolshevism. European and American Jews alike carried deep-seated hatreds for the traditional regimes and religions of the European continent, particularly Czarist Russia and various Eastern European nations due to (real and imagined) "persecution" and "pogroms" that occurred there. Thus, when the Bolsheviks overthrew the Czar, destroyed the hated Orthodox Church, rendered powerless the landed religious peasantry, and replaced traditional Russian authority with a largely Jewish Commissariate, world Jewry (including alleged "capitalists" like the Schiffs and Rothschilds) embraced the Revolution and Marxist ideology alike.

With Russia becoming an effective Jewish colony where "anti-Semitism" was an offense punishable by death and the native gentile culture was effectively stamped out (thanks to a leadership consisting mainly of Jews such as Trotsky, Zinoviev, Kamenev, and Severdlov, held together under the stewardship of the obsequious philosemite Lenin), Jews throughout the world put their hopes in the possibility of similar revolutions elsewhere. Indeed, their comrades in arms were hard at work affecting similar changes in Hungary (Kuhn), Austria (Adler) and Germany (Eisner). The rise of Fascist and Nazi movements only served to further polarize Jewish support in favor of international communism.

This near unanimity would change as a result of two developments: a shift in the character of Soviet Communism on the one hand and the foundation of the State of Israel on the other. Stalin's purges of many of his former Bolshevik colleagues (including Trotsky, who was assassinated while in exile), his 1939 pact with Hitler, and rumors of Stalin's own anti-Jewish prejudices gave many would-be supporters pause. When Hitler invaded the Soviet Union, it became clear the Russian masses would not fight for the sake of Bolshevism, an ideology that brought them so much misery, but rather for the sake of Russian blood and soil. From then on, the Soviet leadership had to court the very Russian nationalist elements that the early Bolsheviks had worked so hard to stamp out. This lead to an increasing tolerance towards the Russian Orthodox Church and a decreased Jewish presence in the Soviet politburo and KGB. Thus, the USSR was "betraying" the very elements that made it attractive to the Jewish establishment to begin with.

Perhaps even more significant a factor in the origins of neoconservatism was the emergence of an independent Israeli state. While many Jewish Marxists eagerly supported the Zionist state, the more intellectually consistent Left opposed Zionism on the grounds that all nationalisms, including Jewish ones, are enemies of global proletarian revolution. Thus, Jewish leftists who once advocated internationalism for gentile nations were forced to come to terms with the implications of this ideology for their own nationalist sentiments. Thus, they needed an ideology which would let them have their cake (opposing gentile nationalism) and eat it too (by supporting Israel), and they found just such a worldview with neoconservatism.

At the same time, although the Soviet Union initially courted Israel during the 1948 wars of independence, it became clear to the Israeli government that in world polarized between the United States and the Soviet Union the former would be wealthier and more pliant cash cow to milk. By the 1950's and the coming of the Suez Wars, regardless of residual Jewish loyalties to Communism, the battle lines were already drawn, with Israel in the US/Western camp and the Arab nations forced to make alliances of convenience with the Soviet Union.

It is hardly a coincidence that the changing character of Soviet Communism and the status of Israel as a US ally came at the same time that neoconservatism was becoming an influential political movement. For all of their talk about "capitalism," "democracy," "freedom," and "free markets," the fact that so many Jewish leftists turned on a dime to back the US in the Cold War because America could serve as a life support system for Israel and a bulwark against resurgent Russian "anti-Semitism" makes their real agenda entirely transparent. One can witness an identical phenomenon taking place today, as many Jewish liberal Democrats switch party ranks and join the GOP because of the latter's stronger support for Israel and harder line with the Arab nations. All of the window dressing about their newfound "patriotism" and "Americanism" is a sham designed to mask the fact that the question for the neocons has always been and will always be "is it good for the Jews?"

The different agendas driving neocon Cold Warriors as opposed to their erstwhile Old Right allies could be seen on any number of fronts. The most obvious one has been the different reactions in the two camps to Russia after the end of the Cold War. While paleoconservative leaning Cold Warriors such as Pat Buchanan have pushed for normalized relations with Russia, the neocons continue to fight on the Cold War, enthusiastically supporting Chechen separatists as "freedom fighters" and advocating NATO expansion. The reasons for this difference are entirely obvious: the Old Right's enemy was Communist ideology, while neoconservative Jews nurtured a hatred for Russian nationalism. Thus post-Communist Russia is still very much a threat to the latter, particularly with resurgent Russian "ultra-nationalism" and "anti-Semitism," while in the absence of Communist rule the above are of little concern to the Old Right.

For all their talk about "anti-Communism," the real engine driving neocon Cold Warrior instincts was punishing the hated Russian goyim for the sin of "anti-Semitism," not any opposition to residual or latent Marxism. As further evidence that this is the case, one need only consider the fact that while the Old Right championed Christian dissidents such as Solzhenitsyn, to the neocons the only legitimate "dissidents" were Zionists like Natan Sharansky, just as the only "refugees" championed by the neos were invariably Jewish (including today's shady Odessa Mafiosi). Solzhenitsyn represented the Russian nationalism and Orthodox Church that made so many of the neocons' predecessors embrace Bolshevism, thus Solzhenitsyn and the plight of Christian dissidents were relegated to obscurity in neocon publications, while Zionist noise-makers in the USSR were given a hero's welcome.

In this regard, the neocons are the true heirs to Leon Trotsky, who condemned Stalin and his followers not so much for their brutality (as commander of the Red Army and overseer of Lenin's terrorist CHEKA, Trotsky was no stranger to brutality and sadism) but for their "anti-Semitism" and "betrayal of the Revolution." Trotsky's main critique of Stalinism seemed to be that Stalin was moving Russia in a nationalist direction rather than working towards the establishment of an international "proletarian" vanguard. The fact that the intellectual ancestors of neoconservatism had not an unkind word to say about Bolshevism while Leninist-Trotskyite goals were being fulfilled suggests that it was not so much ideological reconsideration as tribal self-interest that drove these most unlikely *conversos*.

Because their move from the Left to a pseudo-right was insincere, one would expect to find a whole range of issues where the neocons retain leftist instincts and remain true to their Trotskyite heritage. Indeed this is the case. In their portrayal of the Cold War as a struggle between "capitalism" on the one hand and "socialism" on the other, the neocons try to minimize the fact that in many ways the conflict between the Bolsheviks and the West was over much more than economic systems. To most on the Old Right, the economic issues were at best peripheral: Marxism was opposed because it was materialistic, atheistic, and because it rejected nationalism and patriotism in the name of global revolution.

Most neocons came from a culture that was every bit as materialistic and cosmopolitan as the early Bolshevik leaders, so it is rather unlikely that they would have any quarrel with these aspects of Communist doctrine. The fact that neoconservatism is an ideology which is materialistic in nature and internationalist in focus (with its talk of "global democracy" and "global markets") makes it obvious that the fundamental underpinnings of the Marxist Left are alive and well among the scribblers of Commentary and The Weekly Standard. Their "conservative" pretenses seem limited to the fact that they oppose "socialism" (of the nationalist variety) in the name of "capitalism" (of the internationalist variety), and for all too many naïve people that seems to be sufficient and believable.

Understanding the true nature of the neoconservatives illuminates the essence of the struggle between the Right and the Left. It was never a struggle between "capitalism" and "socialism" as neoconservative or Communist propaganda would have one believe. Rather, it was always a conflict between spiritualism and materialism, between nationalism and globalism, between tradition and subversion, between the defenders of Western Civilization and its enemies. With the battle lines drawn as such, it is abundantly clear where the neocons stand. Many "capitalists" understood that economic means are not significant, only the desired end. Jacob Schiff understood it when he financed the Bolsheviks, just as Rupert Murdoch, Marc Rich, Boris Berezovsky, and George Soros understand that their form of "capitalism" is fully compatible with the essence of the Left, and that they can find friends and allies among the ostensibly conservative neocons.

Unfortunately, many Rightists are not nearly as perceptive in their choice of allies.

Kevin MacDonald's "The Culture of Critique"

reviewed by Stanley Hornbeck

In *The Culture of Critique,* Kevin MacDonald advances a carefully researched but extremely controversial thesis: that certain 20th century intellectual movements – largely established and led by Jews – have changed European societies in fundamental ways and destroyed the confidence of Western man. He claims that these movements were designed, consciously or unconsciously, to advance Jewish interests even though they were presented to non-Jews as universalistic and even utopian. He concludes that the increasing dominance of these ideas has had profound political and social consequences that benefited Jews but caused great harm to gentile societies. This analysis, which he makes with considerable force, is an unusual indictment of a people generally thought to be more sinned against than sinning.

The Culture of Critique is the final title in Prof. MacDonald's massive, three-volume study of Jews and their role in history. The two previous volumes are *A People That Shall Dwell Alone* and *Separation and its Discontents,* published by Praeger in 1994 and 1998. The series is written from a socio-biological perspective that views Judaism as a unique survival strategy that helps Jews compete with other ethnic groups. Prof. MacDonald, who is a psychologist at the University of California at Long Beach, explains this perspective in the first volume, which describes Jews as having a very powerful sense of uniqueness that has kept them socially and genetically separate from other peoples. The second volume traces the history of Jewish-gentile relations, and finds the causes of anti-Semitism primarily in the almost invariable commercial and intellectual dominance of gentile societies by Jews and in their refusal to assimilate. *The Culture of Critique* brings his analysis into the present century, with an account of the Jewish role in the radical critique of traditional culture.

The intellectual movements Prof. MacDonald discusses in this volume are Marxism, Freudian psychoanalysis, the Frankfurt school of sociology, and Boasian anthropology. Perhaps most relevant from a racial perspective, he also traces the role of Jews in promoting multiculturalism and Third World immigration. Throughout his analysis Prof. MacDonald reiterates his view that Jews have promoted these movements *as Jews* and in the interests of Jews, though they have often tried to give the impression that they had no distinctive interests of their own. Therefore Prof. MacDonald's most profound charge against Jews is not ethnocentrism but dishonesty – that while claiming to be working for the good of mankind they have often worked for their own good and to the detriment of others. While attempting to promote the brotherhood of man by dissolving the ethnic identification of gentiles, Jews have maintained precisely the kind of intense group solidarity they decry as immoral in others.

Celebrating Diversity

Prof. MacDonald claims that one of the most consistent ways in which Jews have advanced their interests has been to promote pluralism and diversity – but only for others. Ever since the 19th century, they have led movements that tried to discredit the traditional foundations of gentile society: patriotism, racial loyalty, the Christian basis for morality, social homogeneity, and sexual restraint. At the same time, within their own communities, and with regard to the state of Israel, they have often supported the very institutions they attack in gentile society.

Why is this in the interests of Jews? Because the parochial group loyalty characteristic of Jews attracts far less attention in a society that does not have a cohesive racial and cultural core. The Jewish determination not to assimilate fully, which accounts for their survival as a people for thousands for years – even without a country – has invariably attracted unpleasant and even murderous scrutiny in nations with well-defined national identities. In Prof. MacDonald's view it is therefore in the interest of Jews to dilute and weaken the identity of any people among whom they live. Jewish identity can flower in safety only when gentile identity is weak.

Prof. MacDonald quotes a remarkable passage from Charles Silberman: "American Jews are committed to cultural tolerance because of their belief – one firmly rooted in history – that Jews are safe only in a society acceptant of a wide range of attitudes and behaviors, as well as a diversity of religious and ethnic groups. It is this belief, for example, not approval of homosexuality, that leads an overwhelming majority of American Jews to endorse 'gay rights' and to take a liberal stance on most other so-called 'social' issues."

He is saying, in effect, that when Jews make the diversity-is-our-strength argument it is in support of their real goal of diluting a society's homogeneity so that Jews will feel safe. They are couching a Jewish agenda in terms they think gentiles will accept. Likewise, as the second part of the Silberman quotation suggests, Jews may support deviant movements, not because they think it is good for the country but because it is good for the Jews.

Prof. Silberman also provides an illuminating quote from a Jewish economist who thought that republicans had more sensible economic policies but who voted for the Democratic presidential candidate anyway. His reason? "I'd rather live in a country governed by the faces I saw at the Democratic convention than those I saw at the Republican convention." This man apparently distrusts white gentiles and voted for a racially mixed party even if its economic policies were wrong. What is good for Jews appears to come before what is good for the country.

Earl Raab, former president of heavily Jewish Brandeis University makes the diversity argument in a slightly different way. Expressing his satisfaction with the prediction that by the middle of the next century whites will become a minority, he writes, "We have tipped beyond the point where a Nazi-Aryan party will be able to prevail in this country." He is apparently prepared to displace the people and culture of the founding stock in order to prevent the theoretical rise of an anti-Jewish regime. Prof. Raab appears to see whites mainly as potential Nazis, and is willing to sacrifice their culture and national continuity in order to defuse an imagined threat to Jews. This passage takes for granted the continued future existence of Jews as a distinct community even as gentile whites decline in numbers and influence.

In the same passage, Prof. Raab continues by noting that, "We [Jews] have been nourishing the American climate of opposition to bigotry for about half a century. That climate has not yet been perfected, but the heterogeneous nature of our population tends to make it irreversible…" – just as it tends to make the ultimate displacement of European culture also irreversible.

Prof. MacDonald traces the development of this diversity strategy to several sources. It is widely recognized that the German-Jewish immigrant Franz Boas (1858–1942) almost single-handedly established the current contours of anthropology, ridding it of all biological explanations for differences in human culture or behavior. Prof. MacDonald reports that he and his followers – with the notable exceptions of Margaret Mead and Ruth Benedict – were all Jews with strong Jewish identities: "Jewish identification and the pursuit of perceived Jewish interests, particularly in advocating an ideology of cultural pluralism as a model for Western societies, has been the 'invisible subject' of American anthropology."

By 1915, Boas and his students controlled the American Anthropological Association and by 1926 they headed every major American university anthropology department. From this position of dominance they promoted the idea that race and biology are trivial matters, and that environment counts for everything. They completely recast anthropology so as to provide intellectual support for open immigration, integration, and miscegenation. They also laid the foundation for the idea that because all races have the same potential, the failures of non-whites must be blamed exclusively on white oppression. The ultimate conclusion of Boasian anthropology was that since environment accounts for all human differences, every inequality in achievement can be eliminated by changing the environment. This has been the justification for enormous and wasteful government intervention programs.

The entire "civil rights" movement can be seen as a natural consequence of the triumph of Boasian thinking. Since all races were equivalent, separation was immoral. The color line also sharpened white self-consciousness in ways that might make whites more aware of Jewish parochialism. Thus it was, according to Prof. MacDonald, that Jews almost single-handedly launched the desegregation movement. Without the leadership of Jews, the NAACP might never have been established, and until 1975 every one of its presidents was a Jew. Prof. MacDonald reports that in 1917, when the black separatist Marcus Garvey visited NAACP headquarters, he saw so many white faces that he stormed out, complaining that it was a white organization.

Prof. MacDonald concludes that the efforts of Jews were crucial to the "civil rights" transformation of America. He quotes a lawyer for the American Jewish Congress who claims that "many of these [civil rights] laws were actually written in the offices of Jewish agencies by Jewish staff people, introduced by Jewish legislators and pressured into being by Jewish voters."

While the Boas school was promoting integration and racial equivalence, it was also critical of, in Prof. MacDonald's words, "American culture as overly homogeneous, hypocritical, emotionally and aesthetically repressive (especially with regard to sexuality). Central to this program was creating ethnographies of idyllic [Third-World] cultures that were free of the negatively perceived traits that were attributed to Western culture."

The role of the anthropologist became one of criticizing everything about Western society while glorifying everything primitive. Prof. MacDonald notes that Boasian portrayals of non-Western peoples deliberately ignored barbarism and cruelty or simply attributed it to contamination from the West. He sees this as a deliberate attempt to undermine the confidence of Western societies and to make them permeable to Third World influences and people. Today, this view is enshrined in the dogma that America must remain open to immigration because immigrants bring spirit and energy that natives somehow lack.

Authoritarian Personalities

In order to open European-derived societies to the immigration that would transform them, it was necessary to discredit racial solidarity and commitment to tradition. Prof. MacDonald argues that this was the basic purpose of a group of intellectuals known as the Frankfurt School. What is properly known as the Institute of Social Research was founded in Frankfurt, Germany, during the Weimar period by a Jewish millionaire but was closed down by the Nazis shortly after they took power. Most of its staff emigrated to the United States and the institute reconstituted itself at UC Berkeley. The organization was headed by Max Horkheimer, and its most influential members were T.W. Adorno, Erich Fromm, and Herbert Marcuse, all of whom had strong Jewish identities. Horkheimer made no secret of the partisan nature of the institute's activities: "Research would be able here to transform itself *directly* into propaganda," he wrote. (Italics in the original.)

Prof. MacDonald devotes many pages to an analysis of *The Authoritarian Personality*, which was written by Adorno and appeared in 1950. It was part of a series called *Studies in Prejudice*, produced by the Frankfurt school, which included titles like *Anti-Semitism and Emotional Disorder*. *The Authoritarian Personality* was particularly influential because, according to Prof. MacDonald, the American Jewish Committee heavily funded its promotion and because Jewish academics took up its message so enthusiastically.

The book's purpose is to make every group affiliation sound as if it were a sign of mental disorder. Everything from patriotism to religion to family – and race – loyalty are signs of a dangerous and defective "authoritarian personality." Because drawing distinctions between different groups is illegitimate, all group loyalties – even close family ties! – are "prejudice." As Christopher Lasch has written, the book leads to the conclusion that prejudice "could be eradicated only by subjecting the American people to what amounted to collective psychotherapy – by treating them as inmates of an insane asylum."

But according to Prof. MacDonald it is precisely the kind of group loyalty, respect for tradition, and consciousness of differences central to *Jewish* identity that Horkheimer and Adorno described as mental illness in gentiles. These writers adopted what eventually became a favorite Soviet tactic against dissidents: Anyone whose political views were different from theirs was insane. As Prof. MacDonald explains, the Frankfurt school never criticized or even described Jewish group identity – only that of gentiles: "behavior that is critical to Judaism as a successful group evolutionary strategy is conceptualized as pathological in gentiles."

For these Jewish intellectuals, anti-Semitism was also a sign of mental illness: They concluded that Christian self-denial and especially sexual repression caused hatred of Jews. The Frankfurt school was enthusiastic about psycho-analysis, according to which "Oedipal ambivalence toward the father and anal-sadistic relations in early childhood are the anti-Semite's irrevocable inheritance."

In addition to ridiculing patriotism and racial identity, the Frankfurt school glorified promiscuity and Bohemian poverty. Prof. MacDonald sees the school as a seminal influence: "Certainly many of the central attitudes of the largely successful 1960s countercultural revolution find expression in *The Authoritarian Personality,* including idealizing rebellion against parents, low-investment sexual relationships, and scorn for upward social mobility, social status, family pride, the Christian religion, and patriotism."

Of the interest here, however, is the movement's success in branding ancient loyalties to nation and race as mental illnesses. Although he came later, the French-Jewish "deconstructionist" Jacques Derrida was in the same tradition when he wrote:

"The idea behind deconstruction is to deconstruct the workings of strong nation-states with powerful immigration policies, to deconstruct the rhetoric of nationalism, the politics of place, the metaphysics of native land and native tongue… The idea is to disarm the bombs… of identity that nation-states build to defend themselves against the stranger, against Jews and Arabs and immigrants…"

As Prof. MacDonald puts it, "Viewed at its most abstract level, a fundamental agenda is thus to influence the European-derived peoples of the United States to view concern about their own demographic and cultural eclipse as irrational and as an indication of psychopathology." Needless to say, this project has been successful; anyone opposed to the displacement of whites is routinely treated as a mentally unhinged "hate-monger," and whenever whites defend their group interests they are described as psychologically inadequate. The irony has not escaped Prof. MacDonald: "The ideology that ethnocentrism was a form of psychopathology was promulgated by a group that over its long history had arguably been the most ethnocentric group among all the cultures of the world."

Immigration

Prof. MacDonald argues that it is entirely natural for Jews to promote open immigration. It brings about the "diversity" Jews find comforting and it keeps America open to persecuted co-religionists throughout the world. He says Jews are the only group that has always fought for mass immigration; a few European ethnic organizations have made sporadic efforts to make it easier for their own people to come, but only Jews have consistently promoted open borders for all comers. Moreover, whatever disagreements they may have had on other issues, Jews of every political persuasion have favored high immigration.

This, too, goes back many years, and Prof. MacDonald traces in considerable detail the sustained Jewish pro-immigration effort. Israel Zangwill, author of the eponymous 1908 play *The Melting Pot*, was of the view that "there is only one way to World Peace, and that is the absolute abolition of passports, visas, frontiers, custom houses…" He was nevertheless an ardent Zionist and disapproved of Jewish intermarriage.

Although the statue of liberty, properly known as Liberty Enlightening the World, was a gift to the United States from France as a tribute to American political traditions, the sonnet by the Jewish Emma Lazarus helped change it into a symbol of immigration. Affixed to the base of the statue several decades after its construction, the poem welcomes to America "huddled masses yearning to breath free/The wretched refuse of your teeming shore."

Prof. MacDonald has discovered that implausible arguments about diversity being a quintessentially American strength have been made by Jews for a long time. He reports that in 1948 the American Jewish Committee was urging Congress to believe that "Americanism is the spirit behind the welcome that America has traditionally extended to people of all races, all religions, all nationalities." Of course, there had never been such a tradition. In 1952, the American Jewish Congress argued in hearings on immigration that "our national experience has confirmed beyond a doubt that our very strength lies in the diversity of our peoples." This, too, was at a time when U.S. immigration law was still explicitly designed to maintain a white majority.

It is often said that when the old immigration policy was scrapped in 1965, scarcely anyone knew, and no one predicted, that the new law would change the racial makeup of the country. Prof. MacDonald disputes this, arguing that this had been the objective of Jewish groups from the beginning.

Prof. MacDonald finds that Jews have been the foremost advocates of immigration in England, France, and Canada, and that Jewish groups were the most vocal opponents of independence for Quebec. Australian Jews led the effort to dismantle the "white Australia" policy, one reason for which was cited in an editorial in the *Australian Jewish Democrat:* "The strengthening of multi-cultural or diverse Australia is also our most effective insurance policy against anti-Semitism. The day Australia has a Chinese Australian Governor General I would feel more confident of my freedom to live as a Jewish Australian." Like Earl Raab writing about the United States, this Australian Jew is prepared to sacrifice the traditional culture, people, and identity of Australia to specifically Jewish interests. It would not be surprising if such an openly expressed objective did not have the opposite effect from the intended, and *increase* anti-Jewish sentiment.

Jews and the Left

It is well known that Jews have been traditionally associated with the left, and Prof. MacDonald investigates this connection in some detail. Historically it was understandable that Jews should support movements that advocated overthrowing the existing order. After emancipation, Jews met resistance from gentile elites who did not want to lose ground to competitors, and outsiders easily become revolutionaries. However, in Prof. MacDonald's view, Jewish commitment to leftist causes has often been motivated by the hope that communism, especially, would be a tool for combating anti-Semitism, and by expectation that universalist social solutions would be yet another way to dissolve gentile loyalties that might exclude Jews. The appeal of univeralist ideologies is tied to the implicit understanding that Jewish particularism will be exempt: "At the extreme, acceptance of a universalist ideology by gentiles would result in gentiles not perceiving Jews as in a different social category at all, while nonetheless Jews would be able to maintain a strong personal identity as Jews."

Prof. MacDonald argues that Jews had specifically Jewish reasons for supporting the Bolshevik revolution. Czarist Russia was notorious for its anti-Semitic policies and, during its early years, the Soviet Union seemed to be the promised land for Jews: it ended state anti-Semitism, tried to eradicate Christianity, opened opportunities to individual Jews, and preached a "classless" society in which Jewishness would presumably attract no negative attention. Moreover, since

Marxism taught that all conflict was economic rather than ethnic, many Jews believed it heralded the end of anti-Semitism.

Prof. MacDonald emphasizes that although Jewish Communists preached both atheism and the solidarity of the world's working people, they took pains to preserve a distinct, secular Jewish identity. He reports that Lenin himself (who had one Jewish grandparent) approved the continuation of an explicitly Jewish identity under Communism, and in 1946 the Communist Party of the United States voted a resolution also supporting Jewish peoplehood in Communist countries. Thus, although Communism was supposed to be without borders or religion, Jews were confident that it would make a place for their own group identity. He writes that despite the official view that all men were to be brothers, "very few Jews lost their Jewish identity during the entire soviet era."

Jewish Communists sometimes betrayed remarkable particularism. Prof. MacDonald quotes Charles Rappoport, the French Communist leader: "The Jewish people [are] the bearer of all the great ideas of unity and human community in history... The disappearance of the Jewish people would signify the death of humankind, the final transformation of man into a wild beast." This seems to attribute to Jews an elite position incompatible with "unity and human community."

Prof. MacDonald argues that many Jews began to fall away from Communism only after Stalin showed himself to be anti-Semitic. And just as Jews had been the leading revolutionaries in anti-Semitic pre-Revolutionary Russia, Jews became the leading dissidents in an anti-Semitic Soviet Union. A similar pattern can be found in the imposed Communist governments of Eastern Europe, which were largely dominated by Jews. The majority of the leaders of the Polish Communist Party, for example, spoke better Yiddish than Polish, and they too maintained a strong Jewish identity. After the fall of Communism many stopped being Polish and emigrated to Israel.

Prof. MacDonald writes that in Bela Kun's short-lived 1919 Communist government of Hungary, 95 percent of the leaders were Jews, and that at the time of the 1956 uprising Communism was so

Stanley Hornbeck

closely associated with Jews that the rioting had almost the flavor of a pogrom. He argues that in the United States as well, the hard core among Communists and members of Students for a Democratic Society (SDS) was mainly Jewish. Here, too, a revolutionary, atheist, and universalist world-view was fully compatible with strong identification as Jews. Prof. MacDonald quotes from a study of American leftists:

"Many Communists, for example, state that they could never have married a spouse who was not a leftist. When Jews were asked if they could have married Gentiles, many hesitated, surprised by the question, and found it difficult to answer. Upon reflection, many concluded that they had always taken marriage to someone Jewish for granted." Their commitment as Jews was even more fundamental and unexamined than their commitment to the left.

Prof. MacDonald reports that many American Jews also abandoned Communism as it became increasingly anti-Semitic. For a large number, the Soviet Union's severing of diplomatic ties with Israel during the 1967 war was the last straw. A former SDS activist no doubt spoke for many when he explained, "If I must choose between the Jewish cause and a 'progressive' anti-Israel SDS, I shall choose the Jewish cause. If barricades are erected, I will fight as a Jew." According to Prof. MacDonald, American neoconservatism can also be described as a surface shift in external politics that leaves the more fundamental commitment to Jewish identity unchanged. Thus, former leftists abandoned an ideology that had turned against Israel and refashioned American conservatism into a different movement, the one unshakable theme of which was support for Israel. Neoconservatives also support high levels of immigration and were active in excluding white racial identification from the "respectable" right.

Objections

There are many possible objections to Prof. MacDonald's thesis. The first is that it is largely built on the assumption that Jews are dishon-

384

est. It is always risky to assume one understands the motives of others better than they do themselves. Jews have traditionally thought of themselves as a benevolent presence, even as a "light unto the nations" or a "chosen people." This is echoed today in the Jewish self-image as champions of the excluded and the oppressed. Most of the time what passes for "social justice" has the effect of undermining the traditions and loyalties of gentile society, but are Jews deliberately undermining these things rather than righting what they perceive to be wrongs?

Prof. MacDonald concedes that many Jews are sincere in their support for liberal causes, but then escalates his indictment by arguing that "the best deceivers are those who deceive themselves." In other words, many Jews who are actually working for Jewish interests have first convinced themselves otherwise. A Jew who mainly wants America to become less white may also have convinced himself that America benefits from a multitude of cultures. Having convinced himself he can more effectively convince others.

Many Jews, Prof. MacDonald argues, are not even conscious of the extent to which their Jewishness is central to their identities or their political views. He quotes Rabbi Abraham Joshua Heschel on his surprise at how passionately he embraced the Israeli side during the 1967 war: "I had not known how Jewish I was." This is an arresting statement from a man who was thought to be perhaps the greatest Jewish spiritual leader of his time. And whether or not it affects their politics, Jews certainly appear to have a very vivid sense of peoplehood. Prof. MacDonald quotes theologian Eugene Borowitz as saying, "most Jews claim to be equipped with an interpersonal friend-or-foe sensing device that enables them to detect the presence of another Jew, despite heavy camouflage." Always to think in terms of "friends or foe" is no insignificant matter.

Prof. MacDonald is therefore skeptical of Jewish disavowals: "Surface declarations of a lack of Jewish identity may be highly misleading." He notes that Jewish publications write about the power and influence of American Jews in language Jews would immediately denounce as "anti-Semitic" if used by gentiles. He agrees with Jo-

Stanley Hornbeck

seph Sobran, who has said "they want to be Jews among themselves but resent being seen as Jews by Gentiles. They want to pursue their own distinct interests while pretending that they have no such interests…"

Prof. MacDonald argues that the success of Jewish-led intellectual movements has been possible only because their Jewish character was hidden. If multi-culturalism or mass immigration or *The Authoritarian Personality* had been promoted by Orthodox Jews in black coats the Jewish element would have been clear. Prof. MacDonald writes that in fact, "the Jewish political agenda was not an aspect of the theory and the theories themselves had no overt Jewish content. Gentile intellectuals approaching these theories were therefore unlikely to view them as aspects of Jewish-gentile cultural competition or as an aspect of a specifically Jewish political agenda." Prof. MacDonald also claims that Jews have often tried to conceal the Jewish character of an intellectual movement by recruiting token gentiles for visible positions as spokesmen. He writes that this tactic was so common in the American Communist Party that gentiles often saw through it and resigned.

But how can motives ever be completely known? Prof. MacDonald sets a difficult test: "The best evidence that individuals have really ceased to have a Jewish identity is if they choose a political option that they perceive as clearly not in the interest of Jews as a group. In the absence of a clearly perceived conflict with Jewish interests, it remains possible that different political choices among ethnic Jews are only differences in tactics for how best to achieve Jewish interests."

This standard may seem unduly harsh – until it is applied to white gentiles. Third-World immigration, affirmative action, anti-discrimination laws, and forced integration are clearly not in the interests of whites, yet many whites embrace them, thus demonstrating how completely they have abandoned their racial identity.

Finally, Prof. MacDonald raises the disturbing possibility that some Jews, because of centuries of conflict with gentiles, actively hate gentile society and consciously wish to destroy it: "a fundamental motivation of Jewish intellectuals involved in social criticism has simply been hatred of the gentile-dominated power structure perceived as anti-Semitic." He describes the 19th century German-Jewish poet Heinrich Heine as "using his skill, reputation and popularity to undermine the intellectual confidence of the established order."

In defense of this highly provocative view, Prof. MacDonald quotes Benjamin Disraeli on the effects of centuries of Jewish-gentile relations on Jews: "They may have become so odious and so hostile to mankind as to merit for their present conduct, no matter how occasioned, the obloquy and ill-treatment of the communities in which they dwell and with which they are scarcely permitted to mingle."

Apart from any questions of motives, however, is the question of numbers. Jews are a tiny minority in the United States and within that minority there is disagreement even on matters that clearly affect Jews. How can Jews possibly be responsible for dramatic changes in the intellectual landscape? In Prof. MacDonald's view, the explanation lies in the intelligence, energy, dedication, and cohesiveness of Jews. He attributes a great deal to the average IQ of Jews – at 115*, a full standard deviation above the white gentile average – and to "their hard work and dedication, their desire to make a mark on the world, and their desire to rise in the world, engage in personal promotion, and achieve public acclaim…" He also believes Jews have worked together unfailingly on any question they consider necessary for survival: "Intellectual activity is like any other human endeavor: Cohesive groups out-compete individual strategies." He notes that there has *never* been a time when large numbers of white Americans favored non-white immigration; it was a cohesive, determined minority that beat down the disorganized resistance of the majority.

Prof. MacDonald believes that because of the effectiveness of some Jews, it was not even necessary that most Jews actively support anti-majoritarian movements, but that Jewish activity was still decisive. As he puts it, "Jewish-dominated intellectual movements were a critical factor (necessary condition) for the triumph of the intellectual left in late twentieth-century Western societies." This, of course, can never be tested, but there can be no doubt that American Jews have had a disproportionate effect on the American intellect. Prof. Mac-Donald quotes Walter Kerr, writing in 1968, to the effect that "what has happened since World War II is that the American sensibility has become part Jewish, perhaps as much Jewish as it is anything else... The literate American mind has come in some measure to think Jewishly."

Aside from the question of whether Prof. MacDonald is right is the further question of what difference it makes if he is right. If correct, his thesis certainly sheds light on the rapidity with which whites lost their will. Just a few decades ago whites were a confident race, proud of their achievements, convinced of their fitness to dominate the globe. Today they are a declining, apologetic people, ashamed of their history and not sure even of their claim to lands they have occupied for centuries. It is very rare for fundamental concepts to be stood on their heads in the course of just a generation or two, as has happened with thinking about race. Such speed suggests there has been something more than natural change.

Kevin MacDonald, *The Culture of Critique: An Evolutionary Analysis of Jewish Involvement in Twentieth-Century Intellectual and Political Movements,* Praeger (1998) 379 pp.

This article originally appeared in *American Renaissance,* June 1999, issue 54 entitled 'Cherchez le Juif.' Stanley Hornbeck is the pen name of a Washington, D.C. area businessman.

In light of recent studies, McDonald now estimates that the average Ashkenazi Jewish IQ in America is probably around 110, keeping their measured averages just slightly above other high-IQ nationalities found in Germany, Hong Kong, Holland and Japan. In Israel however, standardized intelligence tests there indicate that the national average IQ is, according to Richard Lynn, somewhere around 94. More rigorous and refined testing may eventually yield different results. —mg

The Jewish Question

by Stojgniev O'Donnell

January 2003

"…that [Dostoevsky] should not have come up with even a single word in the defense or justification of a people persecuted over several thousands of years – could he have been so blind? – or was he perhaps blinded by hatred? – and he did not even refer to the Jews as a people, but as a tribe as though they were a group of natives from the Polynesian Islands or somewhere – and to this tribe I belonged and the many friends and acquaintances of mine with whom I had discussed the subtlest problems of Russian literature…and the many other Jewish literary critics who have gained what amounts to a monopoly in the study of Dostoyevsky." Leonid Tsypkin, Summer in Baden-Baden, 1982, trans. Roger and Angela Keys (London, 1987), 116.

There could be no more appropriate place to begin a discussion of the Jews than with a reference to Russian novelist Fedor Dostoevsky and his attitude toward the Jews. Dostoevsky in his writings displayed little admiration for the Jews. In referring to the Jews, he employed the Russian word zhid, which in modern Russian is interpreted as an ethnic slur (although in other Slavic languages it is the sole word for Jew). Dostoevsky's novel The Brothers Karamazov contains a reference to alleged murder by Jews of Christian children and ritual use of their blood, called blood libel by the Jews.

The topic at hand is Jews and the dramatic growth of Jewish power and influence in America in the twentieth century. The Jewish influence and its perception by non-Jews will have dramatic significance in coming years. I must confess that I find Jews a troubling topic, in part because previously I have observed that some individual Jews feel there is something "not right" in my own feelings towards Jews. With assurance I know that, as I write these words, what I say here will be dismissed and rejected by many Jews who read this. I can regret that, but I cannot prevent it. The best I can offer is to follow my own conscience in approaching the topic of the Jews. Tsypkin asks, not entirely rhetorically, if Dostoevsky was blinded by hatred towards the Jews. Periodically, I pause to consider my own reactions to Jews and their actions, to consider if I am not blinded by some type of irrationality. Such reflection leads always to the same three conclusions: (1) There is something greater and more substantial to the Jews and their history than any human can discern. (2) One cannot discard the notion that the Jews represent the ultimate test for Christians, and Christians, therefore, must act with deference and caution in their dealings with Jews. (3) While Christians are obligated to respect the Jews, one, nevertheless, has an obligation at all times to seek objective truths. In viewing the inevitable conflicts that arise between Jews and non-Jews, one must always attempt to discern the truth. It is in the definition of that truth, and also in my emphasis that the search for truth is the task of both non-Jews and Jews, that many Jews find fault with my attitude.

What does it mean for someone to suggest that Dostoevsky, a writer and thinker of considerable moral insight, the world's greatest novelist for some readers, was blind to truth? Was not the ascertainment of truths one of the tasks of Dostoevsky's life as a writer and as a human being? Taking Tsypkin's question above at face value and considering also his general respect for Dostoevsky's literary work, I would rework his question in this manner: Did it happen somehow that Dostoevsky was guided in his life by some irrational hatred of the Jews, all the while he otherwise pursued in other matters of life a rational search for truth? Such a proposition is itself irrational. How could it be that Dostoevsky demonstrated such insight in all realms of life except that relating to the Jews? And what of Dostoevsky's obligation to "come up with even a single word in the defense or justification of a people persecuted..."? Was Dostoevsky, who wrote bluntly of his characters and their moral imperfections, morally obligated to alter or to falsify his own artistic vision in defense of the Jews?

As a believing Christian, I approach the topic of the Jews with trepidation, conscious that Christ, His Mother and the first disciples came out of the milieu of ethno-religious Judaism. He who despises the Jews must surely despise some aspect of Christ, the first Christians, and Christianity. Russian writer Alexander Solzhenitsyn views the Jews, at times critically, as a catalyst for all humanity. I am inclined to agree with such an interpretation. If we study the history of Jews and Christians, we see that, indeed, the Jews often present the ideal historical moment for the Christian to practice his faith. Often, however, Christians have failed this test. Russian philosopher Vladimir Solov'ev wrote in 1884: "The Jews have always treated us in accordance with the Jewish faith, though we, the Christians, have yet to learn to treat the Jews in the Christian fashion." Evreistvo i christianskii vopros (Moscow 1884, 3).

Many-faceted are the contradictions of Jewishness, so much so that one hardly knows where to begin a conversation on the topic. I am interested in the meaning of Jewish history. Studying the natural processes of assimilation in which ethnic groups have been formed and then eventually, with the passage of time, subsumed within other ethnic groups more recently arisen, one comes to the realization that the Jews have managed to continue as an ethnic group many centuries longer than any other ethnic group.

The Jews themselves disagree on the meaning of their history. There are different interpretations of the meaning of Jewish death and suffering during the Second World War, for example. Some religious Jews view the Jewish tragedies of that period as divine chastisement. Some non-religious Jews see those events as a mark of Jewish singularity, yet they refuse – strangely, in the view of the religious believer – to acknowledge a religious basis for that singularity. Whatever the meaning, it seems certain to me that a divine hand intervenes in the midst of every Jewish generation. It is inconceivable to deny that the Jews occupy a special place in history.

One wonders about individual Nazis, otherwise in some cases exemplary fathers, husbands and local citizens, who faced the moral dilemma of whether or not they could themselves torture or murder another human being because he was a Jew. One recalls the biblical tale of Isaac and Jacob and Isaac's unwavering obedience to God. Many Christians were thus tested and failed, though perhaps under entirely different circumstances, one such individual might have lived out what would have been considered a normal, decent life. In such a case, was it the Jew or the human shortcomings of the Nazi that precipitated the latter's damnation? Perhaps the sincere Christian should heed the frequent criticism that comes from the Jews and should view, accordingly, the Jews as an eternal witness, an eternal reminder of the moral failings of humanity.

Yet in searching for the truth of the Jewish question, we must consider the moral obligation of the Jew towards the non-Jew. Discussion of the conflict between Jews and non-Jews very often revolves around Jewish criticism of the specific actions or expressions of a non-Jew. That criticism typically is a response to what is labeled "anti-Semitism," a term that in my mind has little intellectual validity. Despite its prefix, "anti-Semitism" is a concept without any opposite. Some have suggested that the unhyphenated "antisemitism" is the more correct form, since "anti-Semitism" implies mistakenly that it exists in opposition to "Semitism." There is no logic in any definition of "anti-Semitism." The term itself is a piece of propaganda.

To speak of "anti-Semitism" is to insinuate that only one side in this dispute has morality, objectivity, "decency," and truth. In such a one-sided debate, all the prerogatives of truth and morality belong to the side opposed to "anti-Semitism." In my own experience, I have seen the label "anti-Semite" applied to anyone who criticizes Jews, even when that person is honest and acts with the most sincere motives. In academe and the media, those who are branded "anti-Semites" are blackballed and refused employment. Use of such language in its own right is a political act, and I propose that "anti-Semitism" and its derivatives be avoided by all of those who seek an objective discussion of Jewish issues.

Discourse on the Jewish question typically revolves around an act or expression of "anti-Semitism," to which voices of "morality" and "decency" respond. Yet in introducing the quote from Tsypkin above, I choose to begin my discussion by letting the Jewish side make the first move, so to speak. For a discussion of the Jewish question cannot be limited solely to Jewish responses to the non-Jew, but must also consider the Jew's role and responsibility in that discourse. The Jewish question consists of much more than simple immoral behavior by individual non-Jews.

What is the root of the modern conflict between Jews and non-Jews? I am not a Jew and I cannot know the feelings and intuitions of Jews, though with curiosity often I have observed these first-hand. My interpretation of the Jewish view of the conflict is as follows. Jews, even the majority that does not practice the Jewish religion, tend to view this conflict in moral terms. The positions taken by the non-Jewish side in the conflict are, in Jewish eyes, typically viewed as immoral, irrational. The criticism of Dostoevsky above is often leveled at all non-Jews: non-Jews fail, in various ways, in their obligations towards the Jews. A Christian must agree that such a criticism is sometimes valid, though all sides should also come to terms with the fact that there is a hierarchy of moral issues for Christians and that there are sincere, devout Christians who will not define the practice of their religion primarily by fulfillment of a Christian obligation towards Jews, which varies according to the time and circumstances.

I detect another Jewish sensibility in the Jewish reaction towards non-Jews. Some Jews oppose very firmly any reference by non-Jews to stereotypical Jewish behavior and attitudes. At times, I am left with the impression that Jews are less interested in reaching the objective truths of the Jewish question than they are in insuring the well being of their own community, even if that involves obfuscation of the truth. As I interpret the actions and expressions of Jews, it seems to me that the Jews believe their historical role as the Chosen People absolves them from any obligation of self-criticism. The solidarity of the Jewish community in working towards common goals is remarkable, and it is unrivalled in any other ethnic community in history. Observing the behavior of the Jews I have known, I believe almost every situation in the Jew's life is met with the question "Is it good for the Jews?"

What is the reaction of the non-Jew towards the Jew? There is one very common stance that characterizes much of the historical interaction between the Jew and the non-Jew. This involves a base envy, one of the ugliest of human sins. Envy results from the contrast, visible in every field and every endeavor, between the material successes and rewards of the Jew, on the one hand, and the personal inadequacies of individual Jews, on the other. Such a contrast riles the sense of order and fairness in some non-Jews, especially in those of a baser, simpler nature.

Over the centuries Jews have taken pains to emphasize what they believe is the religious nature of anti-Jewish feeling among Christians, though anti-Jewish expressions actually precede Christianity. Of course, it has been advantageous for Jews to emphasize religious prejudice among their critics, rather than to focus on political, cultural, or economic factors. This is one of the causes of the widespread and deep Jewish hatred for the Catholic Church. As a believing Christian, I do not see religious prejudice on the part of Christians as a significant element of the Jewish question. I take offense at what I interpret as a distortion of history by those Jews who blame Christianity for the moral failings of individuals whom Jews sometimes incorrectly associate with Christianity.

If we acknowledge some genuine moral failings in envious individual non-Jews, and if the Jew can accept my belief that the essence of the Jewish question is not religious prejudice on the part of Christians, are there still, then, other aspects of the historical conflict that deserve our attention? I believe there are. Dostoevsky is not a poor example to follow in interacting with the Jews. In his writings Dostoevsky always pursued what he believed to be truth. There can be no higher goal for any person. While I know that the Jews are at times a controversial topic, one that history demonstrates can transform an otherwise decent human being into a monster, I seek always to be honest in my own feelings and perceptions that relate to Jews.

It would be dishonest for me to deny that my own impressions of the individual Jews I have known in my life are predominately negative. Such a statement for some Jews, unfortunately, disqualifies me, in their eyes, as an objective voice in this discussion. Yet my desire to come to the truth of the Jewish question is stronger than any feeling of moral obligation that I "...come up with even a single word in the defense or justification of a people persecuted." I am troubled by any moral obligation that would demand an obfuscation of the truth. Unfortunately, I have observed that some Jews feel they have an obligation to silence all criticism directed at Jews as individuals and as a group. What kind of world will we create when Dostoevsky is not to be allowed to follow his conscience and describe bluntly life as he sees it?

My contacts with ethnic Jews date to fourth grade, to Nanette, a quiet bespectacled girl whose name and face I still recall. Since adulthood I worked closely with Jews in business and in academe. Only a small fraction of the Jews I have known practiced Judaism. Most were Jews in a complex ethno-cultural-political sense. These non-religious Jews constantly redefined their Jewishness according to the situation of the moment. Of the Jews I have known personally, I respected most the elderly professor who was a member of my dissertation committee, a devout practitioner of the Jewish religion. (Perhaps it is worth mentioning, in regard to the makeup of contemporary American universities, that of the five members of my dissertation committee, one was the aforementioned religious Jew and two were non-practicing Jews. A fourth was a member of an officially recognized minority whose wife, also a professor, was Jewish).

For non-Jews, the Jews are puzzling in so many respects. No other nation on earth exhibits such ethnocentrism. With their vast supplies of energy and intelligence, Jews as a group are like a show of fireworks, unstoppable, inevitably burning themselves out to the last spark and flame. As I learned in academe, criticism of Jews in America and other parts of the Western world today is frowned upon, if not effectively prohibited. Unless one can speak with some accuracy about Jewishness, it is foolish to raise the subject at all, since the Jews are formidable opponents of all in whom they see even a hint of determined opposition to them. Never in my life have I encountered such resistance and such emotional hostility as when I have voiced a criticism of the Jews.

I shall relate a personal anecdote which allows me to introduce the controversial topic of stereotypes and also concerns general questions of truth. I have observed that some non-religious Jews are reluctant to reveal their ethnicity to non-Jews, no doubt a relic of memories of oppression passed down from generation to generation. In order to conceal their ethnicity, some Jews are willing to concoct elaborate subterfuges. It offends me and insults my intelligence when a person whom I know very well to be Jewish indicates or suggests that he is not. One such an experience took place during a foreign study program in Moscow, when my Jewish roommate made an effort to convince me that he celebrated Christmas. At that time I was a doctoral student and my younger roommate was an undergraduate. It really was of no significance to me what holidays, if any, the student celebrated. I was preoccupied then with my own research, and I found his repeated references to his celebration of Christmas distracting. By chance, I later overhead his conversation with his Jewish colleague in which he expressed considerable bitterness towards Christianity, Christians, and their holidays. (More than half of the students participating in that program were Jewish). I was genuinely puzzled by his behavior. What bizarre sense of alienation led him to seek my approval, all the while he despised values that he associated with me? I was repulsed by his dishonesty.

Is it proper to repeat such an anecdote? After all, I have implied that the actions of one individual somehow represent a behavioral pattern of millions of individuals of like ethnicity. We cannot talk about Jews without some reference to the historical Jewish stereotypes that are both despised and denied by Jews. Americans have been educated since the 1960s to believe there is no truth in the traditional ethnic stereotypes. But this is ludicrous. In the stereotypes that apply to my own ethnic background, I recognize some awkward human truths, but I cannot deny that these truths apply broadly to a wide population that shares a common ethnicity and cultural heritage. In speaking about Jewish stereotypes, I acknowledge that there are always exceptions to the rule, some of them remarkable. Yet I have found that my own generalizations formed over years of personal contact with Jews are valid for a great majority of Jewish individuals.

The notion rules today in America that is improper and impolite to criticize Jews. This idea has been promoted by the social engineers who, since the 1960s, have argued that historical truth should be subordinated to efforts to attain ethnic and racial harmony in America. In the twenty-first century "nice" people do not criticize Jews, just as they do not attribute to them any characteristics of the ethnic or racial stereotype. A powerful tool used in the advancement of this idea is film and television. Not only is it almost impossible to find a Jewish character in American film or television that exhibits a negative characteristic, but the "evil of anti-Semitism" was a periodic theme in American films in the twentieth century. One recalls the criticism of Dostoevsky above, that he might have attempted a little social engineering in his novels on behalf of oppressed Jews. This phenomenon, in fact, has been observed for many years in the American entertainment industry and news media. Again, the moral question clashes with the intellectual. Is it more proper to speak honestly about Jews, or to work for their welfare and well-being, as a penance for the past and insurance against any possible future lapses into immorality? My major criticisms of Jews as a collective relate to the question of an objective, verifiable truth. I am troubled that Jews appear willing to distort the truth in the pursuit of what they believe to be noble purposes and that Jews attempt to silence criticism of their own group.

A common criticism of the Jews as a collective is that they promote social turmoil. Like each of the issues in this conflict, there are two sides to be argued. With their dynamic intelligence and abilities, Jews as a group naturally become leaders in any new political and cultural movement. This is clearly a phenomenon based on individual talents, not the workings of a conspiracy. Yet is it proper to ask that the

Jews pause to consider the reaction that their involvement in these movements produces upon non-Jews? Does the Jew have any moral obligation towards the non-Jew? As Polish poet Czeslaw Milosz has described himself, I consider myself an anti-modernist, opposed to the ugliness and dehumanization of modernity. And we must admit that modernity has a Jewish face, whether it is Karl Marx, Sigmund Freud, Bob Dylan, Howard Stern, or the Jewish stars of the galaxy of American pop culture.

There is another troubling issue raised in the Tsypkin quote above. Tsypkin refers to himself and to "...the many other Jewish literary critics who have gained what amounts to a monopoly in the study of Dostoyevsky." Based on Tsypkin's own reservations towards Dostoevsky, one is justified to ask if the non-Jewish public can expect true scholarship and objective analysis from a community of scholars that, according to Tsypkin, is almost exclusively Jewish. My interest in this question is not entirely unbiased, since I was denied academic employment in a field that not only is dominated in America by Jews, but that also increasingly defines itself in terms of Jewish topics and Jewish perspectives. The issue of Jewish bias in academe and in the news media is an essential part of the Jewish question in America, something that relates to its moral equation.

In graduate school I was impressed with the skills of Jewish students who, given a writing assignment, quickly visited the library, consulted or checked out all the best reference works on the subject, distilled the information from those sources, and produced a paper. Typically, the Jewish student is capable of assimilating and convincingly disseminating a great deal of information within a short period of time. Part of the success of those Jewish graduate students was in their familiarity with existing resources. But I found also that much of what my Jewish colleagues produced in graduate school was, in my truthful opinion, quite shallow and lacking in originality. In their efficiency and display of energy, something substantial nearly always was sacrificed. Again, I reference a stereotype, one often proven true in my experiences over the years.

Jews exhibit a constant push for a competitive edge. I do not completely understand that Jewish drive. Perhaps it comes from ancestral fear of ethnic persecution, or perhaps it has its roots in the Jewish ethnocentrism. Throughout history, it has produced tensions between the Jews and their host societies. From one perspective, all can understand the Jewish mother who pushes her son to become a lawyer or doctor. On the other hand, we must recognize that it is pathological to use such an achievement as a measurement against which all Jewish sons are to be judged. Can one ask, in good faith, if the Nazi movement might have been stopped had there been fewer Jewish lawyers and professionals in interwar Germany? For the Jews, such a question is preposterous. Thus, one concludes that the true root of the Jewish problem is in Jewish ethnocentrism and in the Jewish identity masquerade, in which the Jew becomes so emotionally involved that he is blind to the non-Jewish reaction to his ethnocentrism.

To return to my observations on the preponderance of Jewish scholars in my own academic field, I must admit that I find something suffocating and inbred in the networks that develop among Jewish scholars. The Jewish presence in academe leads to a tendency for professors and department heads to count sympathy towards the Jews and Jewish interests as a significant criterion for selecting new employees. It is unthinkable today that any university would hire a professor who refused to profess sympathy towards the Jews.

In the end, Jews are unable to prevent the disastrous effects of their own ethnocentrism, which inevitably produces conflicts with non-Jews. Yet as I understand the Jewish perspective, Jews believe that non-Jews have a moral obligation not to interfere in any way in the affairs of Jews, even when Jewish behavior produces what non-Jews interpret as negative influences in their own community. Considering the immense power and influence wielded in America by Jews, Jewish and non-Jewish Americans must determine how to balance these two obligations: the moral obligation of the Christian towards the Jew, and the intellectual obligation to seek the truth in all matters, even if that truth is unflattering towards the Jew.

Stojgniev O'Donnell

I must confess, finally, to a conviction that surely will bring down upon my person Jewish wrath. This matter does not directly concern the Jewish question as a contemporary issue, although it relates to Dostoevsky and the question of historical truth. I question something that, for the Jews, is considered to be beyond questioning, beyond the realm of discussion by rational people, that is, blood libel. I find it hard to believe that there is no truth in any of the accusations of child murder leveled against Jews over the centuries. Jews refer to these crimes, which have been written about for over two thousand years, as blood libel, implying that as a blatant libel, there could never be any consideration of the truth of such claims. One persuasive argument against the truth of the accusations is that religious prescriptions prohibit the ritual use of blood by Jews.

My suspicions about the validity of at least some of the charges arise, in part, from the absolute refusal of Jews to consider the truth of any of those charges and also from the Jewish label of blood libel. It is a topic on which a remarkable solidarity prevails among Jews. Yet it is puzzling that the charge occurred so many times over the centuries and throughout such a wide geographical territory. While the Jews ridicule conspiracy advocates who blame them for elaborate plans of Jewish political and economic domination, one must consider if the accusations of child murder against the Jews would not represent an even vaster and more complicated conspiracy. To categorically reject all such accusations is to accept an anti-Jewish conspiracy more sinister than even the wildest paranoia of the most determined enemies of the Jews. Of course, if one believes that anti-Jewish feeling is a historical, almost naturally motivated force in the world, then perhaps it does not seem surprising that similar charges against the Jews have been documented so often and in so many places.

Yet, as one generally inclined to reject conspiracy theories, I find it hard to believe that anti-Jewish Christians over the centuries could have displayed such organization and consistency in repeatedly laying such serious similar charges against innocent individual Jews. The issue is complicated by the fact that, in some of the more recent cases, the individual Jews charged with blood libel were, in all probability, innocent of the crimes that were committed. Yet the pattern of the accusations over the centuries arouses my suspicion, as does the Jews' unwillingness to consider any of the evidence. An innocent party, to my mind, would confront the charges. Thus, speaking as a student of history, I am inclined to believe that the circumstances of the crimes and their frequency suggest that at least some individual Jews practiced a type of cultic ritual that required the murder of Christian children. To make this statement is, in the world we live in today, the equivalent of saying "I am an idiot, incapable of reason. I believe in aliens, the physical return of Elvis, the flatness of planet earth." Yet foolish as it is to acknowledge this publicly, in light of the assured response, I must state what I believe. My belief in the validity of at least some of the charges of blood libel comes not from an inherent antagonism towards the Jews, but from my understanding of the historical evidence.

In the final analysis, I am left, still, with the same convictions: (1) The history of the Jews and the successes of individual Jews are the product of divine providence. (2) The Jews often represent a moral test for the non-Jew. In noting the contrast between the rewards granted the Jews and the personal shortcomings of individual Jews, the Christian must always act morally. (3) While the Christian is obligated to show some deference to the Jews, this does not mean that he may obfuscate the truth. Dostoevsky was not obligated by any moral or social responsibility to alter his artistic vision of the Jews. As a student of history, I believe that the behavior of Jews, particularly their disregard for objective, historical truth, will result in disastrous consequences for America. For all their horror of Nazism and the suffering of Jews during the Second World War, there has not come from the Jews any proposal of how that tragedy might have been averted, of what steps Jews themselves might have taken to change the course of history. One suspects that there are Jews who would never prefer, in the final analysis, that history in the 1930s and 1940s had taken any different course. One senses Jewish conviction, and even satisfaction, in the inevitability of Jewish suffering and in the inevitability of an immoral response on the part of the non-Jew.

The Christian, however, cannot accept any such conviction that ignores the teachings of Christianity and that suggests the Christian faith cannot overcome the deepest of hatreds. For the non-Jew, Jewish suffering can never be the central experience of human history, no matter how hard some Jews work towards such an interpretation of history. In good faith, I put the following question to Jews, especially to religious Jews, since I suspect that I, as a believing Christian, share something in common with them. Does the historical role of the Jews absolve them of any moral obligation to attempt to understand the non-Jew's reaction to the Jew? Or do the Jew and the non-Jew inhabit two different universes, the Jew put on earth as the non-Jew's ultimate moral test, to follow always blindly his own conscience and tradition, free of any responsibility in his relation to the non-Jew? And is the non-Jew always to face alone the constant moral dilemma of how to react to the Jew and to his strident ethnocentrism? Should any formulation of moral duties and obligations lead to an end to these ancient antagonisms, surely rational people on both sides of the dispute would embrace such an idea. Yet so long as Jews believe that historical truths relating to their relations with non-Jews have little importance, there is scant chance of averting future conflicts.

Stojgniev O'Donnell is the pseudonym of an American scholar.

Source: Jewish Tribal Review

"Stalin's Willing Executioners"?

by Kevin MacDonald

November 05, 2005

Yuri Slezkine's book "The Jewish Century", which appeared last year to rapturous reviews, is an intellectual tour de force, alternately muddled and brilliant, courageous and apologetic. Slezkine's greatest accomplishment is to set the historical record straight on the importance of Jews in the Bolshevik Revolution and its aftermath. He summarizes previously available data and extends our understanding of the Jewish role in revolutionary movements before 1917 and of Soviet society thereafter. His book provides a fascinating chronicle of the Jewish rise to elite status in all areas of Soviet society—culture, the universities, professional occupations, the media, and government. Indeed, the book is also probably the best, most up-to-date account of Jewish economic and cultural pre-eminence in Europe (and America) that we have.

The once-common view that the Bolshevik Revolution was a Jewish revolution and that the Soviet Union was initially dominated by Jews has now been largely eliminated from modern academic historiography. The current view, accepted by almost all contemporary historians, is that Jews played no special role in Bolshevism and indeed, were uniquely victimized by it.

Slezkine's book provides a bracing corrective to this current view.

Slezkine himself is a Russian immigrant of partially Jewish extraction. Arriving in America in 1983, he moved quickly into elite U.S. academic circles and is now a professor at U.C. Berkeley. This, his second book, is his first on a major theme.

While the greater part of The Jewish Century is an exposition of the Russian experience, Slezkine provides what are in effect sidebars (comparatively flimsy) recounting the Jewish experience in America and the Middle East. Together, these phenomena can in fact be seen as the three great Jewish migrations of the 20th century, since within Russia millions of Jews left the *shtetl* towns of the Pale of Settlement, migrating to Moscow and the other cities to man elite positions in the Soviet state.

Slezkine attempts to understand Jewish history and the rise of Jews to elite status in the 20th century by developing the thesis that the peoples of the world can be classified into two groups.

The successful peoples of the modern world, termed Mercurians, are urban, mobile, literate, articulate, and intellectually sophisticated.

The second group, termed Apollonians, is rooted to the land with traditional agrarian cultures, valuing physical strength and warrior virtues.

Since Slezkine sees Jews as the quintessential Mercurians, modernization is essentially a process of everyone becoming Jewish. Indeed, Slezkine regards both European individualism and the European nation state as imitations of pre-existing Jewish accomplishments— both deeply problematic views, in my opinion.

There are problems with the Mercurian/Apollonian distinction as well. The Gypsies whom he offers as an example of another Mercurian people, are basically the opposite of Jews: having a low-investment, low-IQ reproductive style characterized by higher fertility, earlier onset of reproduction, more unstable pair bonds, and more single parenting.

The Overseas Chinese, another proposed parallel, are indeed highly intelligent and entrepreneurial, like the Jews. But I would argue the aggressiveness of the Jews, compared to the relative political passivity of the Overseas Chinese, invalidates the comparison.

We do not read of Chinese cultural movements dominating the major local universities and media outlets, subjecting the traditional culture of Southeast Asians and anti-Chinese sentiment to radical critique —or of Chinese organizations campaigning for the removal of native cultural and religious symbols from public places.

Moreover, the vast majority of Jews in Eastern Europe in the late nineteenth and early twentieth centuries were hardly the modern Mercurians that Slezkine portrays.

Well into the 20th century, as Slezkine himself notes, most Eastern European Jews could not speak the languages of the non-Jews living around them. Slezkine also ignores their medieval outlook on life, their obsession with the Kabbala—the writings of Jewish mystics— their superstition and anti-rationalism, and their belief in magical remedies and exorcisms.

And these supposedly modern Mercurians had an attitude of absolute faith in the person of the *tsadik*, their *rebbe*, who was a charismatic figure seen by his followers literally as the personification of God in the world.

Slezkine devotes one line to the fact that Jewish populations in Eastern Europe had the highest rate of natural increase of any European population in the nineteenth century. The grinding poverty that this produced caused an upsurge of fundamentalist extremism that coalesced in the Hasidic movement and, later in the nineteenth century, into political radicalism and Zionism as solutions to Jewish problems.

By proposing the basically spurious Mercurian/Apollonian contrast, Slezkine obscures the plain fact that Jewish history in the period he discusses constitutes a spectacularly, arguably uniquely, successful case of what I have described as an ethnocentric group competitive strategy in action.

Slezkine conceptualizes Mercurianism as a worldview and therefore a matter of psychological choice rather than a set of psychological mechanisms, notably general intelligence and ethnocentrism. He appears to be aware of the biological reality of kinship and ethnicity, but he steadfastly pursues a cultural determinism model. As a result of this false premise, he understates the power of ethnocentrism and group competitiveness as unifying factors in Jewish history.

This competitiveness was of course notorious in Eastern Europe before the 1917 revolution. Slezkine ignores, or at least does not spell out, the extent to which Jews were willing agents of exploitative elites in traditional societies, not only in Europe, but in the Muslim world as well. Forming alliances with exploitative elites is arguably the most reliably recurrent theme observable in Jewish economic behavior over the ages.

Indeed, Slezkine shows that this pattern effectively continued in Russia after the Revolution: Jews became part of a new exploitative elite. But here boundaries between Jews and non-Jews were unusually blurred—in traditional societies, barriers between Jews and non-Jews at all social levels were always high.

Slezkine supposes that Jews and other Mercurians performed economic tasks deemed inappropriate for the natives for religious reasons. But this is only part of the story. Often these were situations where the natives were simply comparatively less ruthless in exploiting their fellows, which put them at a competitive disadvantage. This was especially the case in Eastern Europe, where conducive economic arrangements, such as tax farming, estate management, and monopolies on retail liquor distribution, lasted far longer than in the West.

Slezkine also ignores the extent to which Jewish competition may have suppressed – arguably sometimes reversed – the formation of a native middle class in Eastern Europe. He seems instead to simply assume the locals lacked the abilities required.

But the fact is that in most of Western Europe Jews were expelled in the Middle Ages. And, as a result, when modernization occurred, it was accomplished with an indigenous middle class. Perhaps the Christian taxpayers of England made a good investment in their own future when they agreed to pay King Edward I a massive tax of £116,346 in return for expelling 2000 Jews in 1290. If, as in Eastern Europe, Jews had won the economic competition in most of these professions, there might not have been a non-Jewish middle class in England.

Although in the decades immediately before the Russian Revolution Jews had already made enormous advances in social and economic status, a major contribution of Slezkine's book is to document that Communism was, indeed, 'good for the Jews.' After the Revolution, there was active elimination of any remnants of the older order and their descendants. Anti-Semitism was outlawed. Jews benefited from "antibourgeois" quotas in educational institutions and other forms of discrimination against the middle class and aristocratic elements of the old regime, which could have competed with the Jews. While all other nationalities, including Jews, were allowed and encouraged to keep their ethnic identities, the revolution maintained an anti-majoritarian attitude. (Some might argue that this parallels the many changes in the U.S. following our 1965 Civil Rights Act)

Beyond the issue of demonstrating that the Jews benefited from the Revolution lies the more important question of their role in implementing it. Having achieved power and elite status, did their traditional hostility to the leaders of the old regime, and to the peasantry, contribute to the peculiarly ghastly character of the early Soviet era?

On this question, Slezkine's contribution is decisive.

Despite the important role of Jews among the Bolsheviks, most Jews were not Bolsheviks before the Revolution. However, Jews were prominent among the Bolsheviks, and once the Revolution was underway, the vast majority of Russian Jews became sympathizers and active participants.

Jews were particularly visible in the cities and as leaders in the army and in the revolutionary councils and committees. For example, there were 23 Jews among 62 Bolsheviks in the All-Russian Central Executive Committee elected at the Second Congress of Soviets in October, 1917. Jews were leaders of the movement and to a great extent they were its public face.

Their presence was particularly notable at the top levels of the Cheka and OGPU (two successive acronyms for the secret police). Here Slezkine provides statistics on Jewish overrepresentation in these organizations, especially in supervisory roles, and quotes historian Leonard Shapiro's comment that "anyone who had the misfortune to fall into the hands of the Cheka stood a very good chance of finding himself confronted with and possibly shot by a Jewish investigator."

During the 1930s, Slezkine reports, the secret police, now known as the NKVD, "was one of the most Jewish of all Soviet institutions", with 42 of the 111 top officials being Jewish. At this time, 12 of the 20 NKVD directorates were headed by ethnic Jews, including those in charge of State Security, Police, Labor Camps, and Resettlement (deportation).

The Gulag was headed by ethnic Jews from its beginning in 1930 until the end of 1938, a period that encompasses the worst excesses of the Great Terror.

They were, in Slezkine's remarkable phrase, "Stalin's willing executioners".

Slezkine appears to take a certain pride in the drama of the role of the Jews in Russia during these years. Thus he says they were "among the most exuberant crusaders against 'bourgeois' habits during the Great Transformation; the most disciplined advocates of socialist realism during the 'Great Retreat' (from revolutionary internationalism); and the most passionate prophets of faith, hope, and combat during the Great Patriotic War against the Nazis".

Sometimes his juxtapositions between his descriptions of Jewish involvement in the horror of the early Soviet period and the life styles of the Jewish elite seem deliberately jarring. Lev Kopelev, a Jewish writer who witnessed and rationalized the Ukrainian famine in which millions died horrible deaths of starvation and disease as an "historical necessity" is quoted saying "You mustn't give in to debilitating pity. We are the agents of historical necessity. We are fulfilling our revolutionary duty."

On the next page, Slezkine describes the life of the largely Jewish elite in Moscow and Leningrad where they attended the theater, sent their children to the best schools, had peasant women (whose families were often the victims of mass murder) for nannies, spent weekends at pleasant dachas and vacationed at the Black Sea.

Again, Slezkine discusses the heavily Jewish NKVD and the Jewish leadership of the Great Terror of the 1930s. Then, he writes that in 1937 the prototypical Jewish State official "probably would have been living in elite housing in downtown Moscow . . . with access to special stores, a house in the country (dacha), and a live-in peasant nanny or maid". He writes long and lovingly detailed sketches of life at the dachas of the elite—the "open verandas overlooking small gardens enclosed by picket fences..."

The reader is left on his own to recall the horrors of the Ukrainian famine, the liquidation of the Kulaks, and the Gulag.

Slezkine attempts to dodge the issue of the degree to which the horrors perpetrated by the early Soviet state were rooted in the traditional attitudes of the Jews who in fact played such an extensive role in their orchestration. He argues that the Jewish Communists were Communists, not Jews.

This does not survive factual analysis.

One might grant the possibility that the revolutionary vanguard was composed of Jews like Trotsky, apparently far more influenced by a universalist utopian vision than by their upbringing in traditional Judaism. But, even granting this, it does not necessarily follow for the millions of Jews who left the *shtetl* towns, migrated to the cities, and to such a large extent ran the USSR.

It strains credulity to suppose that these migrants completely and immediately threw off all remnants of the Eastern European *shtetl* culture—which, as Slezkine acknowledges, had a deep sense of estrangement from non-Jewish society, a fear and hatred of peasants, hostility toward the Czarist upper class, and a very negative attitude toward Christianity.

In other words, the war against what Slezkine terms "rural backwardness and religion" — major targets of the Revolution — was exactly the sort of war that traditional Jews would have supported wholeheartedly, because it was a war against everything they hated and thought of as oppressing Jews.

However, while Slezkine seems comfortable with the notion of revenge as a Jewish motive, he does not consider traditional Jewish culture itself as a possible contributor to Jewish behavior in the new Communist state.

Moreover, while it was generally true that Jewish servants of the Soviet regime had ceased being religious Jews, this did not mean they ceased having a Jewish identity. (Albert Lindeman made this point when reviewing Slezkine in The American Conservative magazine.)

Slezkine quotes the philosopher Vitaly Rubin speaking of his career at a top Moscow school in the 1930s where over half the students were Jewish:

"Understandably, the Jewish question did not arise there… All the Jews knew themselves to be Jews but considered everything to do with Jewishness a thing of the past…There was no active desire to renounce one's Jewishness. The problem simply did not exist."

In other words, in the early decades of the Soviet Union, the ruling class was so heavily a Jewish milieu, that there was no need to renounce a Jewish identity and no need to aggressively push for Jewish interests. Jews had achieved elite status.

But ethnic networking continued nonetheless. Indeed, Slezkine reports that when a leading Soviet spokesmen on anti-Semitism, Yuri Larin (Lurie), tried to explain the embarrassing fact that Jews were, as he said, "preeminent, overabundant, dominant, and so on" among the elite in the Soviet Union, he mentioned the "unusually strong sense of solidarity and a predisposition toward mutual help and support"—ethnic networking by any other name.

Obviously, "mutual help and support" required that Jews recognize each other as Jews. Jewish identity may not have been much discussed. But it operated nonetheless, even if subconsciously, in the rarified circles at the top of Soviet society.

Things changed. Slezkine shows that the apparent de-emphasis of Jewish identity by many members of the Soviet elite during the 1920s and 1930s turned out to be a poor indicator of whether or not these people identified as Jews—or would do so when Jewish and Soviet identities began to diverge in later years: when National Socialism reemphasized Jewish identity, and when Israel emerged as a magnet for Jewish sentiment and loyalty.

In the end, despite the rationalizations of many Soviet Jews on Jewish identity in the early Soviet period, it was blood that mattered.

After World War II, in a process which remains somewhat obscure, the Russian majority began taking back their country. One method was 'massive affirmative action' aimed at giving greater representation to underrepresented ethnic groups. Jews became targets of suspicion because of their ethnic status. They were barred from some elite institutions, and had their opportunities for advancement limited. Overt anti-Semitism was encouraged by the more covert official variety apparent in the limits on Jewish advancement.

Under these circumstances, Slezkine says that Jews became "in many ways, the core of the anti-regime intelligentsia". Applications to leave the USSR increased dramatically after Israel's Six-Day War of 1967 which, as in the United States and Eastern Europe, resulted in an upsurge of Jewish identification and ethnic pride. The floodgates were eventually opened by Gorbachev in the late 1980s. By 1994,

1.2 million Soviet Jews had emigrated—43% of the total. By 2002, there were only 230,000 Jews remaining in the Russian Federation, 0.16% of the population.

Nevertheless these remaining Jews continue to remain overrepresented among the elite. Six of the seven "oligarchs" who emerged in control of the Soviet economy and media in the period of denationalization of the 1990s were Jews.

As mentioned above, Slezkine's discussions of the Jewish experience in the Middle East and America are quite perfunctory in comparison.

Slezkine views the Jewish migration to Israel as heroic and believes the moral debt owed to Jews by Western societies justifies the most extreme expressions of Jewish racialism: "The rhetoric of ethnic homogeneity and ethnic deportations, tabooed elsewhere in the West is a routine element of Israeli political life... no other European state can have as strong a claim on the West's moral imagination."

He sees the moral taboo on European ethnocentrism, the designation of Nazism as the epitome of absolute evil, and the identification of Jews as what he calls "the Chosen people of the postwar Western world" as simply the inevitable results of the events of World War II. In fact, of course, the creation and maintenance of the culture of the Holocaust and the special moral claims of Jews and Israel might be more fairly viewed the intended result of Jewish ethnic activism.

Slezkine's caricature of American history is close to preposterous. He sees the United States as a Jewish promised land precisely because it is not defined tribally and "has no state-bearing natives". In fact, of course, the Founding Fathers very explicitly saw themselves as Englishmen defending a specific political tradition. But (somewhat like the Soviet Union's Jews in the early decades) they felt no need to assert the cultural and ethnic parameters of their creation; they assumed the racial and cultural homogeneity of the Republic and perceived no threat to its control by themselves and their descendants.

And when the Founding Fathers' descendents did perceive such a threat, they reacted powerfully and decisively, with the Know-Nothing movement in the 1850s and the Immigration Restriction (and associated "Americanization" requirements) in the early 20th Century. Slezkine's acceptance of the "Proposition Nation" myth reflects the triumph of intellectuals and propagandists, many of them Jewish, led by Horace Kallen in the 1920s. They successfully replaced the previously standard view by which many Americans thought of themselves as members of a very successful ethnic group derived from Great Britain and with strong cultural and ethnic connections to Europe, particularly Northern Europe.

The fate of Russia in the first two decades following the Revolution prompts reflection on what might have happened in the United States had American communists and their sympathizers assumed power. Sectors of American society might perhaps have been deemed unacceptably backward and superstitious and even worthy of liquidation by the American counterparts of the Jewish elite in the Soviet Union—the ones who journeyed to Ellis Island instead of Moscow.

Those "red state" voters who have loomed so important in recent national elections would have been the enemy. The cultural and religious attitudes of "red state" America are precisely those attitudes that have been deemed change-worthy by the left, particularly by the Jewish community, which has been the driving force of the left in America throughout the 20th century.

As Joel Kotkin points out, "for generations, [American] Jews have viewed religious conservatives with a combination of fear and disdain."

And, as [Reagan and Bush appointee] Elliott Abrams has noted, the American Jewish community "clings to what is at bottom a dark vision of America, as a land permeated with anti-Semitism…"

The dark view of traditional Slavs and their culture that caused so many Eastern European *shtetl* Jews to become "willing executioners" in the name of international socialism is unmistakably related, however remotely, to the views of some contemporary American Jews about a majority of their fellow countrymen.

Slezkine's main point is that the most important factor for understanding the history of the 20th century is the rise of the Jews in the West and the Middle East, and their rise and decline in Russia. I think he is absolutely right about this.

If there is any lesson to be learned, it is that Jews not only became an elite in all these areas, they became a hostile elite—hostile to the traditional people and cultures of all three areas they came to dominate.

So far, the greatest human tragedies have occurred in the Soviet Union. But the presence of Israel in the Middle East is creating obvious dangers there. And alienation remains a potent motive for the disproportionate Jewish involvement in the transformation of the U.S. into a non-European society through non-traditional immigration.

Given this record of Jews as a very successful but hostile elite, it is possible that the continued demographic and cultural dominance of Western European peoples will not be retained, either in Europe or the United States, without a decline in Jewish influence.

But the lesson of the Soviet Union (as also of Spain from the 15th–17th centuries) is that Jewish influence does wane as well as wax. Unlike the attitudes of the utopian ideologies of the 20th century, there is no end to history.

Kevin MacDonald is Professor of Psychology at California State University-Long Beach. He is the author of numerous books and articles, including a three volume trilogy on Judaism: "A People That Shall Dwell Alone", "Separation and its Discontents" and "The Culture of Critique". This article is adapted from a longer one published in the Fall 2005 issue of The Occidental Quarterly.

Exploring The 'Shell Game' of Ideology

"The Ordeal of Civility: Freud, Marx, Levi-Strauss, and the Jewish Struggle with Modernity" by John Murray Cuddihy; Basic Books, 1974.

Reviewed by Hugh Lincoln

Decades before Kevin MacDonald embarked on his Jewish trilogy, a little-known sociology professor at New York City's Hunter College came to suspect that the Jewish intellectual movements of the 19th and 20th centuries weren't quite the marvels of universal application imagined by academia and later by wider society. Rather, they were elaborate coping mechanisms designed to de-racialize the social conflicts between Gentile Europe and newly emancipated Jewry. It was MacDonald who expanded "coping" to "undermining" in the context of Jewish-Gentile relations, but John Murray Cuddihy is to be credited for one of history's more thoroughgoing, if obscure, exposures of Jewish deception.

Cuddihy, who retired in 1998, is presumably not a racialist. He speaks more of "culture" than ethnicity or even race, and might even consider himself sympathetic to Jews. The book, *The Ordeal of*

Civility: Freud, Marx, Levi-Strauss, and the Jewish Struggle with Modernity,
was published in 1974. Some racially conscious Whites confess that
the book does not speak to them. Inaccessibly dense and academic,
they say – a sentiment with which I came to sympathize as I read
the book. *The Ordeal of Civility* is not light reading. It is also difficult
to find. But within the yellowed pages of my used copy, purchased
over the Internet, I found a surprisingly damning analysis of Jewish
motivations.

Cuddihy's thesis goes roughly as follows: Upon the granting of emancipation to the Jews of Europe*, their less-refined ways, developed
over centuries within their tightly bound tribal lives, bumped rudely
into the carefully cultivated behavioral codes of the larger Gentile communities of Europe. The closer Jews tried to get, the more
intense the conflict became. The Jewish intellectual elite cringed
when the *ostjuden,* or unassimilated Jews, made a spectacle of themselves in European civil society. Cuddihy cites the example of the
Victorian-era social reformer Beatrice Potter, who found herself disgusted by the Jews of London's East End: "… the immigrant Jew,
though possessed of many first-class virtues, is deficient in that highest and latest development of human sentiment – social morality…
He totally ignores all social obligations other than keeping the law
of the land, the maintenance of his own family, and the charitable
relief of coreligionists."

Jewish intellectuals were well aware that views such as Potter's prevailed. Their minds raced to concoct explanations for the conflict that
steered clear of the most obvious one: race. Karl Marx described it as
a class conflict rooted in economic maldistribution. Sigmund Freud
described it as a medical malady rooted in suppressed natural urges.
The "structuralism" of French anthropologist Claude Levi-Strauss,
propounded in the 1960s and 1970s, asserted that no one culture was
better than any another, leaving open the possibility that, if anything,
Western culture was loaded with hypocrisy and trivial etiquette while
non-Western cultures were more admirably "natural."

[*Prussian Jewry's Emancipation Edict, for instance, was granted on
March 11, 1812.]

The propounding of such ideas, Cuddihy says, sprang from Jewish "status humiliations of modernity," the "wound in the heart" suffered by their encounter with a larger and more refined Gentile society, an encounter that left them feeling inferior. "Structuralism, like Marxism, is an ideology of subcultural despair, an uneasy mélange of cognitive relativism and ethical absolutism," Cuddihy says. By Gentile "modernity," Cuddihy meant the separation of the private from the public that evolved as Gentile Europe moved from animal skin-wearing tribalism to civil societies with public institutions. The transition saw the development of new social rituals that would have been unnecessary in a close-knit society in which everyone was intimately acquainted with everyone else. Jews, not having undergone such changes, developed no such rituals.

As I imagine it, the Jewish intelligentsia were prompted into a "fight or flight" mental reaction. In application, it combined both fighting and 'flighting'. The fighting was the criticism of Gentiles for living their lives in ways that were, to us, completely natural. The 'flighting' was the deceptive aspect of that fighting: Jews did not confront Gentiles qua Gentiles. Rather, they sought alternate explanations that served to mollify their embarrassment at the behavior of their own people. From the introduction: "As we shall see, the ideology of the Jewish intellectual is frequently a projection onto the general, Gentile culture of a forbidden ethnic self-criticism. Shame for 'one's own kind' is universalized into anger at the ancestral enemy... 'Neither Jew nor Gentile is to be blamed for the tsursis (trouble) of the Diaspora: it is but a symptom of the capitalist exploitation (Marx) or a medical symptom of anxiety (Freud),'" Cuddihy says, echoing the hoped-for reception of the Jewish ideas. The analysis rings true. I am convinced (no, not by reference to Freud) that a primary motivator for the human thought process is the desire to "get comfortable" with any given situation, from the immediate and personal to larger social or political realities. Getting comfortable need not be mere self-adjustment – it can also mean the alteration of the environment itself, like a prehistoric human smashing down grasses to make a bed. As I understand Cuddihy, Jews were doing both: creating ideologies that comforted them with reassurances of equality, and, if accepted by Gentiles, made for pliant enemies.

Cuddihy is short on vivid examples of the culture clash that so motivated (and was misunderstood by) the Jewish intelligentsia, but several emerge in his treatment of Freud. Consider Freud's reaction to privacy. Within the insulated Jewish community of the *shtetl,* or Jewish ghetto, "privacy" was seen as abnormal – anyone desiring personal space must be hiding something and is suspect. It did not occur to Freud that Gentile culture, having developed into a larger society, may well have had good reasons for respecting the personal space of others. In the nineteenth century, Eastern European Jewry "mistakes privacy for secrecy." The ways in which European Gentiles institutionalized the need to be private in public, or the need for decorum, is "lost on the Jewish intelligentsia of the nineteenth century. To them, it appears as so much hypocrisy." Cuddihy quotes Philip Rieff's *Freud: The Mind of the Moralist:* "What is for Freud 'repression' psychologically understood, is 'secrecy' morally understood. Secrecy is the category moral illness, for it provides a hiding place for false motives."

In other words, Freud described as "sick" Gentile behavior that was, to us, healthy and necessary. But it was not out of mere misunderstanding that Freud came to his conclusions. Animosity toward Gentiles played no small part. Freud, laid out on Cuddihy's couch, recalls a childhood episode that burned into him a desire to "get even" with the exclusionary enemy. Freud's father, Jacob Freud, was walking down the sidewalk in Moravia and bumped into a Gentile. "Jew! Get off the pavement!" snarled the Gentile. The elder Freud's hat was knocked into the gutter. His reaction is not to leap to the Gentile's throat, but to calmly retrieve his hat from the gutter and continue on his way. Freud, as it happens, didn't witness any of this. The recounting by his father was enough. Is it possible that this episode created Freud's fantasy that by developing "psychoanalysis," he would become the Semitic conqueror of Gentile Europe? Like Hannibal astride his elephant, he would storm Rome and exact vengeance on the hated goyim.

Freud on Hannibal

When I finally came to realize the consequences of belonging to an alien race, and was forced by the anti-Semitic feeling among my classmates to take a definite stand, the figure of the Semitic commander assumed still greater proportions in my imagination. Hannibal and Rome symbolized, in my youthful eyes, the struggle between the tenacity of the Jews and the organization of the Catholic Church. The significance for our emotional life which the anti-Semitic movement has since assumed helped to fix the thoughts and impressions of those earlier days. Thus the desire to go to Rome has in my dream-life become the mask and symbol for a number of warmly cherished wishes, for whose realization one had to work with the tenacity and single-mindedness of the Punic general, though their fulfillment at times seemed as remote as Hannibal's life-long wish to enter Rome.

And now, for the first time, I happened upon the youthful experience which even today still expresses its power in all these emotions and dreams. I might have been ten or twelve years old when my father began to take me with him on his walks, and in his conversation to reveal his views on the things of this world. Thus it was that he once told me the following incident, in order to show me that I had been born into happier times than he: "When I was a young man, I was walking one Saturday along the street in the village where you were born; I was well-dressed, with a new fur cap on my head. Up comes a Christian, who knocks my cap into the mud, and shouts, 'Jew, get off the pavement!'" – "And what did you do?" – "I went into the street and picked up the cap," he calmly replied. That did not seem heroic on the part of the big, strong man who was leading me, a little fellow, by the hand. I contrasted this situation, which did not please me, with another, more in harmony with my sentiments – the scene in which Hannibal's father, Hamilcar Barcas, made his son swear before the household alter to take vengeance on the Romans. Ever since then Hannibal has had a place in my phantisies.

It is no accident that "id" mimics "Yid." "In psychoanalysis, the 'id' is the functional equivalent of the 'Yid' in social intercourse," Cuddihy says. "The id, in other words, was a moral equalizer legitimating 'scientifically' social equality between Jew and Gentile in late nineteenth-century Europe." Cuddihy quotes Howard Morley Sacher on "the unconscious desire of Jews, as social pariahs, to unmask the respectability of the European society which closed them out," adding that in Freud's case, it was the conscious desire of a conscious pariah. "There was no more effective way of doing this," Sacher is quoted as saying, "than by dredging up from the human psyche the sordid and infantile sexual aberrations that were frequently the sources of human behavior. Even Jews who were not psychiatrists must have taken pleasure in the fact of social equalization performed by Freud's 'new thinking.' The B'nai B'rith Lodge of Vienna, for example, delighted in listening to Freud air his theories."

Cuddihy's presentation ironically draws upon the same motivation exposition techniques employed by Freud. When Jews sneer that Gentiles are embarrassed by sex and need to be "unmasked," Cuddihy points out that what they're trying to do is strip all humanity to base commonalities in an effort to make their crude, uncivilized selves feel more acceptable, all the while rudely ignoring the evolved and genuine social need for Gentile conventions. The Gentile is left shamed and confused, convinced that he must "let it all hang out" if he is to achieve mental health. Freud is revealed as a clever Jew pleased with himself for having pulled the Gentile's pants down to point out to the assembled crowd that, like other mammals, this one's got genitalia. Cuddihy coolly returns the favor. Freud himself might have had some insight on this, as he was reported to have once wondered: am I an original scientist or just a dirty Jew?

What Freud sought by subversion, Marx sought by revolution. Jewish-Gentile conflict for Marx was seen not as a racial battle but as class struggle. In this respect, Marxism found a parallel with Zionism. "Jewish radicals analyzed anti-Semitism as incidental to the class struggle and expected it to disappear in the ruins of the capitalist system," Cuddihy quotes a Ben Halpern as saying. Cuddihy continues: "Zionists planned to heal at one stroke the wound to national self-esteem by leaving Europe – and by leaving behind the invidious comparisons fatal to remaining there. Marxists planned to kill the 'Jewish question' by revolution, not emigration: at one stroke, all would be changed, changed utterly, as a species-humane community is born." History, of course, would not bear out anything "humane" resulting from Marxism, socialism or communism.

Toward the end of the book, Cuddihy offers a revealing account of the "Chicago Seven" trial, featuring a showdown between Jewish radical Abbie Hoffman and the assimilated Jewish judge, also named Hoffman. The exchanges ("You're a disgrace to the Jews, runt!" Abbie Hoffman yells at the judge. "You should have served Hitler better!") are seen by Cuddihy as revealing the very clashes Marx and Freud witnessed and sought to explain away.

Today, excluding college campuses, Marxism holds little sway. Freud's ideas find a few purist adherents, though many therapists have distanced themselves from his theories. But observe the damage done, and how Jews have deftly avoided blame for the misery caused. To the untutored, they are tough to spot, darting quickly from movement to movement under a cover of proclaimed universalism. Since once an intellectual or political movement loses utility for Jews, they abandon it. I believe that the Jewish tendency so well described by Cuddihy finds its fiercest manifestation today in "neoconservatism," a two-headed beast of race-denying social liberalism and pro-Israel warmongering.

Jews in government and media line up to feed this beast, which serves them nicely at the dawn of the new century. It looks "conservative" and thus beats the charge that Jews are liberals, yet pushes simultaneously for the American multiculturalism that makes them comfortable in the U.S., and the Jewish exclusionism that makes them comfortable in Israel. If there is a deviation from Cuddihy's thesis, it is this: Neo-conservatism and other Jewish maneuvering is no "Jewish struggle" evocative of sympathy for a "Diaspora people." It is child's play for Jews. Jews no longer struggle with modernity, they define it.

Hugh Lincoln is an attorney living in New York City.

US Makes it Illegal for US Firms and Individuals to Boycott Israel

-Penalty: Up to 10 Years in Prison-

U.S. Office of Antiboycott Compliance Washington, D.C.

http://www.bis.doc.gov/complianceandenforcement/
AnitboycottCompliance.htm

Antiboycott Laws:

During the mid-1970's the United States adopted two laws that seek to counteract the participation of U.S. citizens in other nation's economic boycotts or embargoes. These "antiboycott" laws are the 1977 amendments to the Export Administration Act (EAA) and the Ribicoff Amendment to the 1976 Tax Reform Act (TRA).

Objectives:

The antiboycott laws were adopted to encourage, and in specified cases, require U.S. firms to refuse to participate in foreign boycotts that the United States does not sanction. They have the effect of preventing U.S. firms from being used to implement foreign policies of other nations which run counter to U.S. policy.

Primary Impact:

The Arab League boycott of Israel is the principal foreign economic boycott that U.S. companies must be concerned with today. The antiboycott laws, however, apply to all boycotts imposed by foreign countries that are unsanctioned by the United States.

Who Is Covered by the Laws?

The antiboycott provisions of the Export Administration Regulations (EAR) apply to all "U.S. persons," defined to include individuals and companies located in the United States and their foreign affiliates. These persons are subject to the law when their activities relate to the sale, purchase, or transfer of goods or services (including information) within the United States or between the U.S. and a foreign country. This covers U.S. exports and imports, financing, forwarding and shipping, and certain other transactions that may take place wholly offshore.

Generally, the TRA applies to all U.S. taxpayers (and their related companies). The TRA's reporting requirements apply to taxpayers' "operations" in, with, or related to boycotting countries or their nationals. Its penalties apply to those taxpayers with foreign tax credit, foreign subsidiary deferral, FSC (Foreign Sales Corporation), and IC-DISC (Interest Charge-Domestic International Sales Corporation) benefits.

What do the Laws Prohibit?

Conduct that may be penalized under the TRA and/or prohibited under the EAR includes:

Agreements to refuse or actual refusal to do business with or in Israel or with blacklisted companies.

Agreements to discriminate or actual discrimination against other persons based on race, religion, sex, national origin or nationality.

Agreements to furnish or actual furnishing of information about business relationships with or in Israel or with blacklisted companies.

Agreements to furnish or actual furnishing of information about the race, religion, sex, or national origin of another person.

Implementing letters of credit containing prohibited boycott terms or conditions.

The TRA does not "prohibit" conduct, but denies tax benefits ("penalizes") for certain types of boycott-related agreements.

What Must Be Reported?

The EAR requires U.S. persons to report quarterly requests they have received to take certain actions to comply with, further, or support an unsanctioned foreign boycott.

The TRA requires taxpayers to report "operations" in, with, or related to a boycotting country or its nationals and requests received to participate in or cooperate with an international boycott. The Treasury Department publishes a quarterly list of "boycotting countries."

How To Report:

EAR reports are filed quarterly on form BIS 621-P for single requests or BIS 6051-P for multiple requests available from the Department of Commerce's Office of Antiboycott Compliance (OAC) in Washington, D.C. To obtain these forms, telephone OAC,s Reports Processing Unit at (202) 482-2448. TRA reports are filed with tax returns on IRS Form 5713. This form is available from local IRS offices.

Penalties:

The EAR prescribe the penalties for violations of the Antiboycott Regulations as well as export control violations. These can include:

Criminal:

The penalties imposed for each "knowing" violation can be a fine of up to $50,000 or five times the value of the exports involved, whichever is greater, and imprisonment of up to five years. During periods when the EAR are continued in effect by an Executive Order issued pursuant to the International Emergency Economic Powers Act, the criminal penalties for each "willful" violation can be a fine of up to $50,000 and imprisonment for up to ten years.

Administrative:

For each violation of the EAR any or all of the following may be imposed:

General denial of export privileges;

The imposition of fines of up to $12,000 per violation; and/or

Exclusion from practice.

Boycott agreements under the TRA involve the denial of all or part of the foreign tax benefits discussed above.

The $10,000 maximum per violation specified in the EAA is adjusted periodically pursuant to law for inflation.

The maximum civil penalty for any violation committed from October 23, 1996 through November 1, 2000 is $11,000 per violation.

The maximum civil penalty for any violation committed after November 1, 2000 is $12,000 per violation.

Where to Get More Information:

U.S. Department of Commerce BIS/Office of Antiboycott Compliance, Room 6098, Washington, D.C. 20230 (202) 482-2381 or by E-Mail

http://www.bxa.doc.gov/AntiboycottCompliance/OAC Requirements.html

BRAVE, NEW *Jewish-friendly* WORLD

U.S. To Rate Countries On Their Treatment Of Jews

"Today, I signed the Global Anti-Semitism Review Act of 2004. This law commits the government to keep a record of anti-Semitic acts throughout the world, and also a record of responses to those acts," –President George W. Bush, Oct. 14, 2004

By Maxim Kniazkov, *Agence France Presse*

(10-13-04)

WASHINGTON – US Jewish organizations have hailed final Congressional approval of a bill that compels the State Department to create a special office to monitor anti-Semitic abuses around the world and compile annual reports rating countries on their treatment of Jews.

The bill, known as the Global Anti-Semitism Awareness Act, was introduced by Democratic Representative Tom Lantos, the only Holocaust survivor in the US Congress, in response to recent acts of anti-Semitism in Europe and the Middle East.

The measure quietly cleared both the Senate and the House of Representatives by agreement and voice vote late last week "over objections by the State Department." The department has opposed the bill because it felt it would be seen as giving preferential treatment to Jews over other religious or ethnic groups in human rights reporting.

But last month, it received an angry letter from more than 100 prominent Americans, including former Republican vice presidential nominee Jack Kemp and ex-UN Ambassador Jeane Kirkpatrick, saying that US diplomats were "wrong."

"It is the anti-Semites who are singling out Jews, and that is why the fight against anti-Semitism deserves specific, focused attention," the letter said.

Under the legislation, the State Department will have to produce an annual report on anti-Semitism around the world and publish it as part of its annual review of human rights. Moreover, the bill creates a specific office within the department that would document anti-Semitic abuses and design strategies to combat them. It would be headed by a special envoy to spearhead the worldwide fight against anti-Semitism.

"Considering that anti-Semitism plagues all regions of the world, this special office will ensure that the United States resolutely denounces acts of anti-Semitism across the board, including state-sponsored anti-Semitism in Syria and elsewhere," said Republican Congressman Chris Smith, a co-sponsor of the legislation.

Rafael Medoff, director of the Pennsylvania-based David S. Wyman Institute for Holocaust Studies, praised members of Congress on Monday for their "vision, courage and determination in overcoming the State Department's obstacles and achieving this crucial step in the battle against anti-Semitism."

Joel Schindler, president of the National Council of Soviet Jewry, said Congress "has now provided new avenues" for combating anti-Semitism around the world.

Barbara Balser, national chairwoman of the Anti-Defamation League (ADL), and Abraham Foxman, its national director, said acts of anti-Semitism witnessed over the last two years have underscored the need for greater monitoring of such crimes.

"As more governments take on this responsibility, strong US reporting on anti-Semitism as a human rights and religious freedom issue is vitally important," Balser and Foxman said. The measure, which is largely expected to be signed by President George W. Bush, requires that the State Department document acts of physical violence against Jews, their property, cemeteries and places of worship abroad, as well as local governments, responses to them.

The report will also take note of instances of anti-Jewish propaganda and governments, readiness to promote unbiased school curricula emphasizing tolerance.

Among the attacks that prompted passage of the bill, the sponsors mentioned the burning of a Jewish synagogue in Toulon, France, last March, the desecration of about 50 Jewish gravestones in St. Petersburg, Russia, in February, and the recent claim by former Malaysian Prime Minister Mahathir Mohamad that Jews "rule the world by proxy."